Black Rose ALICE

Black Rose ALICE

4

Story & Art by
Setona Mizushiro

Black Rose ALICE

Characters & Story

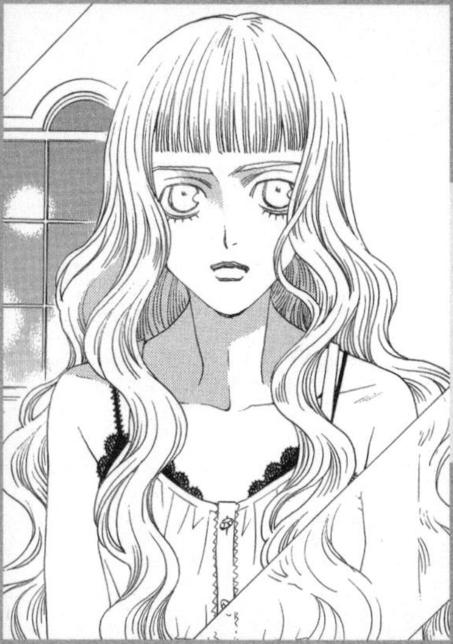

Alice
Azusa in Agnieszka's body. She has decided to cooperate in propagating with four vampires.

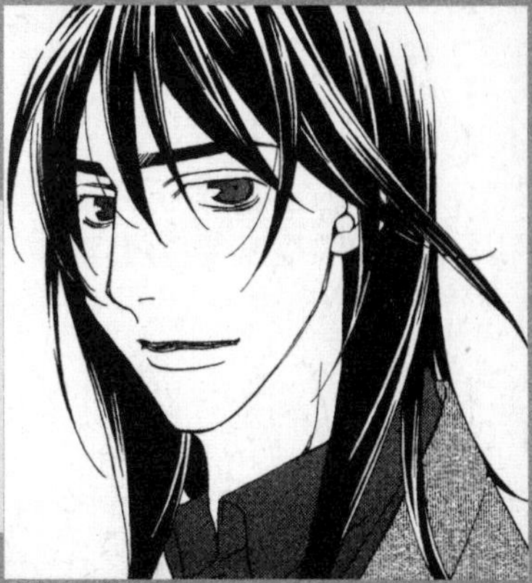

Dimitri
A tenor vocalist. After an accident, he became a vampire.

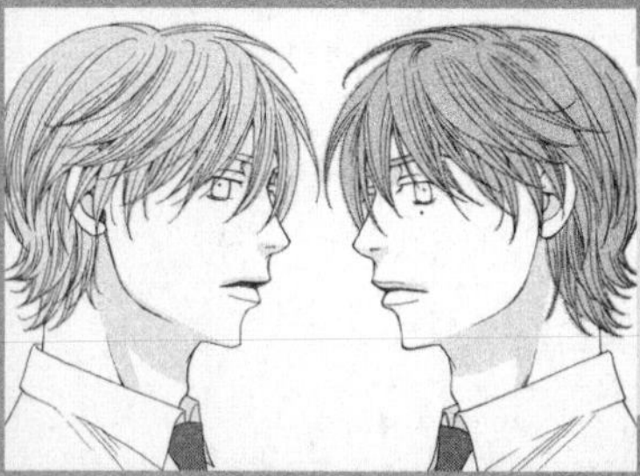

Kai & Reiji
Twin vampires born from Maximilian's seed.

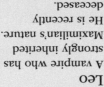

Maximilian
A vampire. Dimitri's servant in the past.

Leo
A vampire who has strongly inherited Maximilian's nature. He is recently deceased.

Toko Narusawa
A novelist who suffers from an incurable disease. Leo has helped extend her life.

Vienna, 1908. Dimitri dies in an accident but is reborn as a vampire. He tries to sleep with his beloved Agnieszka by force, but she kills herself. Taking Agnieszka's soulless body with him, Dimitri leaves Vienna.

Tokyo, a century later. High school teacher Azusa and her student Koya are in a car accident. As she lies severely injured, Dimitri appears and proposes a bargain: he will save Koya if she offers him her soul. When she accepts, her soul enters Agnieszka's body and sleeps...

Waiting for Azusa when she awakes are four vampires: Dimitri, Leo and the twins Kai and Reiji. They want her to choose the best vampire from among them for propagation. Azusa changes her name to Alice and begins observing them. However, Leo reaches the end of his life span, and Alice must accept the harsh truth...

CONTENTS

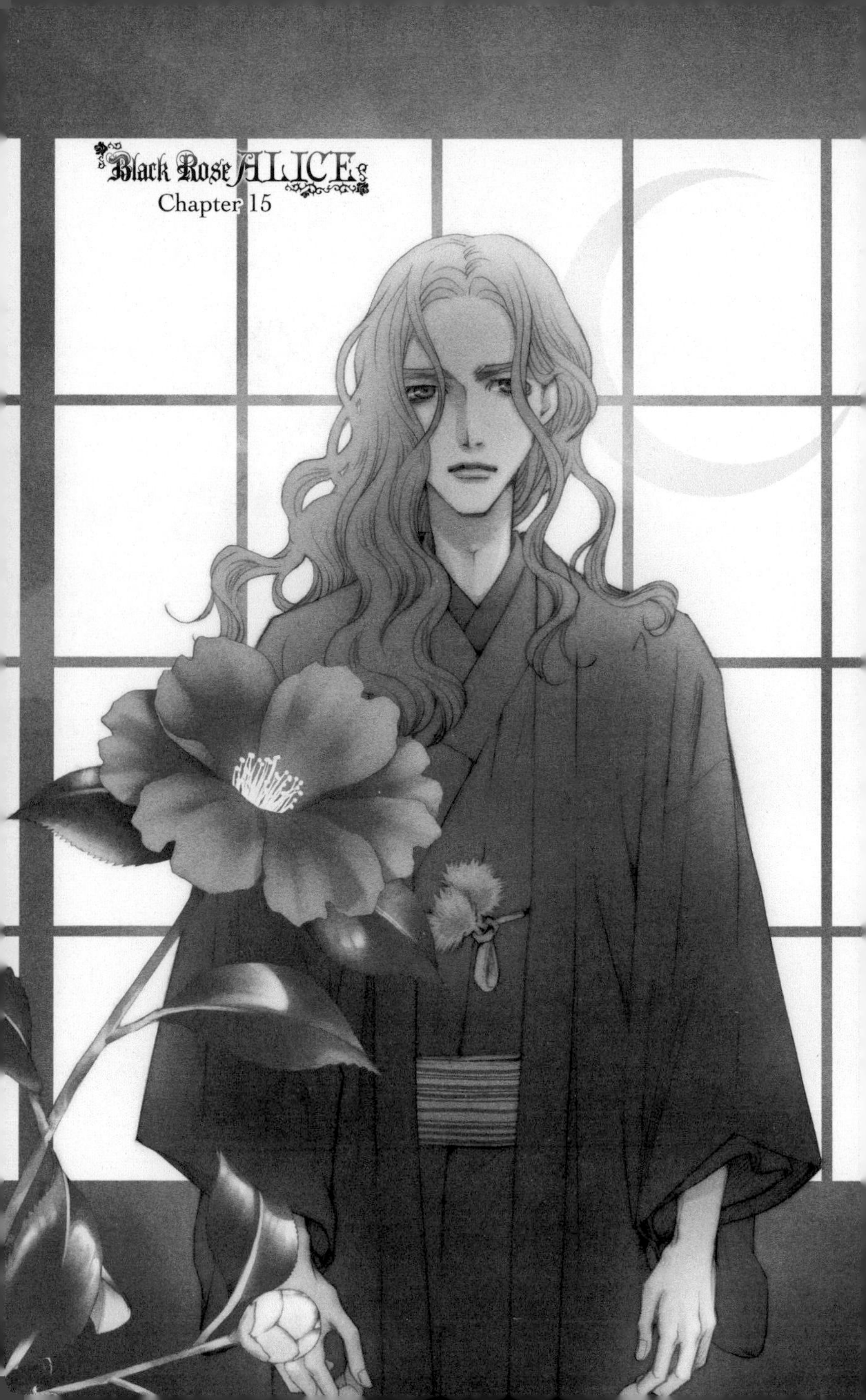
Black Rose Alice
Chapter 15

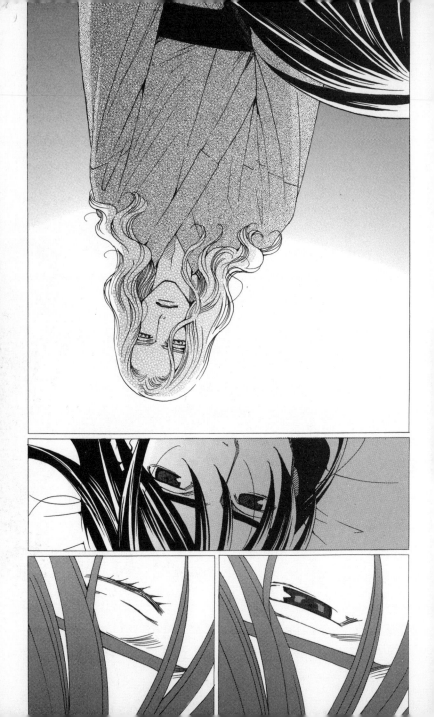

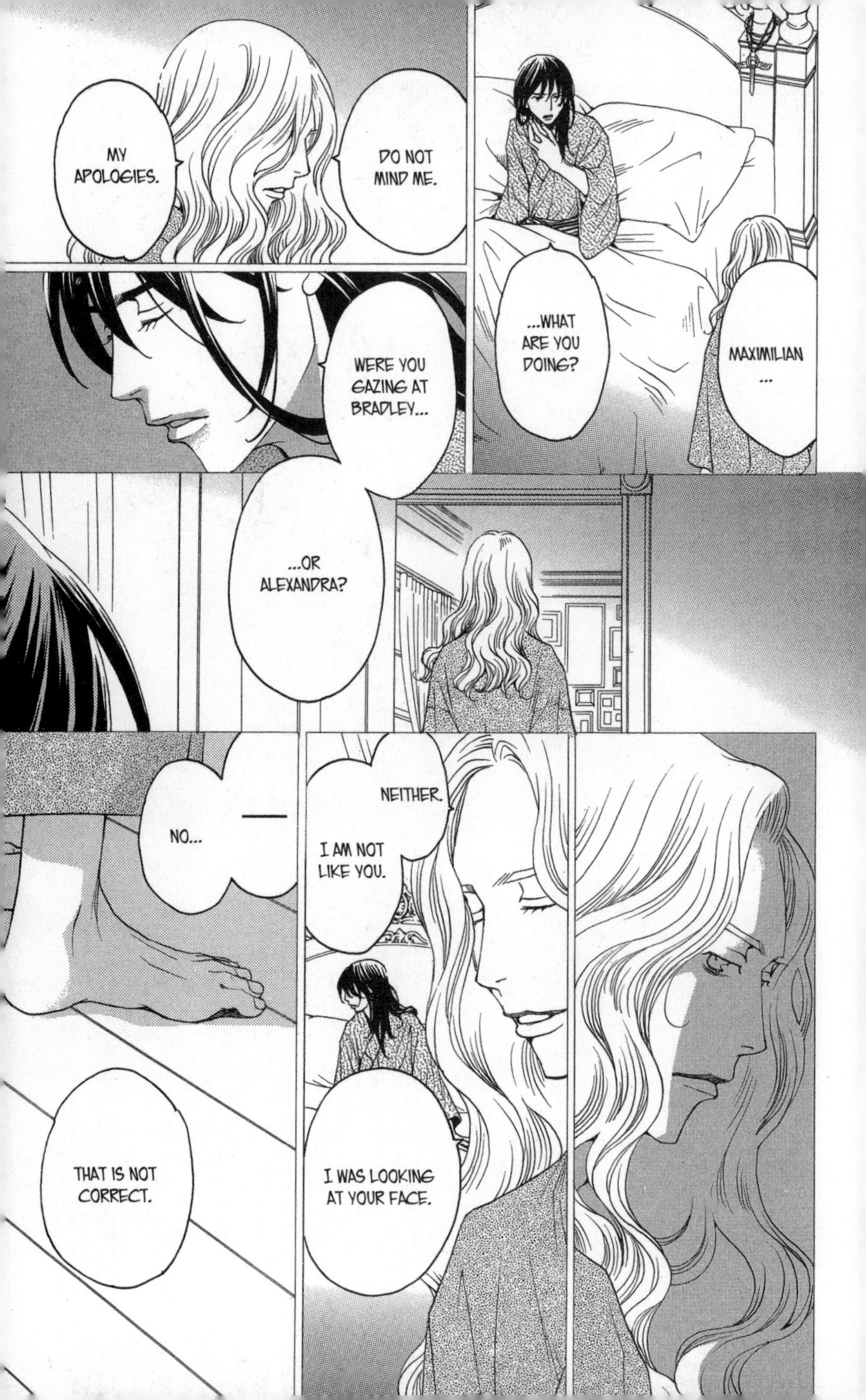
MAXIMILIAN
...
...WHAT ARE YOU DOING?
DO NOT MIND ME.
MY APOLOGIES.
WERE YOU GAZING AT BRADLEY...
...OR ALEXANDRA?
NEITHER.
I AM NOT LIKE YOU.
I WAS LOOKING AT YOUR FACE.
—
NO...
THAT IS NOT CORRECT.

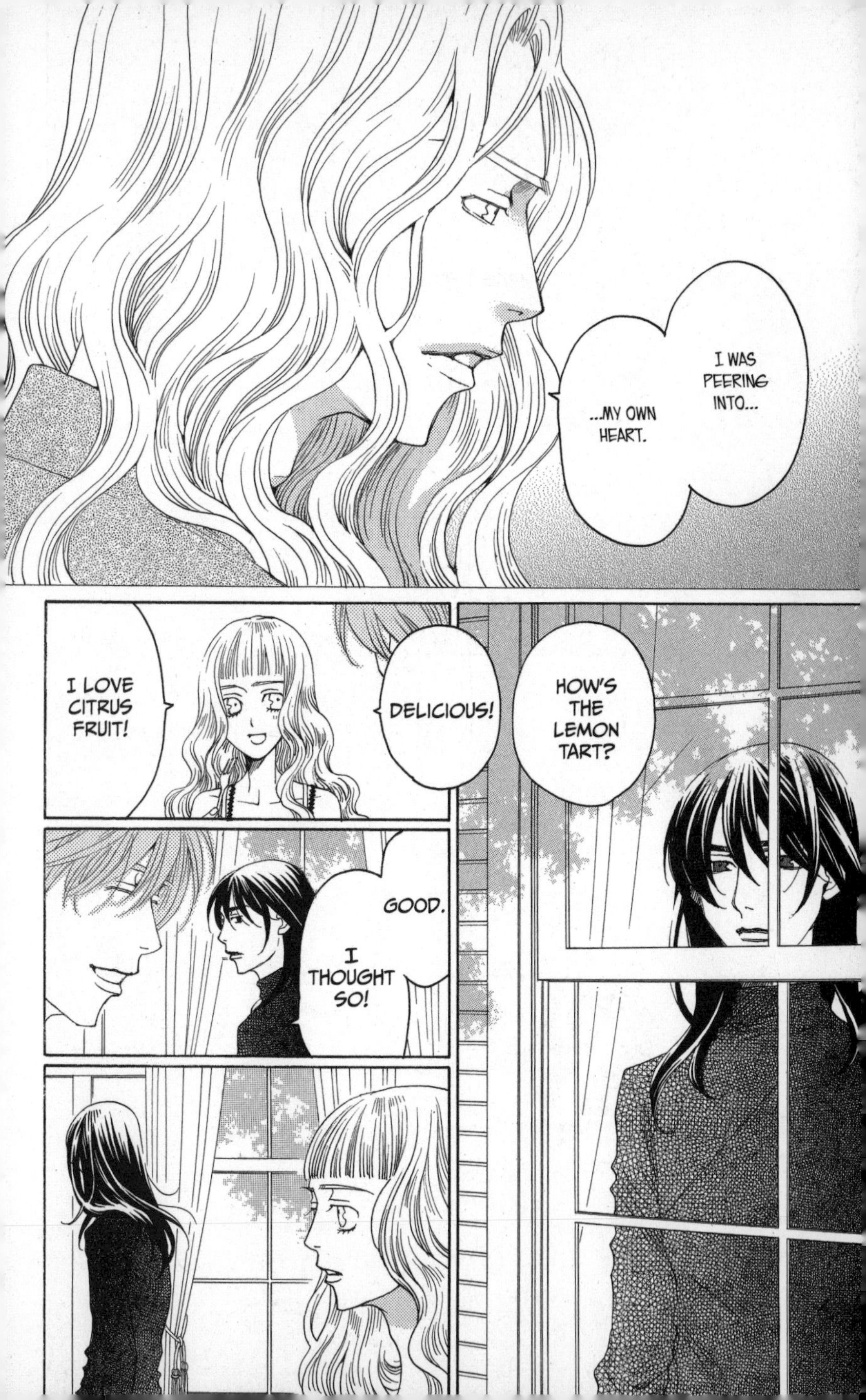
I WAS PEERING INTO...
...MY OWN HEART.
HOW'S THE LEMON TART?
DELICIOUS!
I LOVE CITRUS FRUIT!
GOOD.
I THOUGHT SO!

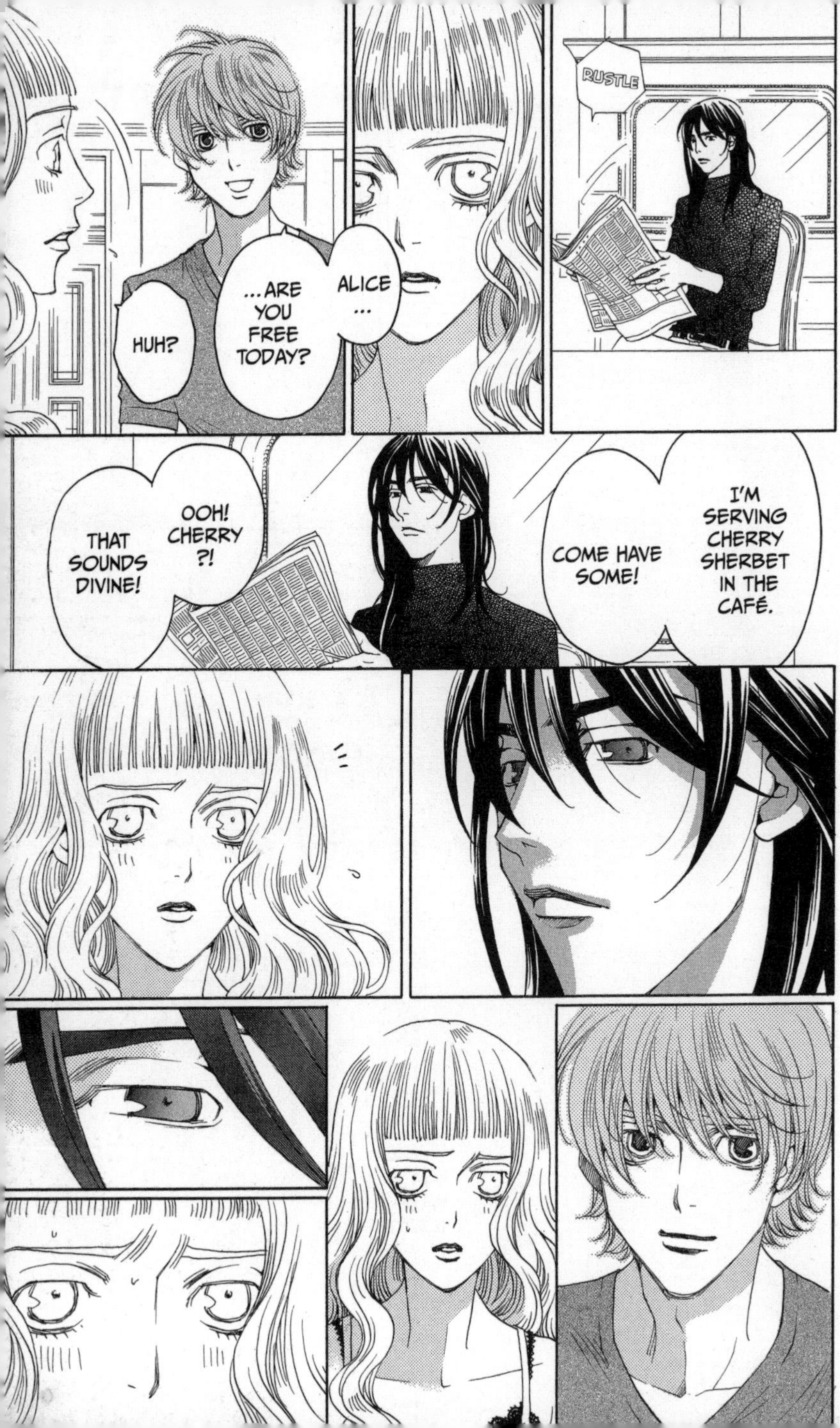
RUSTLE
ALICE ...
...ARE YOU FREE TODAY?
HUH?
I'M SERVING CHERRY SHERBET IN THE CAFÉ.
COME HAVE SOME!
OOH! CHERRY ?!
THAT SOUNDS DIVINE!

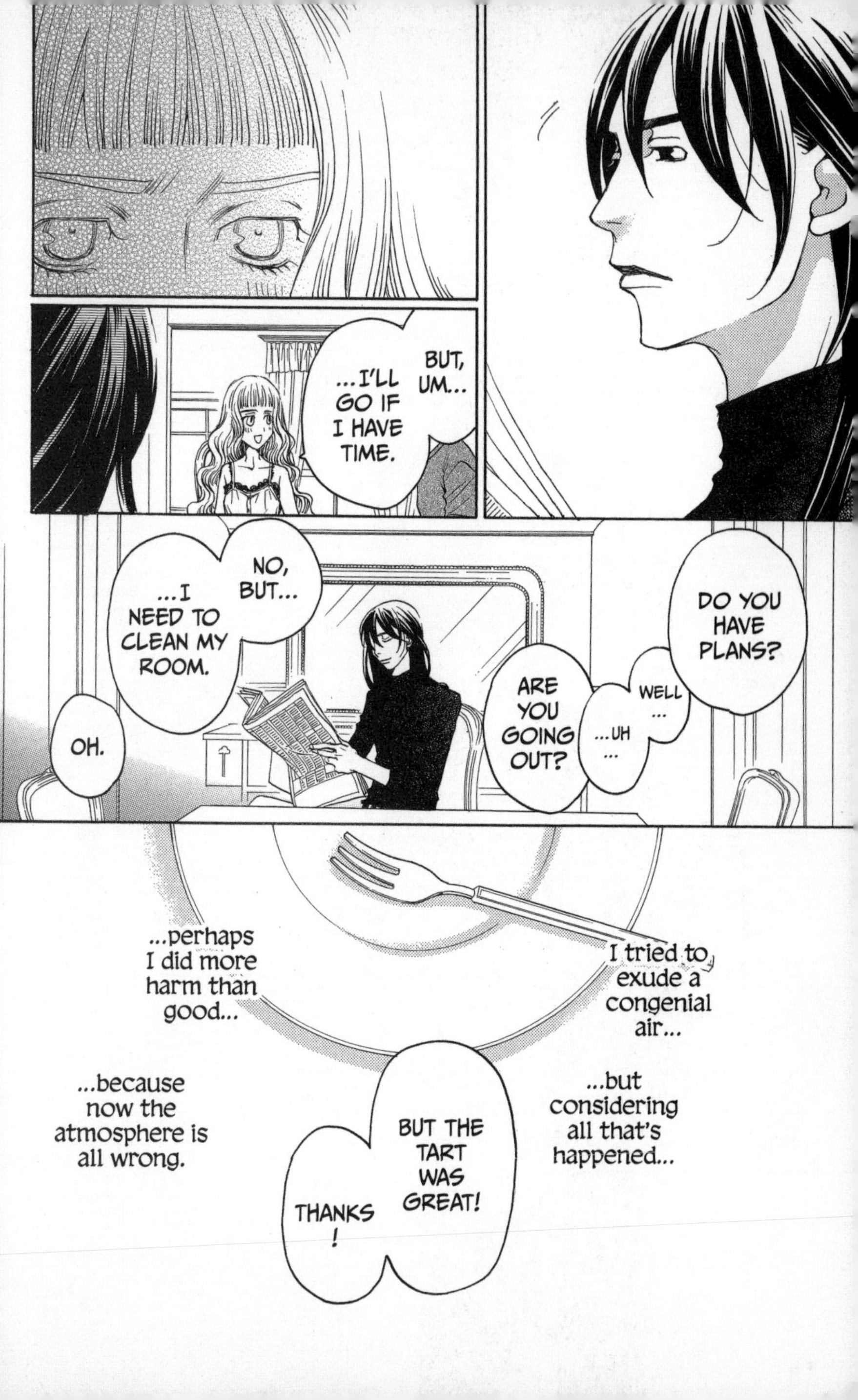
BUT, UM...
...I'LL GO IF I HAVE TIME.
DO YOU HAVE PLANS?
WELL ...
...UH ...
ARE YOU GOING OUT?
NO, BUT...
...I NEED TO CLEAN MY ROOM.
OH.
I tried to exude a congenial air...
...but considering all that's happened...
BUT THE TART WAS GREAT!
THANKS!
...perhaps I did more harm than good...
...because now the atmosphere is all wrong.

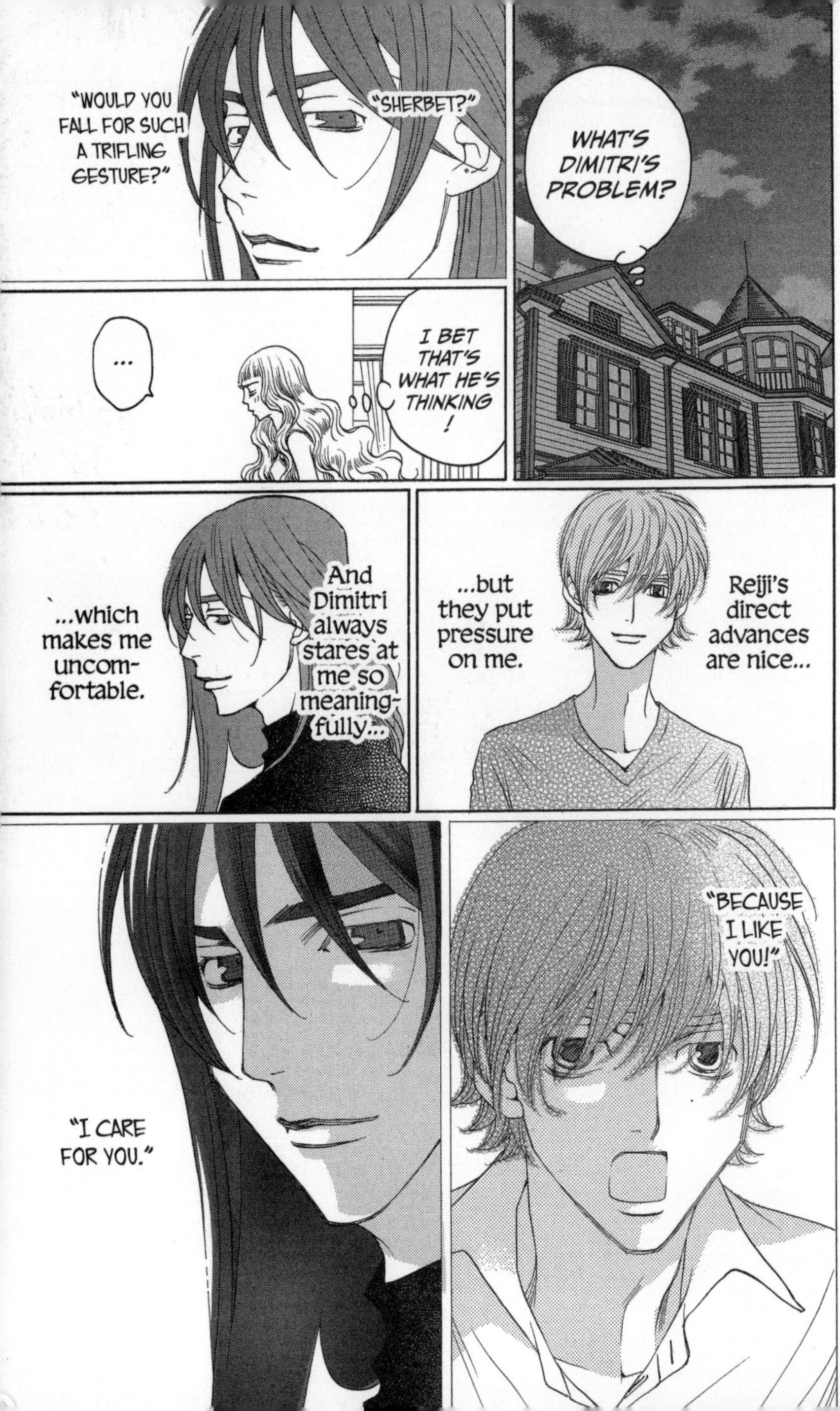
WHAT'S DIMITRI'S PROBLEM?
"SHERBET?"
"WOULD YOU FALL FOR SUCH A TRIFLING GESTURE?"
I BET THAT'S WHAT HE'S THINKING!
...
Reiji's direct advances are nice...
...but they put pressure on me.
And Dimitri always stares at me so meaningfully...
...which makes me uncomfortable.
"BECAUSE I LIKE YOU!"
"I CARE FOR YOU."

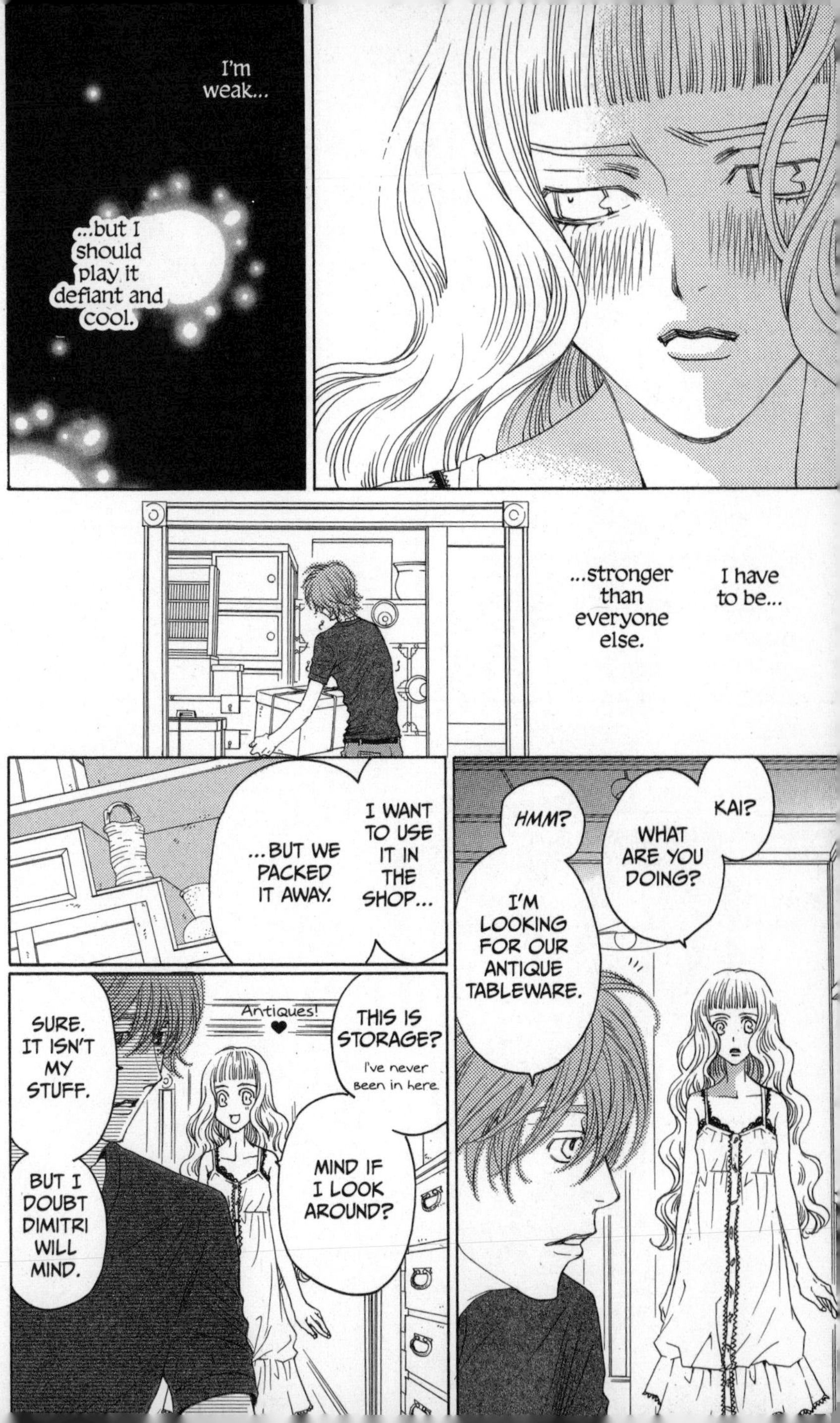
I'm weak...
...but I should play it defiant and cool.
I have to be...
...stronger than everyone else.
KAI?
WHAT ARE YOU DOING?
HMM?
I'M LOOKING FOR OUR ANTIQUE TABLEWARE.
I WANT TO USE IT IN THE SHOP...
...BUT WE PACKED IT AWAY.
THIS IS STORAGE?
Antiques!
I've never Been in here.
MIND IF I LOOK AROUND?
SURE. IT ISN'T MY STUFF.
BUT I DOUBT DIMITRI WILL MIND.

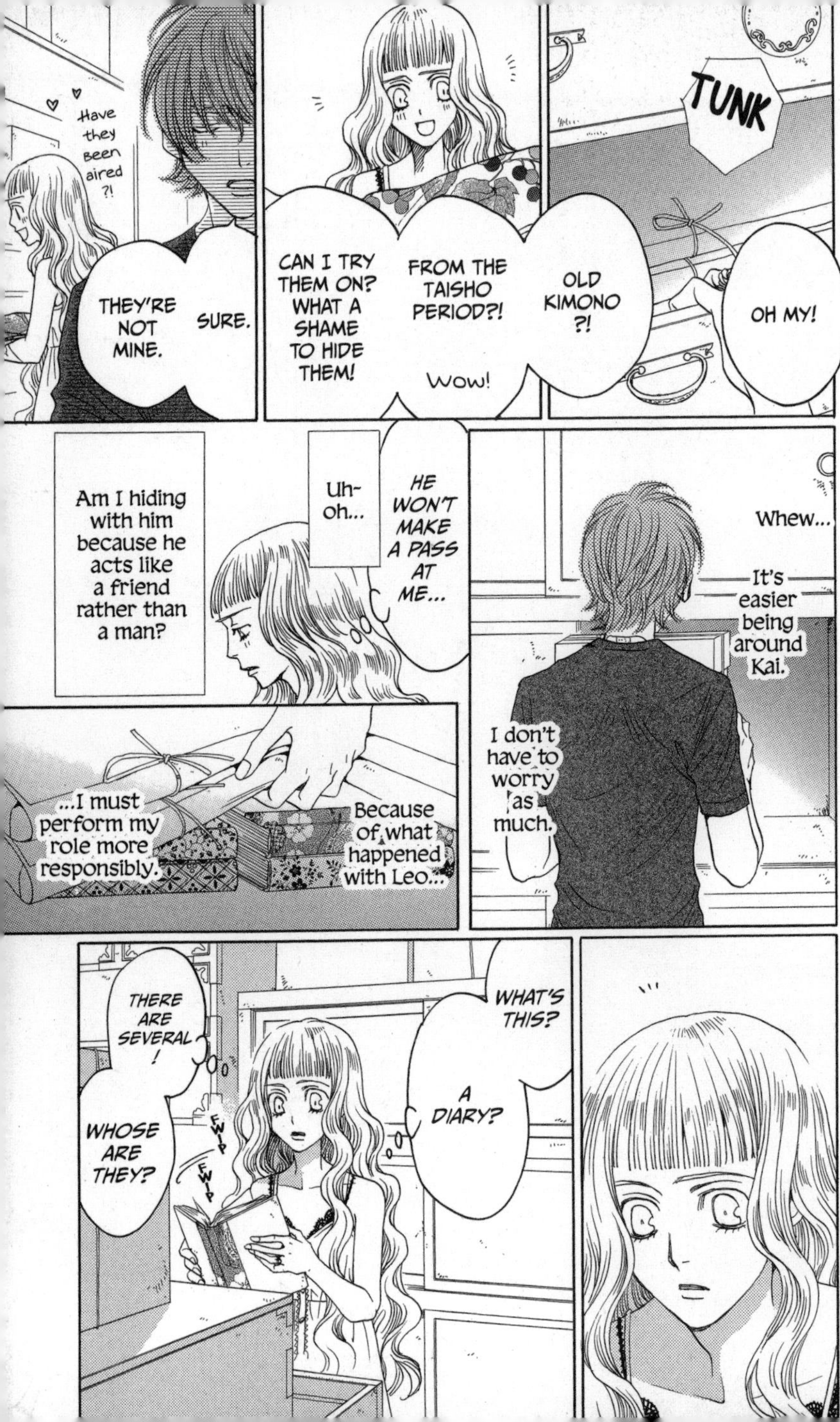
TUNK
OH MY!
OLD KIMONO ?!
FROM THE TAISHO PERIOD?!
Wow!
CAN I TRY THEM ON? WHAT A SHAME TO HIDE THEM!
SURE.
THEY'RE NOT MINE.
Have they been aired ?!
Whew...
It's easier being around Kai.
I don't have to worry as much.
HE WON'T MAKE A PASS AT ME...
Uh-oh...
Am I hiding with him because he acts like a friend rather than a man?
Because of what happened with Leo...
...I must perform my role more responsibly.
WHAT'S THIS?
A DIARY?
FWIP
FWIP
THERE ARE SEVERAL!
WHOSE ARE THEY?

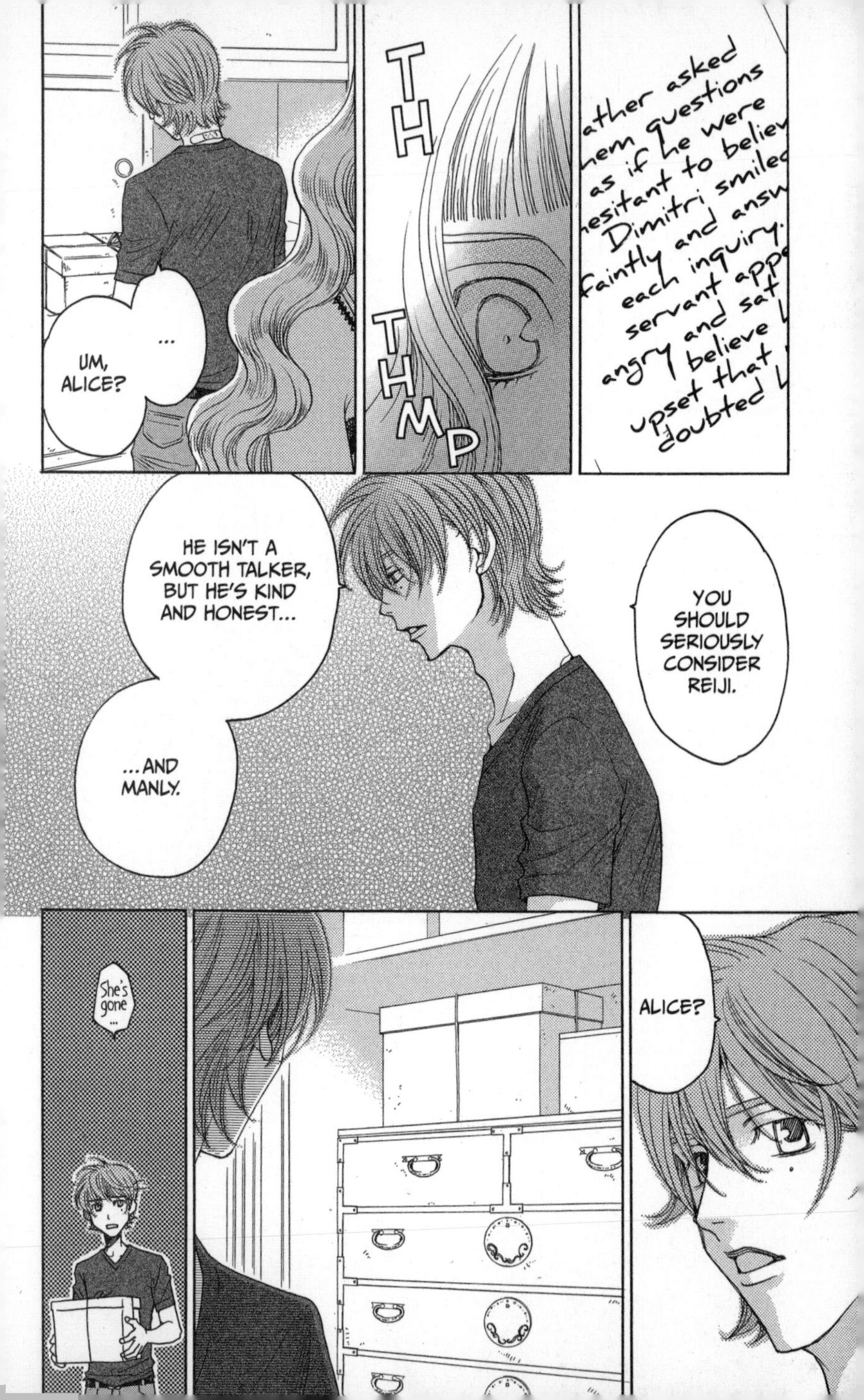
ather asked
hem questions
as if he were
esitant to believ
Dimitri smiled
faintly and answ
each inquiry.
servant app
angry and sat
believe
upset that
doubted
THTHMP
...
UM, ALICE?
YOU SHOULD SERIOUSLY CONSIDER REIJI.
HE ISN'T A SMOOTH TALKER, BUT HE'S KIND AND HONEST...
...AND MANLY.
ALICE?
She's gone...

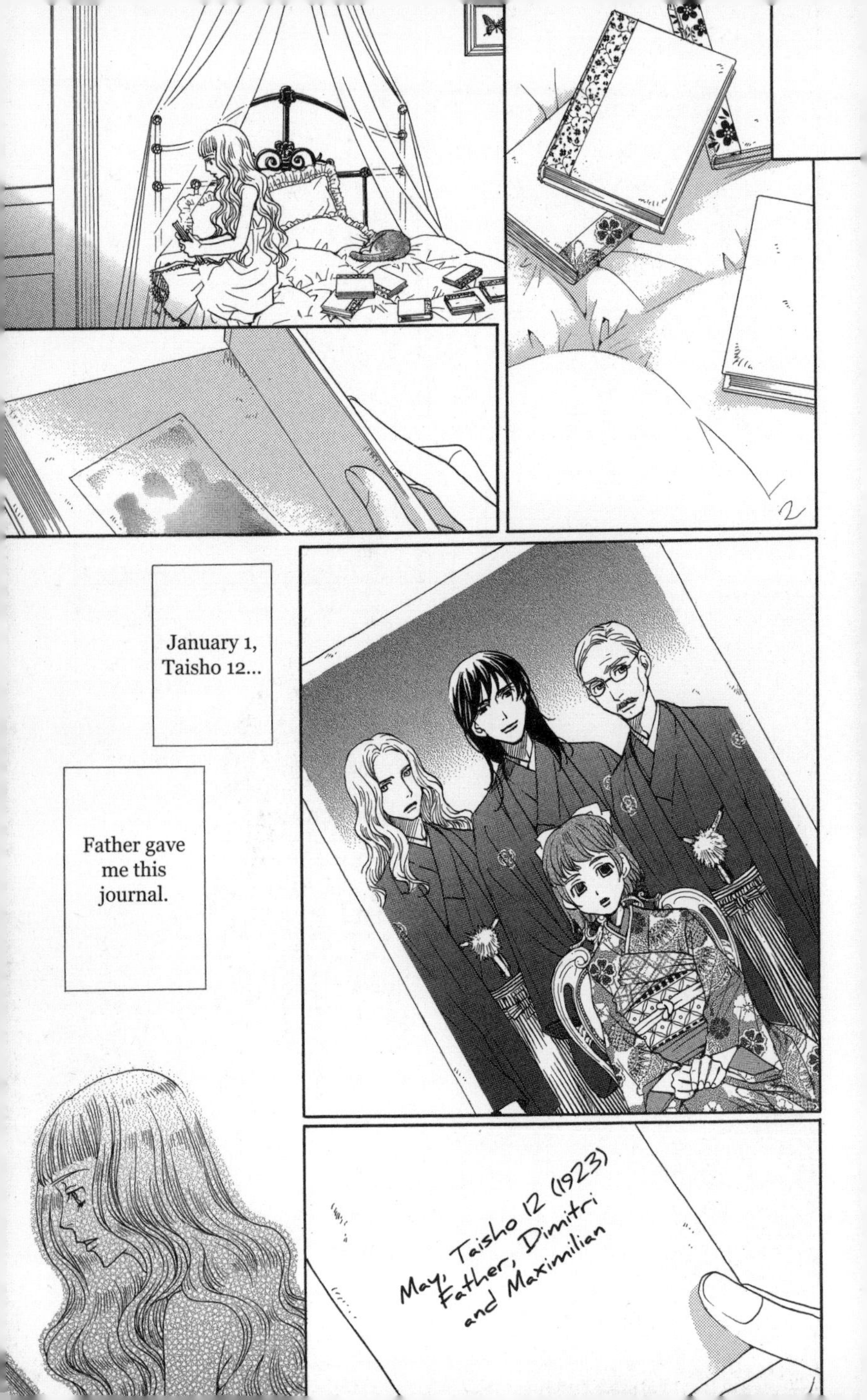
January 1, Taisho 12...
Father gave me this journal.
May, Taisho 12 (1923)
Father, Dimitri and Maximilian

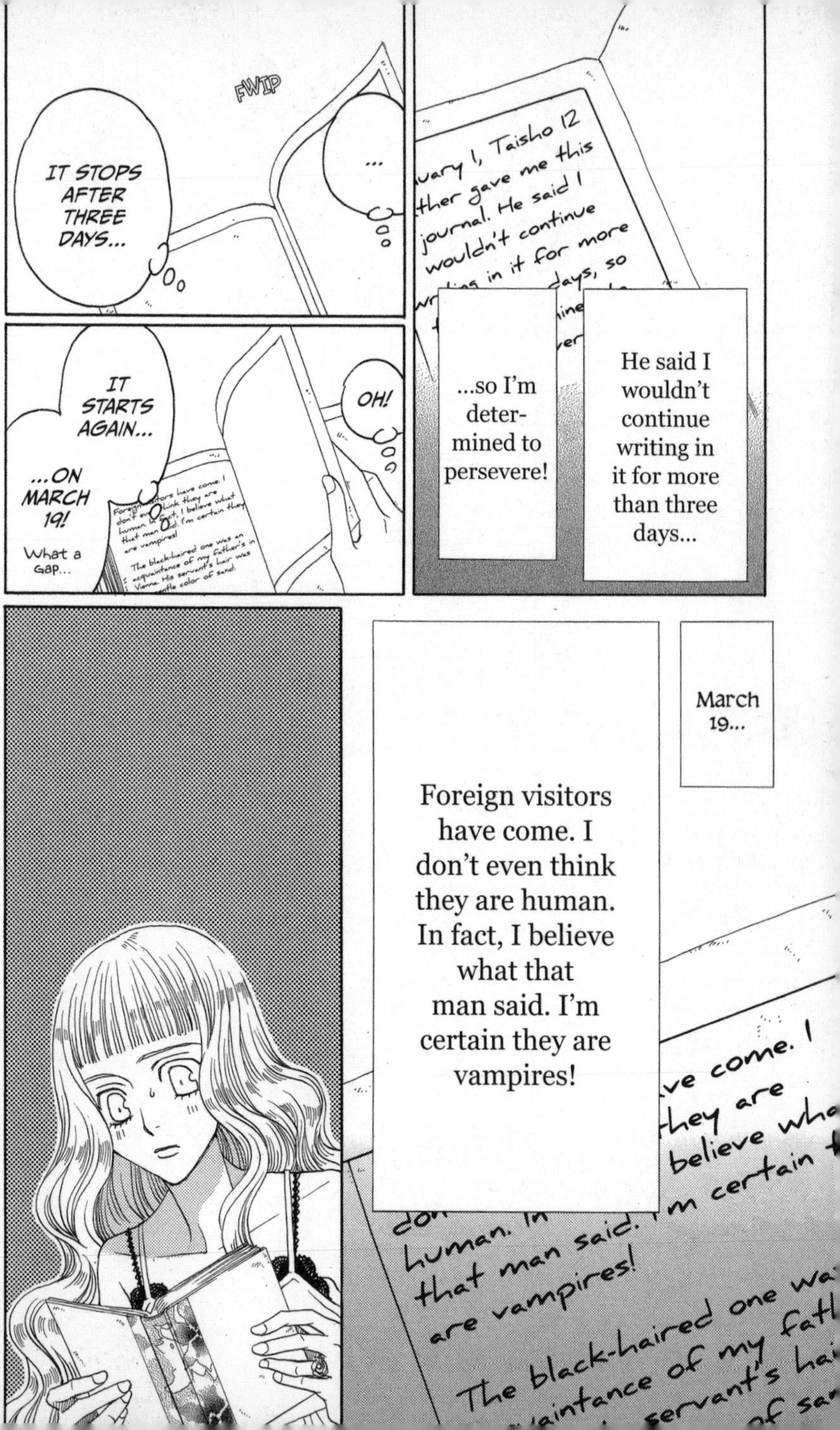

uary 1, Taisho 12
ther gave me this journal. He said I wouldn't continue wouldn't continue in it for more days, so
He said I wouldn't continue writing in it for more than three days...
...so I'm deter-mined to persevere!
...
FWIP
IT STOPS AFTER THREE DAYS...
OH!
IT STARTS AGAIN...
...ON MARCH 19!
What a Gap...
March 19...
Foreign visitors have come. I don't even think they are human. In fact, I believe what that man said. I'm certain they are vampires!
ve come. I
they are
believe wha
m certain t
human. In
that man said.
are vampires!
The black-haired one wa
aintance of my fath
servant's hai

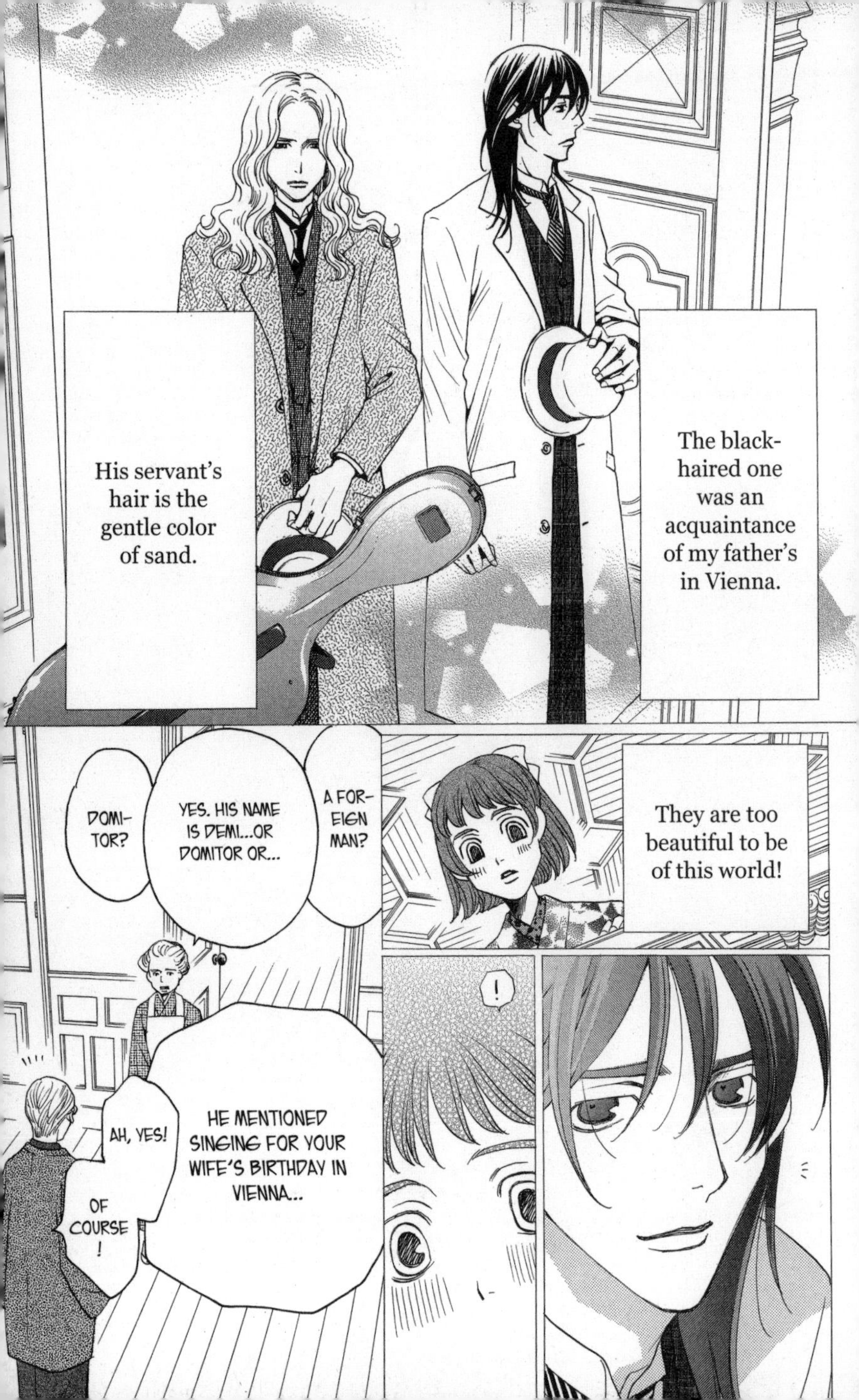
The black-haired one was an acquaintance of my father's in Vienna.
His servant's hair is the gentle color of sand.
They are too beautiful to be of this world!
!
A FOR-EIGN MAN?
YES. HIS NAME IS DEMI...OR DOMITOR OR...
DOMI-TOR?
HE MENTIONED SINGING FOR YOUR WIFE'S BIRTHDAY IN VIENNA...
AH, YES!
OF COURSE!

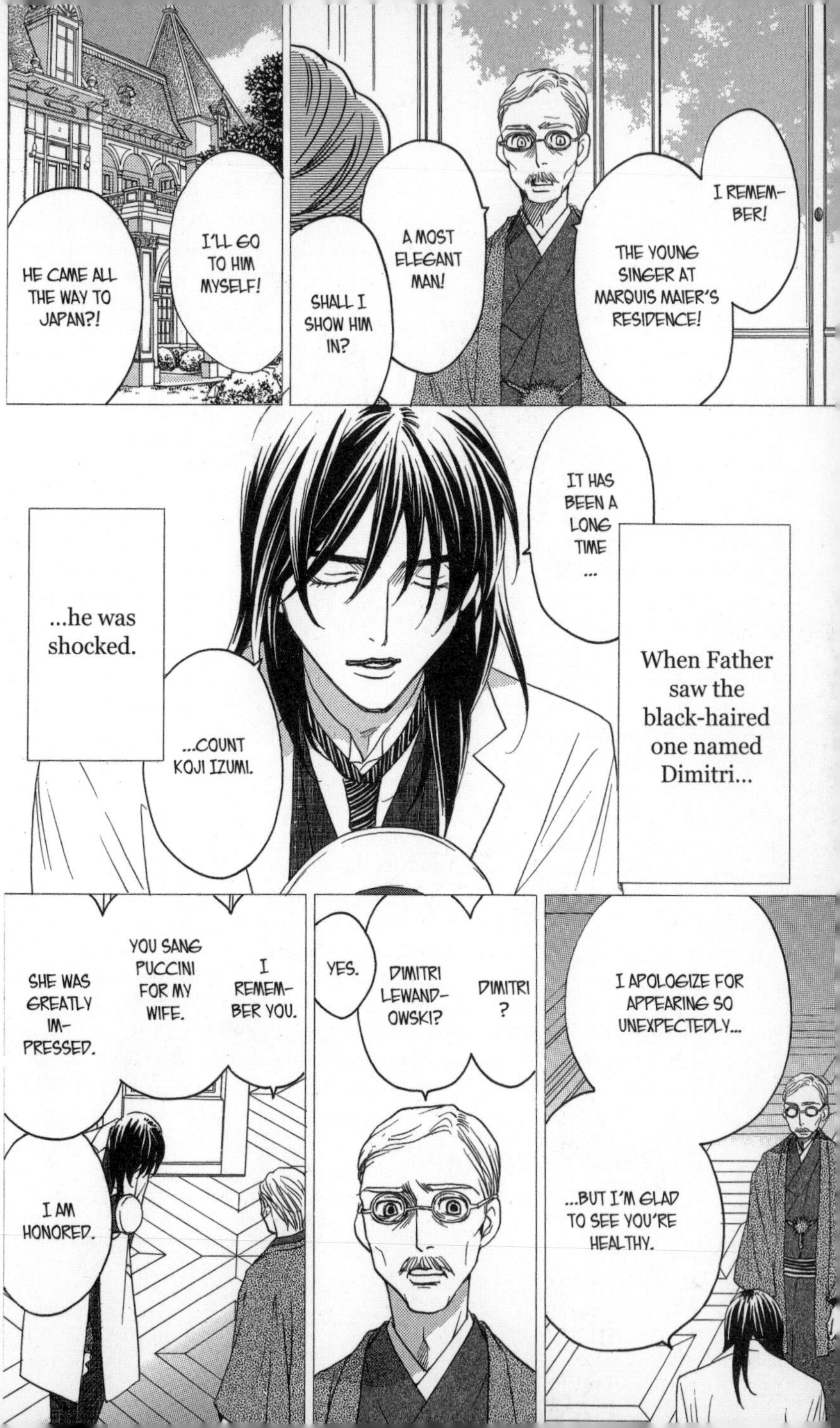
I REMEMBER!
THE YOUNG SINGER AT MARQUIS MAIER'S RESIDENCE!
A MOST ELEGANT MAN!
SHALL I SHOW HIM IN?
I'LL GO TO HIM MYSELF!
HE CAME ALL THE WAY TO JAPAN?!
When Father saw the black-haired one named Dimitri...
IT HAS BEEN A LONG TIME...
...COUNT KOJI IZUMI.
...he was shocked.
I APOLOGIZE FOR APPEARING SO UNEXPECTEDLY...
...BUT I'M GLAD TO SEE YOU'RE HEALTHY.
DIMITRI?
DIMITRI LEWANDOWSKI?
YES.
I REMEMBER YOU.
YOU SANG PUCCINI FOR MY WIFE.
SHE WAS GREATLY IMPRESSED.
I AM HONORED.

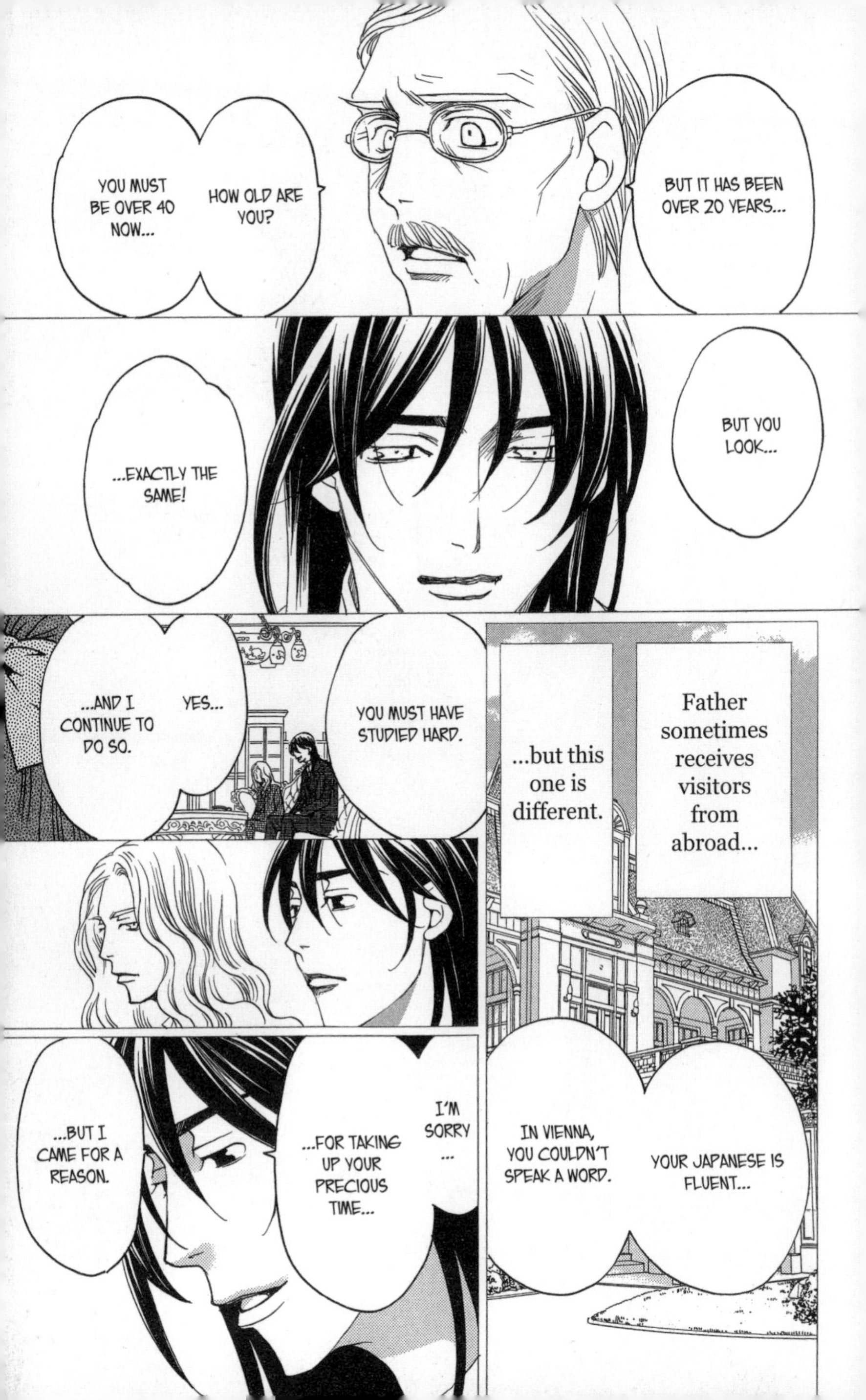
BUT IT HAS BEEN OVER 20 YEARS...
HOW OLD ARE YOU?
YOU MUST BE OVER 40 NOW...
BUT YOU LOOK...
...EXACTLY THE SAME!
Father sometimes receives visitors from abroad...
...but this one is different.
YOUR JAPANESE IS FLUENT...
IN VIENNA, YOU COULDN'T SPEAK A WORD.
YOU MUST HAVE STUDIED HARD.
YES...
...AND I CONTINUE TO DO SO.
I'M SORRY ...
...FOR TAKING UP YOUR PRECIOUS TIME...
...BUT I CAME FOR A REASON.

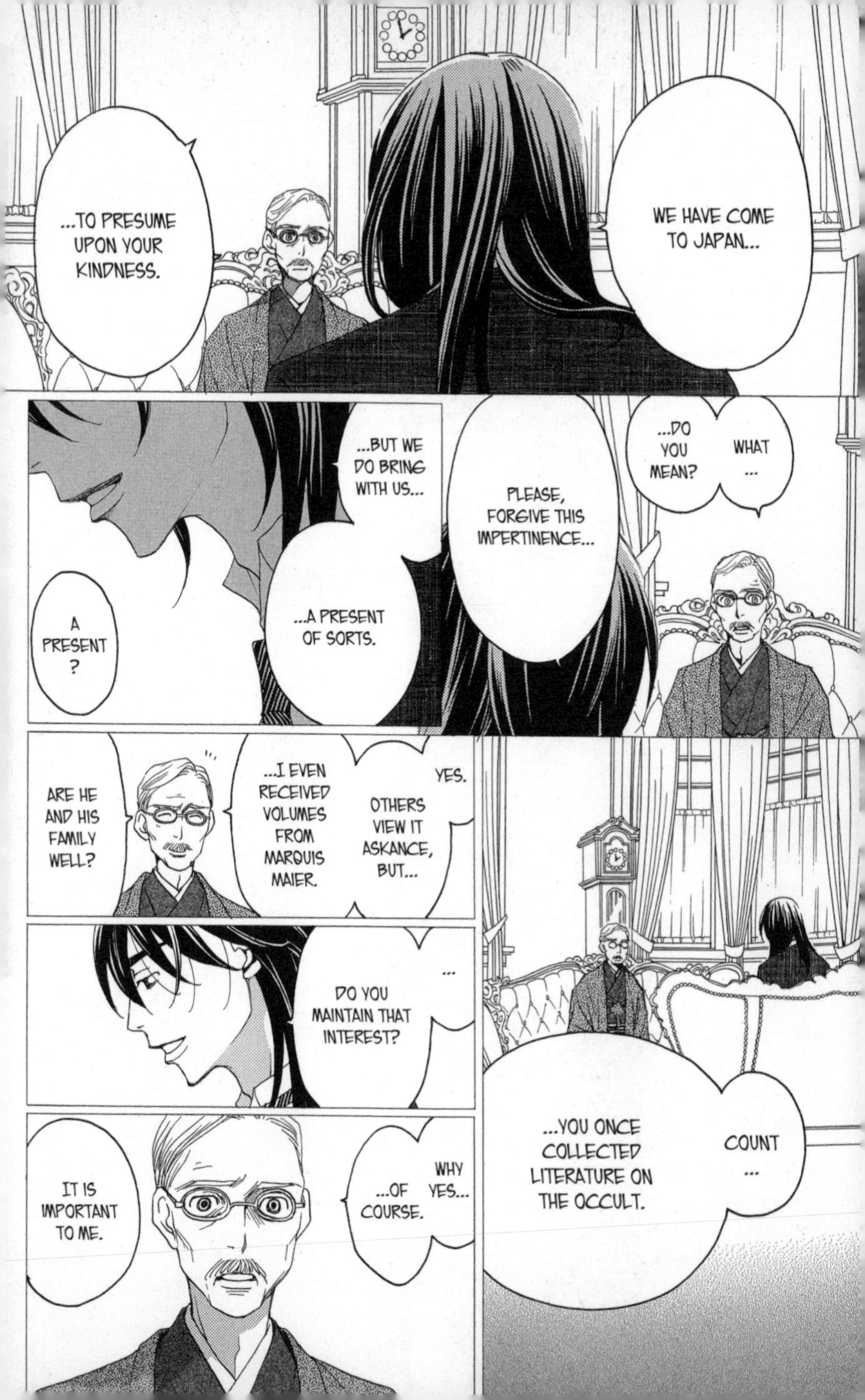
WE HAVE COME TO JAPAN...
...TO PRESUME UPON YOUR KINDNESS.
WHAT ...
...DO YOU MEAN?
PLEASE, FORGIVE THIS IMPERTINENCE...
...BUT WE DO BRING WITH US...
...A PRESENT OF SORTS.
A PRESENT ?
COUNT ...
...YOU ONCE COLLECTED LITERATURE ON THE OCCULT.
YES.
OTHERS VIEW IT ASKANCE, BUT...
...I EVEN RECEIVED VOLUMES FROM MARQUIS MAIER.
ARE HE AND HIS FAMILY WELL?
...
DO YOU MAINTAIN THAT INTEREST?
WHY YES...
...OF COURSE.
IT IS IMPORTANT TO ME.

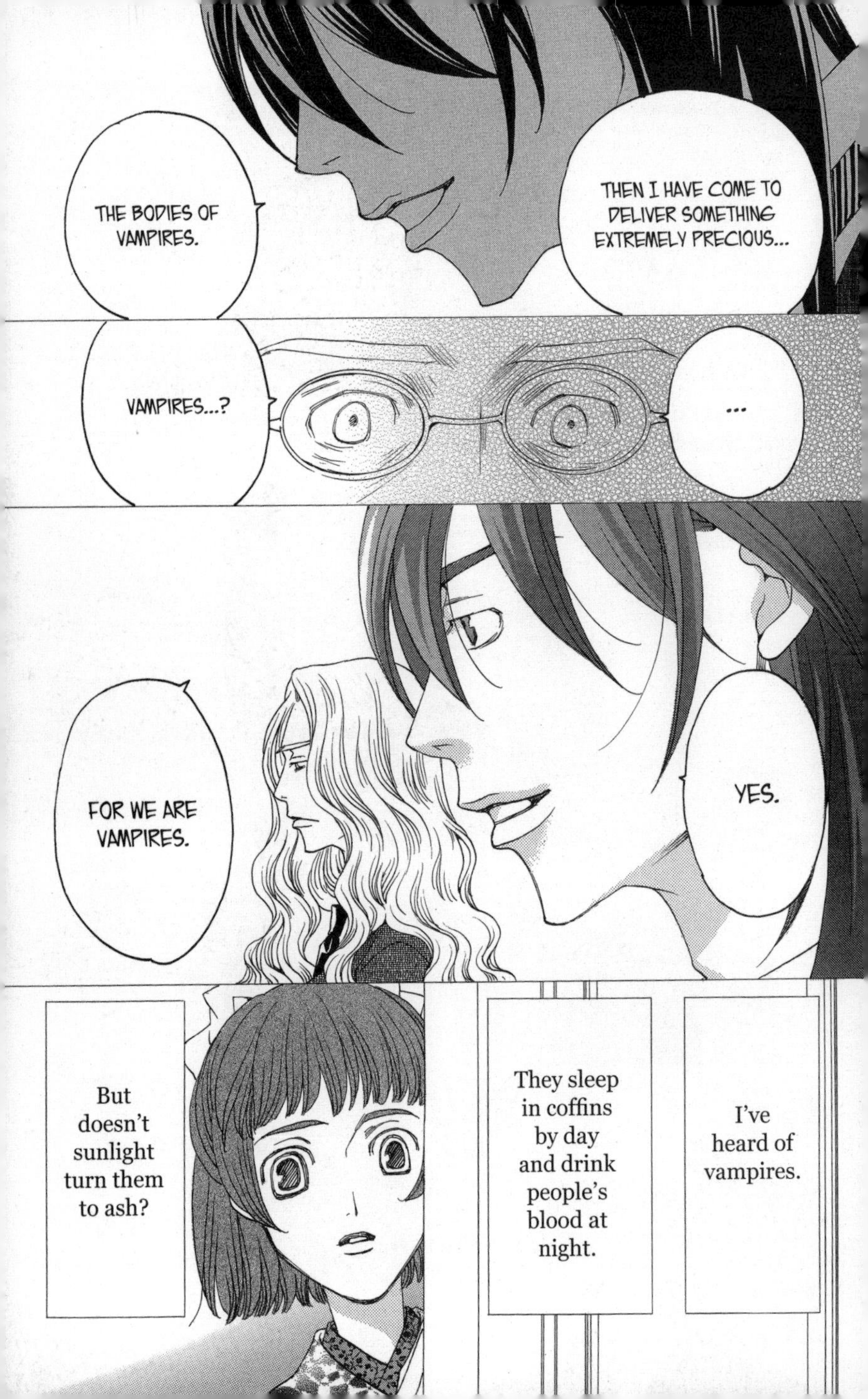
THEN I HAVE COME TO DELIVER SOMETHING EXTREMELY PRECIOUS...
THE BODIES OF VAMPIRES.
...
VAMPIRES...?
YES.
FOR WE ARE VAMPIRES.
I've heard of vampires.
They sleep in coffins by day and drink people's blood at night.
But doesn't sunlight turn them to ash?

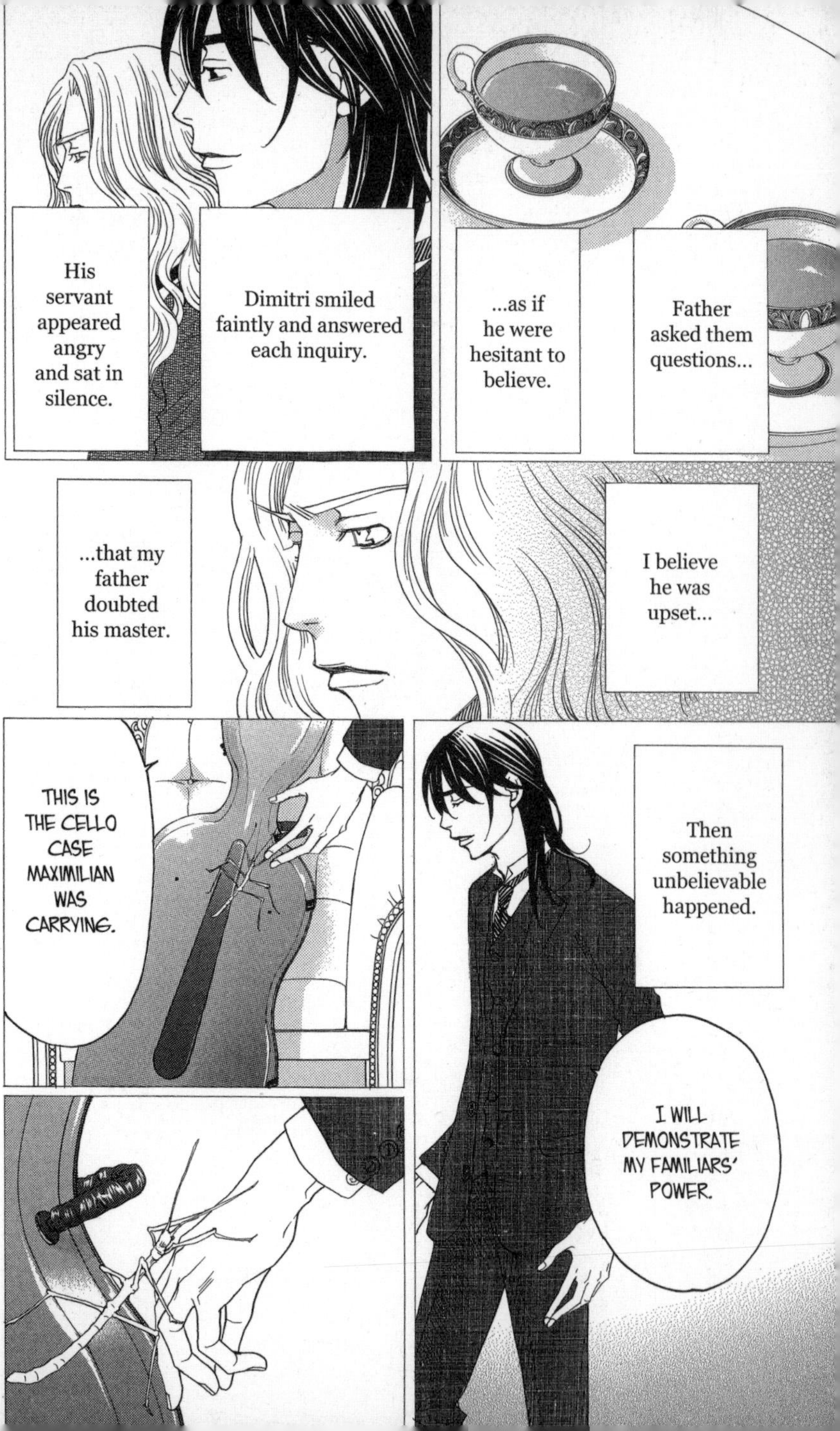
Father asked them questions...
...as if he were hesitant to believe.
Dimitri smiled faintly and answered each inquiry.
His servant appeared angry and sat in silence.
I believe he was upset...
...that my father doubted his master.
Then something unbelievable happened.
I WILL DEMONSTRATE MY FAMILIARS' POWER.
THIS IS THE CELLO CASE MAXIMILIAN WAS CARRYING.

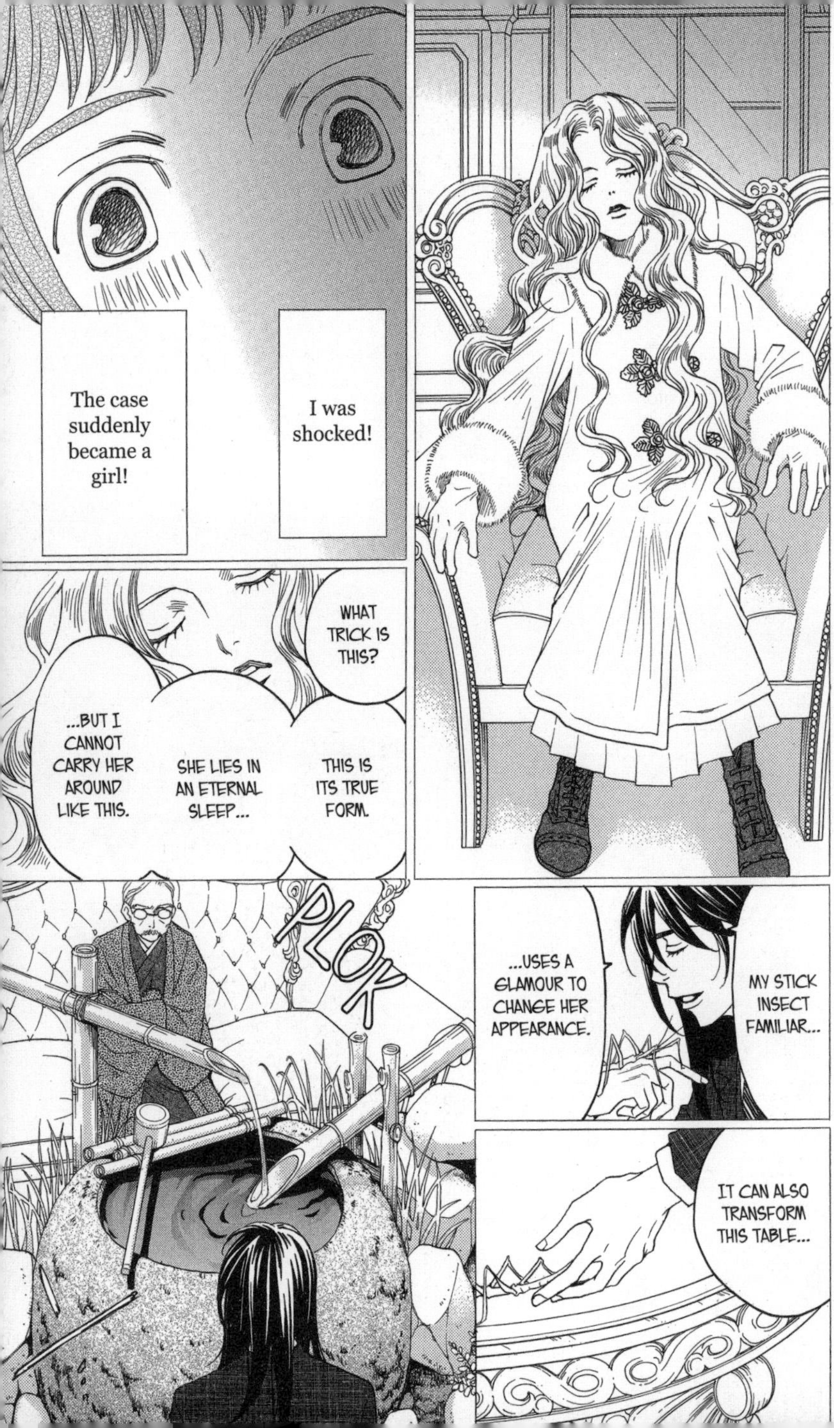
I was shocked!
The case suddenly became a girl!
WHAT TRICK IS THIS?
THIS IS ITS TRUE FORM.
SHE LIES IN AN ETERNAL SLEEP...
...BUT I CANNOT CARRY HER AROUND LIKE THIS.
MY STICK INSECT FAMILIAR...
...USES A GLAMOUR TO CHANGE HER APPEARANCE.
IT CAN ALSO TRANSFORM THIS TABLE...
PLOK

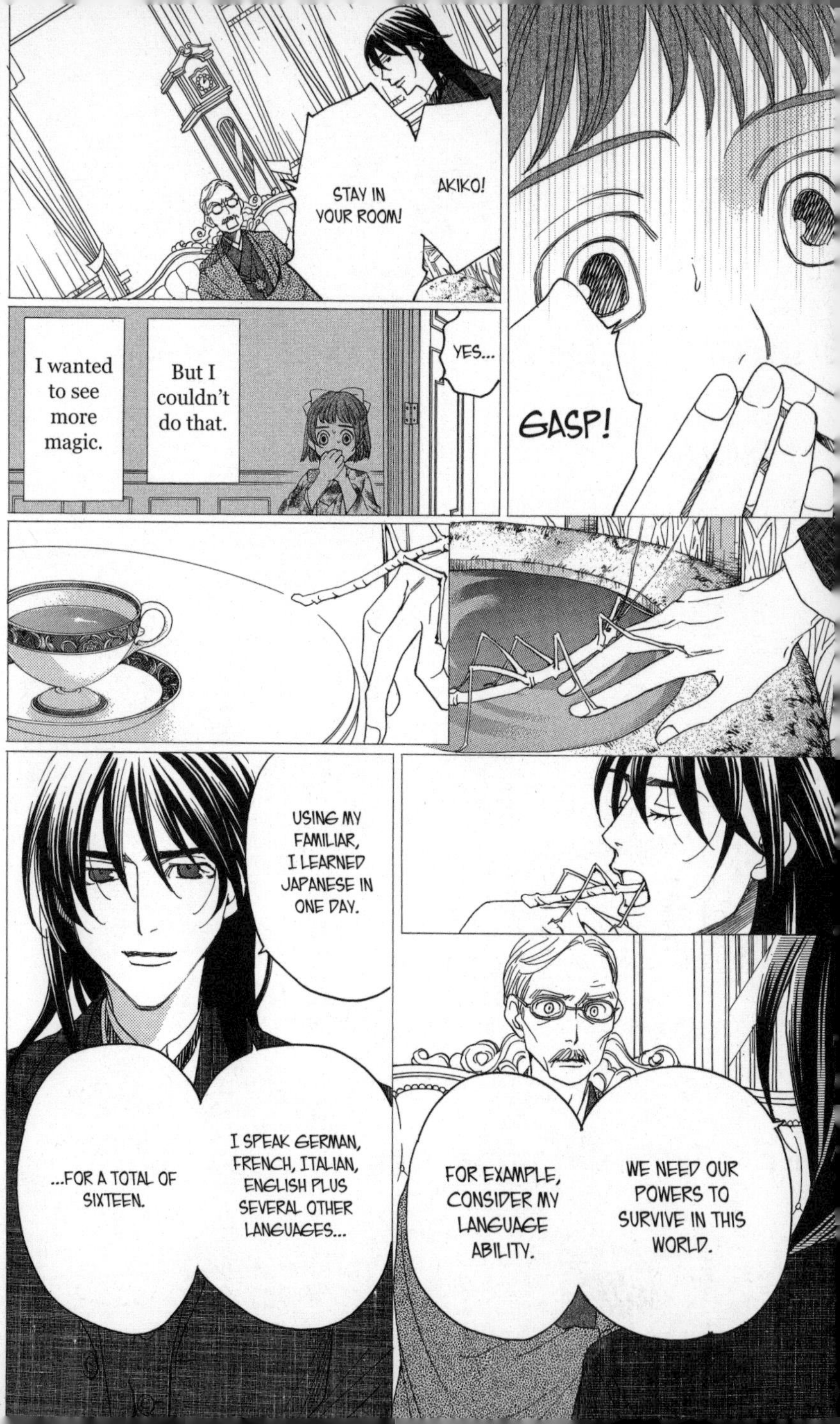
GASP!
AKIKO!
STAY IN YOUR ROOM!
YES...
I wanted to see more magic.
But I couldn't do that.
WE NEED OUR POWERS TO SURVIVE IN THIS WORLD.
FOR EXAMPLE, CONSIDER MY LANGUAGE ABILITY.
USING MY FAMILIAR, I LEARNED JAPANESE IN ONE DAY.
I SPEAK GERMAN, FRENCH, ITALIAN, ENGLISH PLUS SEVERAL OTHER LANGUAGES...
...FOR A TOTAL OF SIXTEEN.

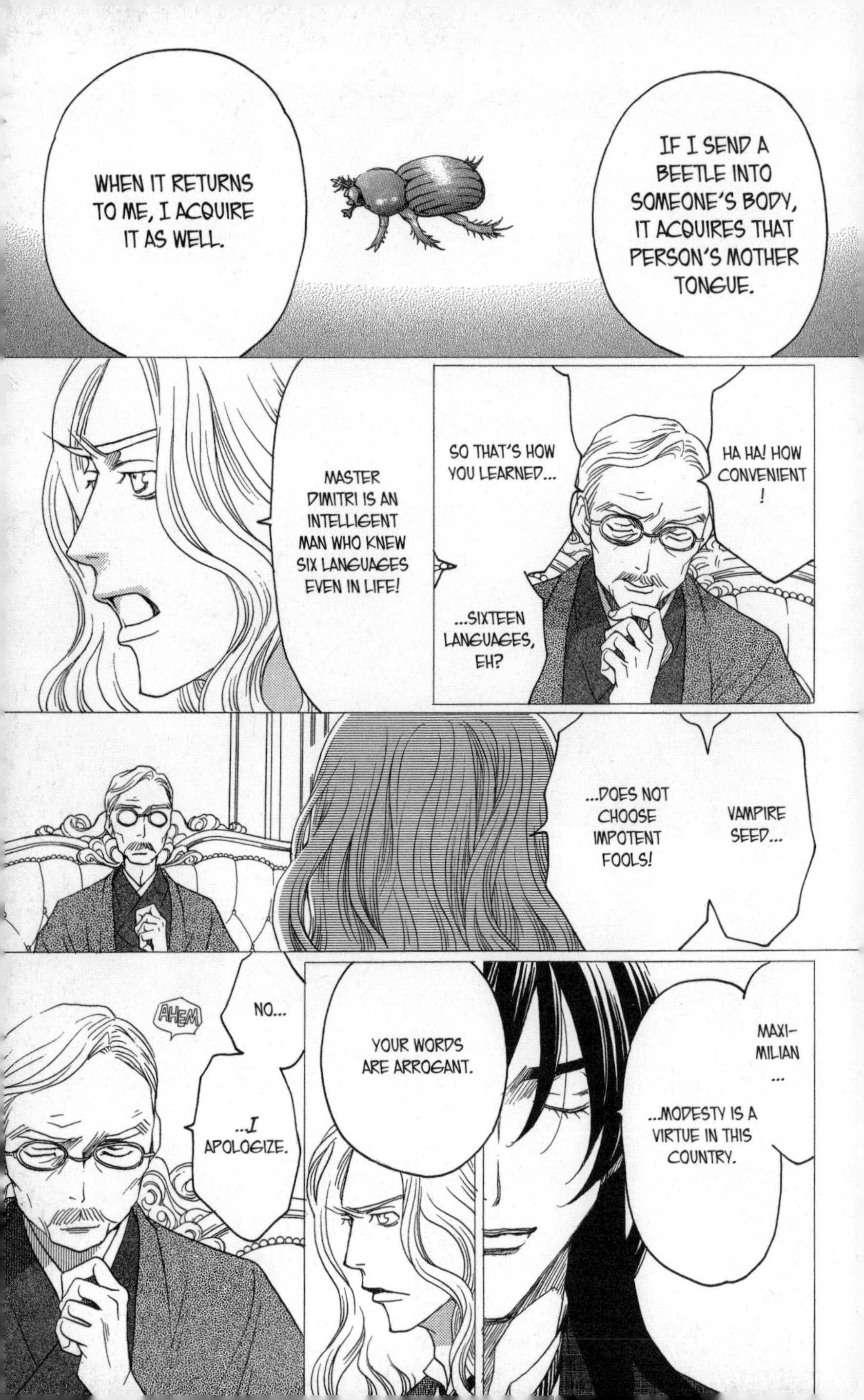
IF I SEND A BEETLE INTO SOMEONE'S BODY, IT ACQUIRES THAT PERSON'S MOTHER TONGUE.
WHEN IT RETURNS TO ME, I ACQUIRE IT AS WELL.
HA HA! HOW CONVENIENT!
SO THAT'S HOW YOU LEARNED...
...SIXTEEN LANGUAGES, EH?
MASTER DIMITRI IS AN INTELLIGENT MAN WHO KNEW SIX LANGUAGES EVEN IN LIFE!
VAMPIRE SEED...
...DOES NOT CHOOSE IMPOTENT FOOLS!
MAXI-MILIAN...
...MODESTY IS A VIRTUE IN THIS COUNTRY.
YOUR WORDS ARE ARROGANT.
NO...
AHEM
...I APOLOGIZE.

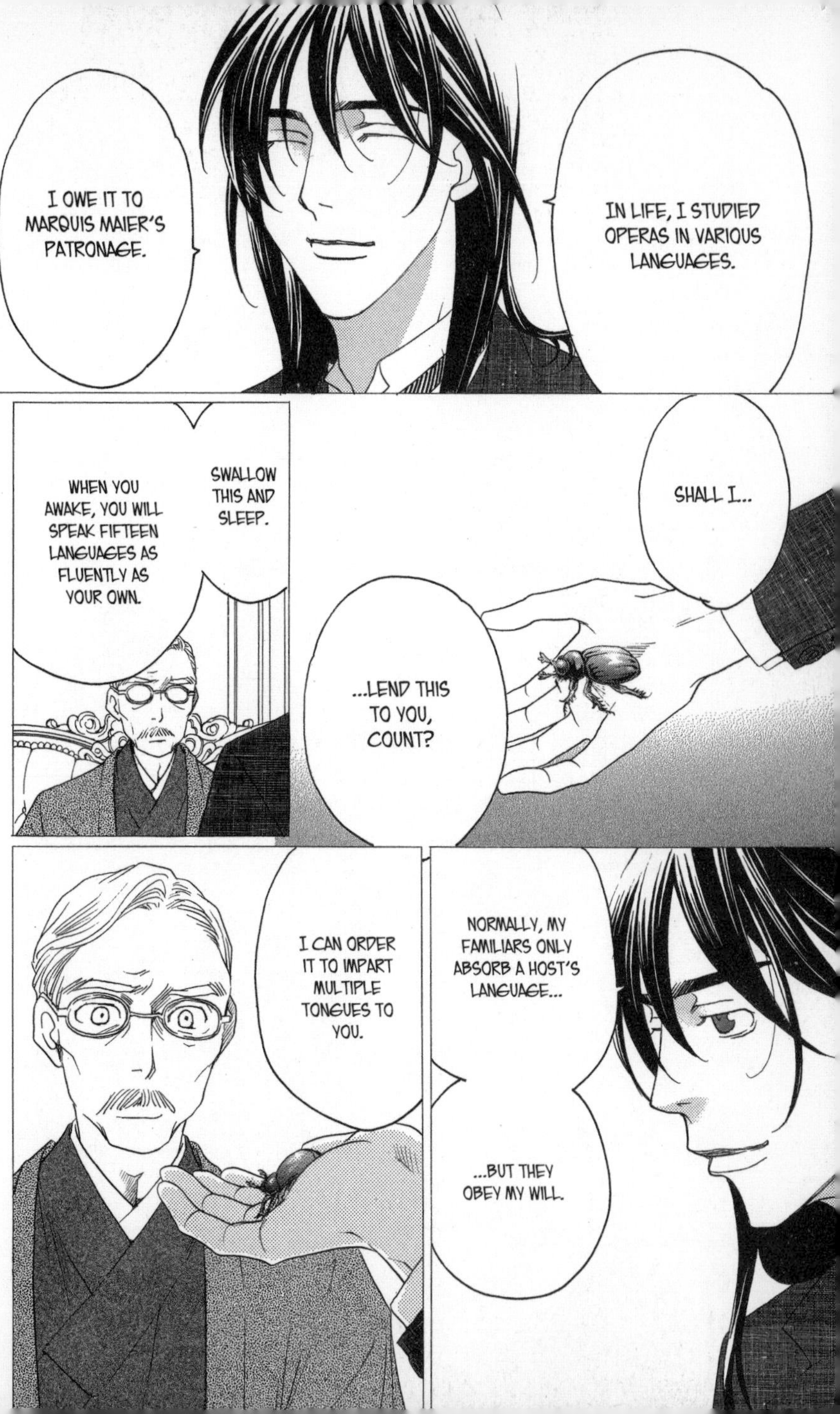
IN LIFE, I STUDIED OPERAS IN VARIOUS LANGUAGES.
I OWE IT TO MARQUIS MAIER'S PATRONAGE.
SHALL I...
...LEND THIS TO YOU, COUNT?
SWALLOW THIS AND SLEEP.
WHEN YOU AWAKE, YOU WILL SPEAK FIFTEEN LANGUAGES AS FLUENTLY AS YOUR OWN.
NORMALLY, MY FAMILIARS ONLY ABSORB A HOST'S LANGUAGE...
...BUT THEY OBEY MY WILL.
I CAN ORDER IT TO IMPART MULTIPLE TONGUES TO YOU.

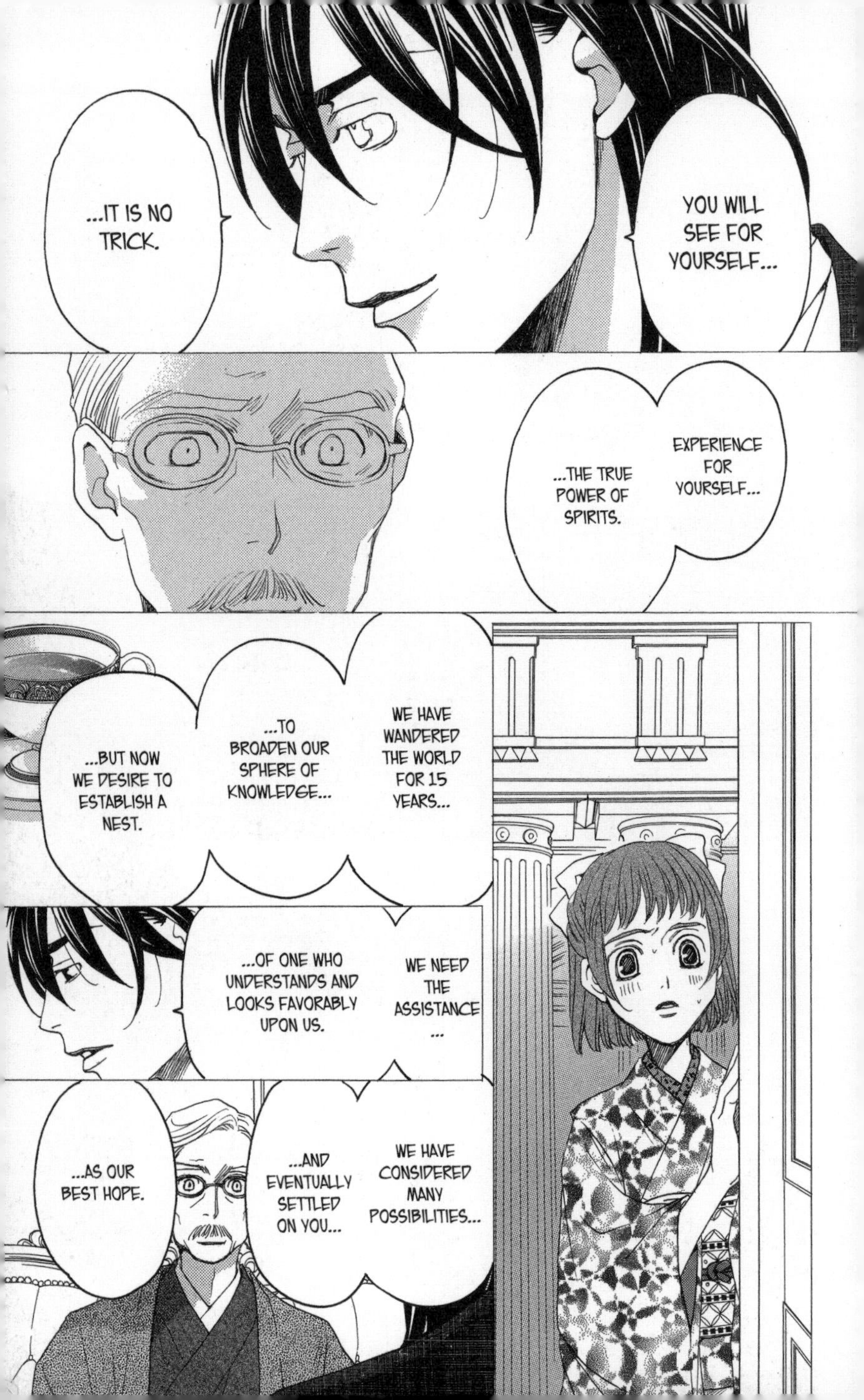
YOU WILL SEE FOR YOURSELF...
...IT IS NO TRICK.
EXPERIENCE FOR YOURSELF...
...THE TRUE POWER OF SPIRITS.
WE HAVE WANDERED THE WORLD FOR 15 YEARS...
...TO BROADEN OUR SPHERE OF KNOWLEDGE...
...BUT NOW WE DESIRE TO ESTABLISH A NEST.
WE NEED THE ASSISTANCE...
...OF ONE WHO UNDERSTANDS AND LOOKS FAVORABLY UPON US.
WE HAVE CONSIDERED MANY POSSIBILITIES...
...AND EVENTUALLY SETTLED ON YOU...
...AS OUR BEST HOPE.

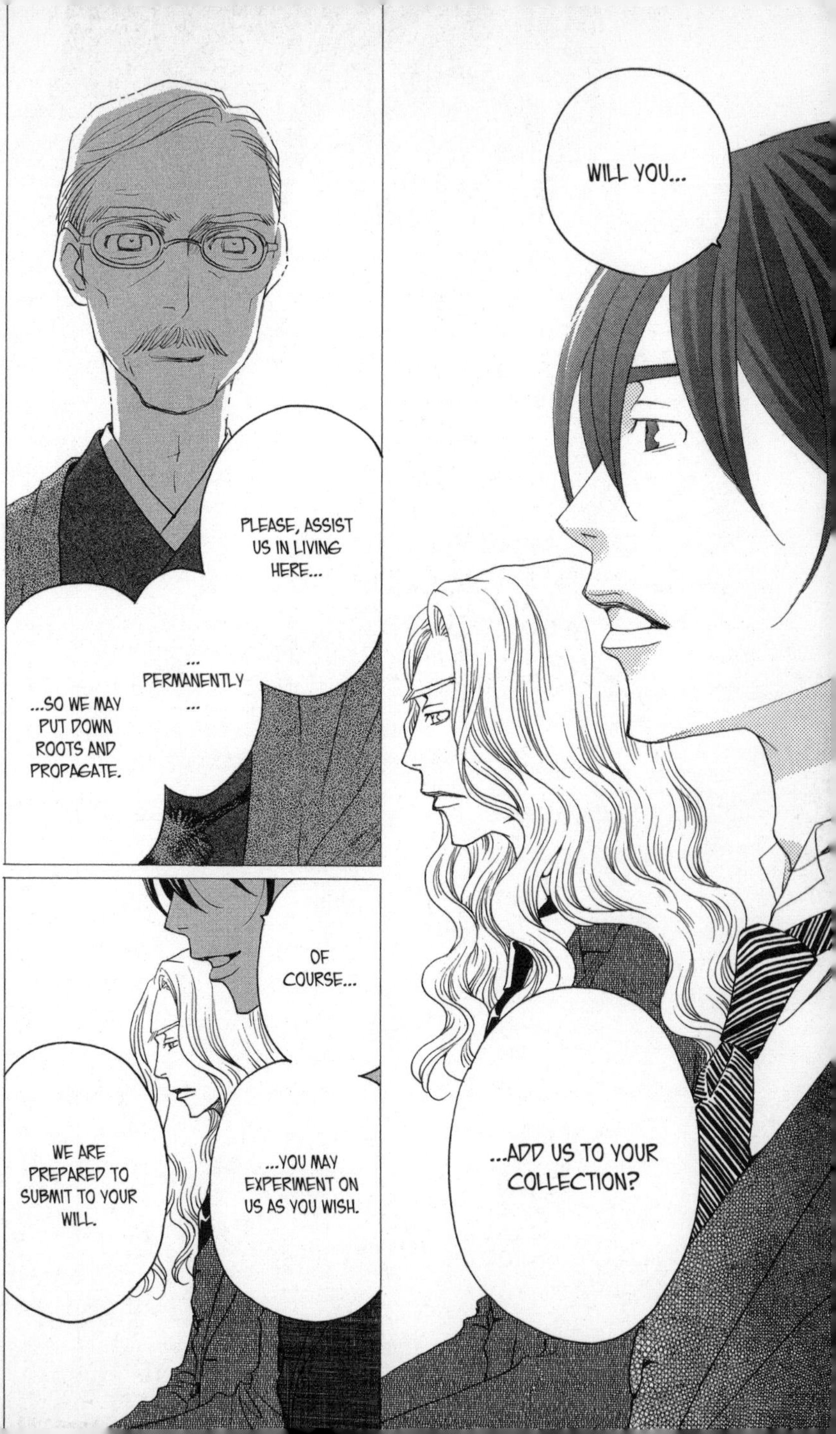
WILL YOU...
...ADD US TO YOUR COLLECTION?
PLEASE, ASSIST US IN LIVING HERE...
... PERMANENTLY ...
...SO WE MAY PUT DOWN ROOTS AND PROPAGATE.
OF COURSE...
...YOU MAY EXPERIMENT ON US AS YOU WISH.
WE ARE PREPARED TO SUBMIT TO YOUR WILL.

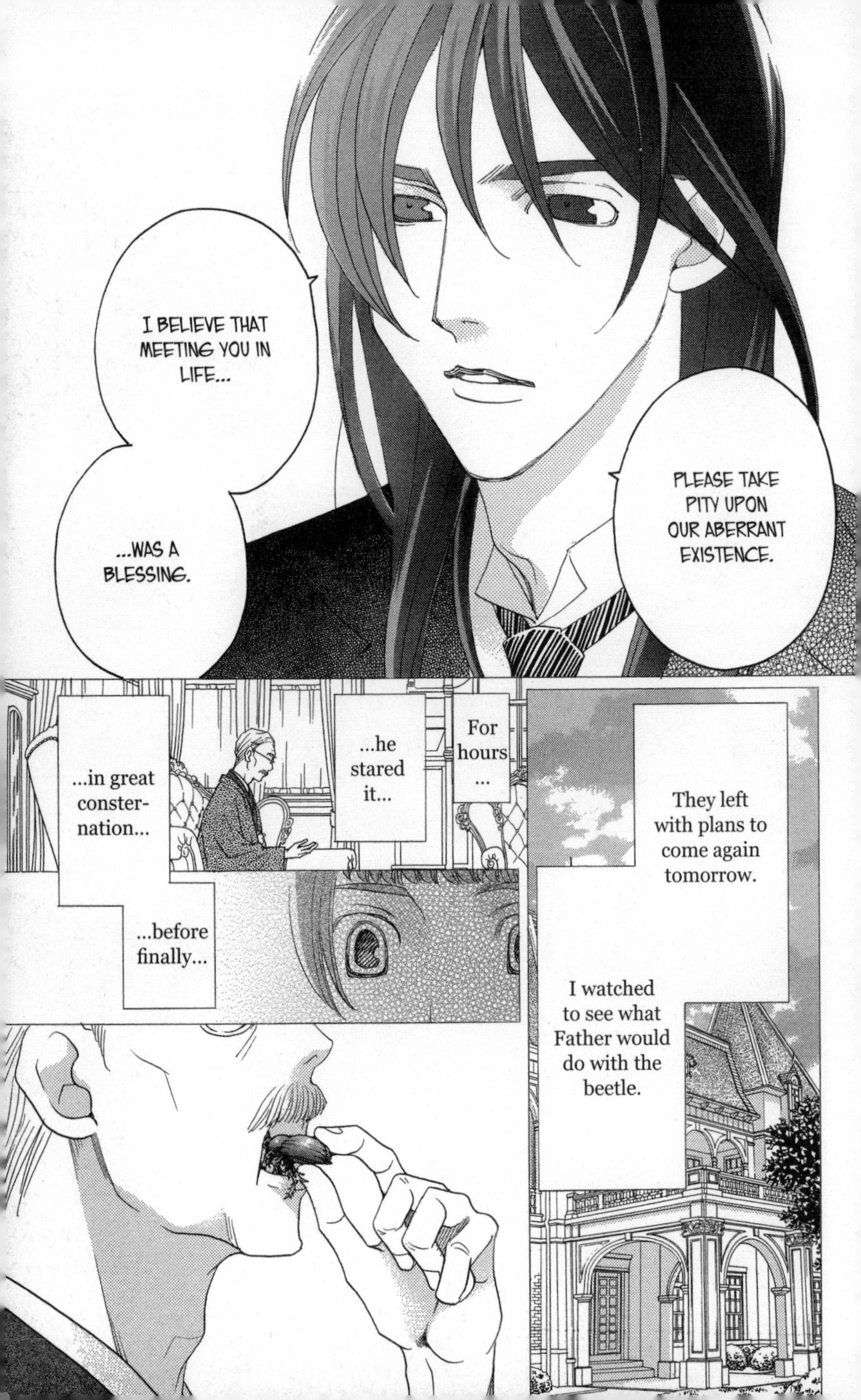
PLEASE TAKE PITY UPON OUR ABERRANT EXISTENCE.
I BELIEVE THAT MEETING YOU IN LIFE...
...WAS A BLESSING.
They left with plans to come again tomorrow.
I watched to see what Father would do with the beetle.
For hours ...
...he stared it...
...in great conster-nation...
...before finally...

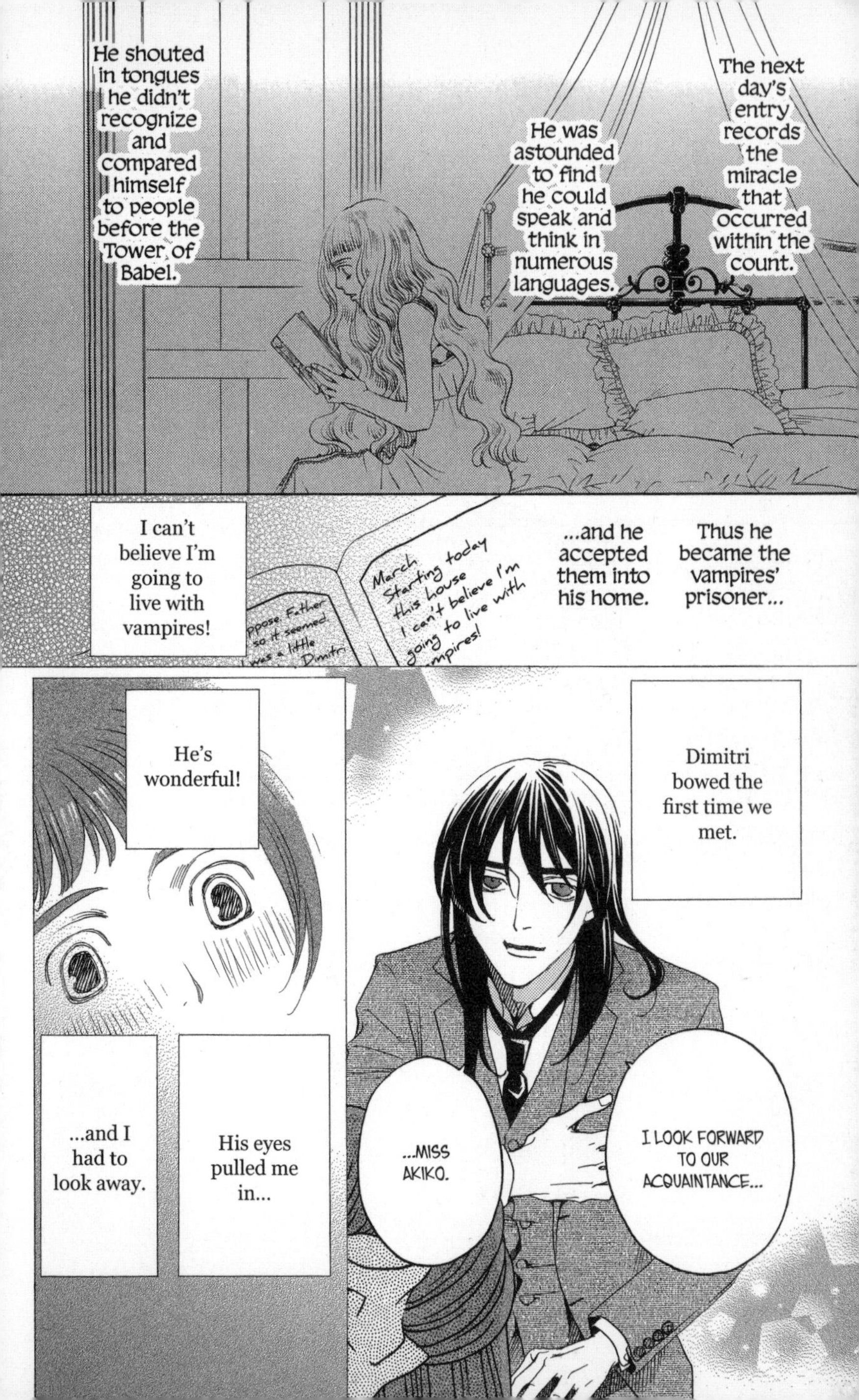
The next day's entry records the miracle that occurred within the count.
He was astounded to find he could speak and think in numerous languages.
He shouted in tongues he didn't recognize and compared himself to people before the Tower of Babel.
Thus he became the vampires' prisoner...
...and he accepted them into his home.
March
Starting today
this house
I can't believe I'm
going to live with
I can't believe I'm going to live with vampires!
Dimitri bowed the first time we met.
I LOOK FORWARD TO OUR ACQUAINTANCE...
...MISS AKIKO.
He's wonderful!
His eyes pulled me in...
...and I had to look away.

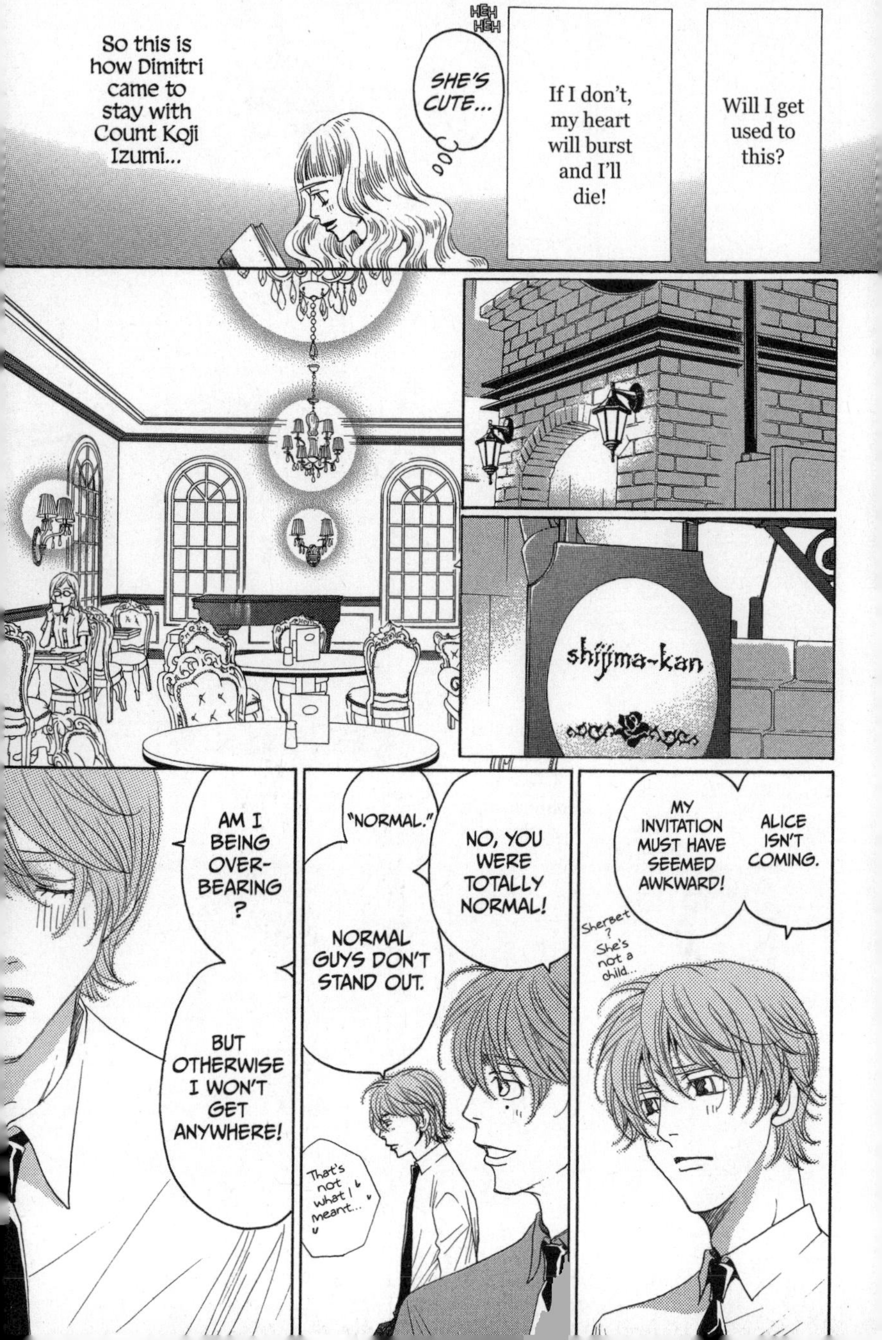
Will I get used to this?
If I don't, my heart will burst and I'll die!
HEH HEH
SHE'S CUTE...
So this is how Dimitri came to stay with Count Koji Izumi...
shijima-kan
ALICE ISN'T COMING.
MY INVITATION MUST HAVE SEEMED AWKWARD!
Sherbet? She's not a child...
NO, YOU WERE TOTALLY NORMAL!
"NORMAL."
NORMAL GUYS DON'T STAND OUT.
That's not what I meant...
AM I BEING OVER-BEARING?
BUT OTHERWISE I WON'T GET ANYWHERE!

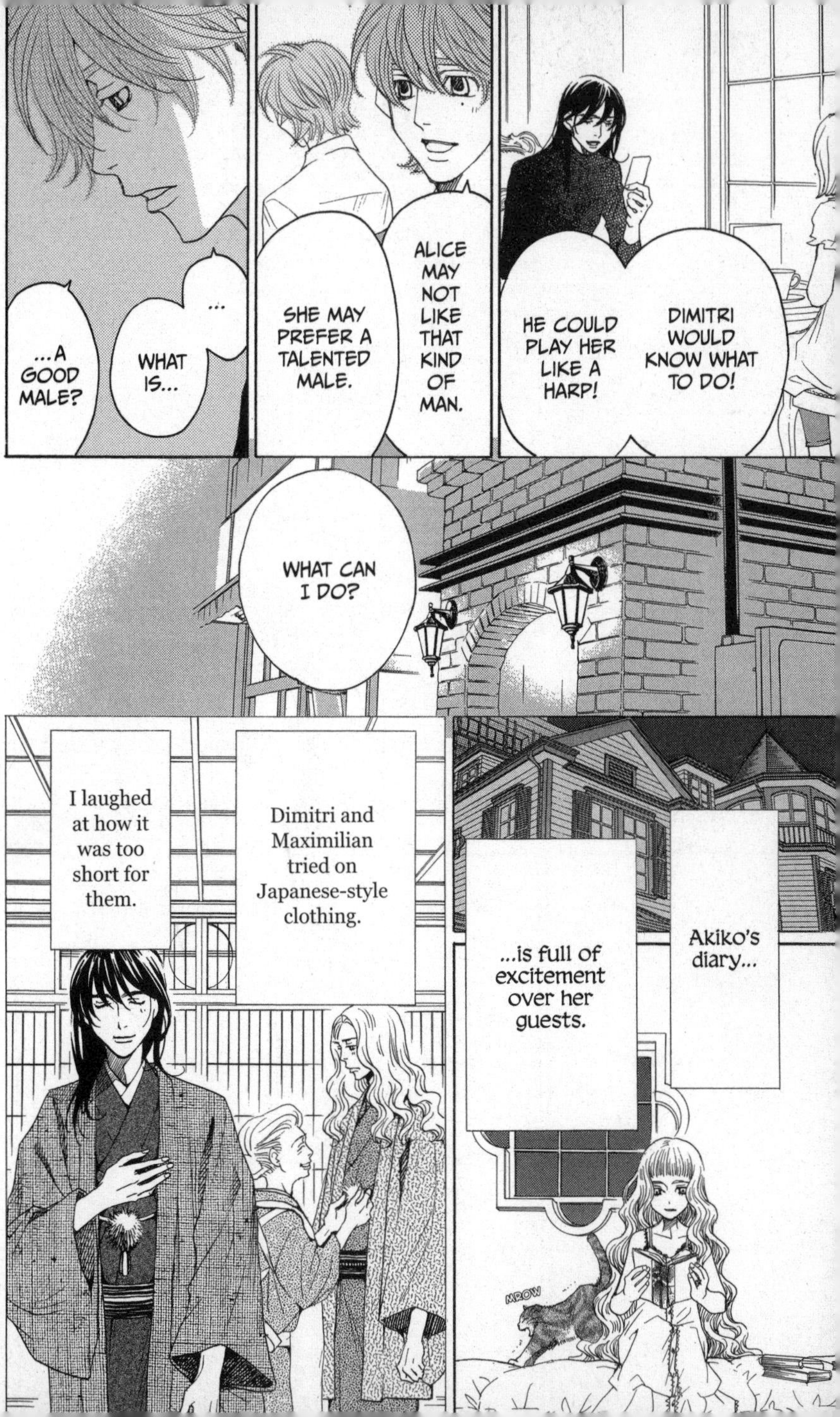
DIMITRI WOULD KNOW WHAT TO DO!
HE COULD PLAY HER LIKE A HARP!
ALICE MAY NOT LIKE THAT KIND OF MAN.
SHE MAY PREFER A TALENTED MALE.
...
WHAT IS...
...A GOOD MALE?
WHAT CAN I DO?
Akiko's diary...
...is full of excitement over her guests.
MROW
Dimitri and Maximilian tried on Japanese-style clothing.
I laughed at how it was too short for them.

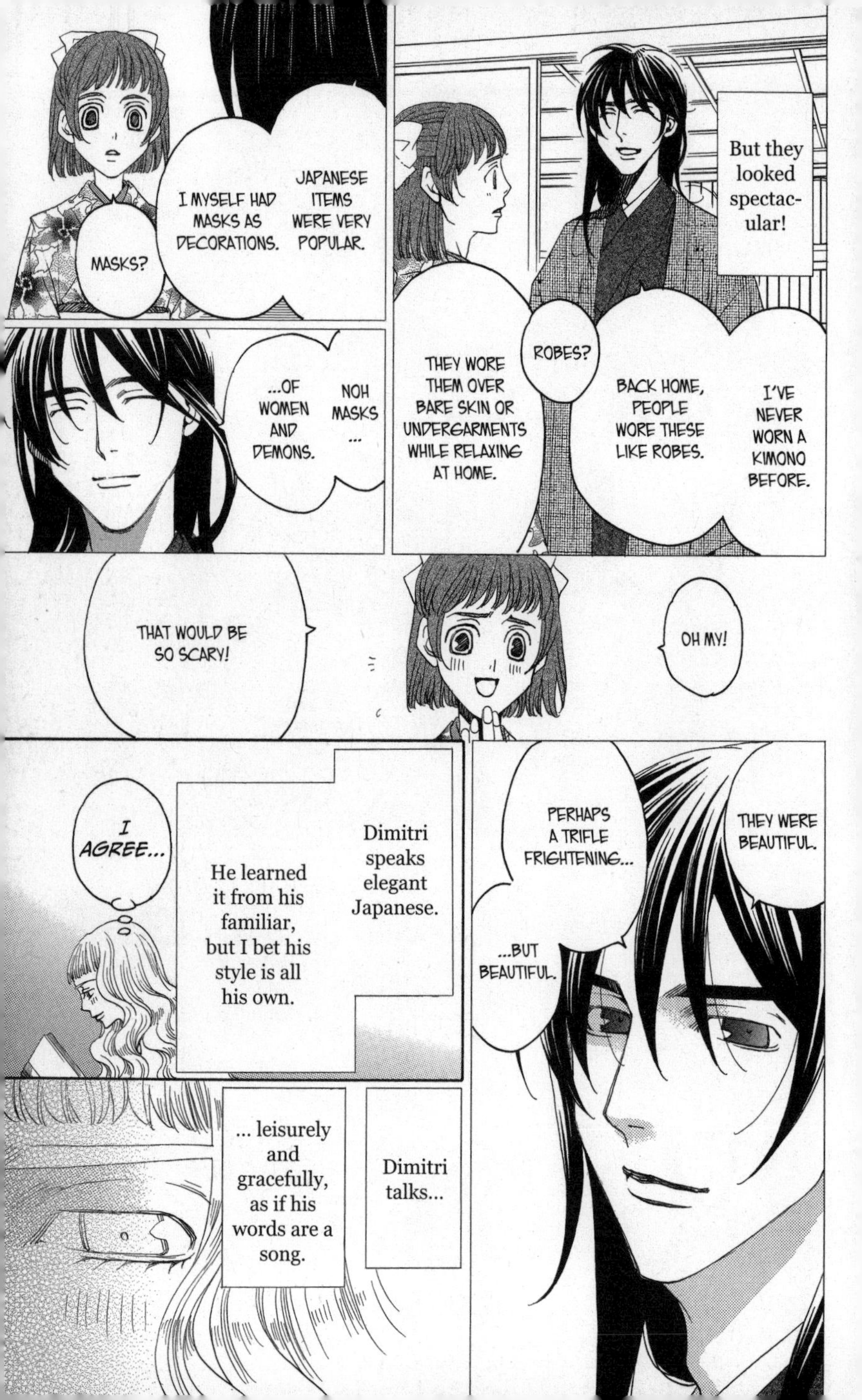
But they looked spectac-ular!
I'VE NEVER WORN A KIMONO BEFORE.
BACK HOME, PEOPLE WORE THESE LIKE ROBES.
ROBES?
THEY WORE THEM OVER BARE SKIN OR UNDERGARMENTS WHILE RELAXING AT HOME.
JAPANESE ITEMS WERE VERY POPULAR.
I MYSELF HAD MASKS AS DECORATIONS.
MASKS?
NOH MASKS...
...OF WOMEN AND DEMONS.
OH MY!
THAT WOULD BE SO SCARY!
THEY WERE BEAUTIFUL.
PERHAPS A TRIFLE FRIGHTENING...
...BUT BEAUTIFUL.
Dimitri speaks elegant Japanese.
He learned it from his familiar, but I bet his style is all his own.
I AGREE...
Dimitri talks...
... leisurely and gracefully, as if his words are a song.

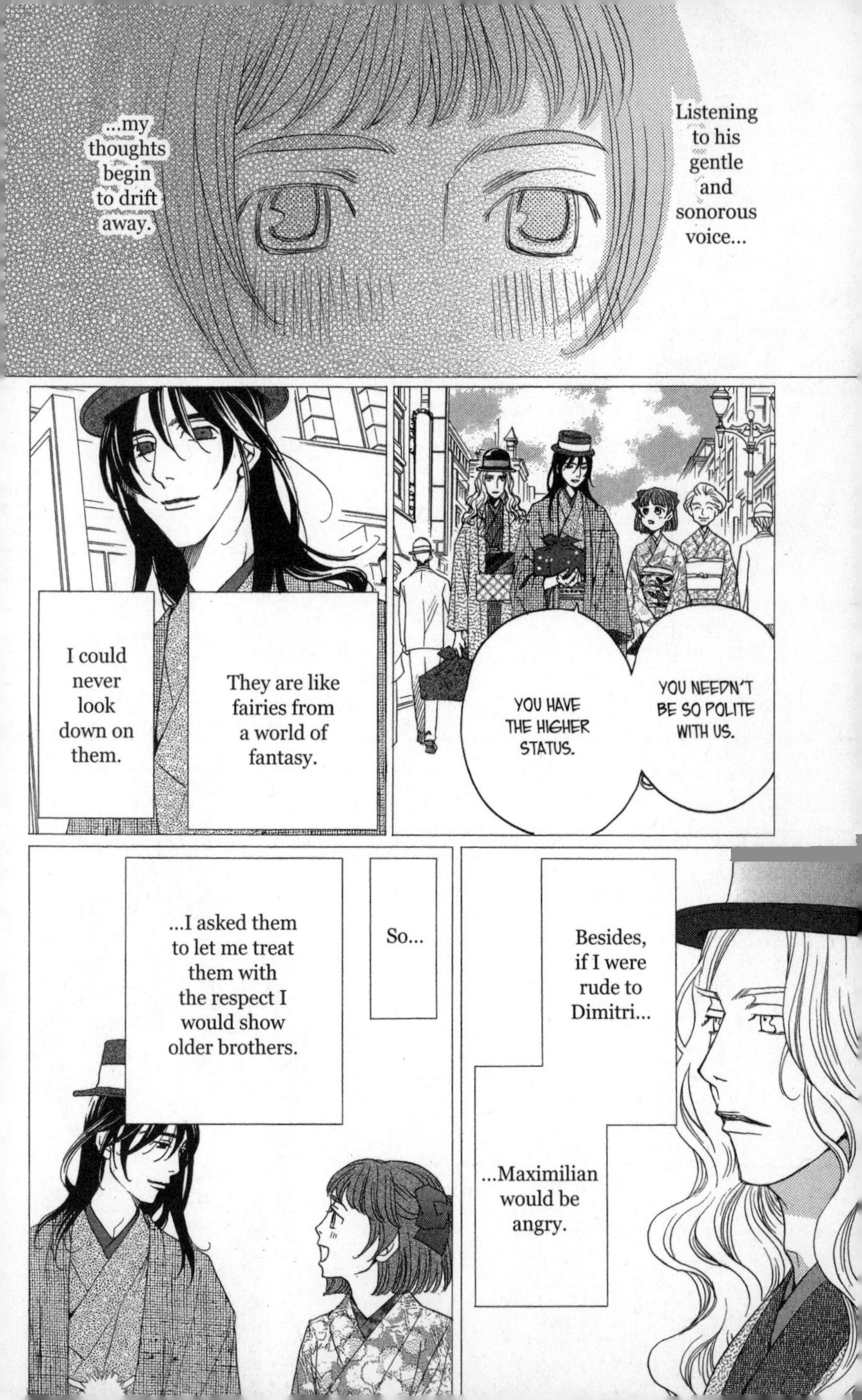
Listening to his gentle and sonorous voice...
...my thoughts begin to drift away.
You needn't be so polite with us.
You have the higher status.
They are like fairies from a world of fantasy.
I could never look down on them.
Besides, if I were rude to Dimitri...
...Maximilian would be angry.
So...
...I asked them to let me treat them with the respect I would show older brothers.

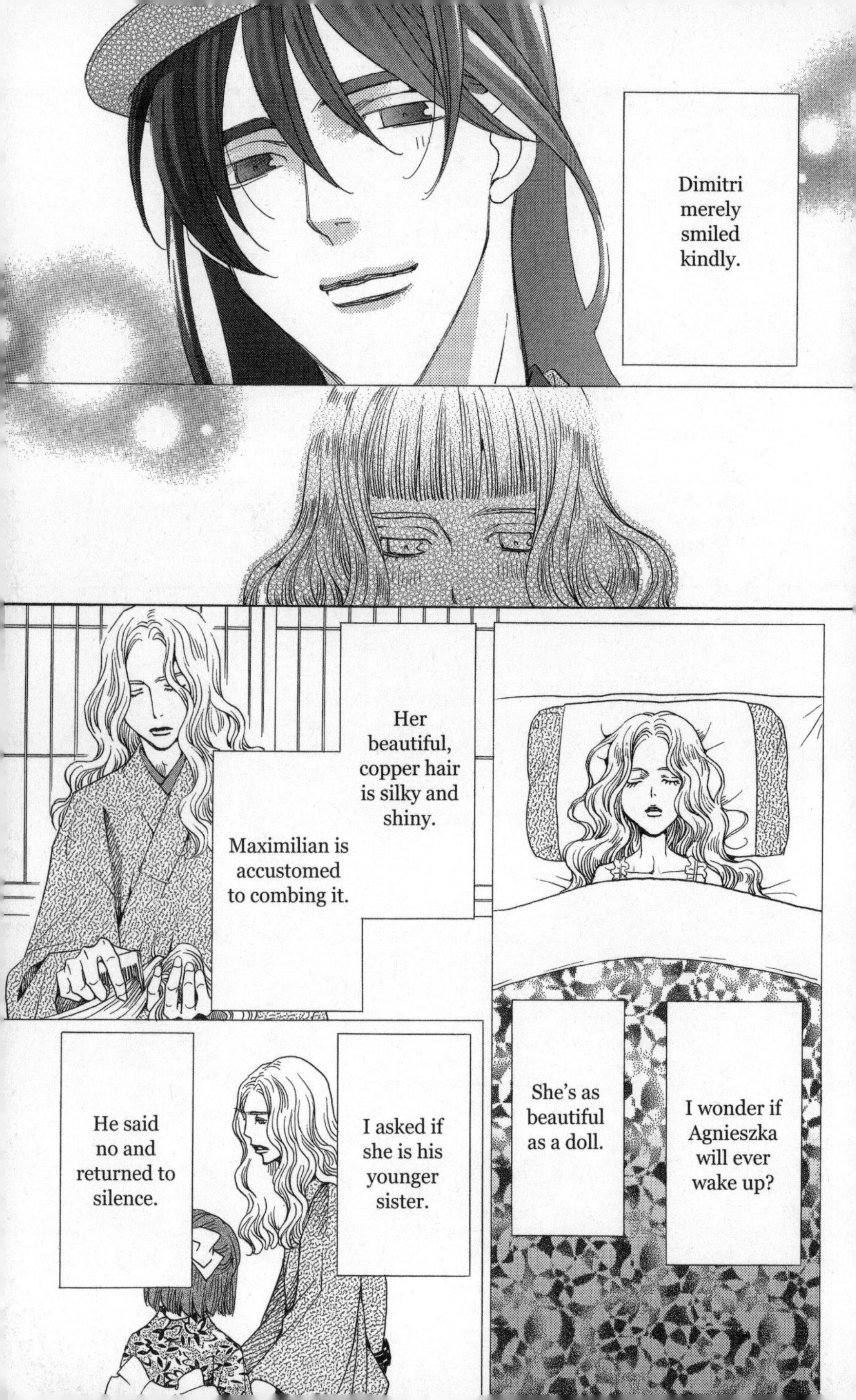
Dimitri merely smiled kindly.
I wonder if Agnieszka will ever wake up?
She's as beautiful as a doll.
Her beautiful, copper hair is silky and shiny.
Maximilian is accustomed to combing it.
I asked if she is his younger sister.
He said no and returned to silence.

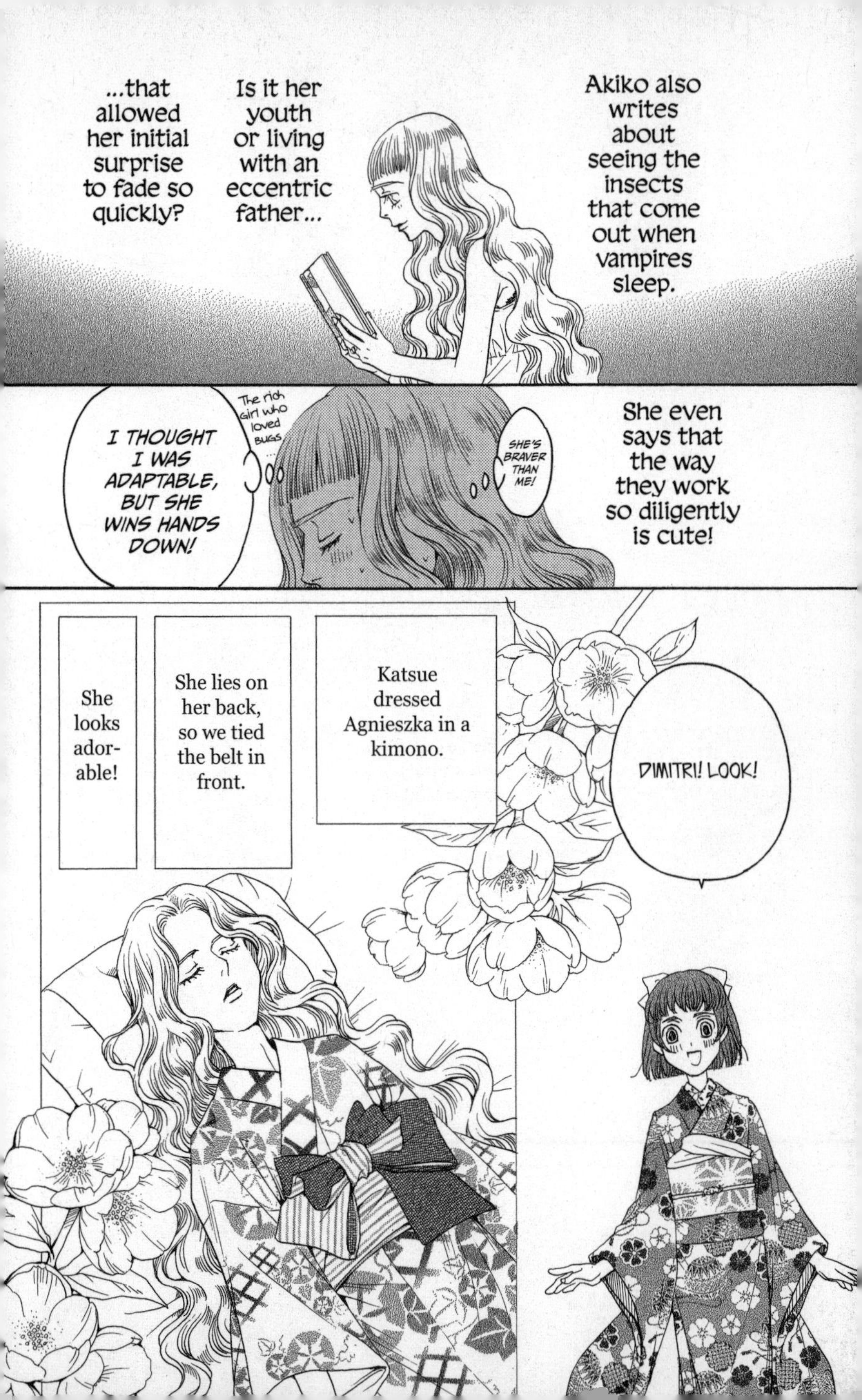
Akiko also writes about seeing the insects that come out when vampires sleep.
Is it her youth or living with an eccentric father...
...that allowed her initial surprise to fade so quickly?
She even says that the way they work so diligently is cute!
SHE'S BRAVER THAN ME!
The rich girl who loved bugs...
I THOUGHT I WAS ADAPTABLE, BUT SHE WINS HANDS DOWN!
DIMITRI! LOOK!
Katsue dressed Agnieszka in a kimono.
She lies on her back, so we tied the belt in front.
She looks ador-able!

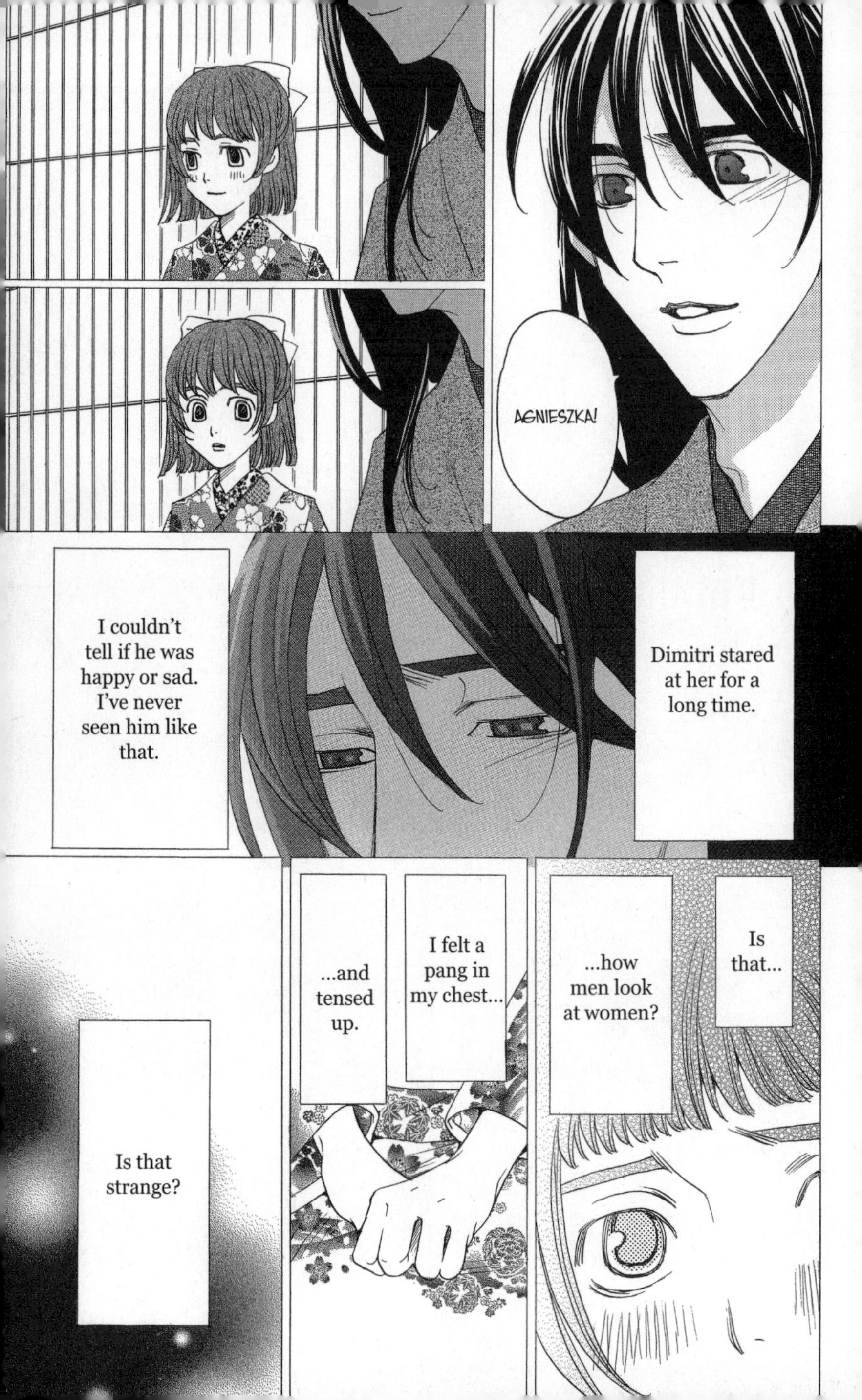
AGNIESZKA!
Dimitri stared at her for a long time.
I couldn't tell if he was happy or sad. I've never seen him like that.
Is that...
...how men look at women?
I felt a pang in my chest...
...and tensed up.
Is that strange?

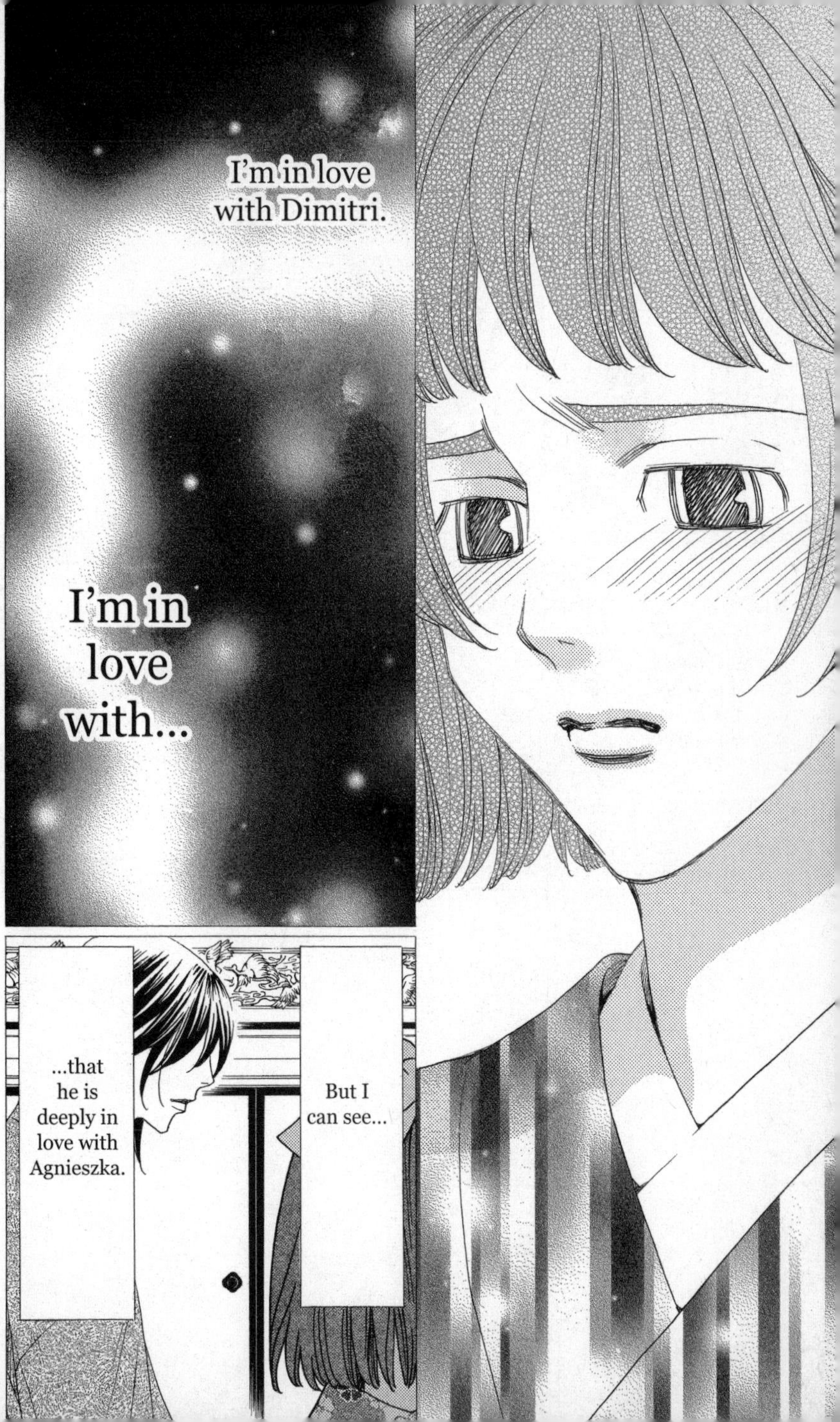
I'm in love with Dimitri.
I'm in love with...
But I can see...
...that he is deeply in love with Agnieszka.

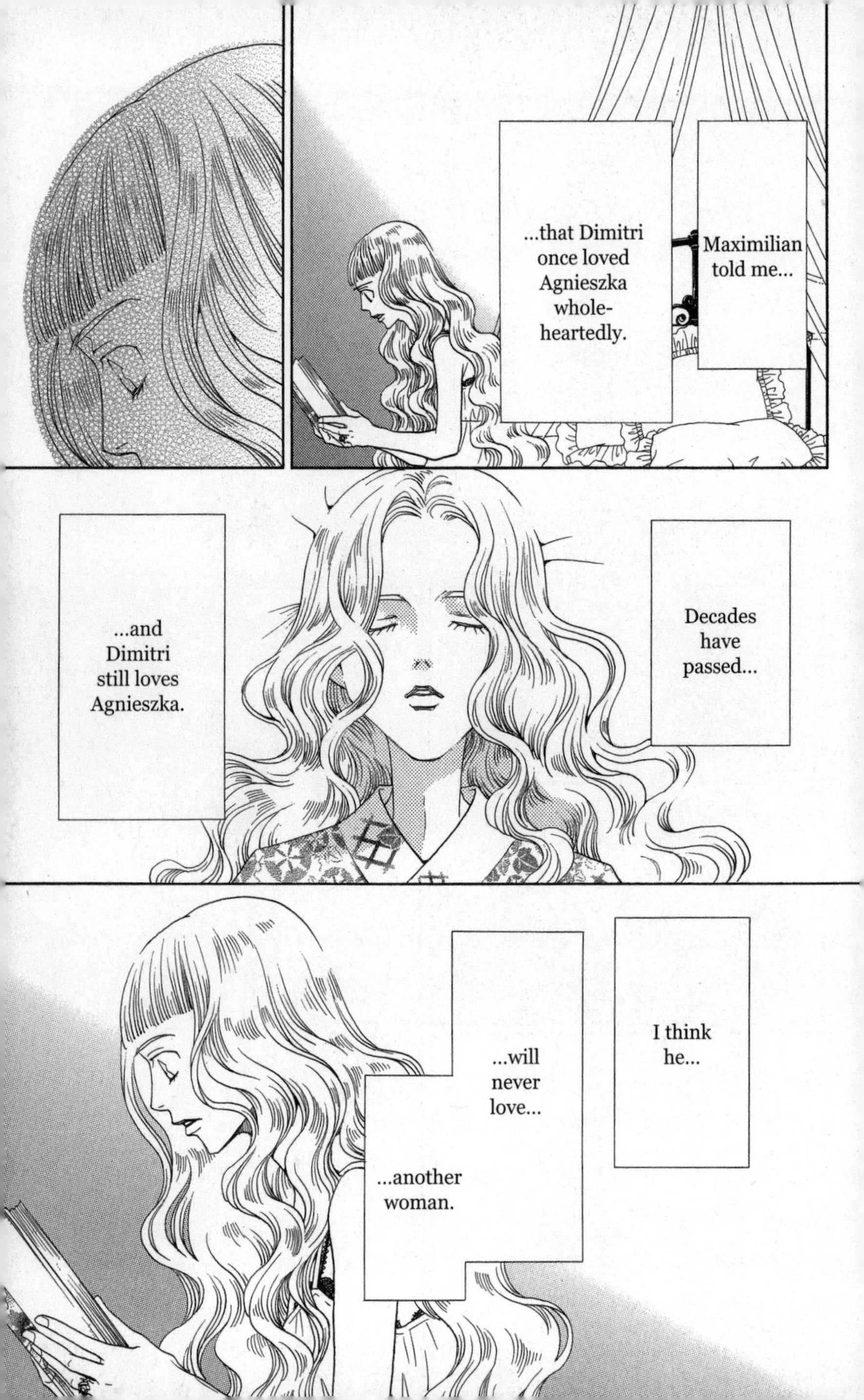
Maximilian told me...
...that Dimitri once loved Agnieszka whole-heartedly.
Decades have passed...
...and Dimitri still loves Agnieszka.
I think he...
...will never love...
...another woman.

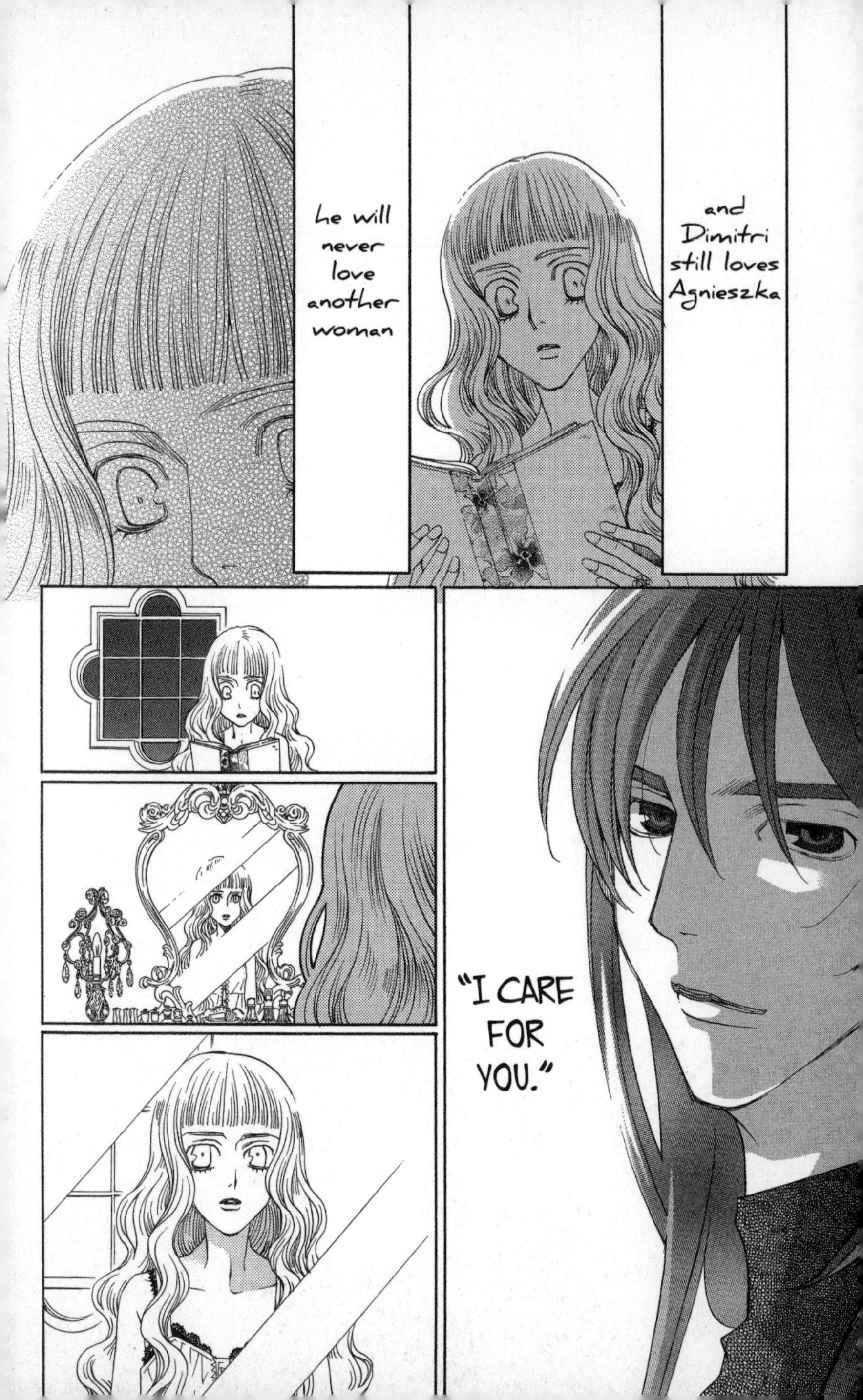
and Dimitri still loves Agnieszka
he will never love another woman
"I CARE FOR YOU."

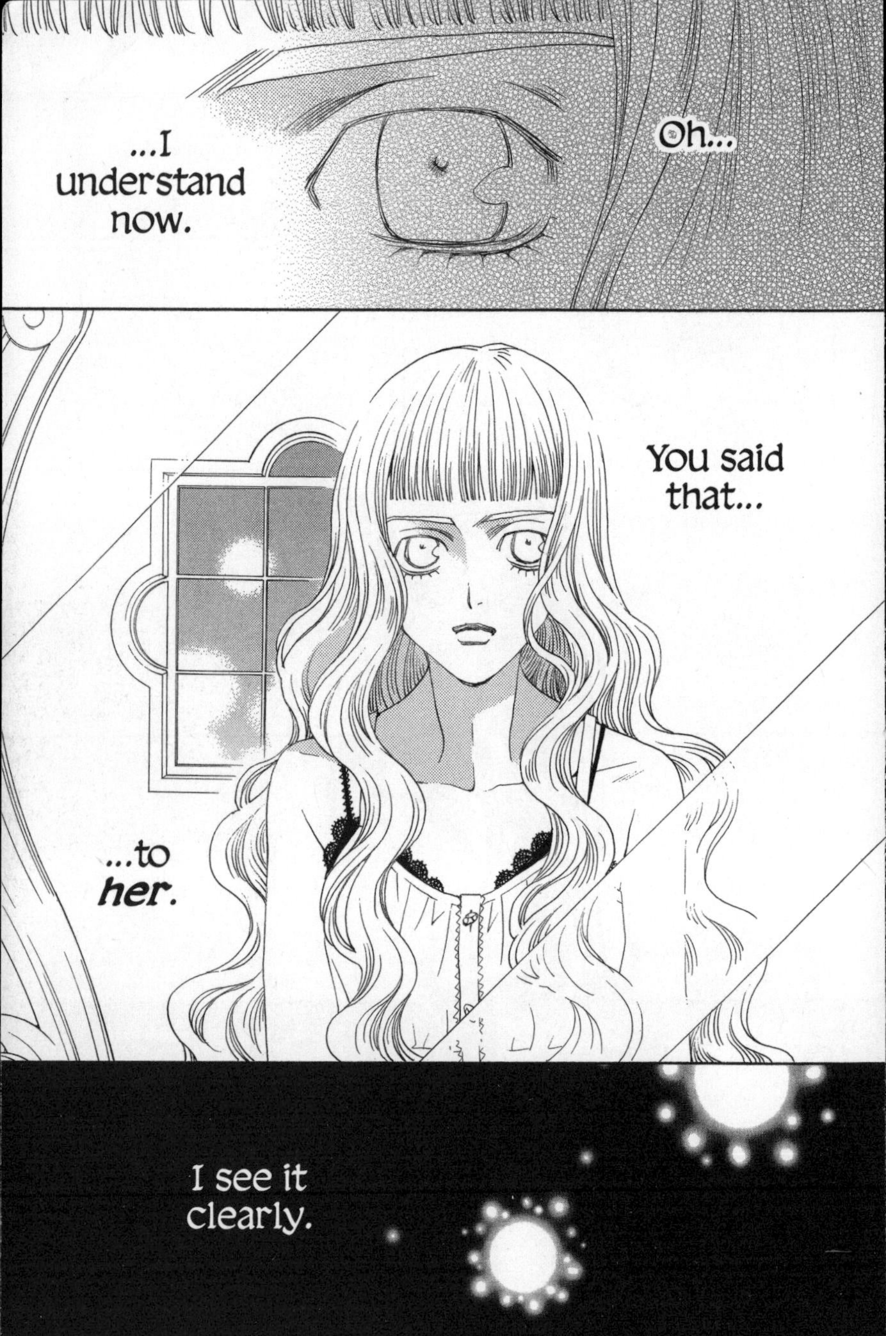
Oh...
...I understand now.
You said that...
...to *her*.
I see it clearly.

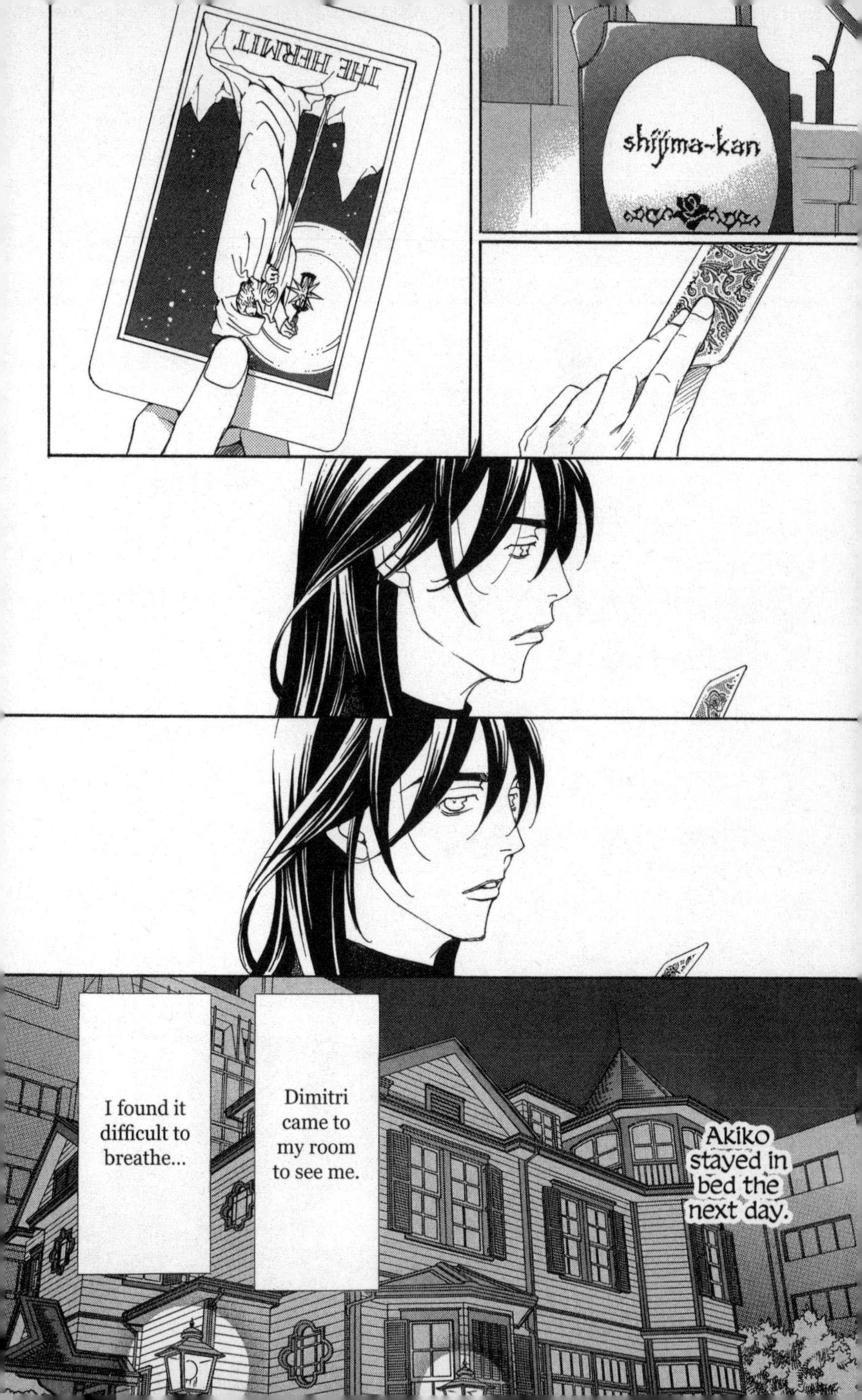
shijima-kan
THE HERMIT
Akiko stayed in bed the next day.
Dimitri came to my room to see me.
I found it difficult to breathe...

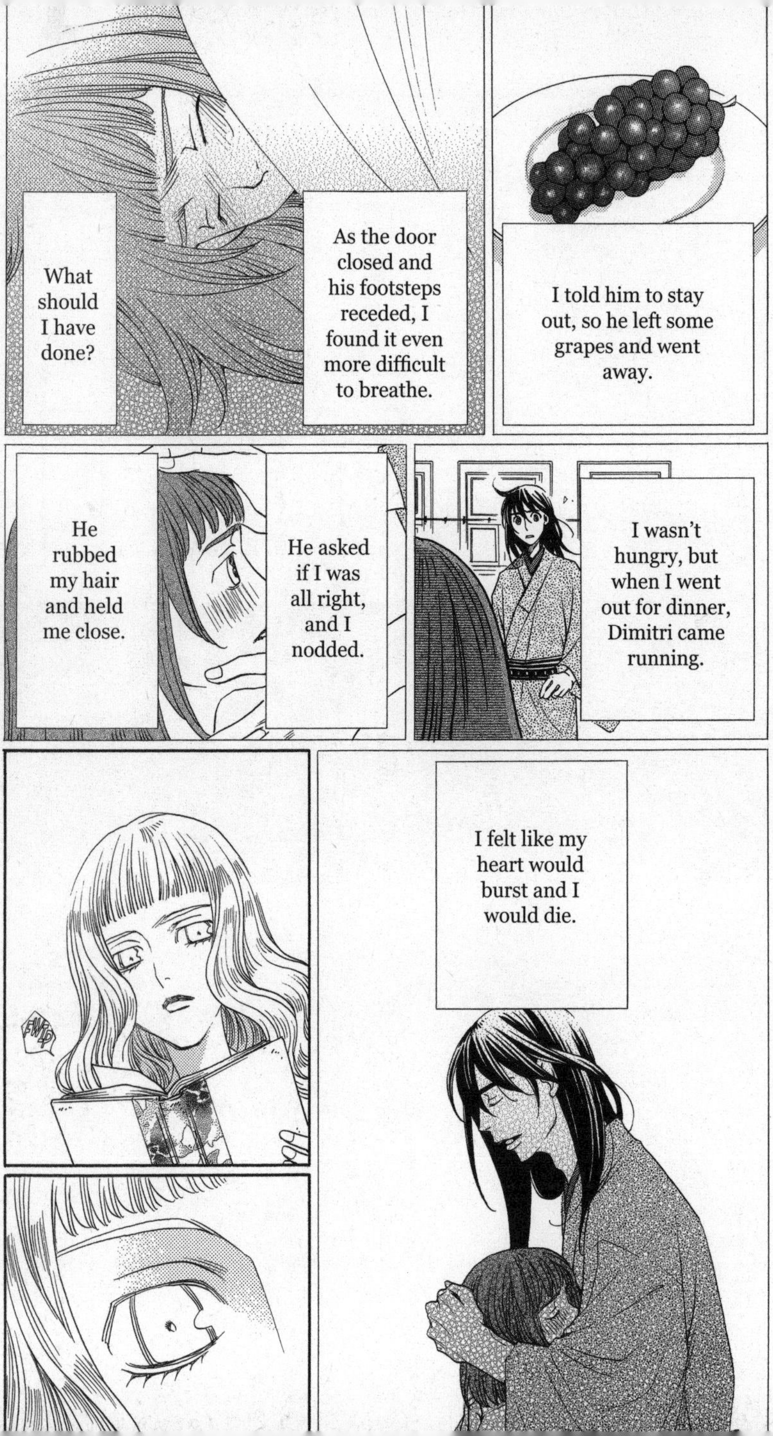
I told him to stay out, so he left some grapes and went away.
As the door closed and his footsteps receded, I found it even more difficult to breathe.
What should I have done?
I wasn't hungry, but when I went out for dinner, Dimitri came running.
He asked if I was all right, and I nodded.
He rubbed my hair and held me close.
I felt like my heart would burst and I would die.
FWIP

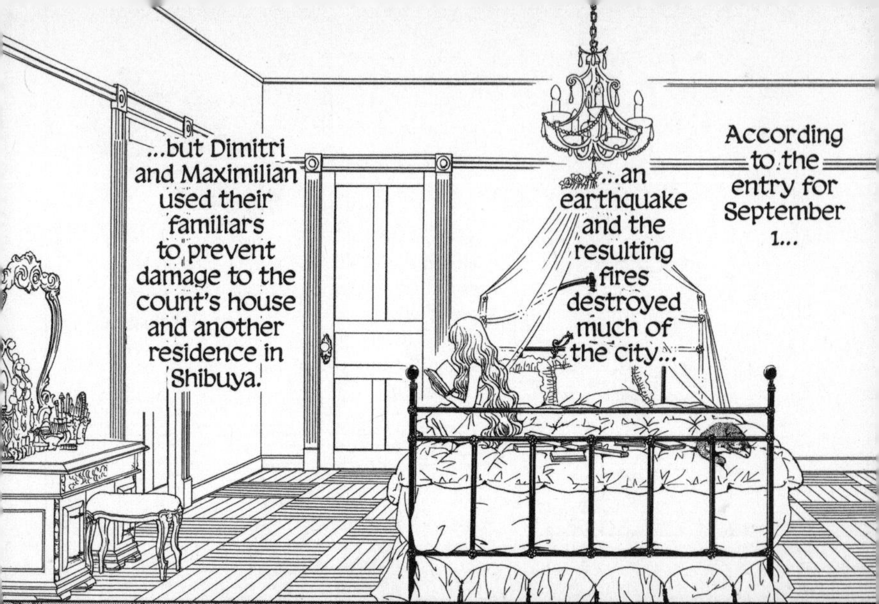
According to the entry for September 1...
...an earthquake and the resulting fires destroyed much of the city...
...but Dimitri and Maximilian used their familiars to prevent damage to the count's house and another residence in Shibuya.

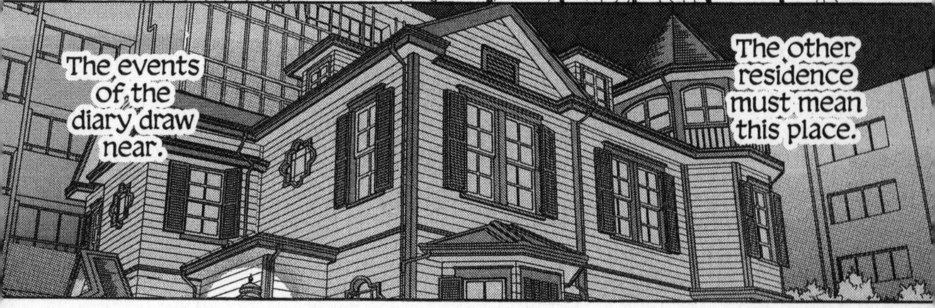
The other residence must mean this place.
The events of the diary draw near.

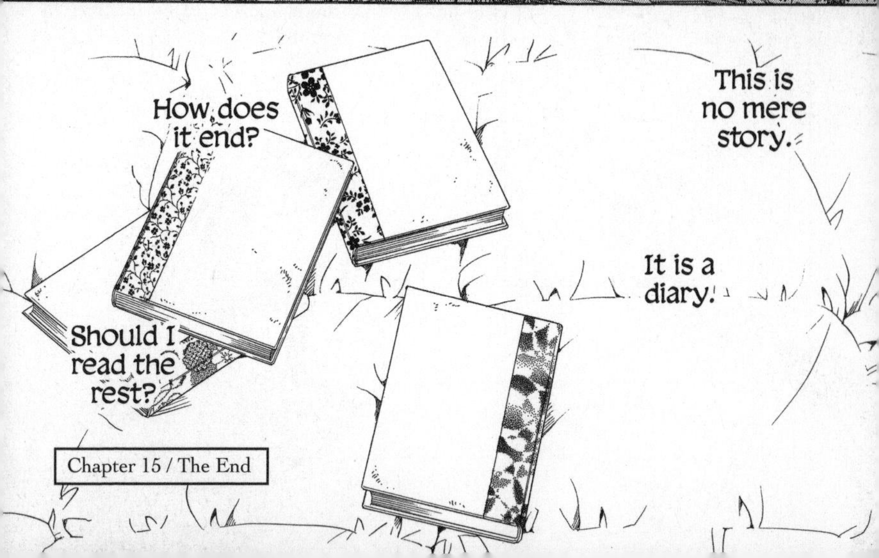
This is no mere story.
It is a diary.
How does it end?
Should I read the rest?

Chapter 15 / The End

Black Rose ALICE
Chapter 16

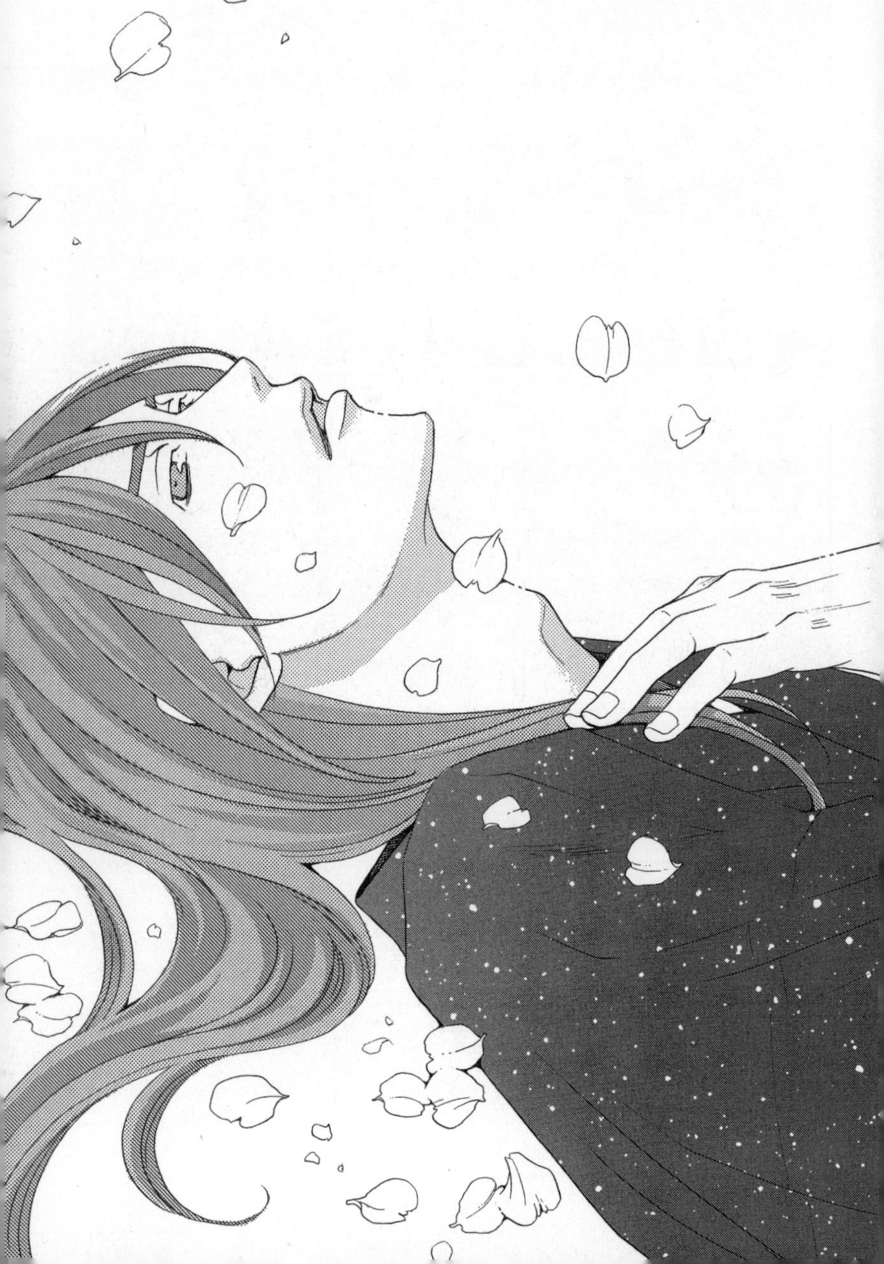

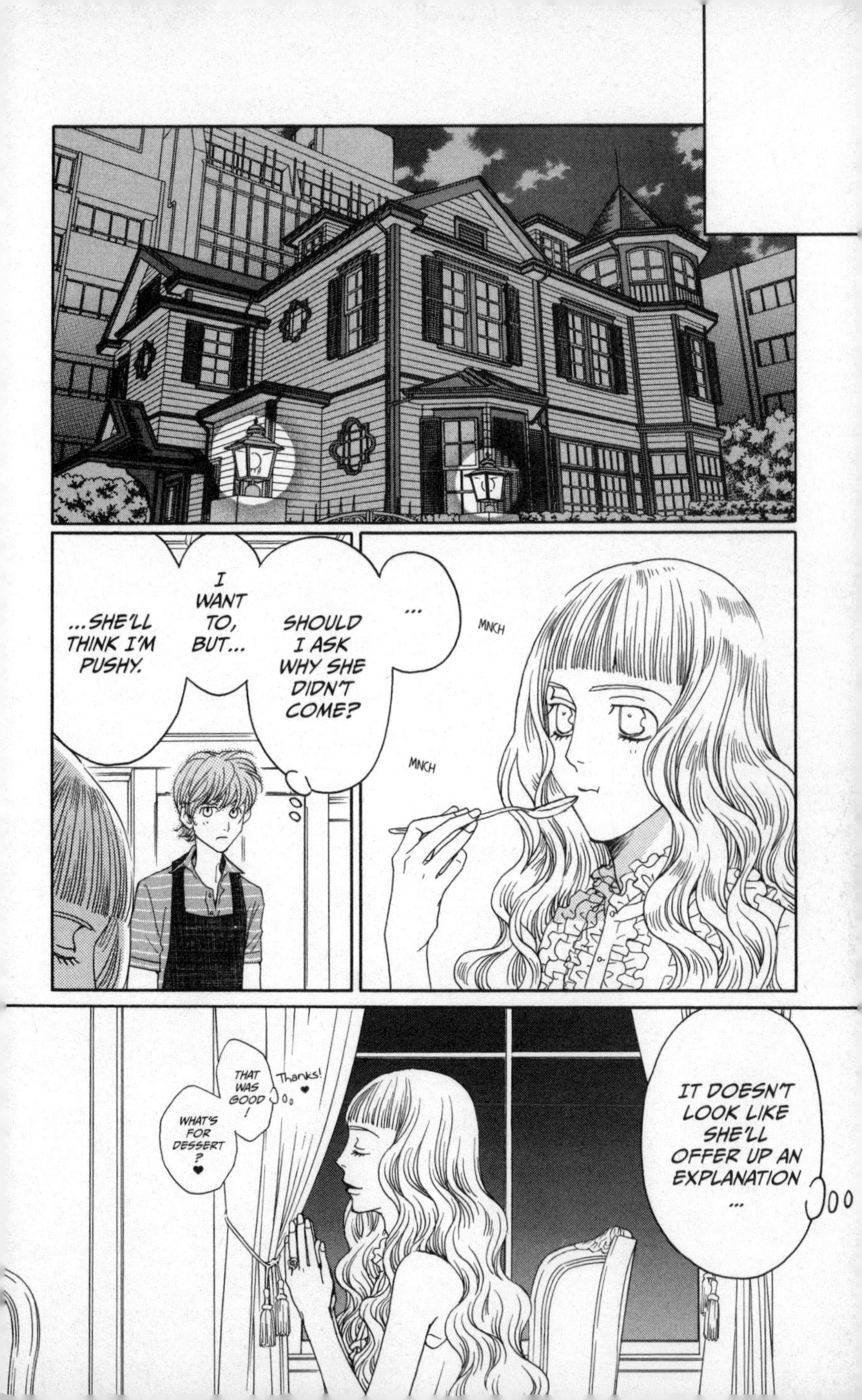
MNCH
MNCH
...
SHOULD I ASK WHY SHE DIDN'T COME?
I WANT TO, BUT...
...SHE'LL THINK I'M PUSHY.
IT DOESN'T LOOK LIKE SHE'LL OFFER UP AN EXPLANATION ...
THAT WAS GOOD!
Thanks! ♥
WHAT'S FOR DESSERT? ♥

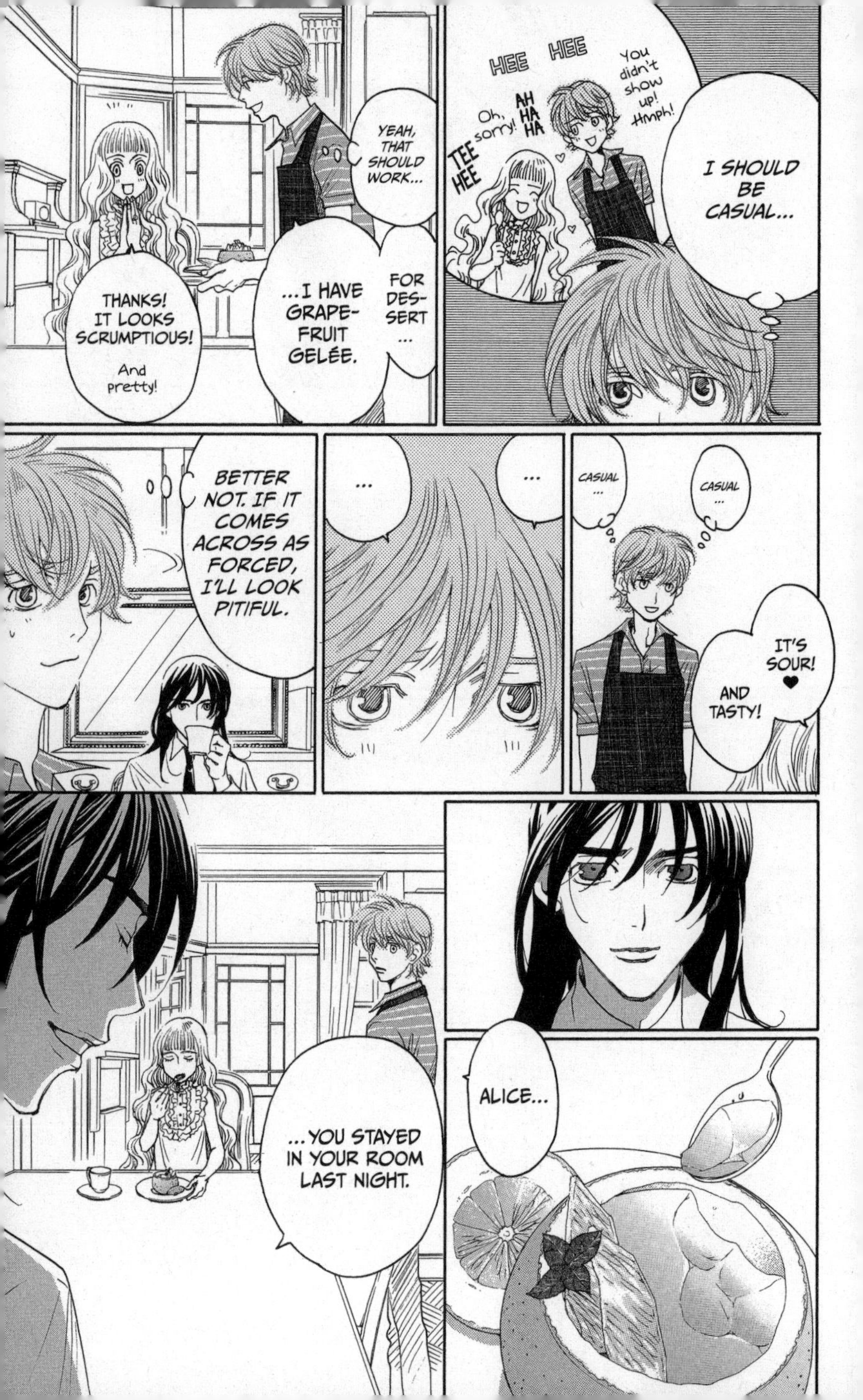
HEE HEE
You didn't show up! Hmph!
Oh, sorry! AH HA HA
TEE HEE
I SHOULD BE CASUAL...
YEAH, THAT SHOULD WORK...
FOR DES-SERT...
...I HAVE GRAPE-FRUIT GELÉE.
THANKS! IT LOOKS SCRUMPTIOUS!
And pretty!
CASUAL...
CASUAL...
IT'S SOUR! ♥
AND TASTY!
...
...
BETTER NOT. IF IT COMES ACROSS AS FORCED, I'LL LOOK PITIFUL.
ALICE...
...YOU STAYED IN YOUR ROOM LAST NIGHT.

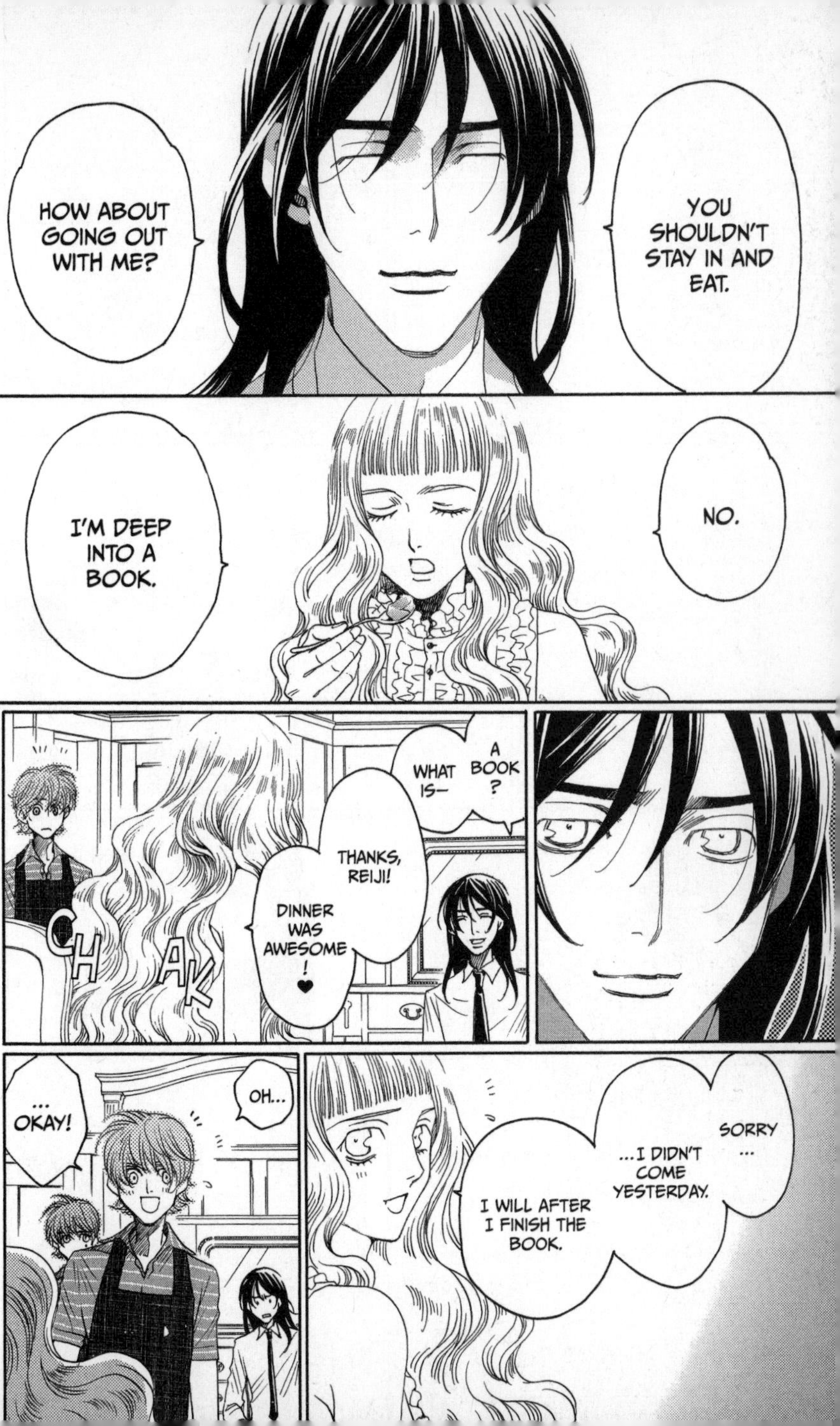
YOU SHOULDN'T STAY IN AND EAT.
HOW ABOUT GOING OUT WITH ME?
NO.
I'M DEEP INTO A BOOK.
A BOOK?
WHAT IS—
THANKS, REIJI!
DINNER WAS AWESOME! ♥
CHAK
SORRY...
...I DIDN'T COME YESTERDAY.
I WILL AFTER I FINISH THE BOOK.
OH...
...OKAY!

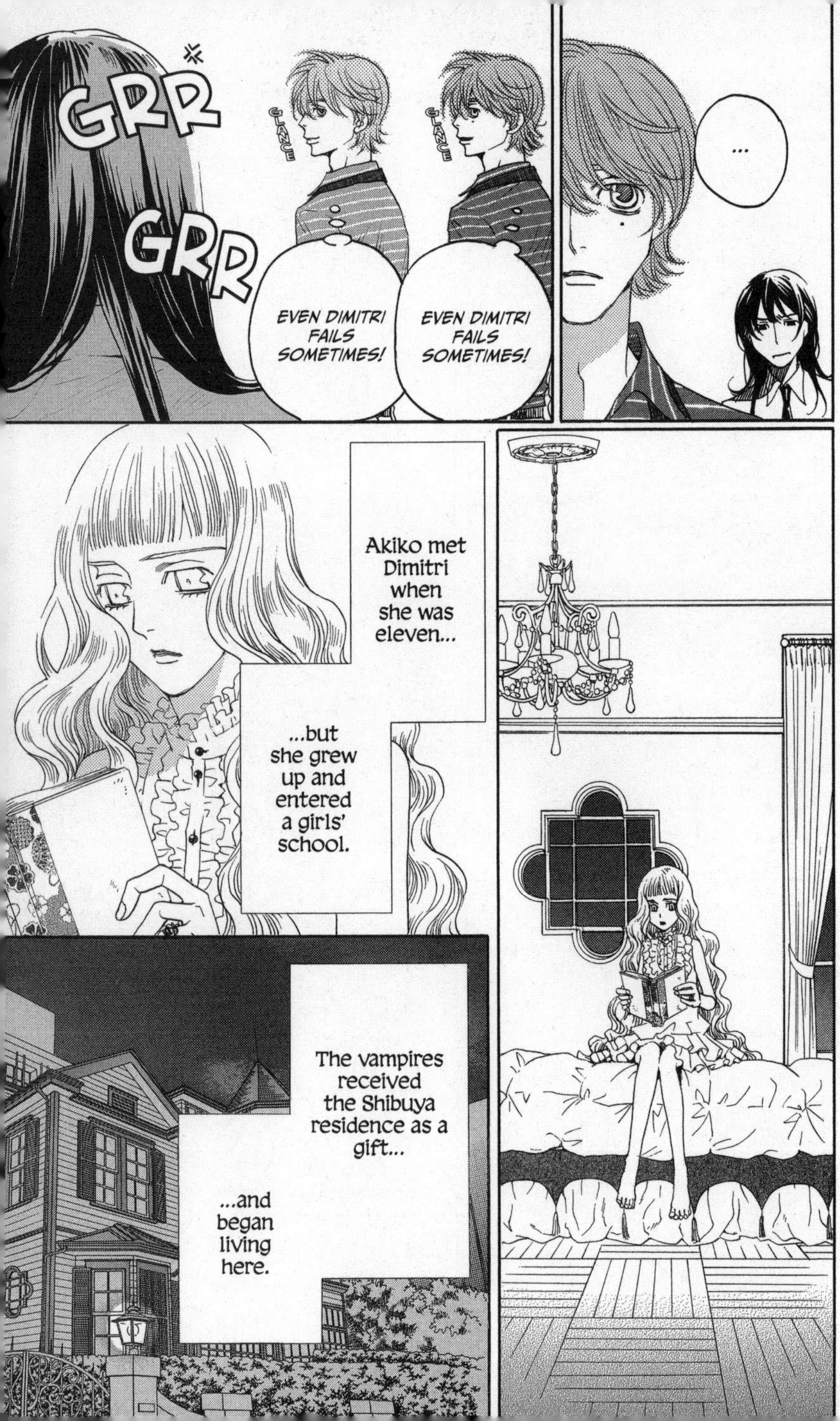
...
GRR
GRR
GLANCE
GLANCE
EVEN DIMITRI FAILS SOMETIMES!
EVEN DIMITRI FAILS SOMETIMES!
Akiko met Dimitri when she was eleven...
...but she grew up and entered a girls' school.
The vampires received the Shibuya residence as a gift...
...and began living here.

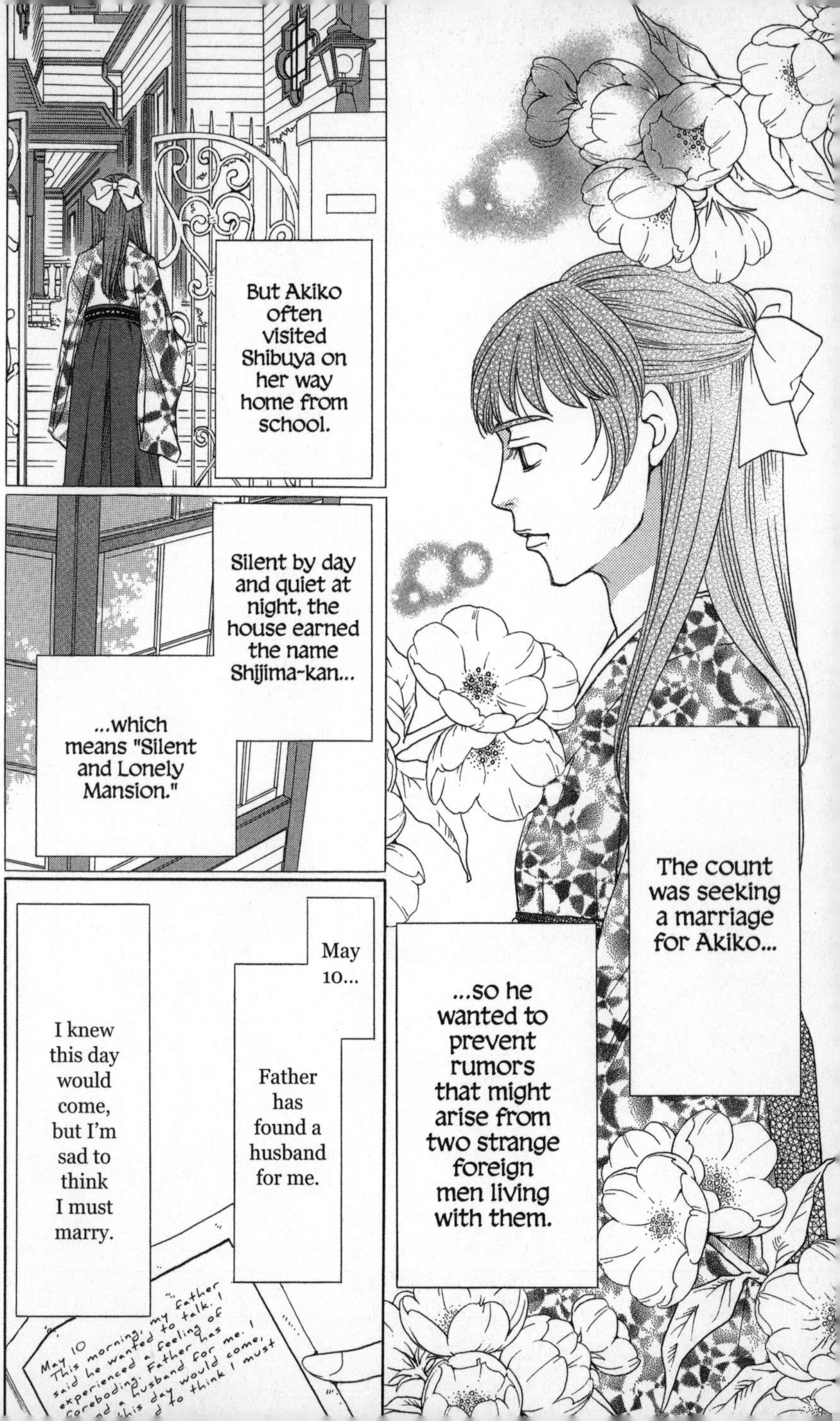
The count was seeking a marriage for Akiko...
...so he wanted to prevent rumors that might arise from two strange foreign men living with them.
But Akiko often visited Shibuya on her way home from school.
Silent by day and quiet at night, the house earned the name Shijima-kan...
...which means "Silent and Lonely Mansion."
May 10...
Father has found a husband for me.
I knew this day would come, but I'm sad to think I must marry.
May 10
This morning, my father
said he wanted to talk. I
experienced a feeling of
foreboding. Father has
a husband for me. I
this day would come,
d to think I must

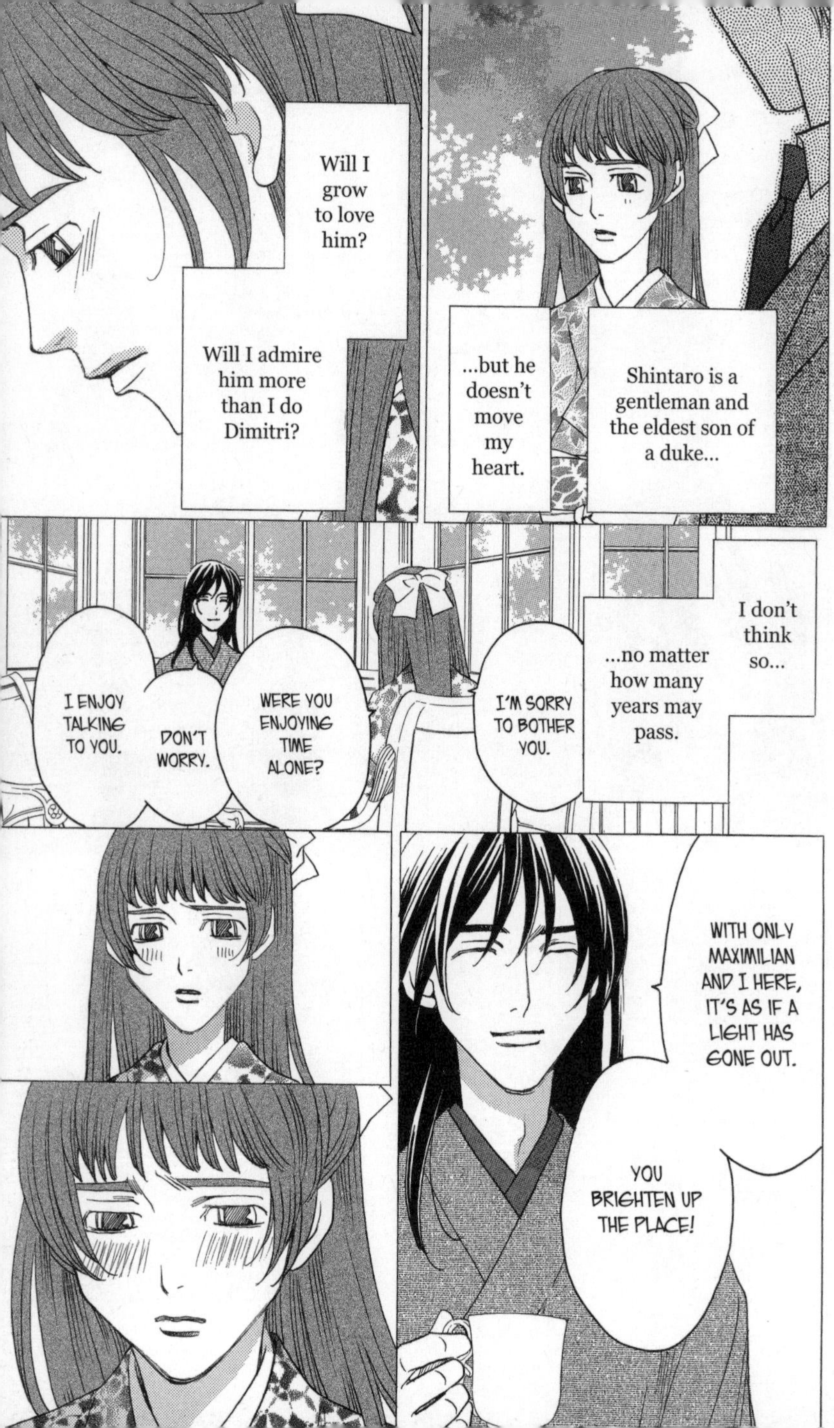
Shintaro is a gentleman and the eldest son of a duke...
...but he doesn't move my heart.
Will I grow to love him?
Will I admire him more than I do Dimitri?
I don't think so...
...no matter how many years may pass.
I'M SORRY TO BOTHER YOU.
WERE YOU ENJOYING TIME ALONE?
DON'T WORRY.
I ENJOY TALKING TO YOU.
WITH ONLY MAXIMILIAN AND I HERE, IT'S AS IF A LIGHT HAS GONE OUT.
YOU BRIGHTEN UP THE PLACE!

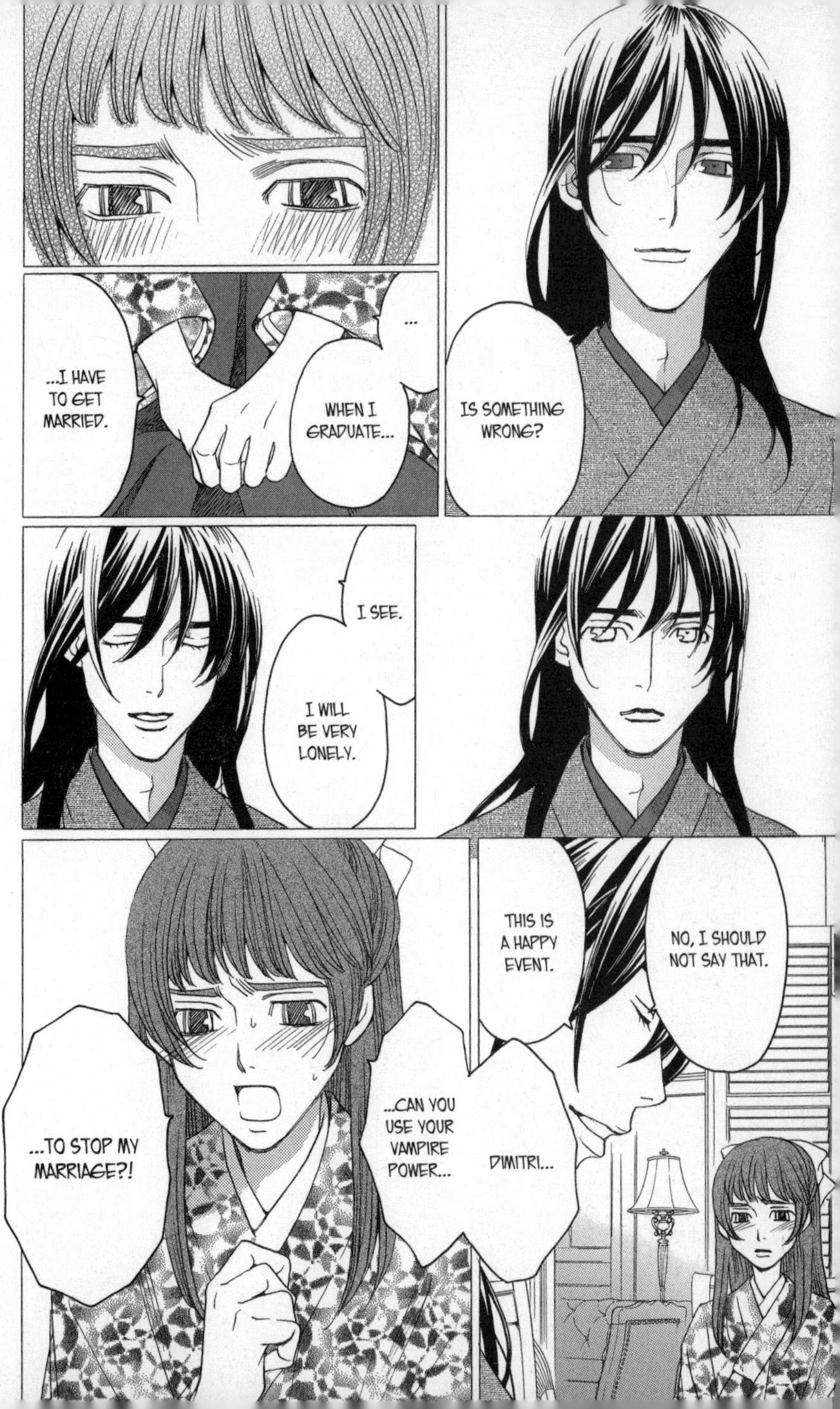
IS SOMETHING WRONG?
...
WHEN I GRADUATE...
...I HAVE TO GET MARRIED.
I SEE.
I WILL BE VERY LONELY.
NO, I SHOULD NOT SAY THAT.
THIS IS A HAPPY EVENT.
DIMITRI...
...CAN YOU USE YOUR VAMPIRE POWER...
...TO STOP MY MARRIAGE?!

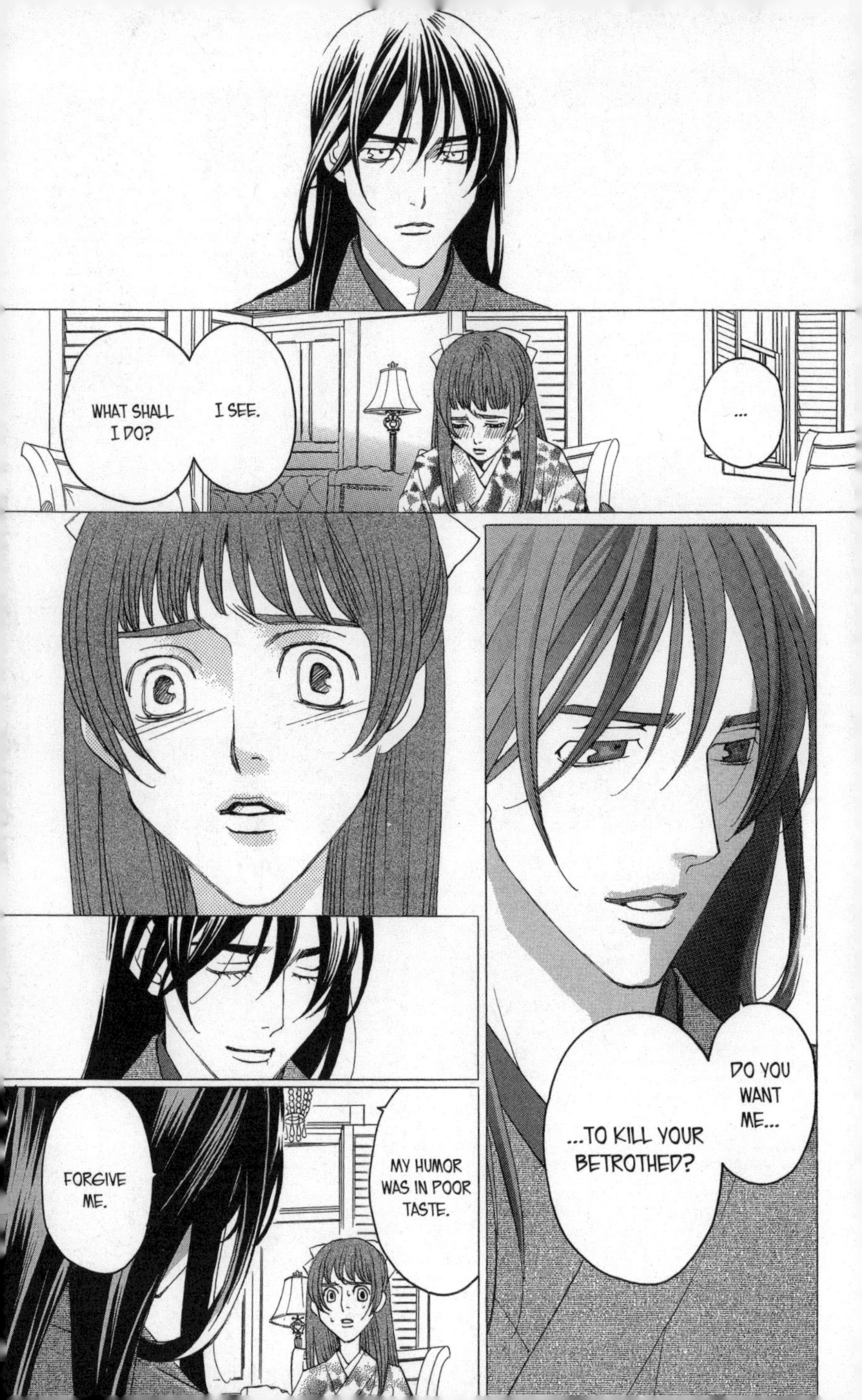
...
I SEE.
WHAT SHALL I DO?
DO YOU WANT ME...
...TO KILL YOUR BETROTHED?
MY HUMOR WAS IN POOR TASTE.
FORGIVE ME.

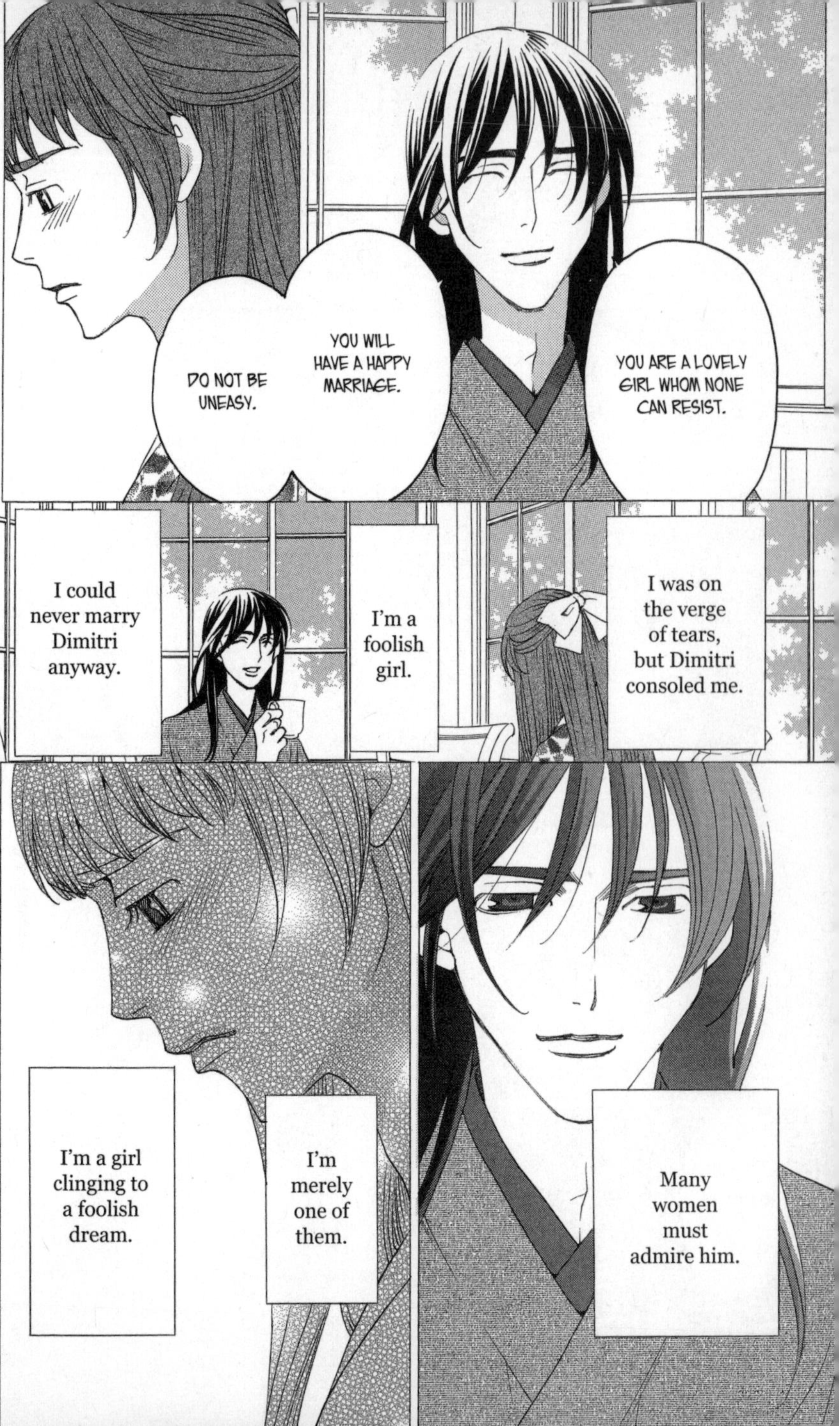
YOU ARE A LOVELY GIRL WHOM NONE CAN RESIST.
YOU WILL HAVE A HAPPY MARRIAGE.
DO NOT BE UNEASY.
I was on the verge of tears, but Dimitri consoled me.
I'm a foolish girl.
I could never marry Dimitri anyway.
Many women must admire him.
I'm merely one of them.
I'm a girl clinging to a foolish dream.

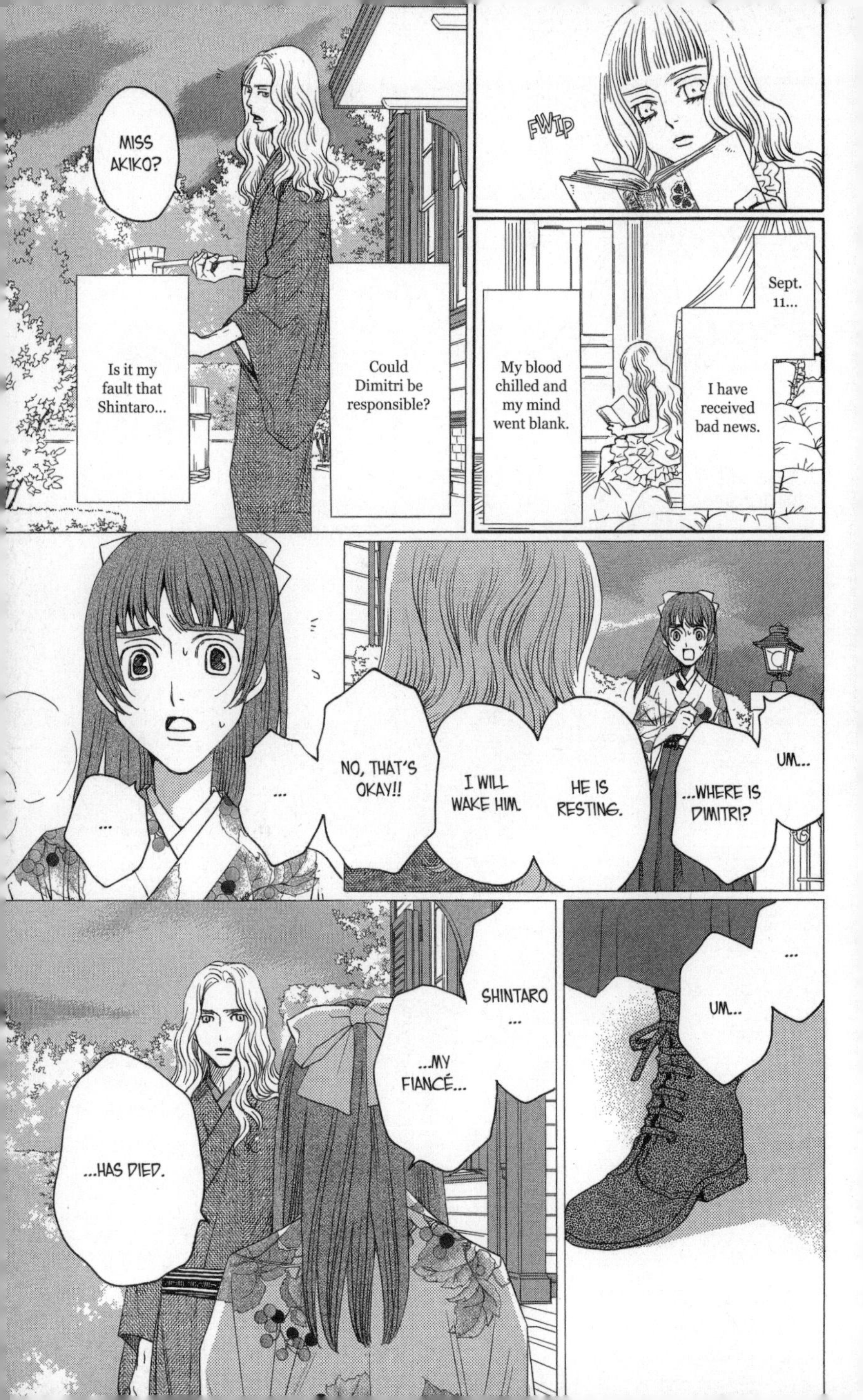
FWIP
Sept. 11...
I have received bad news.
My blood chilled and my mind went blank.
Could Dimitri be responsible?
Is it my fault that Shintaro...
MISS AKIKO?
UM...
...WHERE IS DIMITRI?
HE IS RESTING.
I WILL WAKE HIM.
NO, THAT'S OKAY!!
...
...
...
UM...
SHINTARO ...
...MY FIANCÉ...
...HAS DIED.

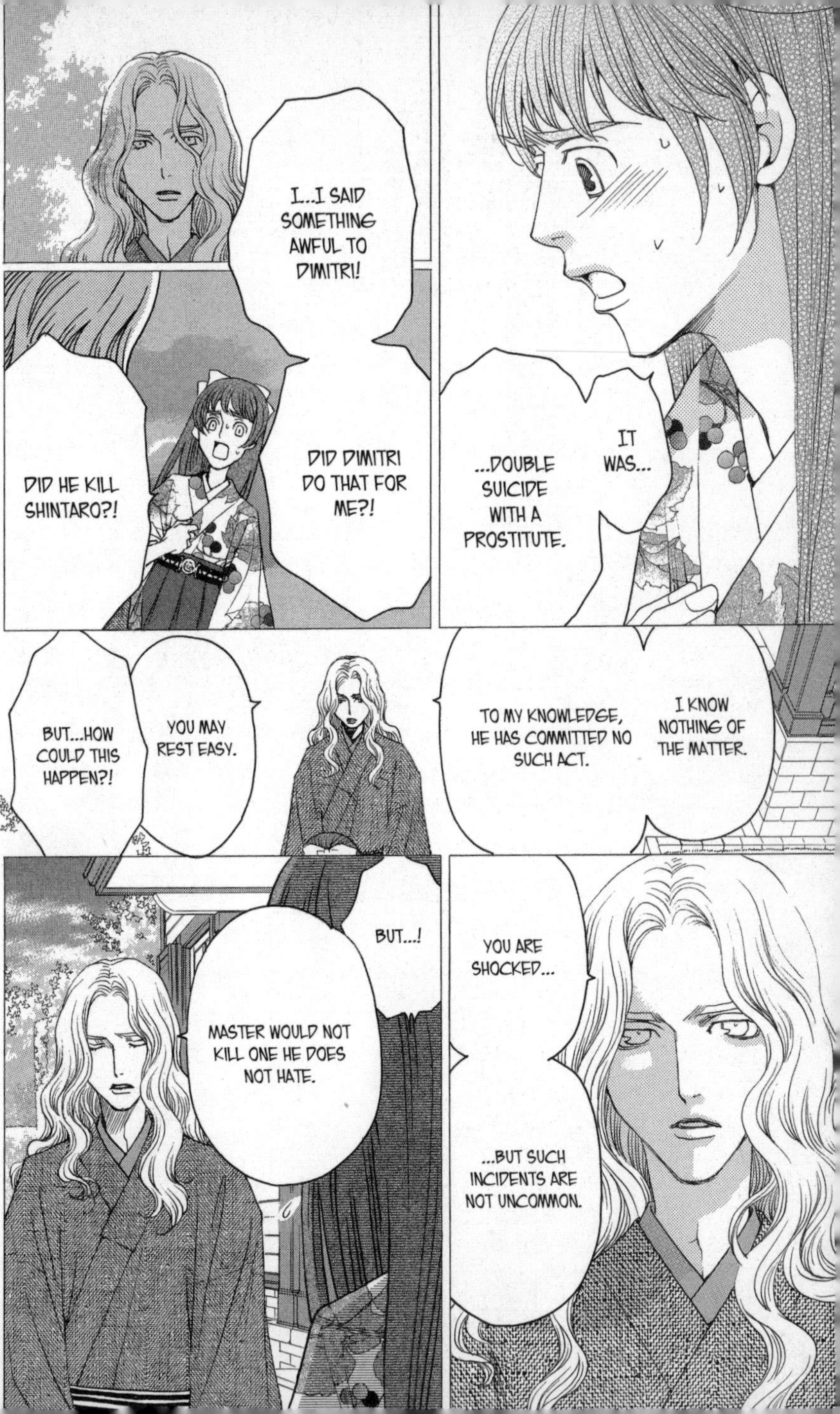
IT WAS...
...DOUBLE SUICIDE WITH A PROSTITUTE.
I...I SAID SOMETHING AWFUL TO DIMITRI!
DID DIMITRI DO THAT FOR ME?!
DID HE KILL SHINTARO?!
I KNOW NOTHING OF THE MATTER.
TO MY KNOWLEDGE, HE HAS COMMITTED NO SUCH ACT.
YOU MAY REST EASY.
BUT...HOW COULD THIS HAPPEN?!
YOU ARE SHOCKED...
...BUT SUCH INCIDENTS ARE NOT UNCOMMON.
BUT...!
MASTER WOULD NOT KILL ONE HE DOES NOT HATE.

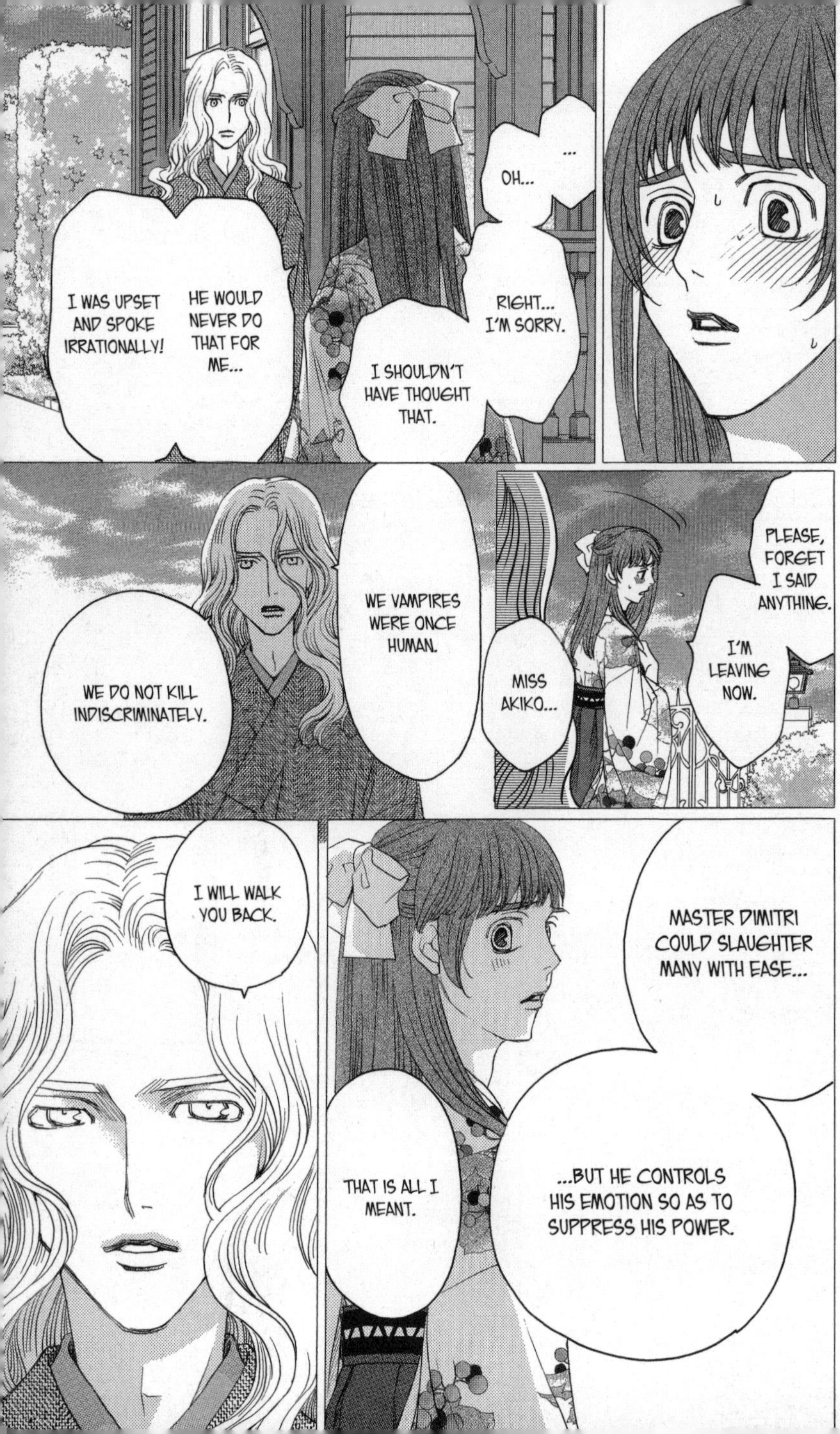
...
OH...
RIGHT... I'M SORRY.
I SHOULDN'T HAVE THOUGHT THAT.
HE WOULD NEVER DO THAT FOR ME...
I WAS UPSET AND SPOKE IRRATIONALLY!
PLEASE, FORGET I SAID ANYTHING.
I'M LEAVING NOW.
MISS AKIKO...
WE VAMPIRES WERE ONCE HUMAN.
WE DO NOT KILL INDISCRIMINATELY.
MASTER DIMITRI COULD SLAUGHTER MANY WITH EASE...
...BUT HE CONTROLS HIS EMOTION SO AS TO SUPPRESS HIS POWER.
THAT IS ALL I MEANT.
I WILL WALK YOU BACK.

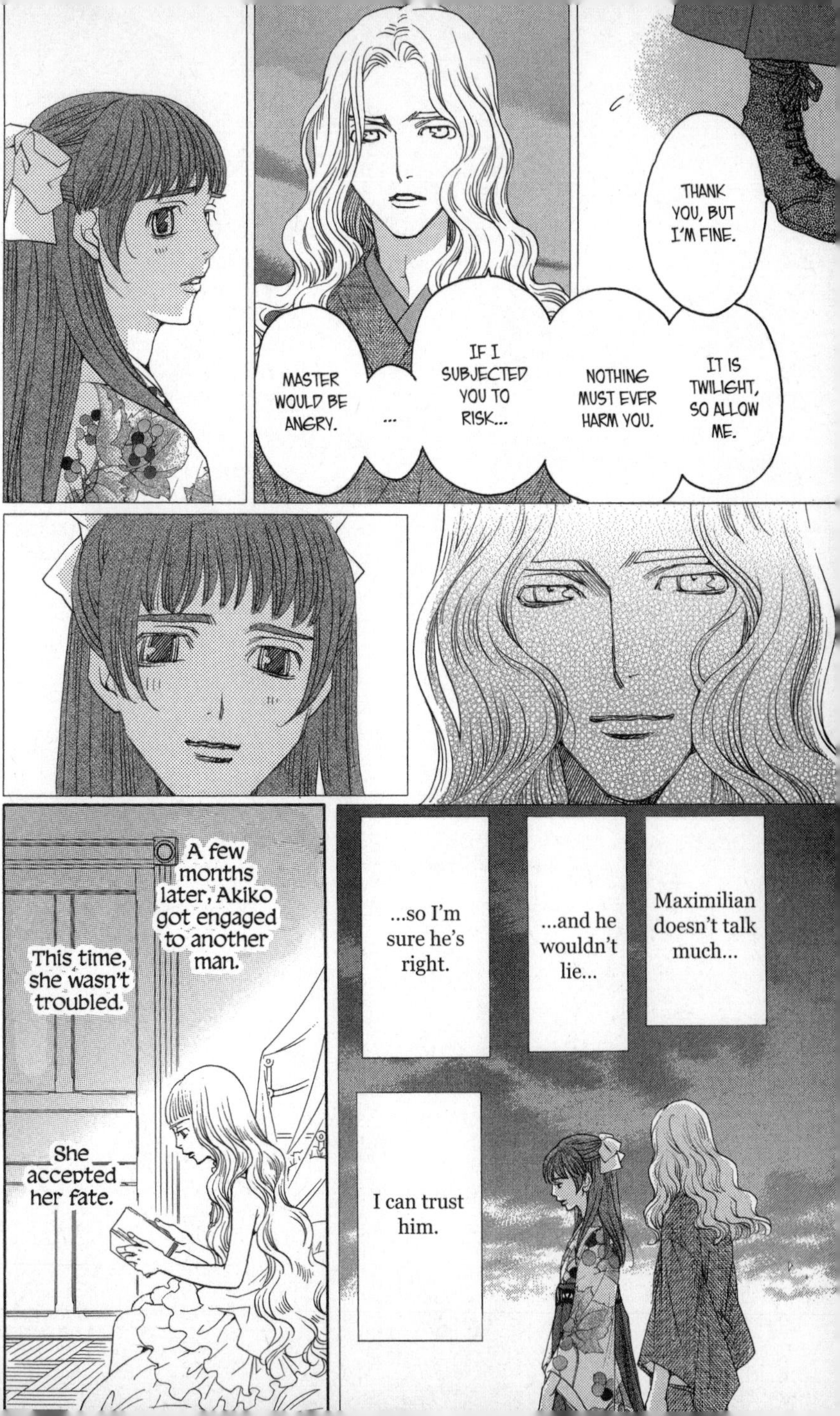
THANK YOU, BUT I'M FINE.
IT IS TWILIGHT, SO ALLOW ME.
NOTHING MUST EVER HARM YOU.
IF I SUBJECTED YOU TO RISK...
...
MASTER WOULD BE ANGRY.
Maximilian doesn't talk much...
...and he wouldn't lie...
...so I'm sure he's right.
I can trust him.
A few months later, Akiko got engaged to another man.
This time, she wasn't troubled.
She accepted her fate.

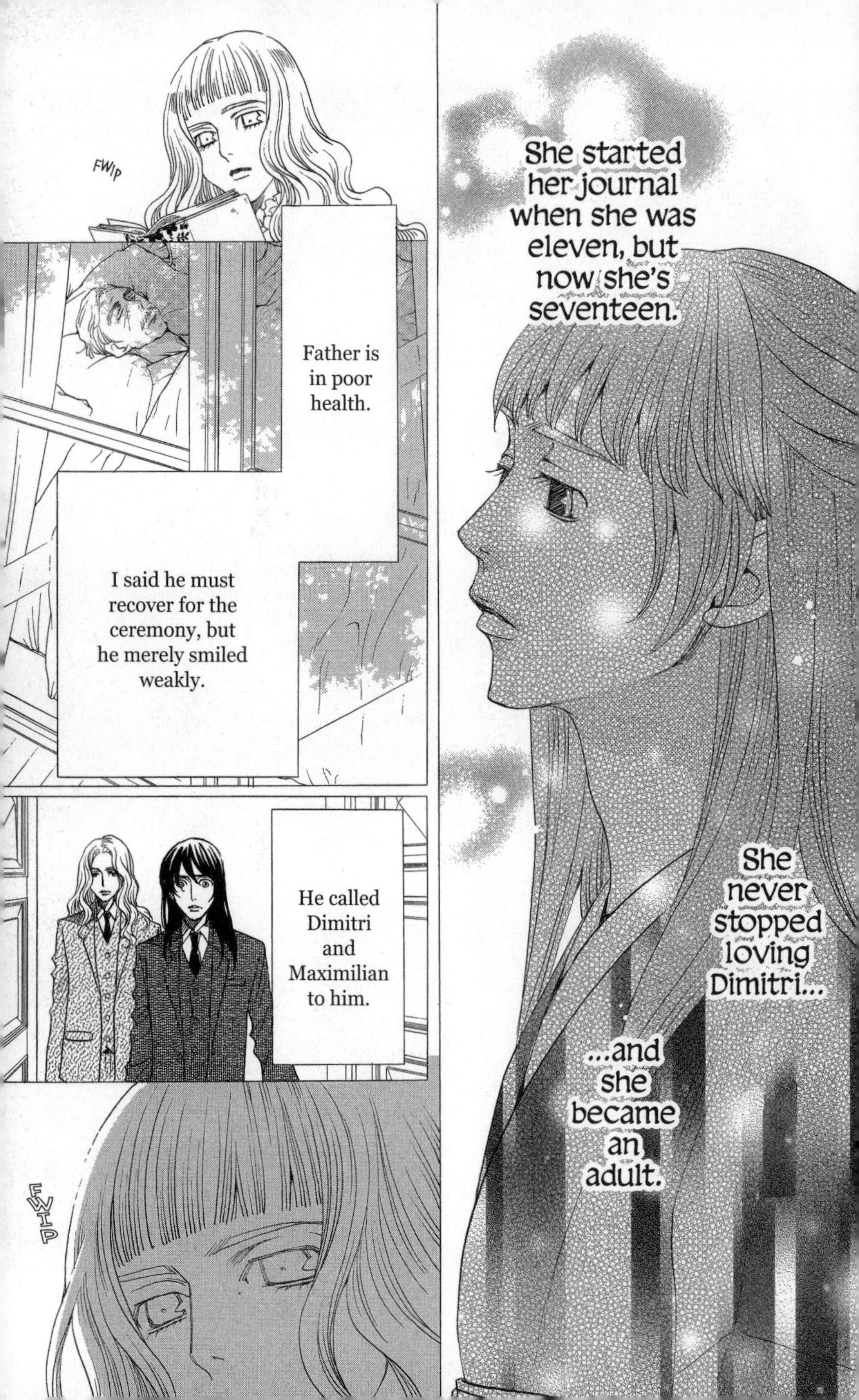

She started her journal when she was eleven, but now she's seventeen.
She never stopped loving Dimitri...
...and she became an adult.
FWIP
Father is in poor health.
I said he must recover for the ceremony, but he merely smiled weakly.
He called Dimitri and Maximilian to him.
FWIP

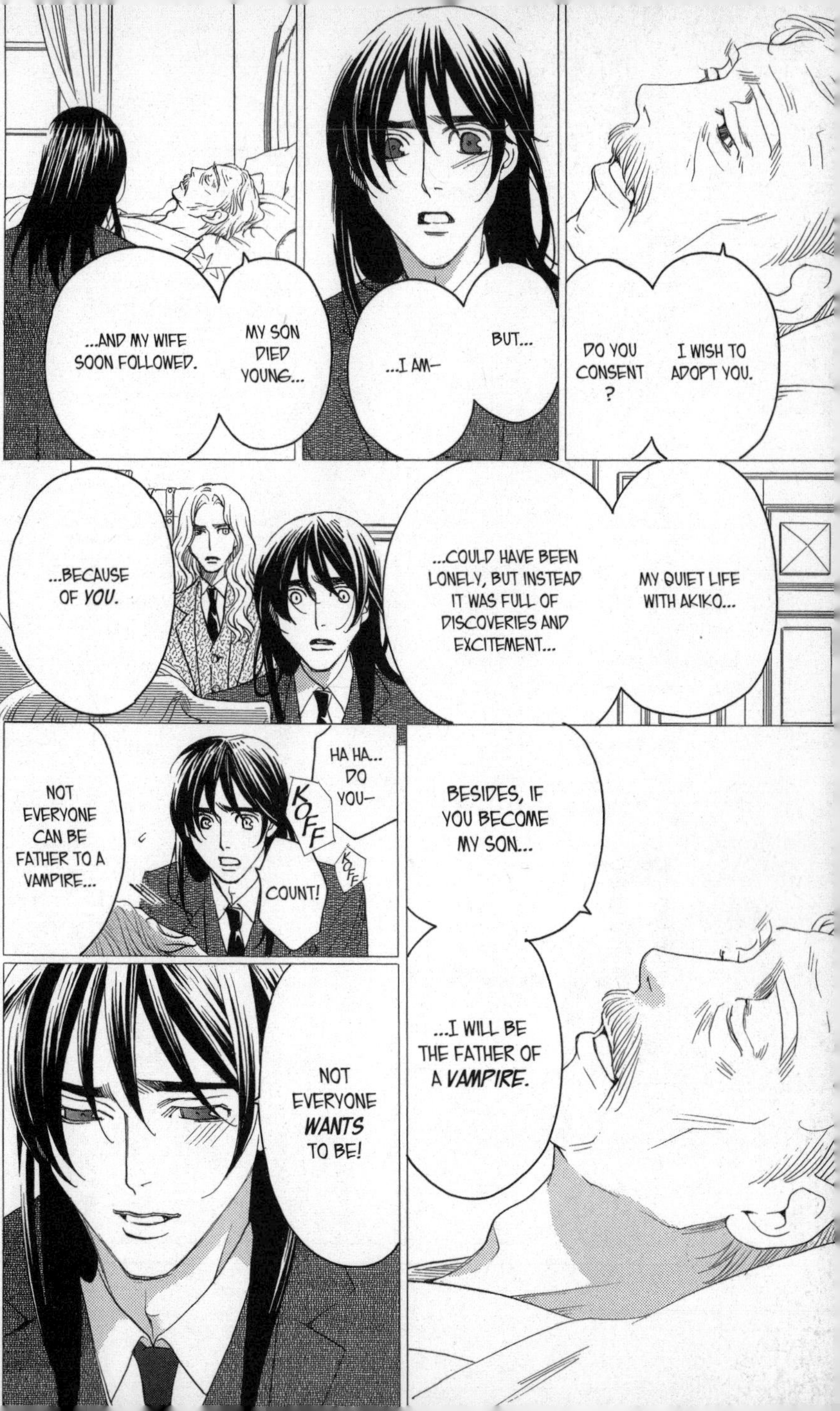
I WISH TO ADOPT YOU.
DO YOU CONSENT ?
BUT...
...I AM—
MY SON DIED YOUNG...
...AND MY WIFE SOON FOLLOWED.
MY QUIET LIFE WITH AKIKO...
...COULD HAVE BEEN LONELY, BUT INSTEAD IT WAS FULL OF DISCOVERIES AND EXCITEMENT...
...BECAUSE OF *YOU*.
BESIDES, IF YOU BECOME MY SON...
...I WILL BE THE FATHER OF A *VAMPIRE*.
HA HA... DO YOU—
KOFF
KOFF
COUNT!
NOT EVERYONE CAN BE FATHER TO A VAMPIRE...
NOT EVERYONE *WANTS* TO BE!

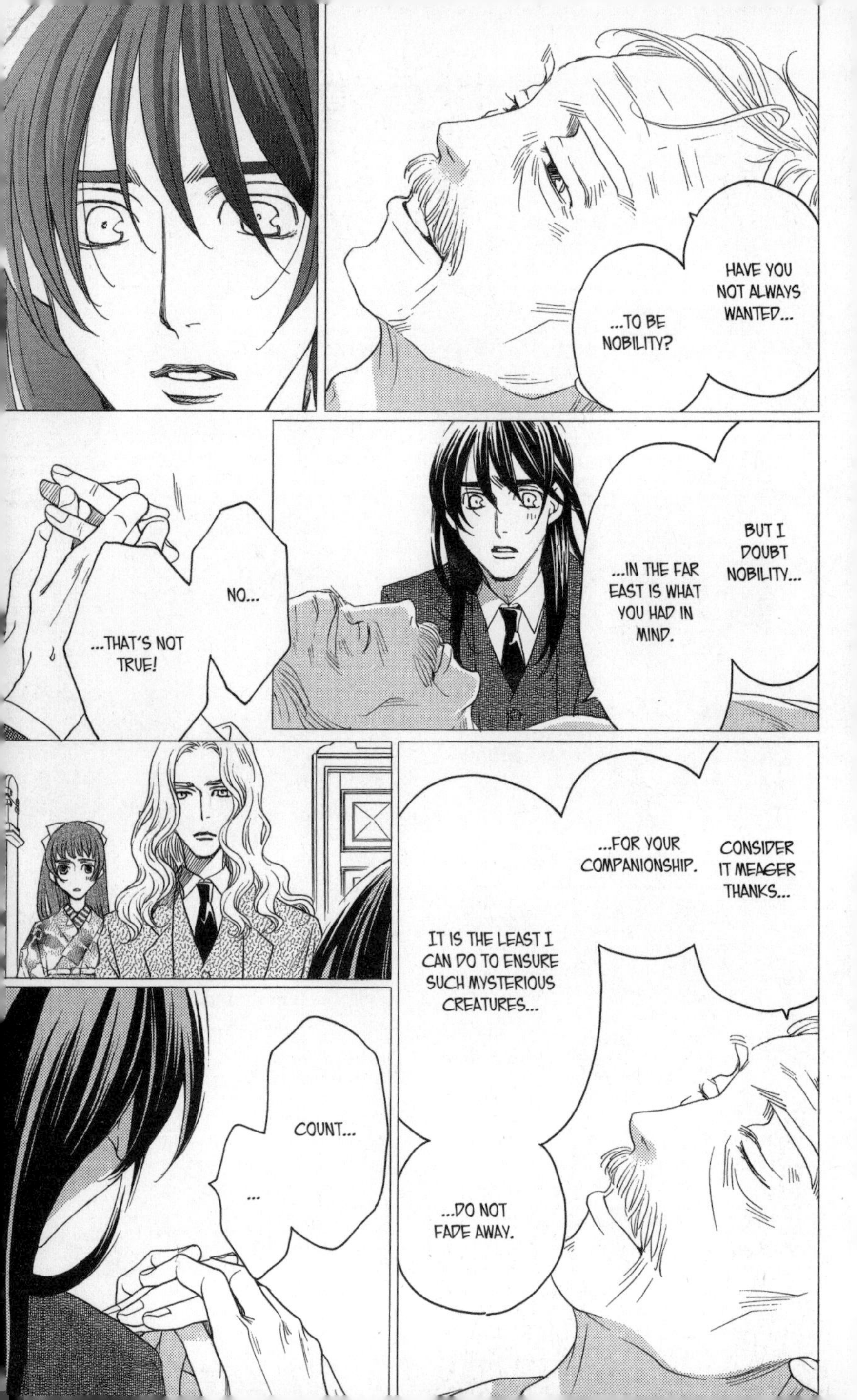
HAVE YOU NOT ALWAYS WANTED...
...TO BE NOBILITY?
BUT I DOUBT NOBILITY...
...IN THE FAR EAST IS WHAT YOU HAD IN MIND.
NO...
...THAT'S NOT TRUE!
CONSIDER IT MEAGER THANKS...
...FOR YOUR COMPANIONSHIP.
IT IS THE LEAST I CAN DO TO ENSURE SUCH MYSTERIOUS CREATURES...
...DO NOT FADE AWAY.
COUNT...
...

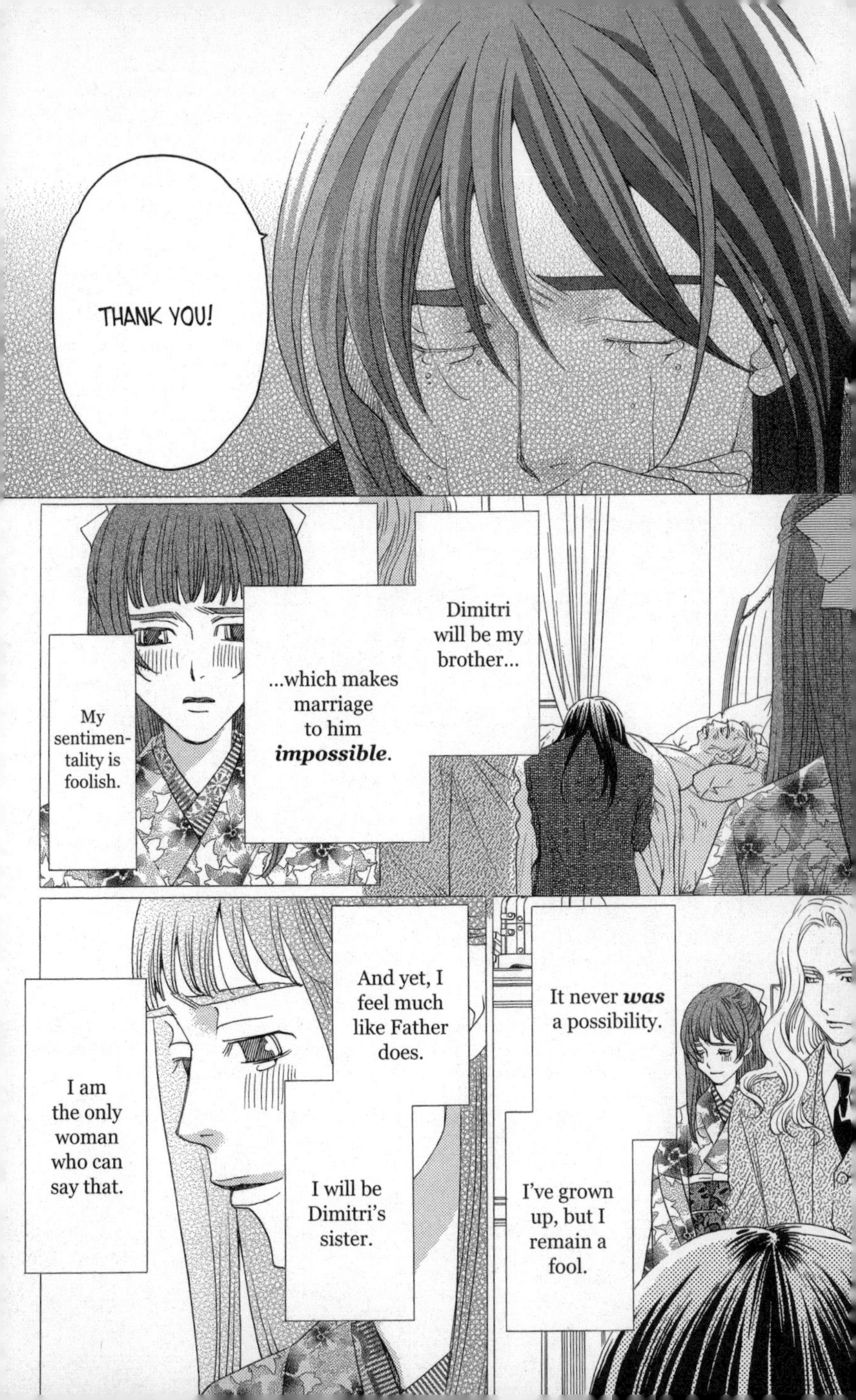
THANK YOU!
Dimitri will be my brother...
...which makes marriage to him *impossible*.
My sentimentality is foolish.
It never *was* a possibility.
I've grown up, but I remain a fool.
And yet, I feel much like Father does.
I will be Dimitri's sister.
I am the only woman who can say that.

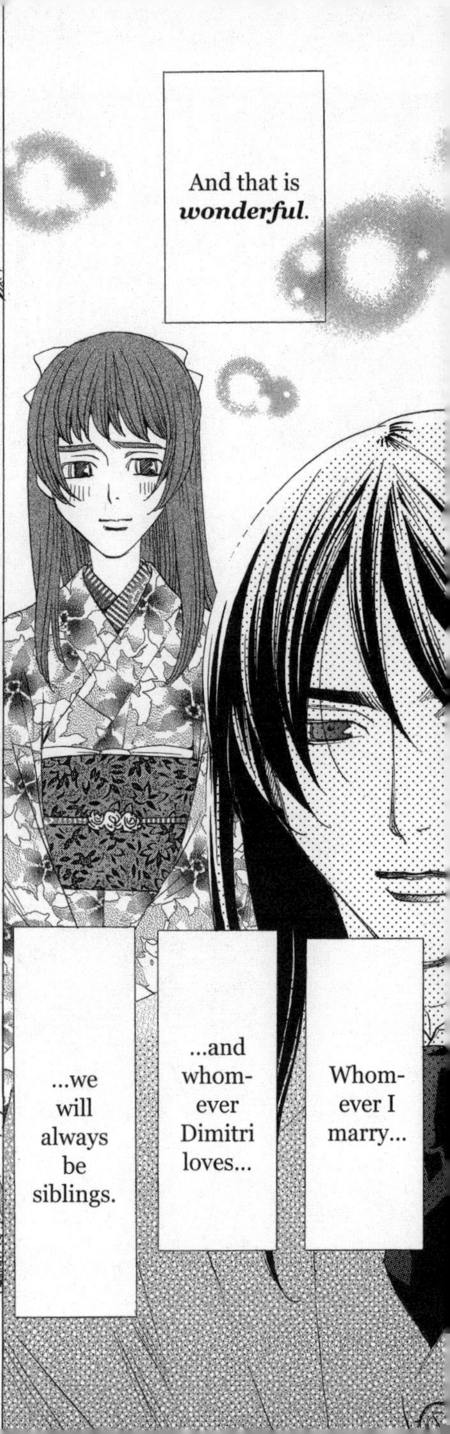
Whom-
ever I
marry...
...and
whom-
ever
Dimitri
loves...
...we
will
always
be
siblings.
And that is
wonderful.

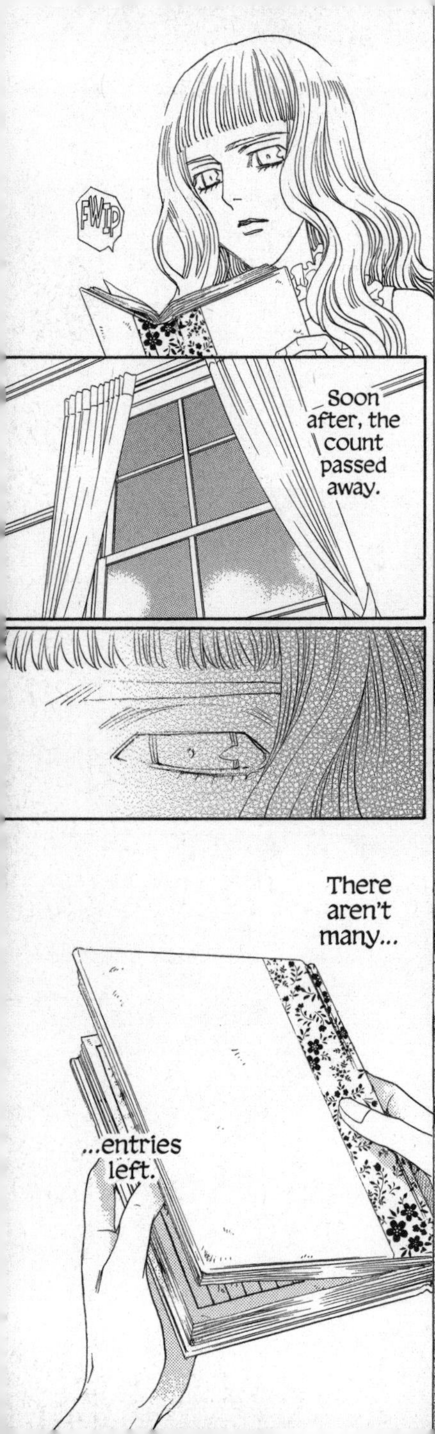
FWIP
Soon
after, the
count
passed
away.
There
aren't
many...
...entries
left.

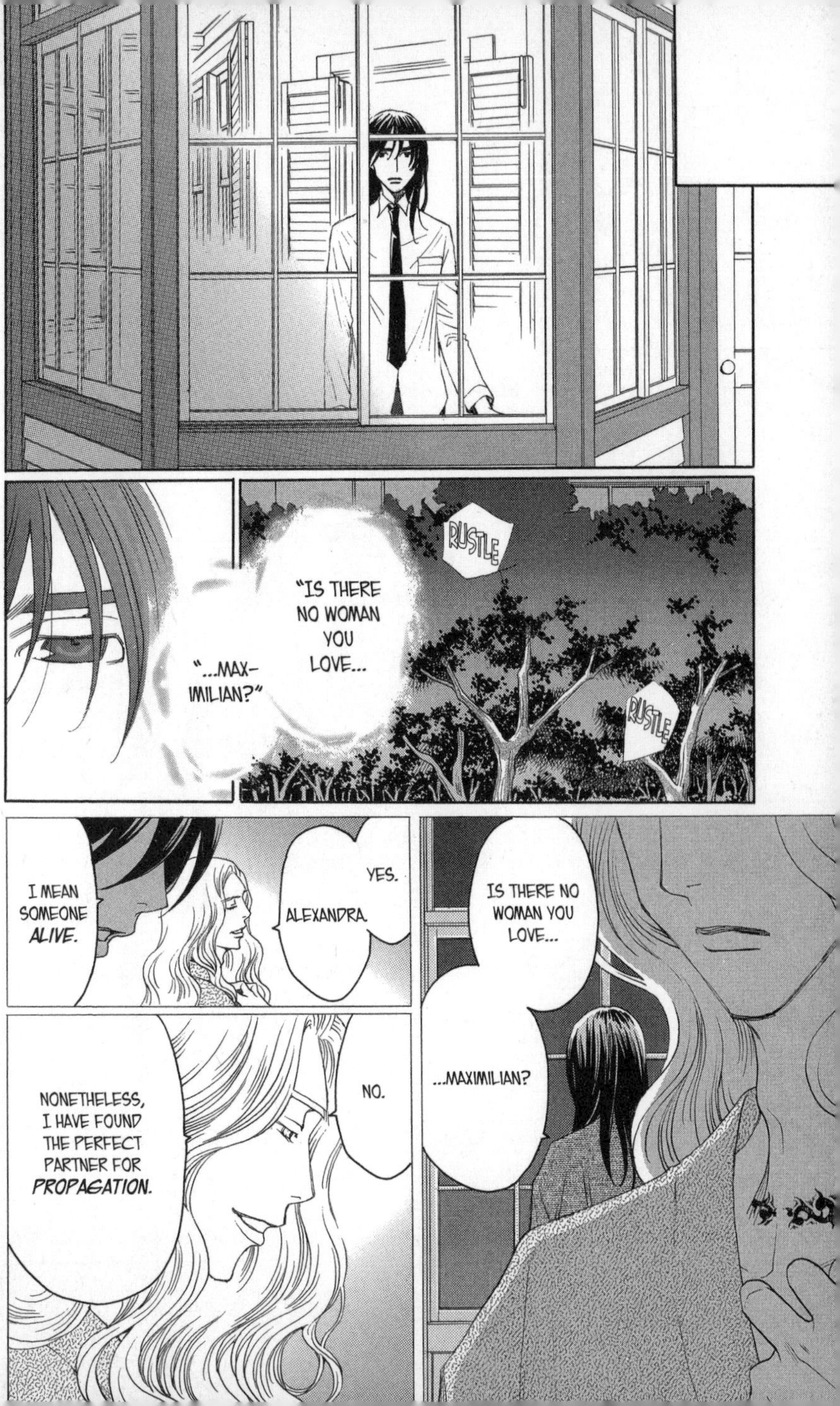
RUSTLE
"IS THERE NO WOMAN YOU LOVE...
"...MAX-IMILIAN?"
RUSTLE
IS THERE NO WOMAN YOU LOVE...
...MAXIMILIAN?
YES.
ALEXANDRA.
I MEAN SOMEONE *ALIVE.*
NO.
NONETHELESS, I HAVE FOUND THE PERFECT PARTNER FOR *PROPAGATION.*

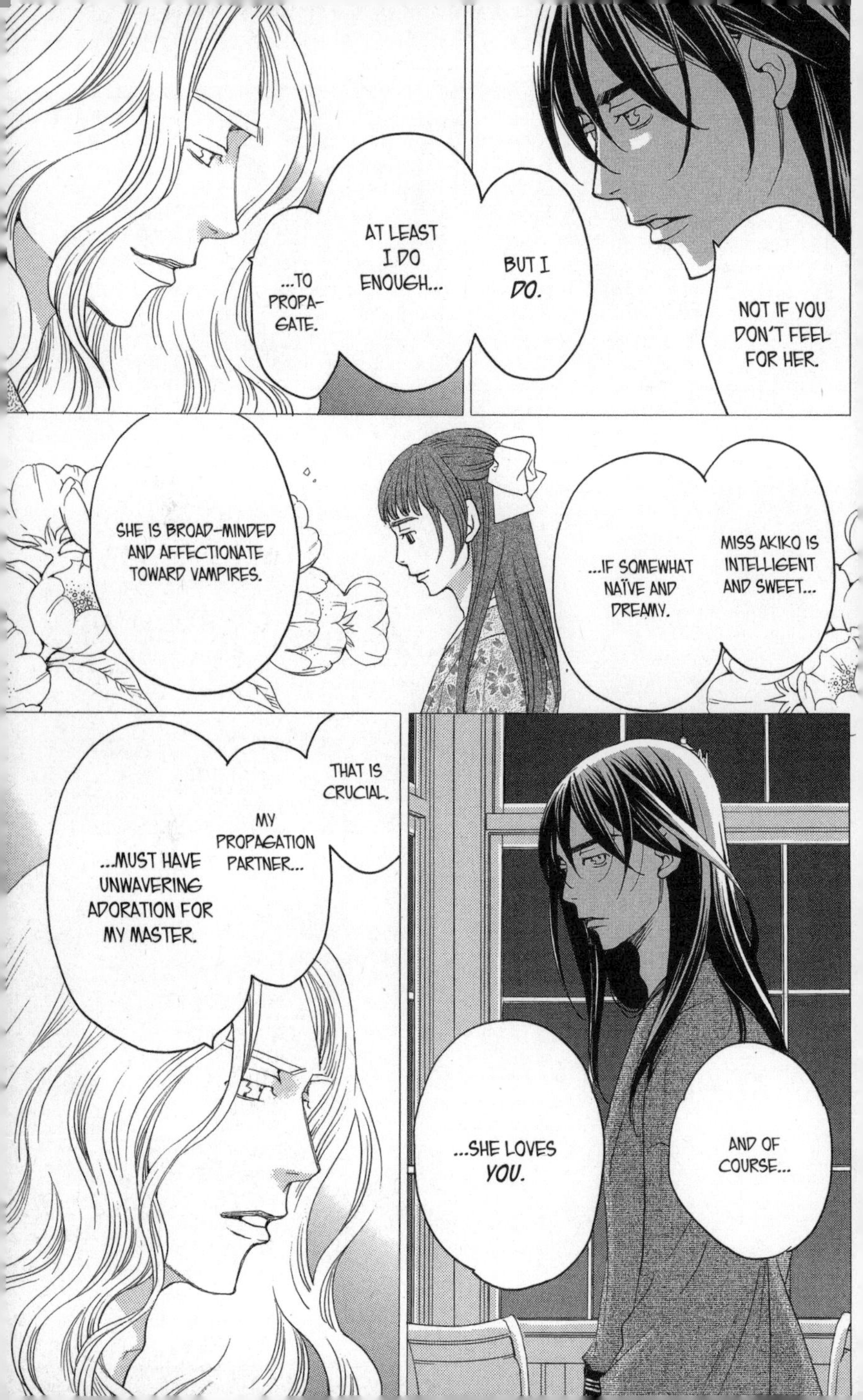
NOT IF YOU DON'T FEEL FOR HER.
BUT I *DO*.
AT LEAST I DO ENOUGH...
...TO PROPAGATE.
MISS AKIKO IS INTELLIGENT AND SWEET...
...IF SOMEWHAT NAÏVE AND DREAMY.
SHE IS BROAD-MINDED AND AFFECTIONATE TOWARD VAMPIRES.
AND OF COURSE...
...SHE LOVES *YOU*.
THAT IS CRUCIAL.
MY PROPAGATION PARTNER...
...MUST HAVE UNWAVERING ADORATION FOR MY MASTER.

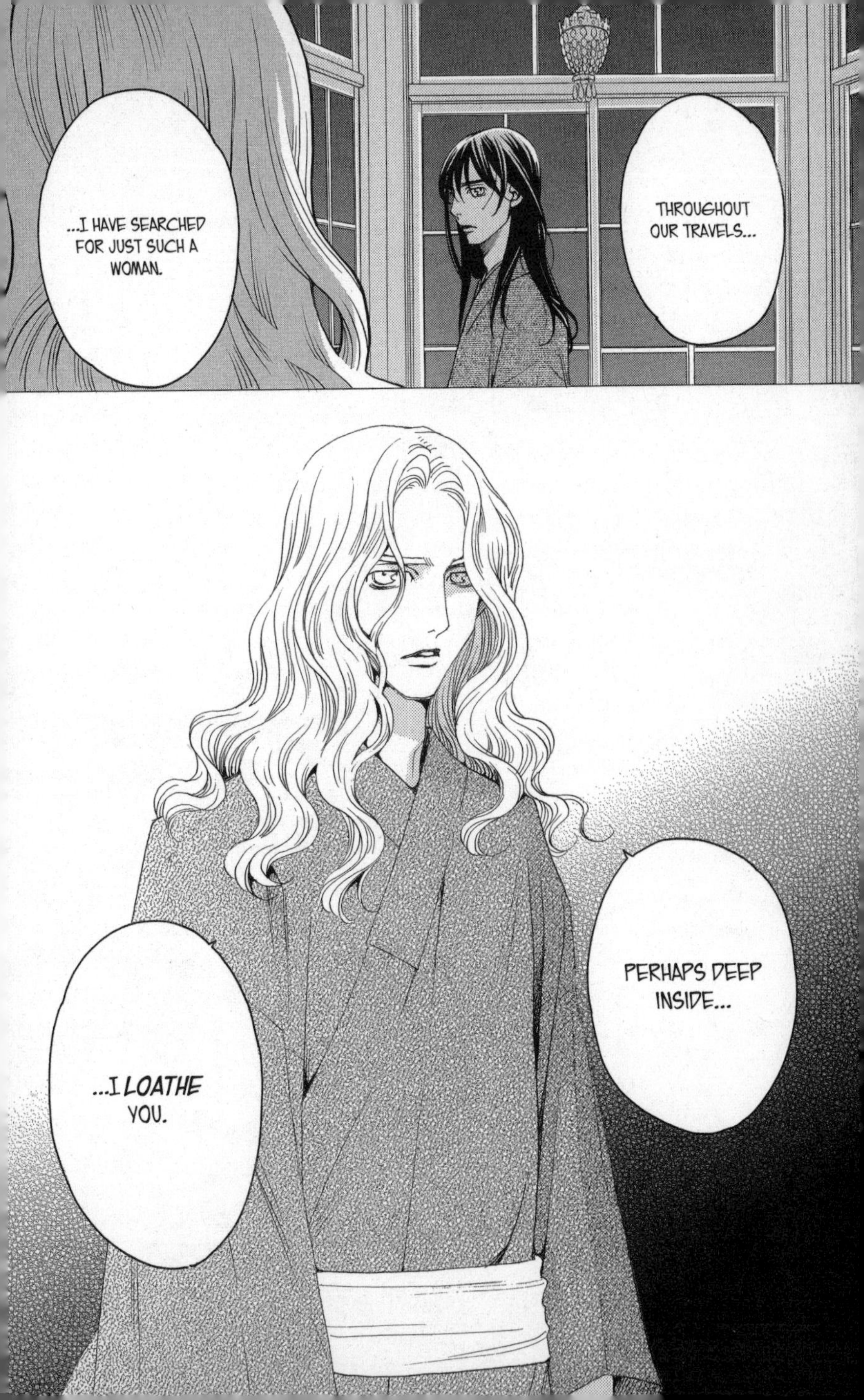
THROUGHOUT OUR TRAVELS...
...I HAVE SEARCHED FOR JUST SUCH A WOMAN.
PERHAPS DEEP INSIDE...
...I LOATHE YOU.

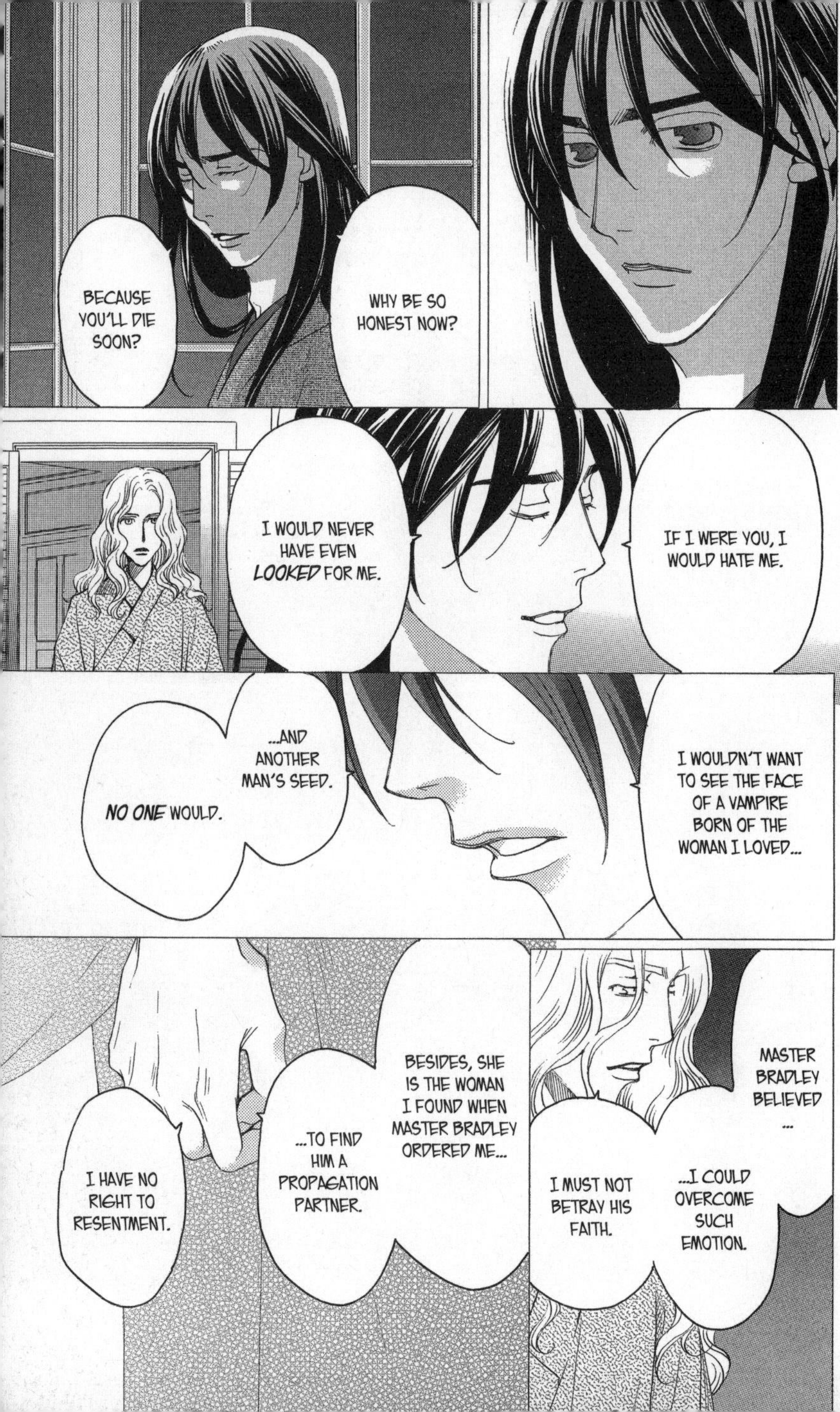
WHY BE SO HONEST NOW?
BECAUSE YOU'LL DIE SOON?
IF I WERE YOU, I WOULD HATE ME.
I WOULD NEVER HAVE EVEN *LOOKED* FOR ME.
I WOULDN'T WANT TO SEE THE FACE OF A VAMPIRE BORN OF THE WOMAN I LOVED...
...AND ANOTHER MAN'S SEED.
NO ONE WOULD.
MASTER BRADLEY BELIEVED ...
...I COULD OVERCOME SUCH EMOTION.
I MUST NOT BETRAY HIS FAITH.
BESIDES, SHE IS THE WOMAN I FOUND WHEN MASTER BRADLEY ORDERED ME...
...TO FIND HIM A PROPAGATION PARTNER.
I HAVE NO RIGHT TO RESENTMENT.

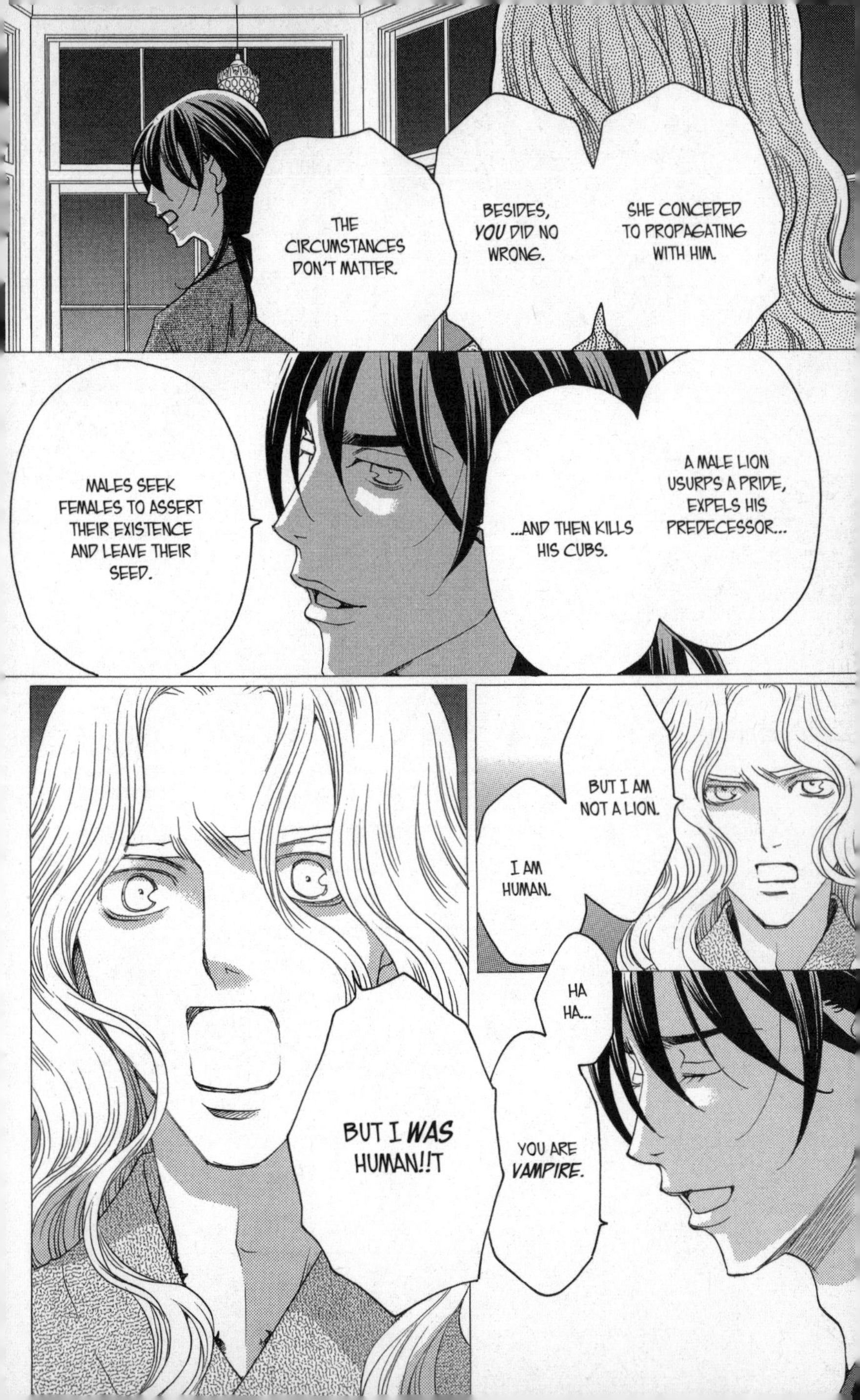
SHE CONCEDED TO PROPAGATING WITH HIM.
BESIDES, **YOU** DID NO WRONG.
THE CIRCUMSTANCES DON'T MATTER.
A MALE LION USURPS A PRIDE, EXPELS HIS PREDECESSOR...
...AND THEN KILLS HIS CUBS.
MALES SEEK FEMALES TO ASSERT THEIR EXISTENCE AND LEAVE THEIR SEED.
BUT I AM NOT A LION.
I AM HUMAN.
HA HA...
YOU ARE **VAMPIRE**.
BUT I **WAS** HUMAN!!

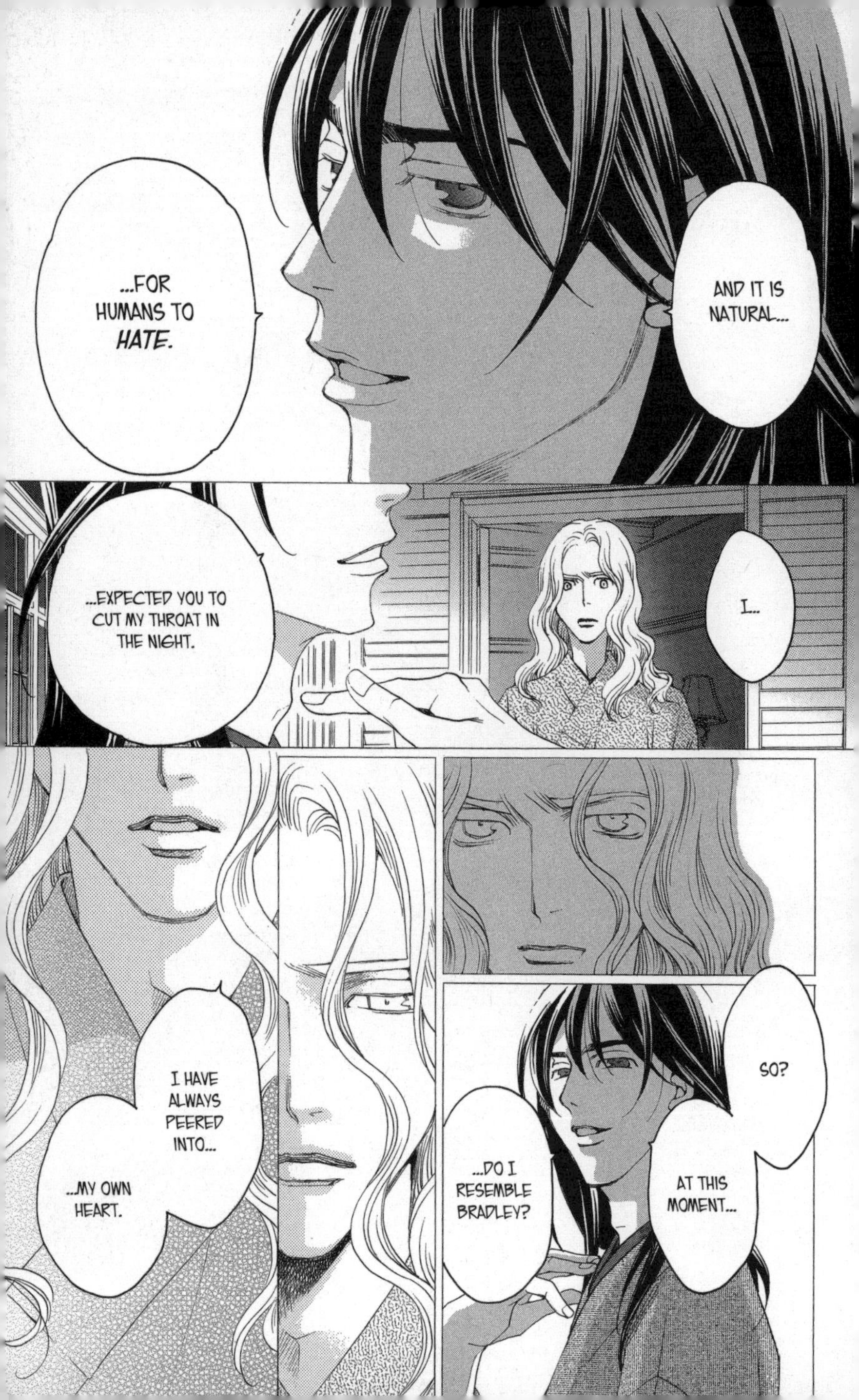
AND IT IS NATURAL...
...FOR HUMANS TO HATE.
I...
...EXPECTED YOU TO CUT MY THROAT IN THE NIGHT.
SO?
AT THIS MOMENT...
...DO I RESEMBLE BRADLEY?
I HAVE ALWAYS PEERED INTO...
...MY OWN HEART.

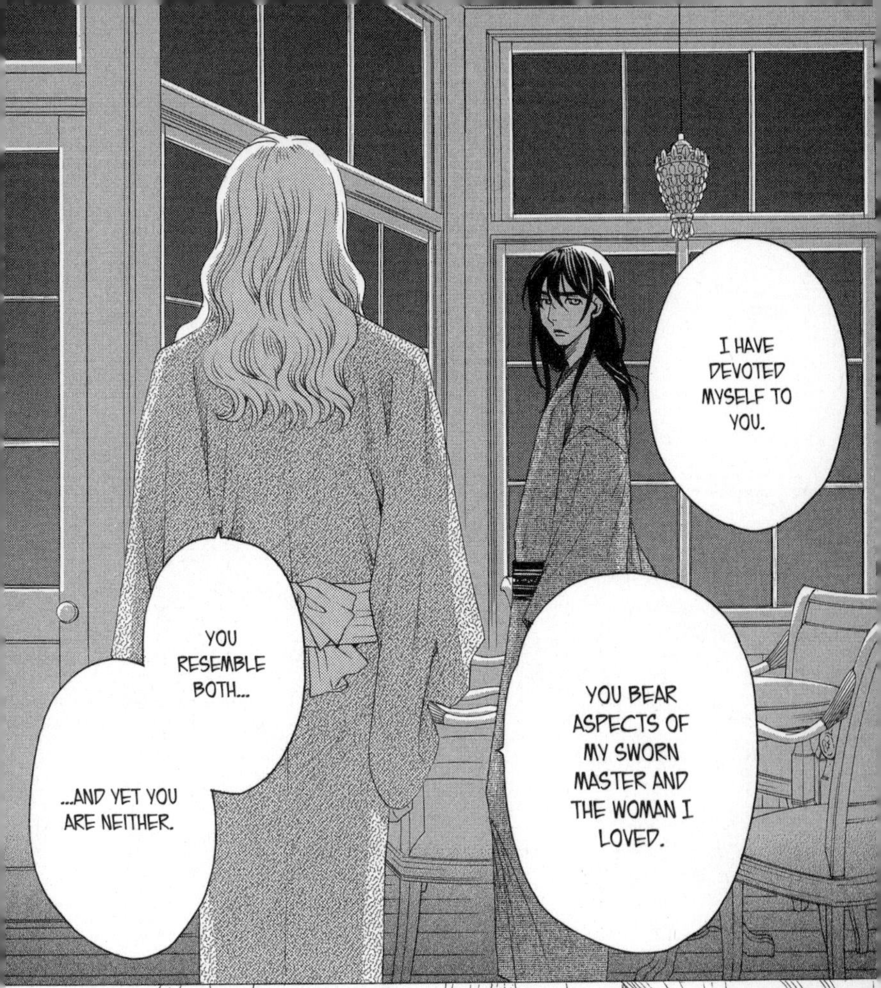
I HAVE DEVOTED MYSELF TO YOU.
YOU BEAR ASPECTS OF MY SWORN MASTER AND THE WOMAN I LOVED.
YOU RESEMBLE BOTH...
...AND YET YOU ARE NEITHER.
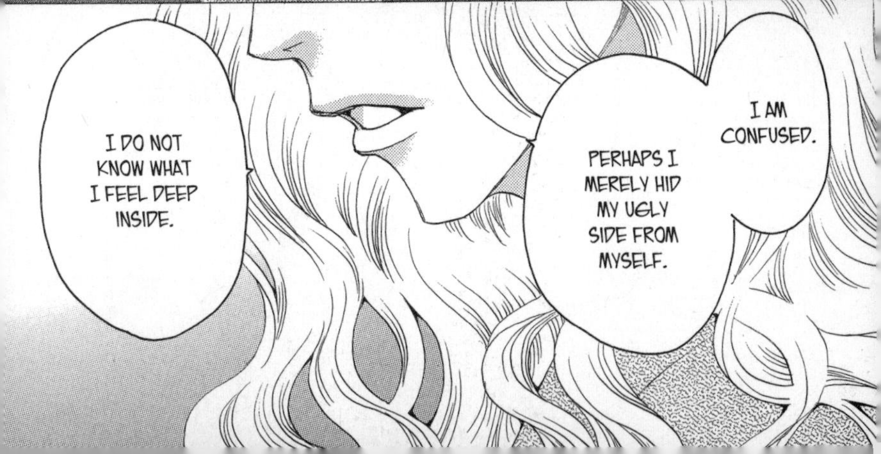
I AM CONFUSED.
PERHAPS I MERELY HID MY UGLY SIDE FROM MYSELF.
I DO NOT KNOW WHAT I FEEL DEEP INSIDE.

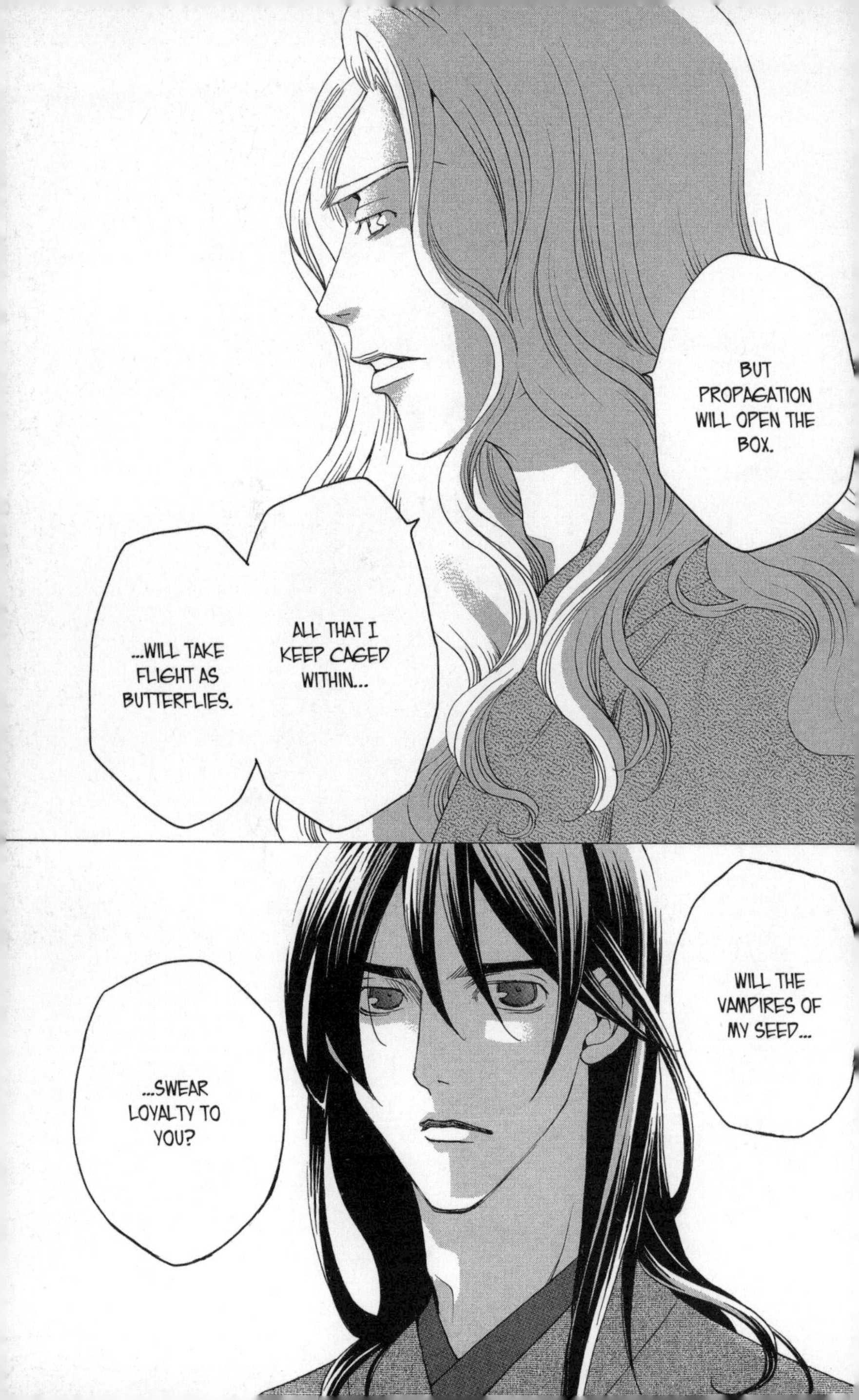
BUT PROPAGATION WILL OPEN THE BOX.
ALL THAT I KEEP CAGED WITHIN...
...WILL TAKE FLIGHT AS BUTTERFLIES.
WILL THE VAMPIRES OF MY SEED...
...SWEAR LOYALTY TO YOU?

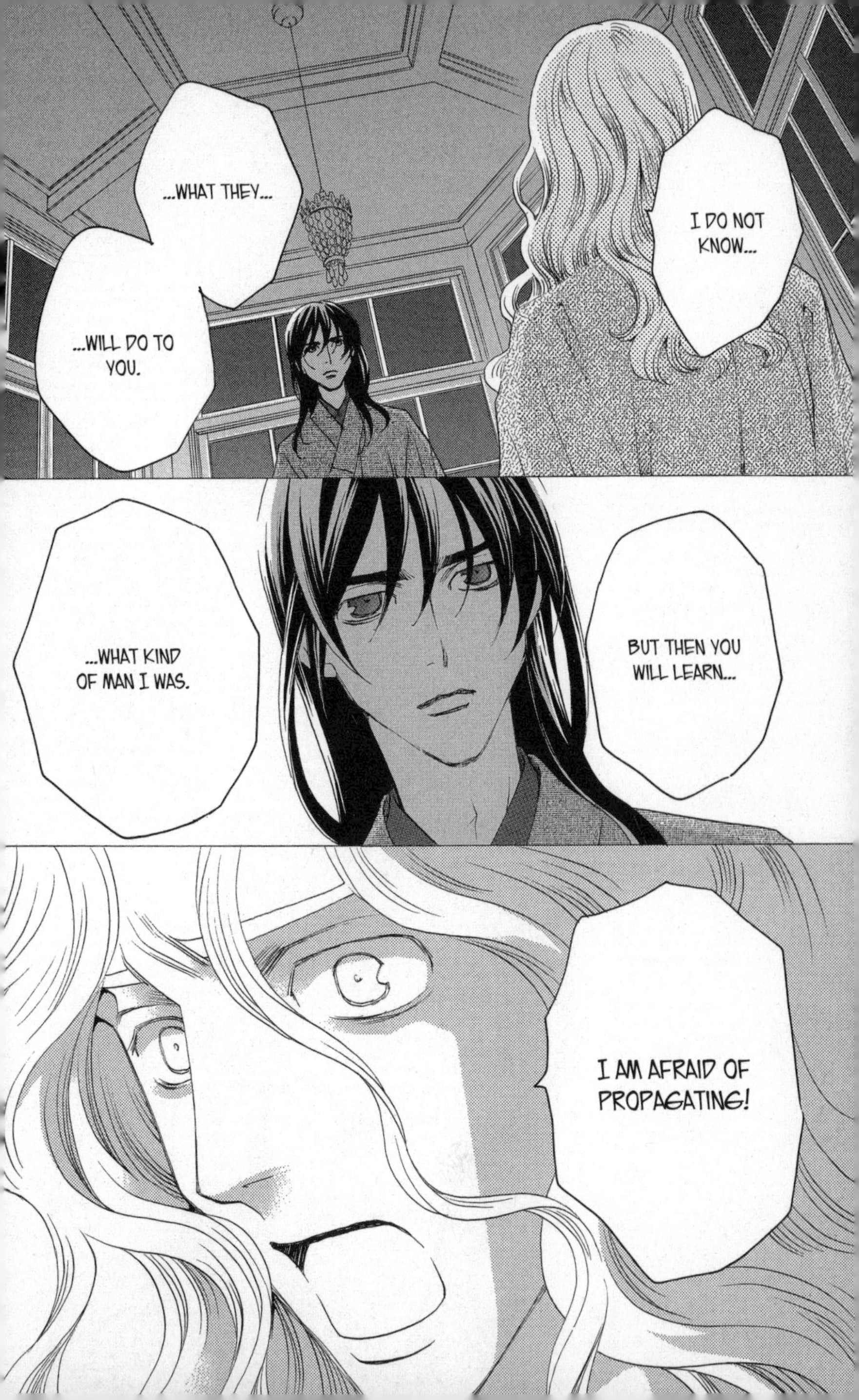
I DO NOT KNOW...
...WHAT THEY...
...WILL DO TO YOU.
BUT THEN YOU WILL LEARN...
...WHAT KIND OF MAN I WAS.
I AM AFRAID OF PROPAGATING!

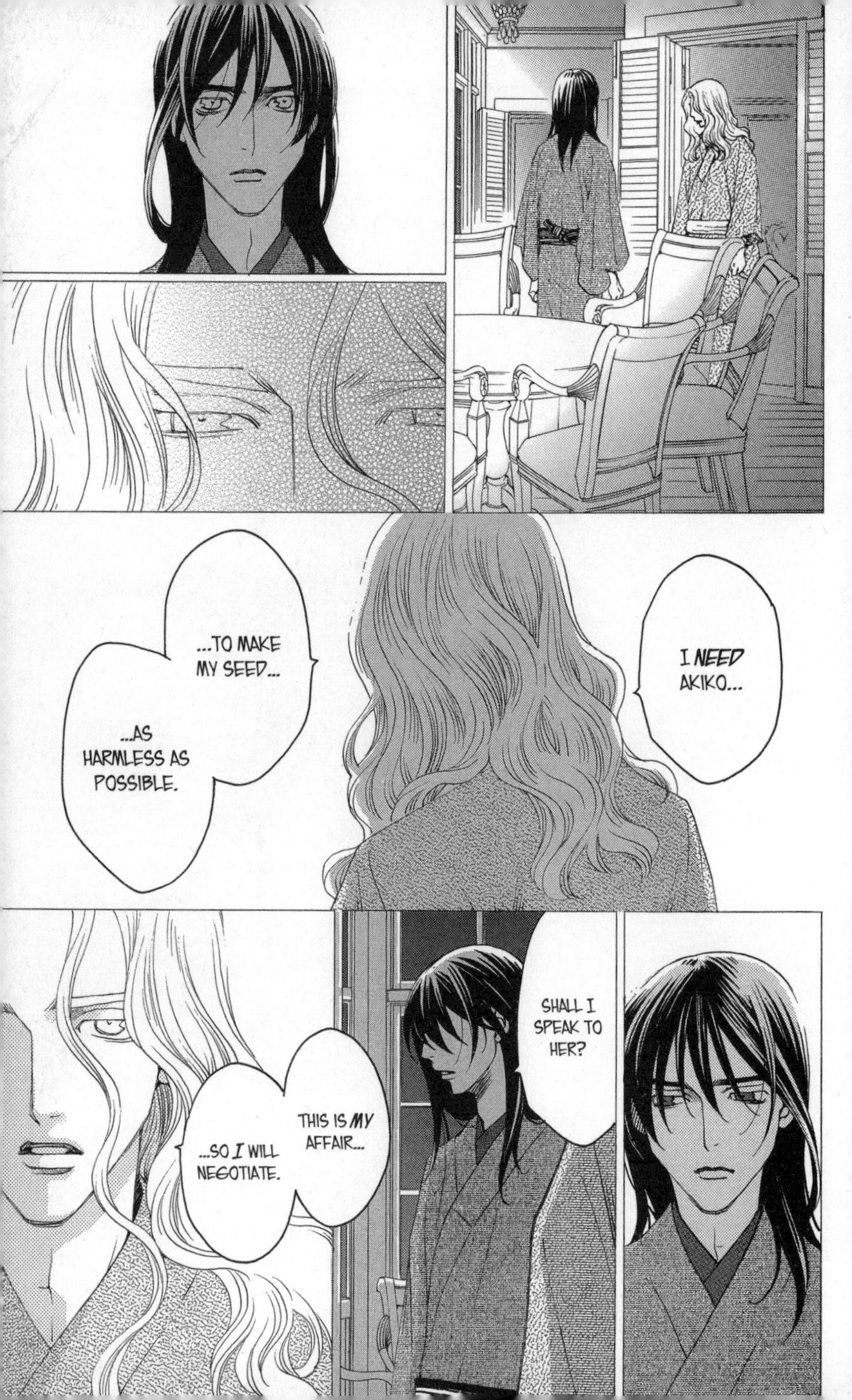
I NEED AKIKO...
...TO MAKE MY SEED...
...AS HARMLESS AS POSSIBLE.
SHALL I SPEAK TO HER?
THIS IS MY AFFAIR...
...SO I WILL NEGOTIATE.

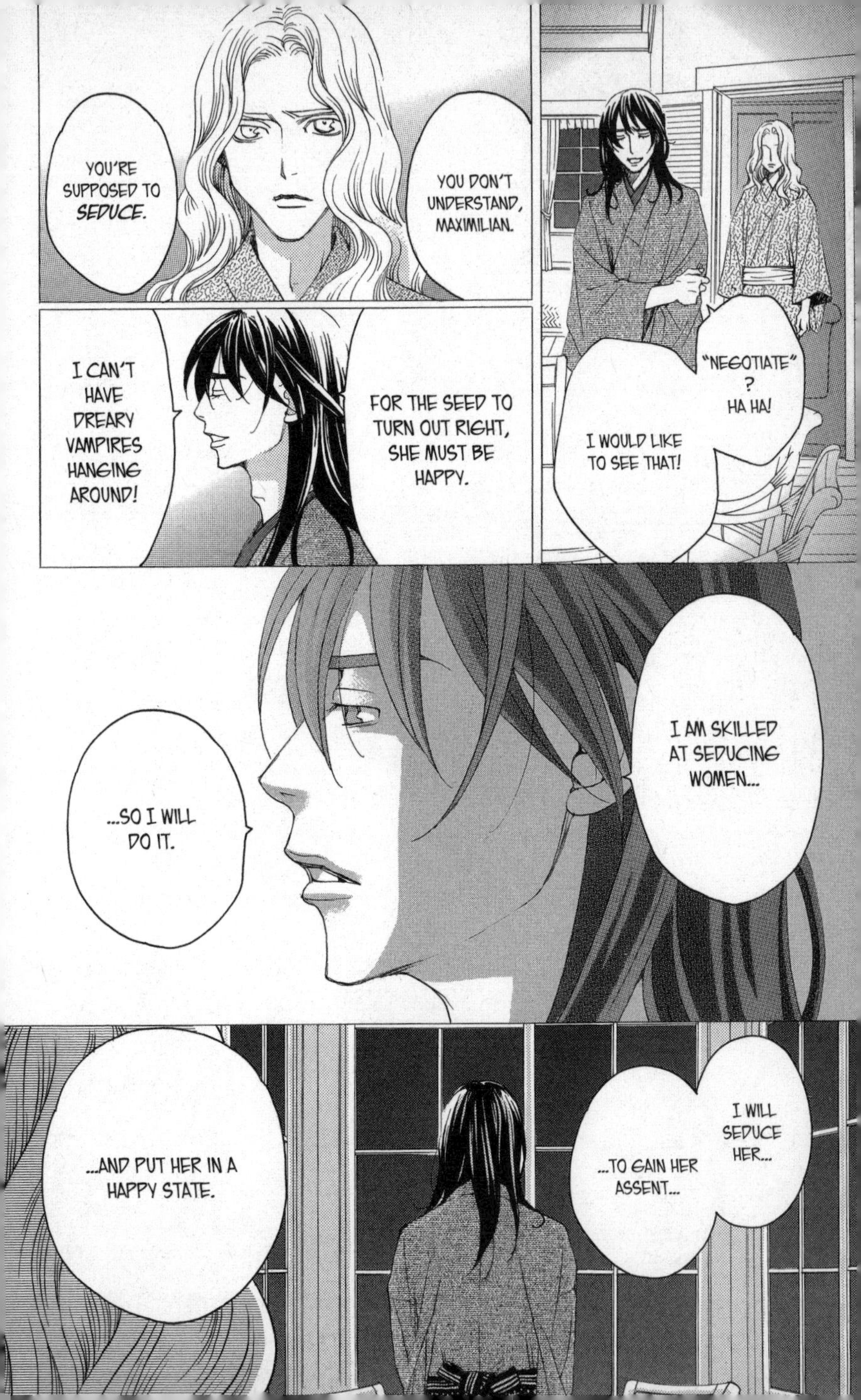
"NEGOTIATE" ? HA HA!
I WOULD LIKE TO SEE THAT!
YOU DON'T UNDERSTAND, MAXIMILIAN.
YOU'RE SUPPOSED TO SEDUCE.
FOR THE SEED TO TURN OUT RIGHT, SHE MUST BE HAPPY.
I CAN'T HAVE DREARY VAMPIRES HANGING AROUND!
I AM SKILLED AT SEDUCING WOMEN...
...SO I WILL DO IT.
I WILL SEDUCE HER...
...TO GAIN HER ASSENT...
...AND PUT HER IN A HAPPY STATE.

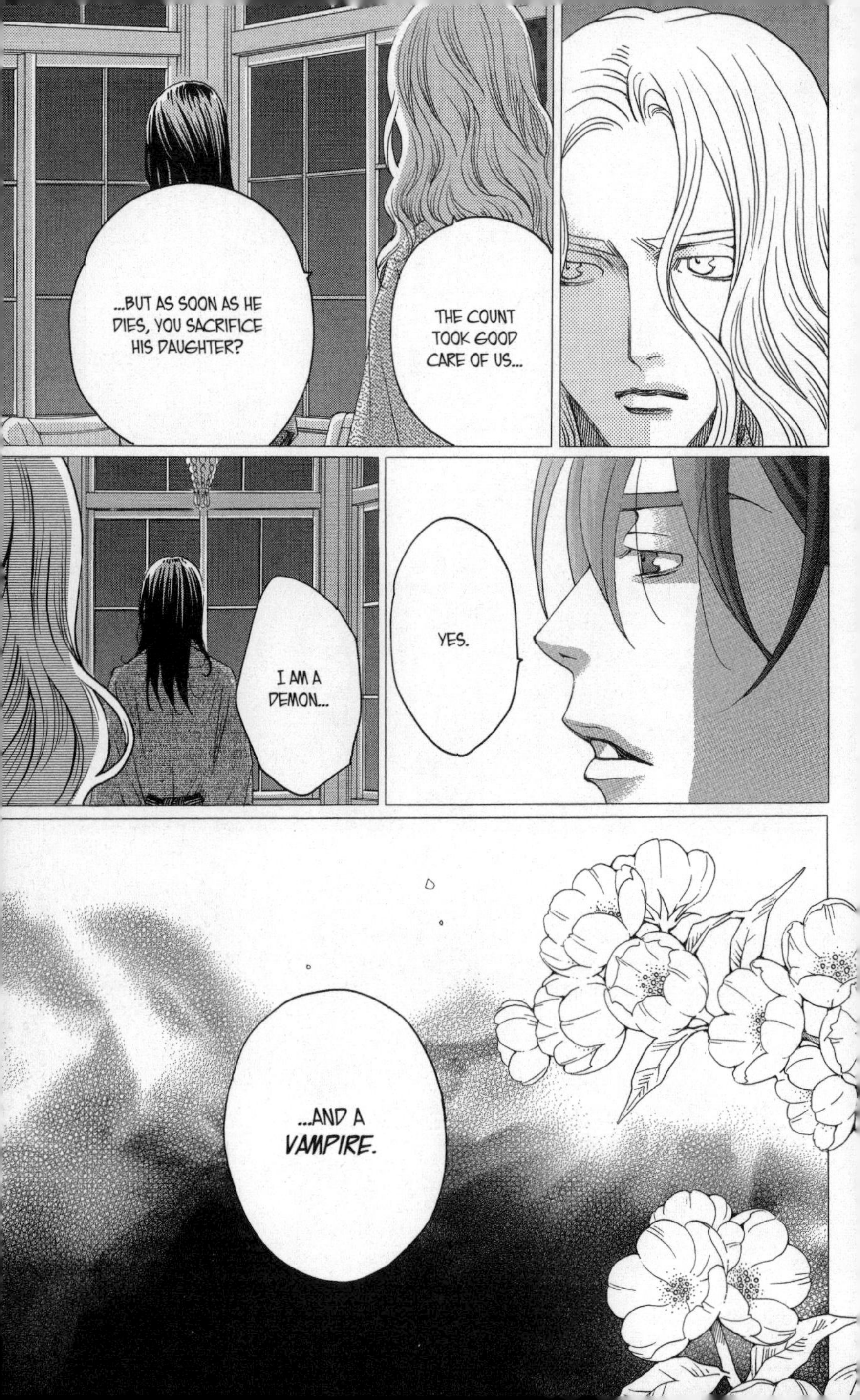
THE COUNT TOOK GOOD CARE OF US...
...BUT AS SOON AS HE DIES, YOU SACRIFICE HIS DAUGHTER?
YES.
I AM A DEMON...
...AND A *VAMPIRE*.

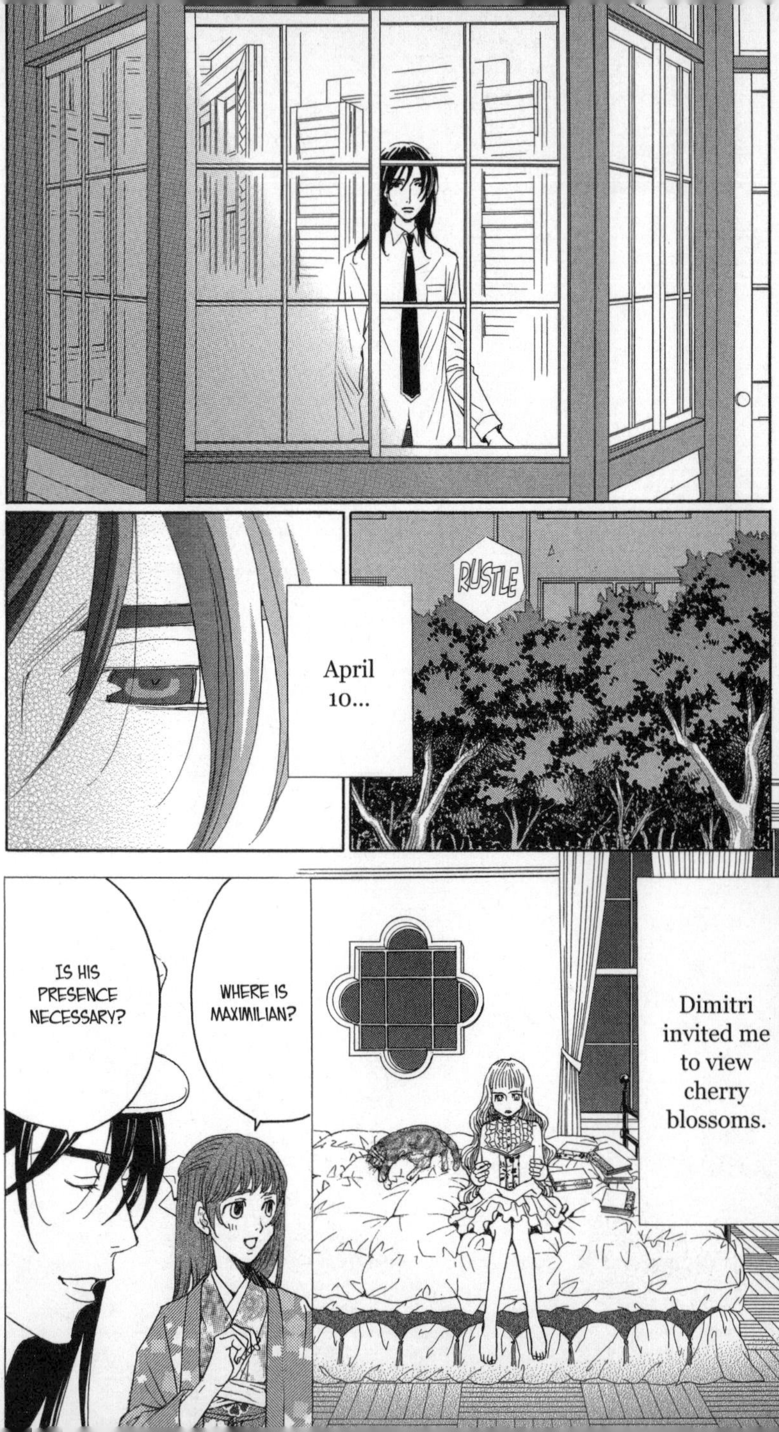
RUSTLE
April 10...
Dimitri invited me to view cherry blossoms.
WHERE IS MAXIMILIAN?
IS HIS PRESENCE NECESSARY?

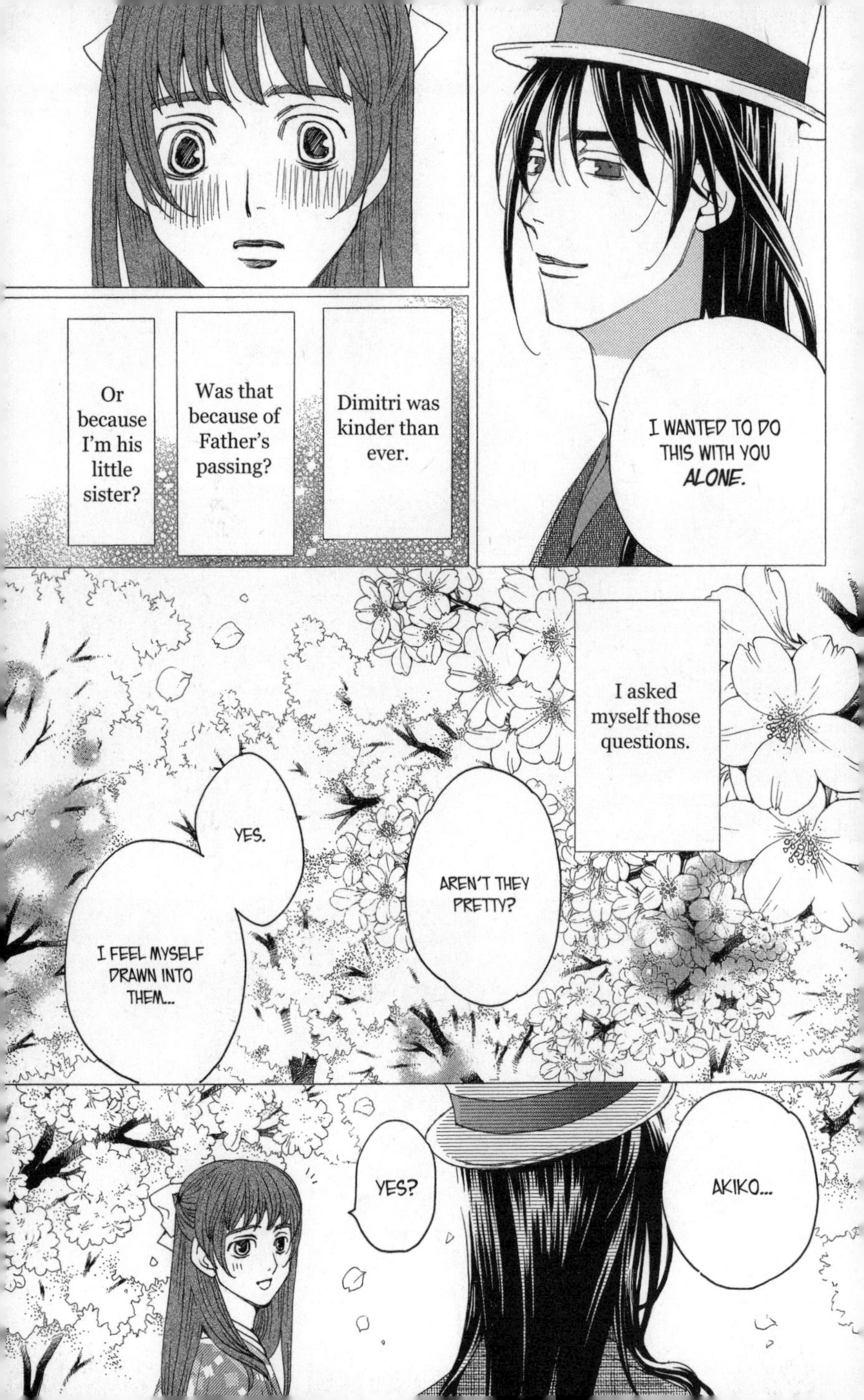
I WANTED TO DO THIS WITH YOU *ALONE*.
Dimitri was kinder than ever.
Was that because of Father's passing?
Or because I'm his little sister?
I asked myself those questions.
AREN'T THEY PRETTY?
YES.
I FEEL MYSELF DRAWN INTO THEM...
AKIKO...
YES?

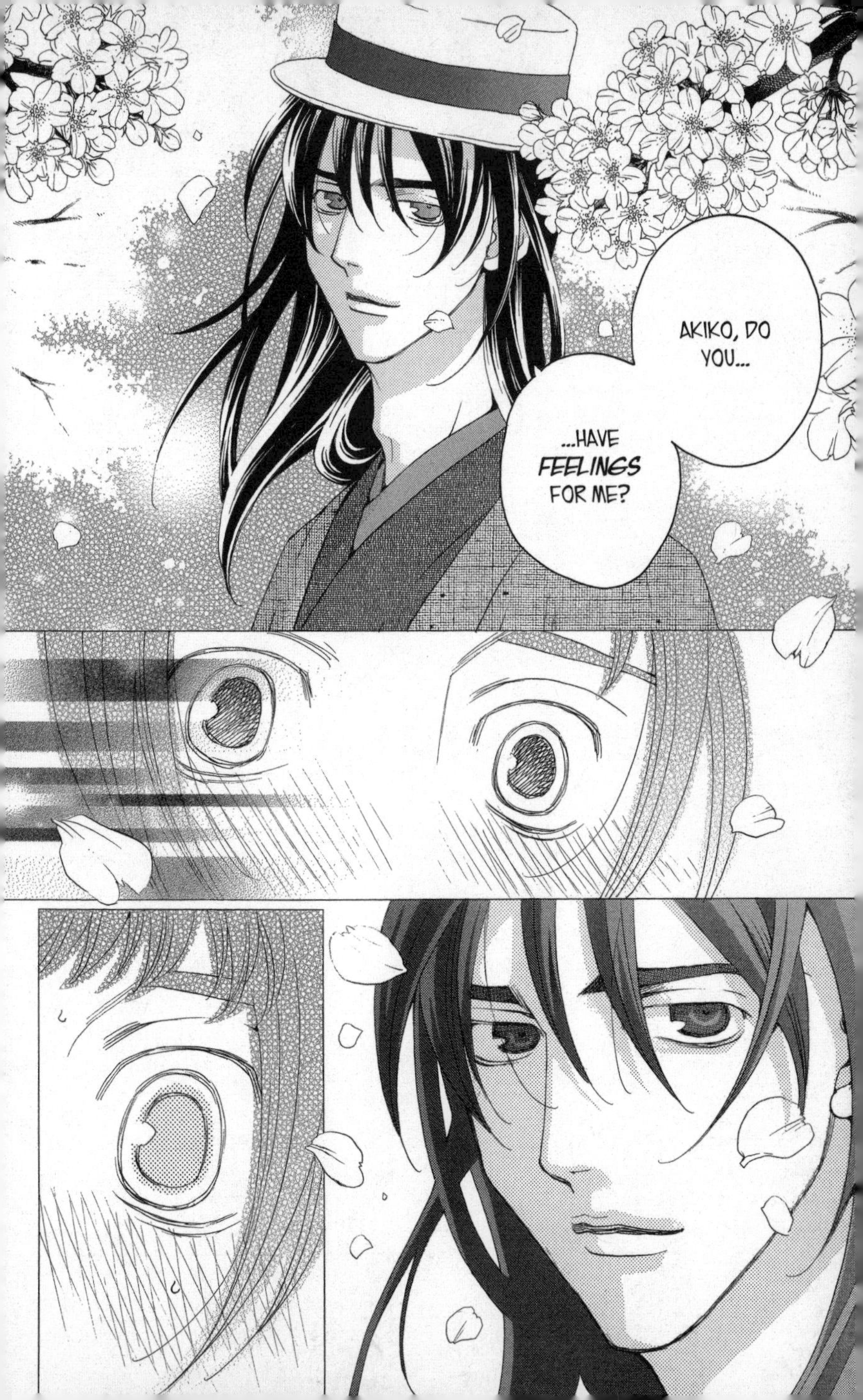
AKIKO, DO YOU...
...HAVE FEELINGS FOR ME?

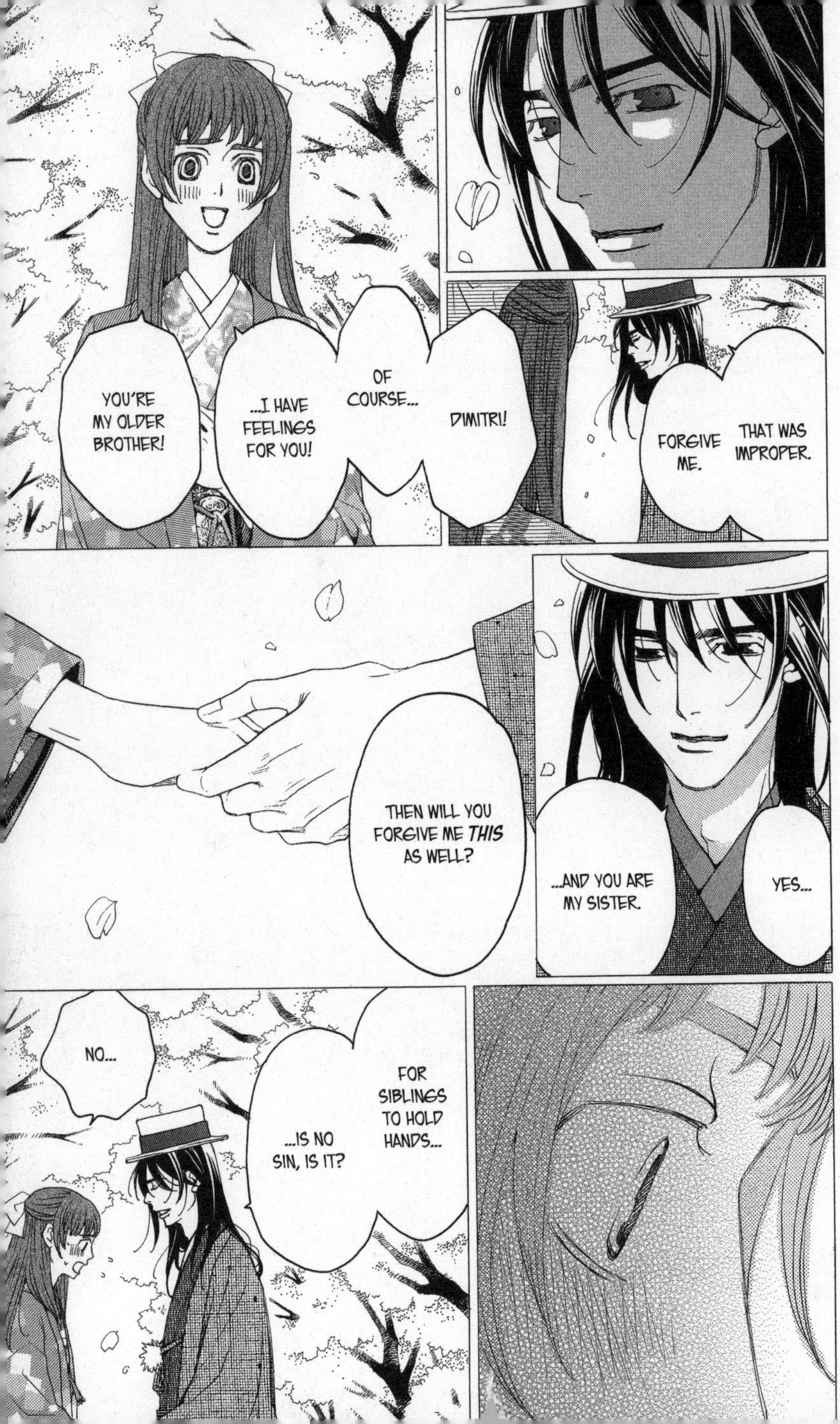
THAT WAS IMPROPER.
FORGIVE ME.
DIMITRI!
OF COURSE...
...I HAVE FEELINGS FOR YOU!
YOU'RE MY OLDER BROTHER!
YES...
...AND YOU ARE MY SISTER.
THEN WILL YOU FORGIVE ME *THIS* AS WELL?
FOR SIBLINGS TO HOLD HANDS...
...IS NO SIN, IS IT?
NO...

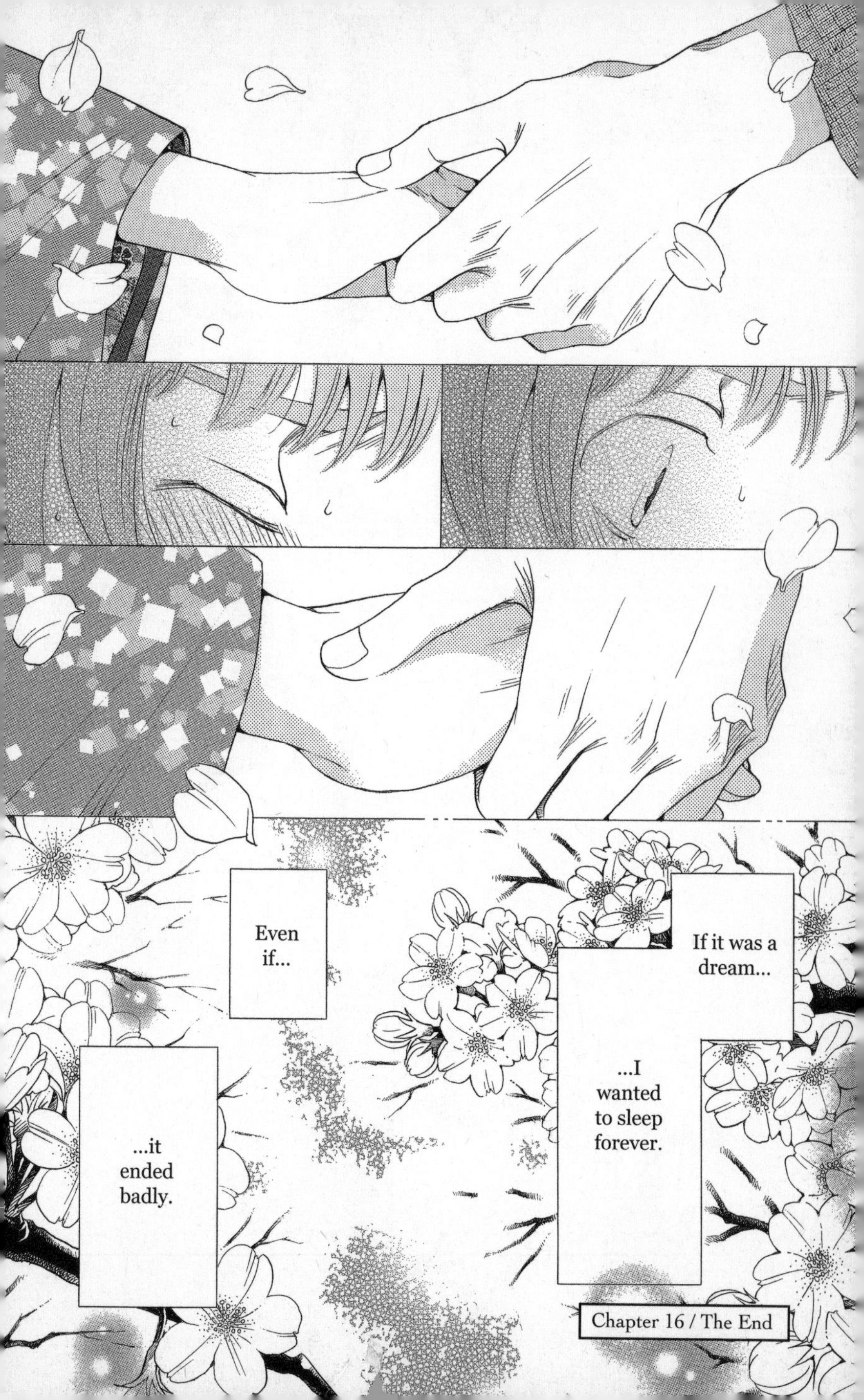
If it was a dream...
...I wanted to sleep forever.
Even if...
...it ended badly.
Chapter 16 / The End

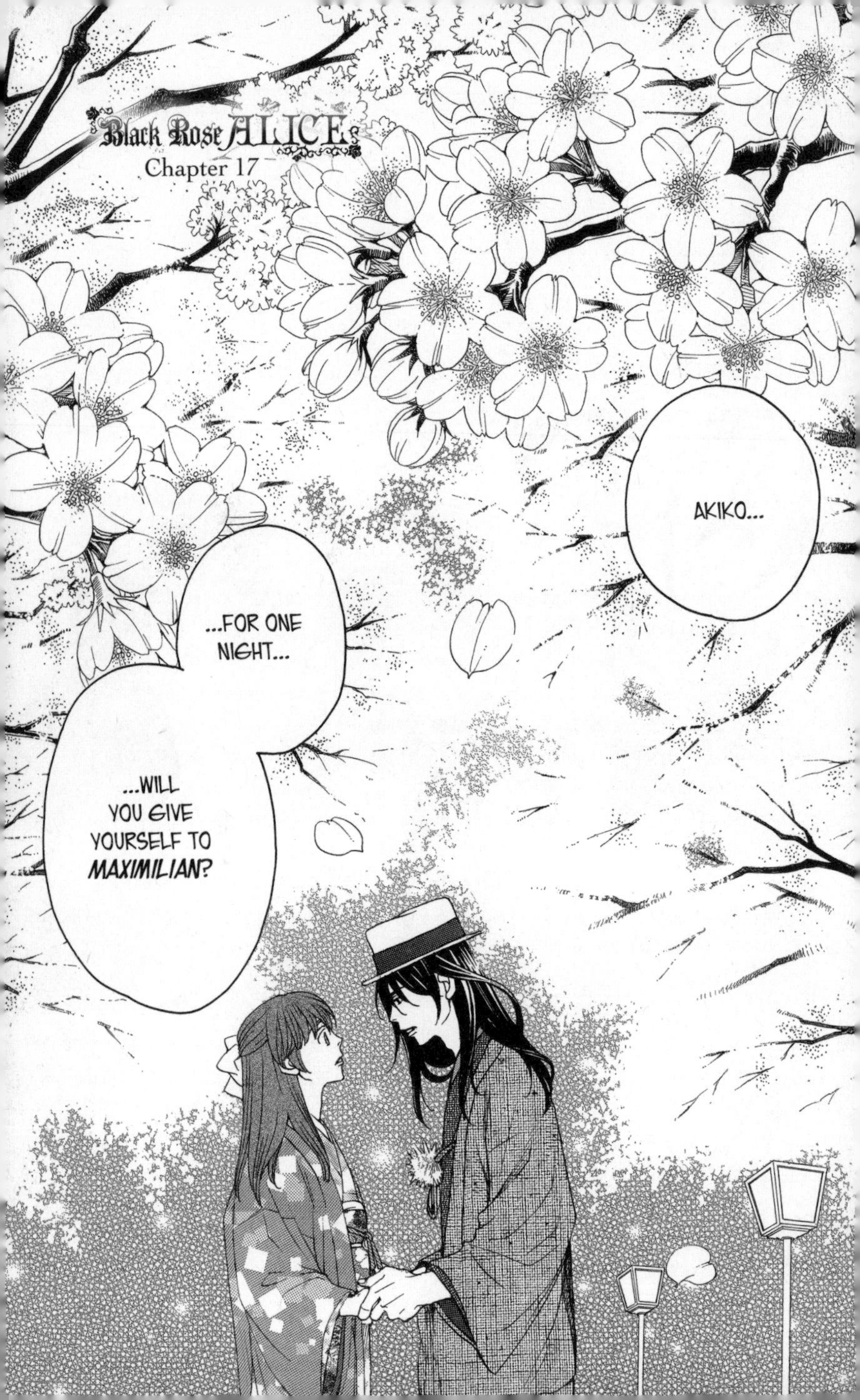
Black Rose ALICE
Chapter 17
AKIKO...
...FOR ONE NIGHT...
...WILL YOU GIVE YOURSELF TO MAXIMILIAN?

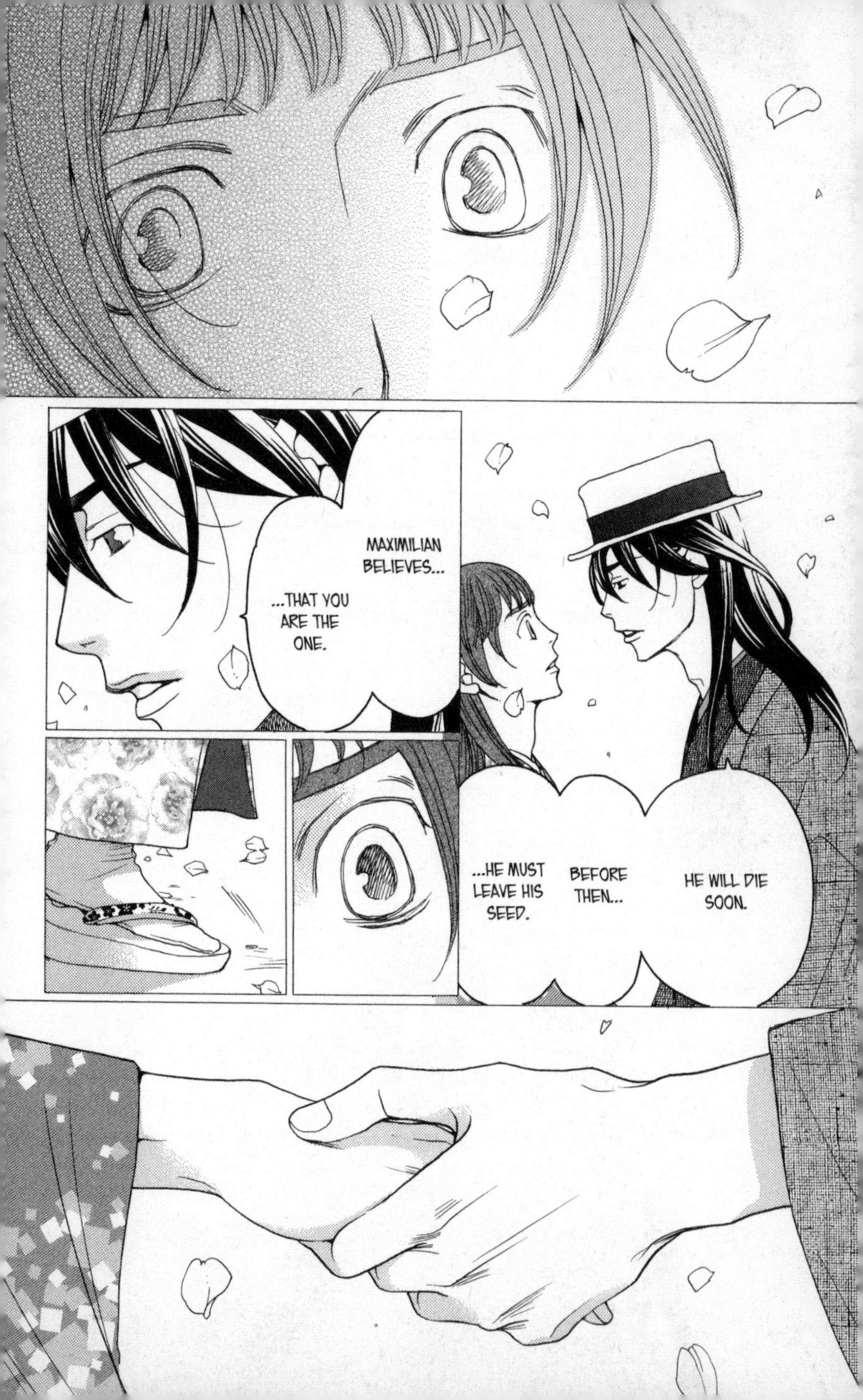
HE WILL DIE SOON.
BEFORE THEN...
...HE MUST LEAVE HIS SEED.
MAXIMILIAN BELIEVES...
...THAT YOU ARE THE ONE.

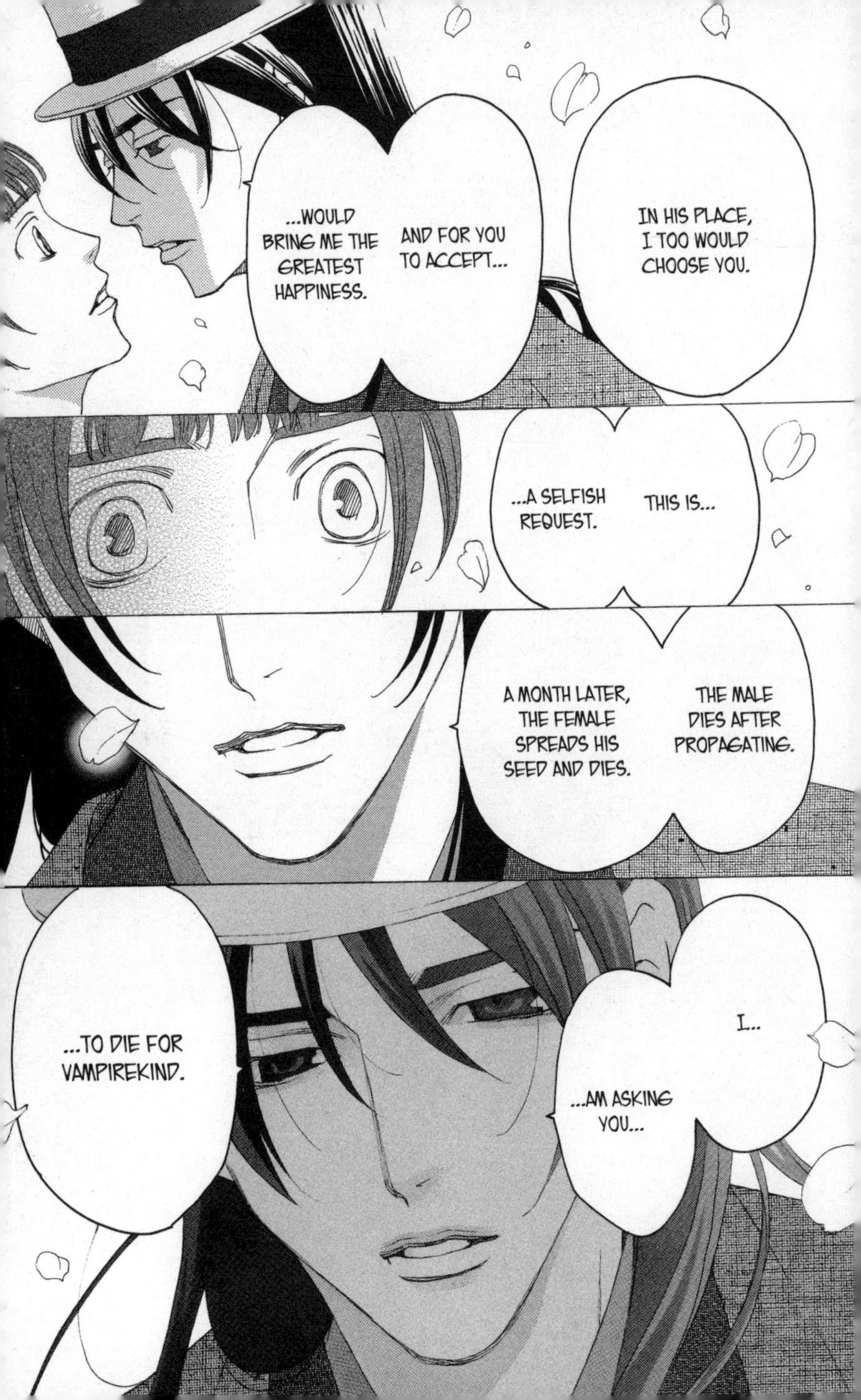
IN HIS PLACE, I TOO WOULD CHOOSE YOU.
AND FOR YOU TO ACCEPT...
...WOULD BRING ME THE GREATEST HAPPINESS.
THIS IS...
...A SELFISH REQUEST.
THE MALE DIES AFTER PROPAGATING.
A MONTH LATER, THE FEMALE SPREADS HIS SEED AND DIES.
I...
...AM ASKING YOU...
...TO DIE FOR VAMPIREKIND.

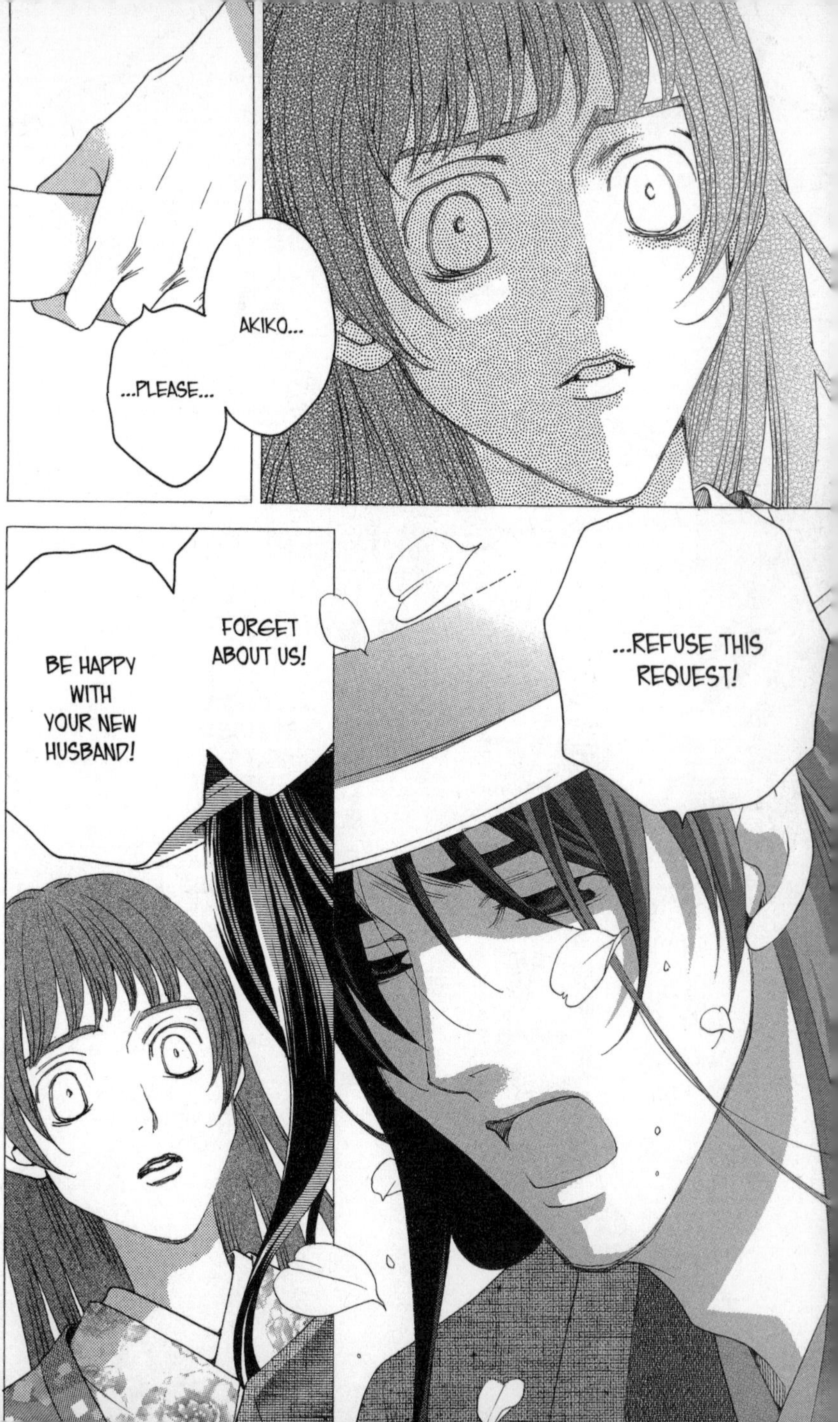
AKIKO...
...PLEASE...
...REFUSE THIS REQUEST!
FORGET ABOUT US!
BE HAPPY WITH YOUR NEW HUSBAND!

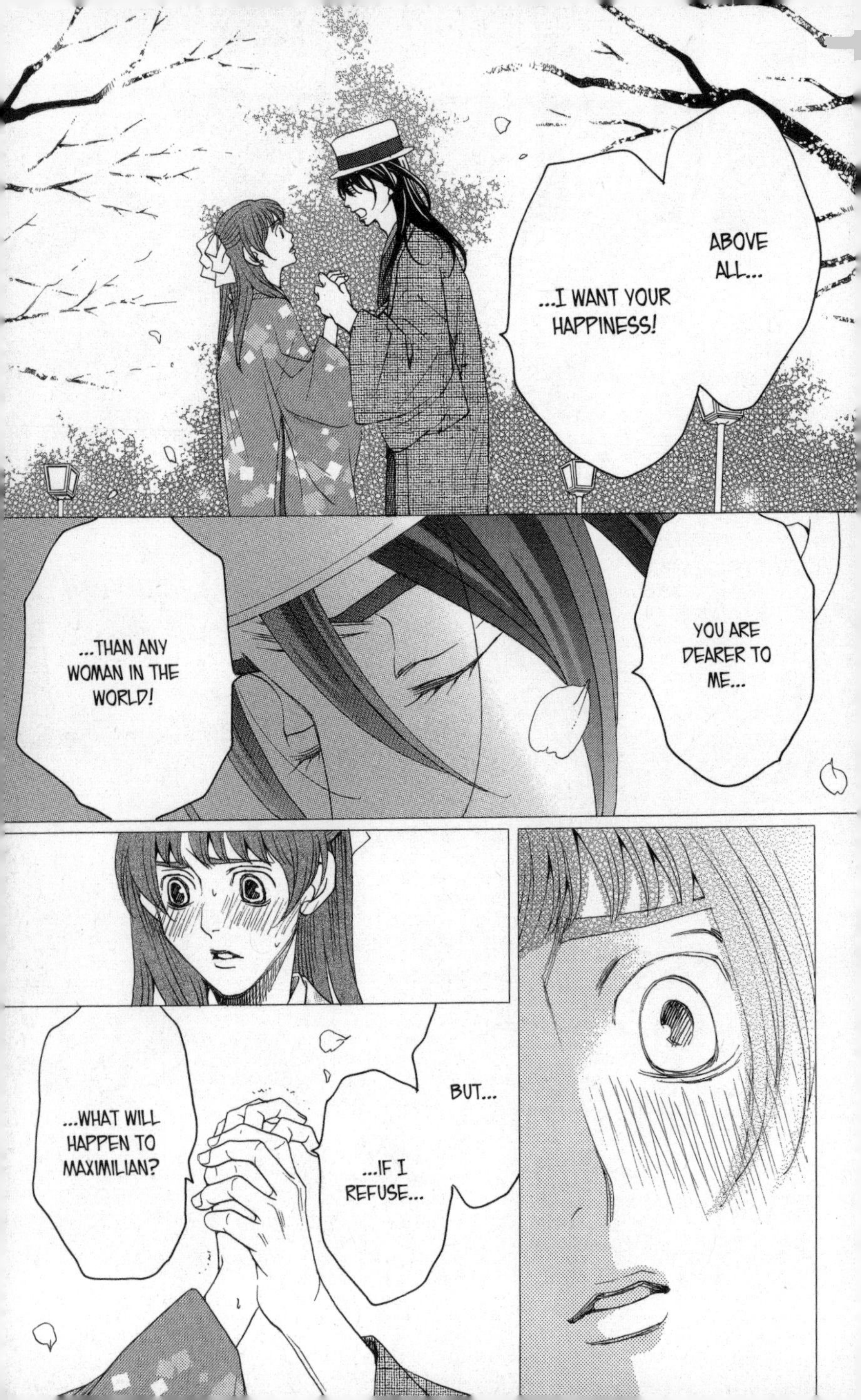
ABOVE ALL...
...I WANT YOUR HAPPINESS!
YOU ARE DEARER TO ME...
...THAN ANY WOMAN IN THE WORLD!
BUT...
...IF I REFUSE...
...WHAT WILL HAPPEN TO MAXIMILIAN?

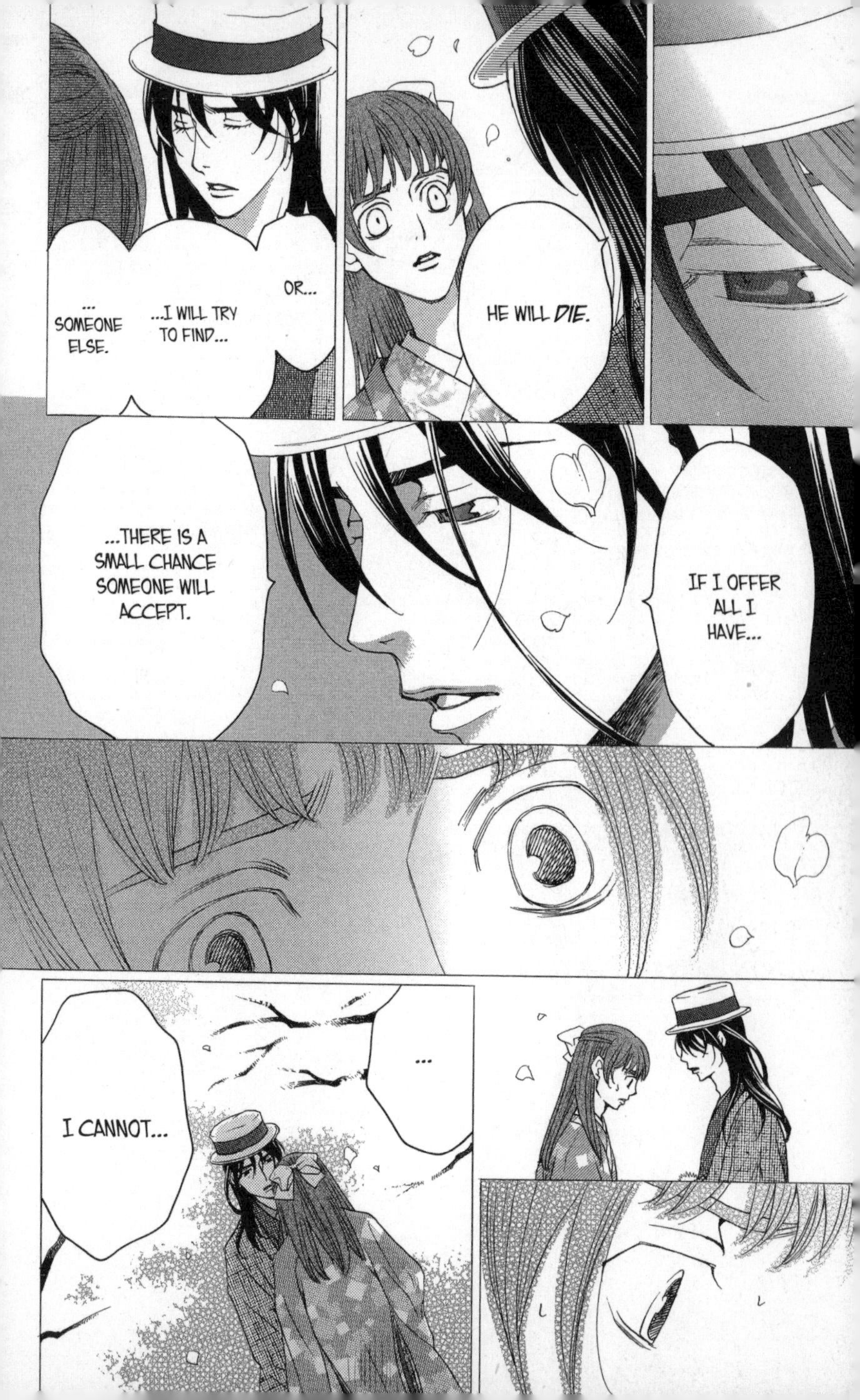
HE WILL *DIE*.
OR...
...I WILL TRY TO FIND...
... SOMEONE ELSE.
IF I OFFER ALL I HAVE...
...THERE IS A SMALL CHANCE SOMEONE WILL ACCEPT.
...
I CANNOT...

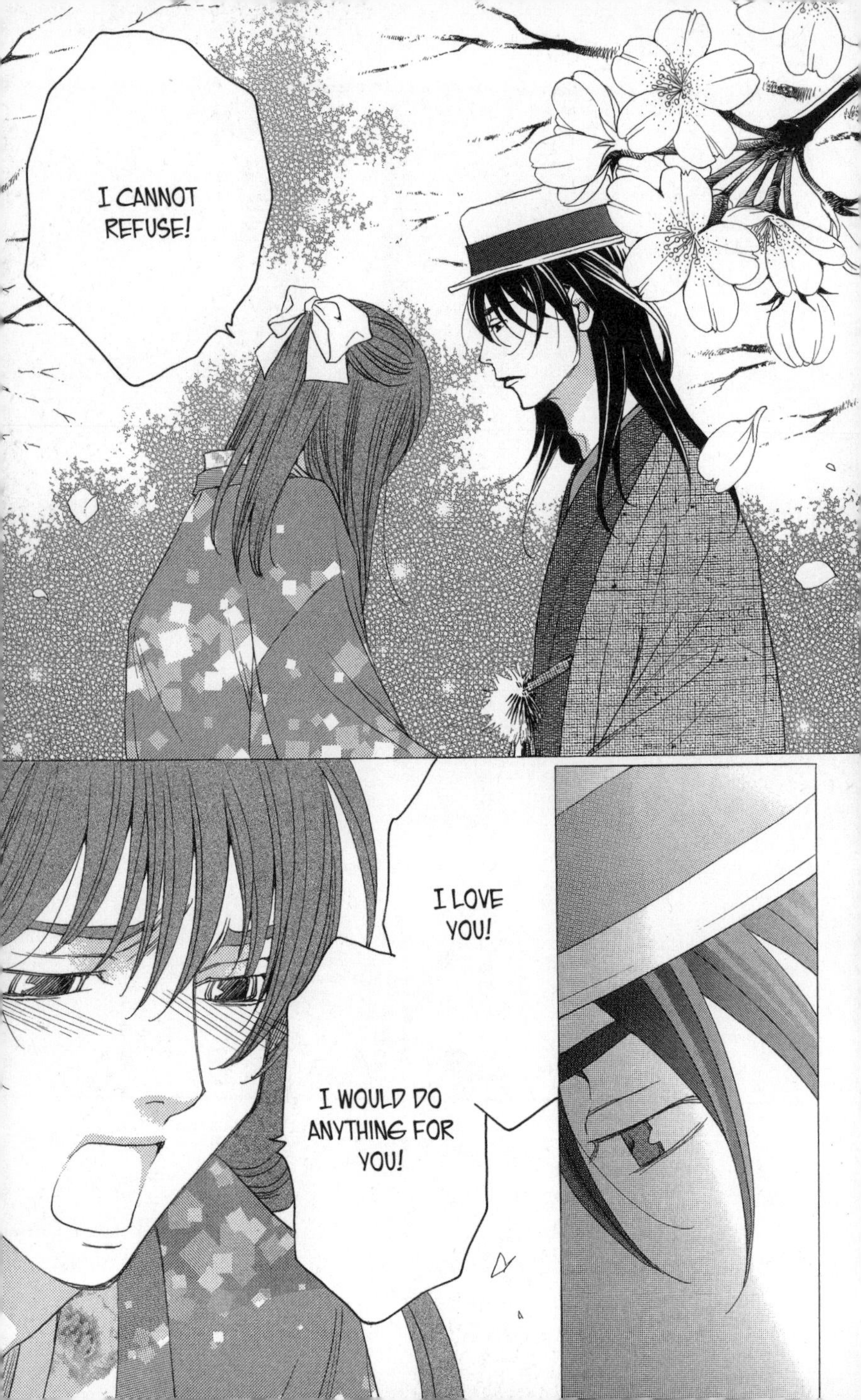
I CANNOT REFUSE!
I LOVE YOU!
I WOULD DO ANYTHING FOR YOU!

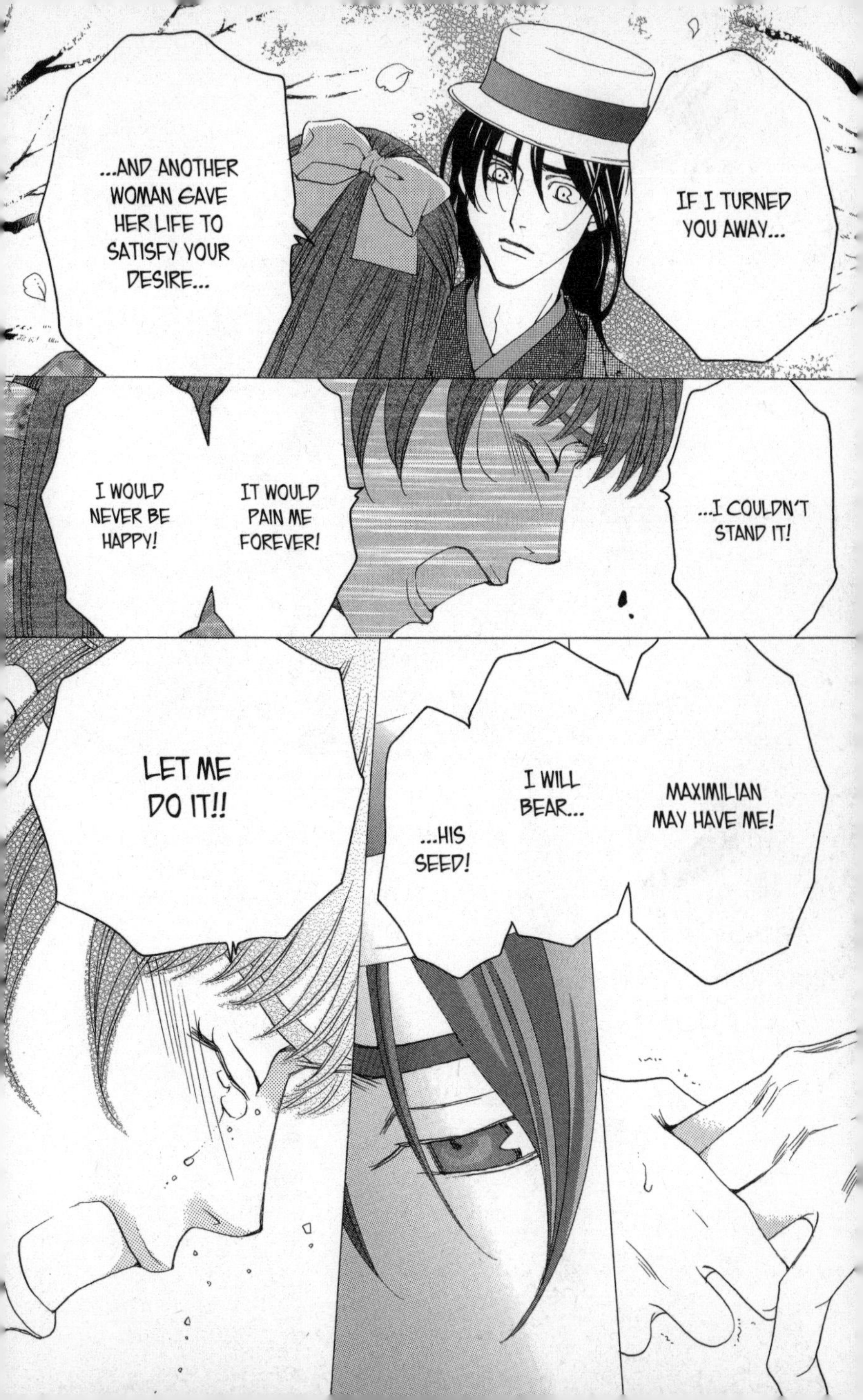
IF I TURNED YOU AWAY...
...AND ANOTHER WOMAN GAVE HER LIFE TO SATISFY YOUR DESIRE...
...I COULDN'T STAND IT!
IT WOULD PAIN ME FOREVER!
I WOULD NEVER BE HAPPY!
MAXIMILIAN MAY HAVE ME!
I WILL BEAR...
...HIS SEED!
LET ME DO IT!!

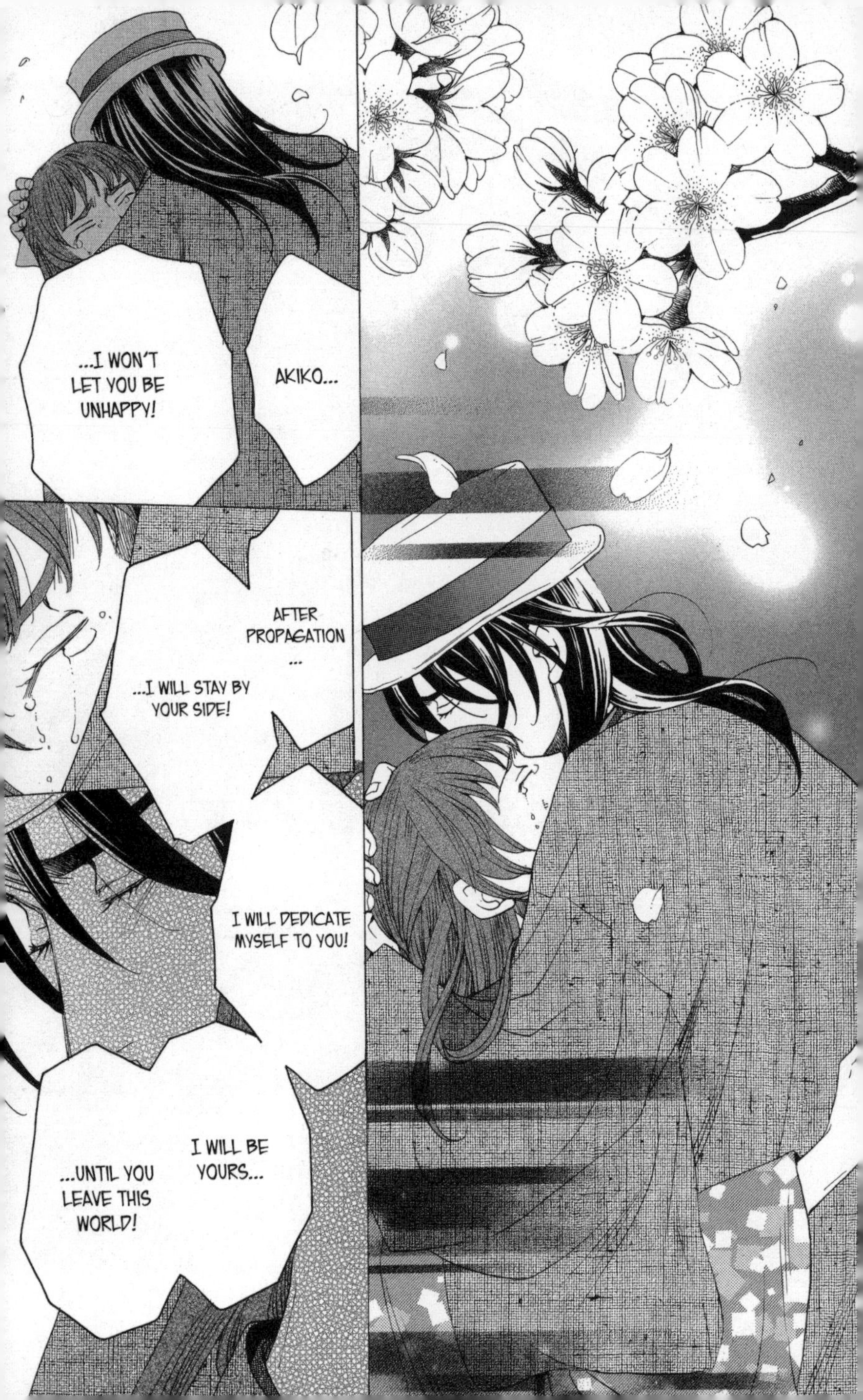
AKIKO...
...I WON'T LET YOU BE UNHAPPY!
AFTER PROPAGATION ...
...I WILL STAY BY YOUR SIDE!
I WILL DEDICATE MYSELF TO YOU!
I WILL BE YOURS...
...UNTIL YOU LEAVE THIS WORLD!

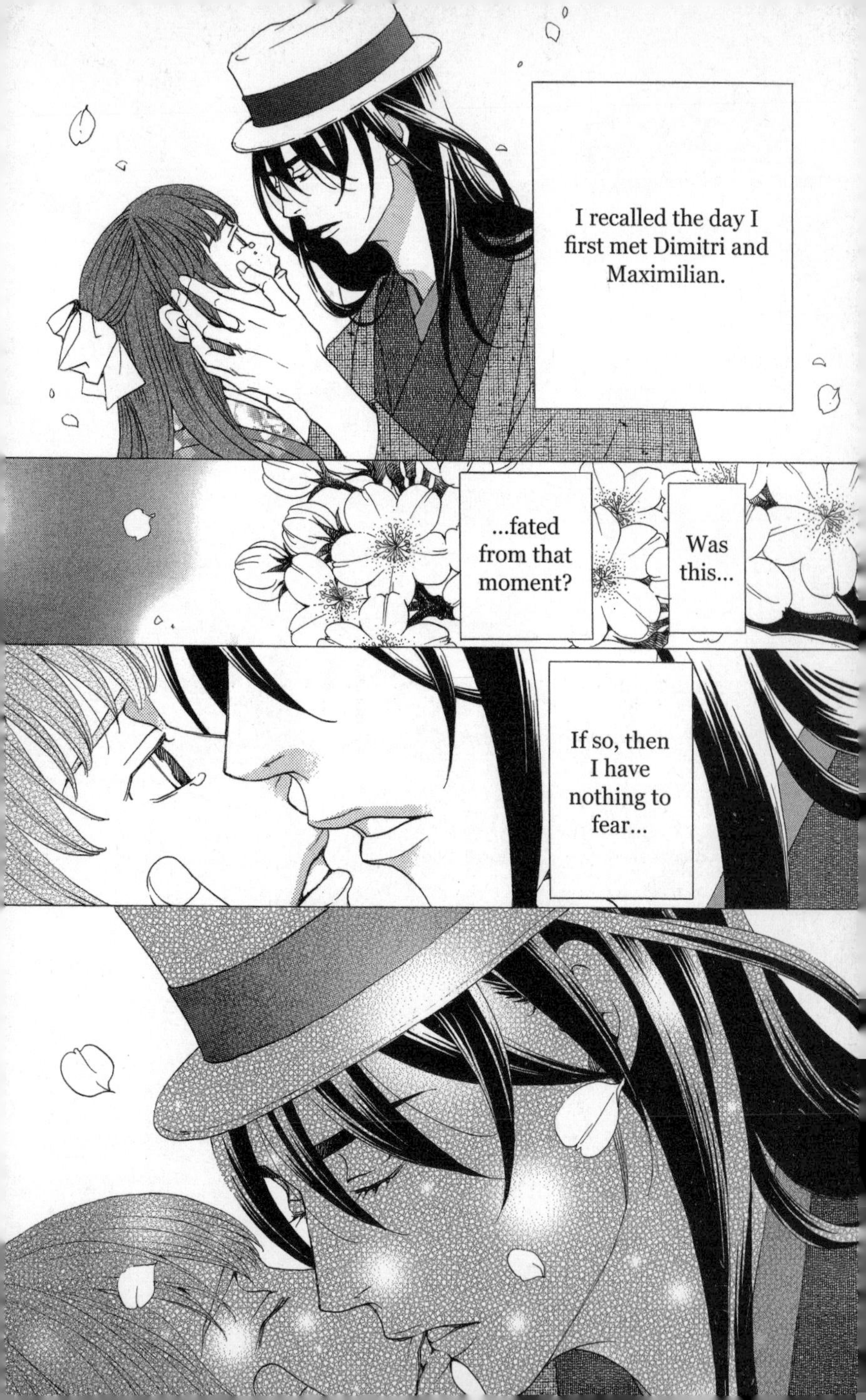
I recalled the day I first met Dimitri and Maximilian.
Was this...
...fated from that moment?
If so, then I have nothing to fear...

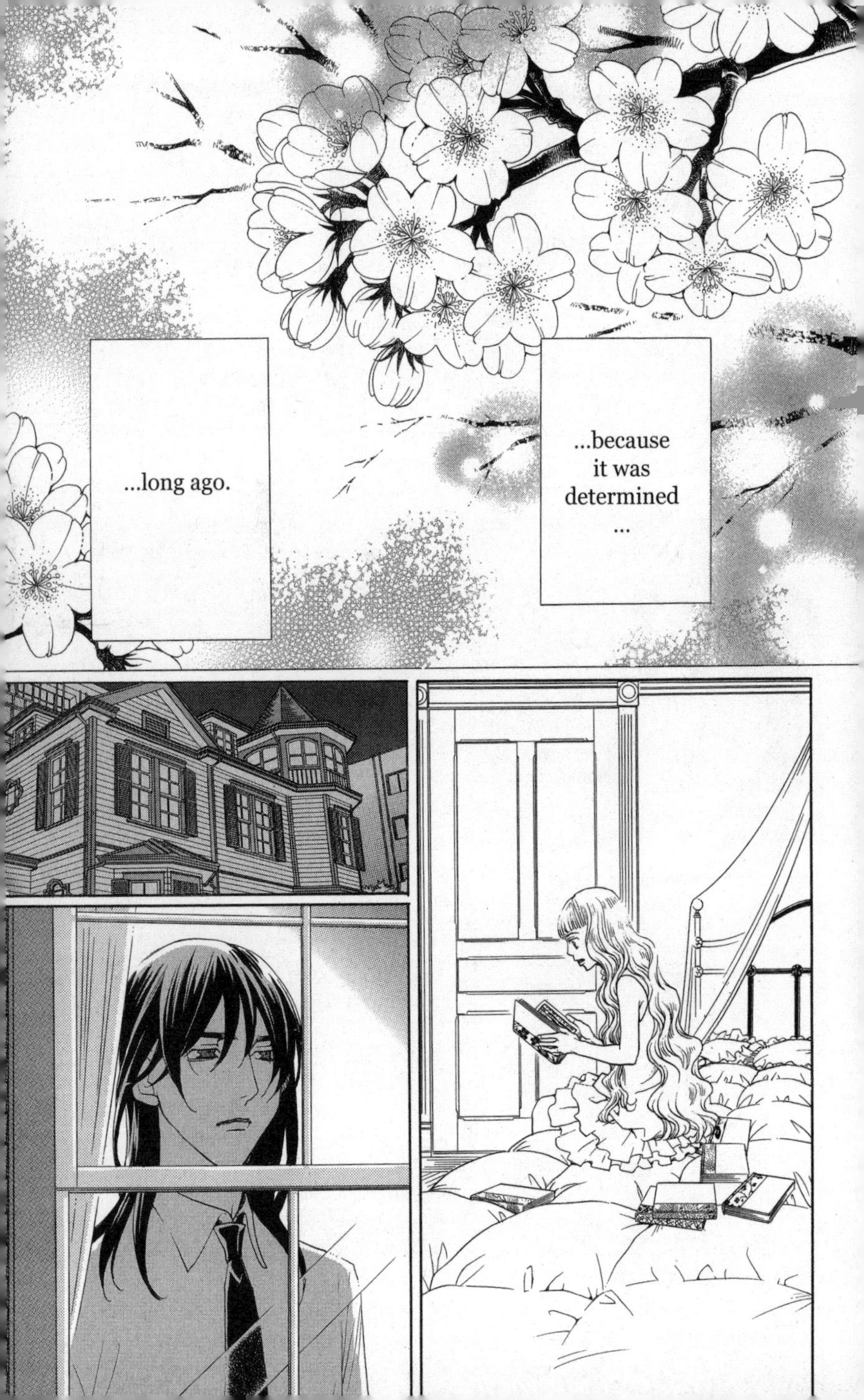
...because it was determined ...
...long ago.

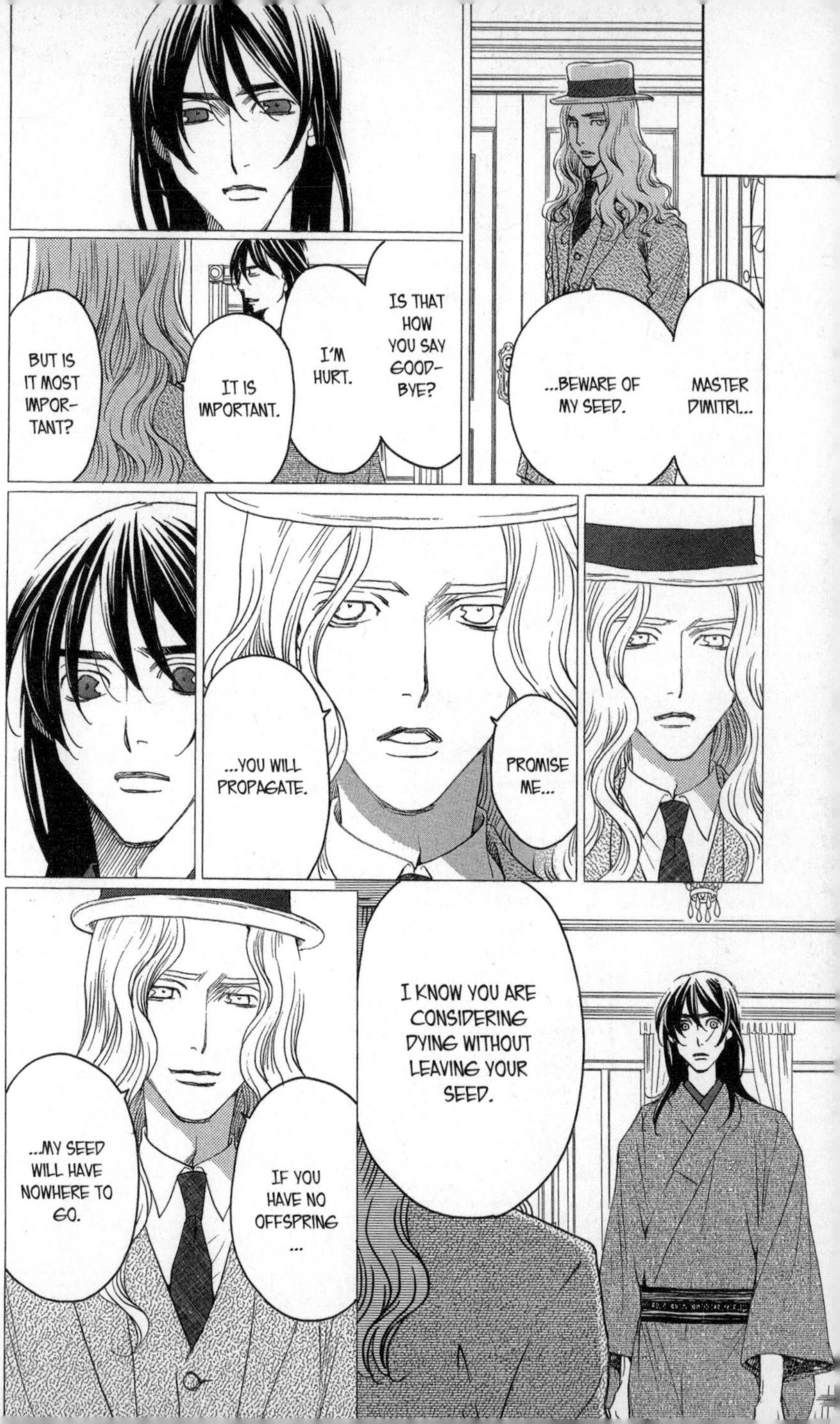
MASTER DIMITRI...
...BEWARE OF MY SEED.
IS THAT HOW YOU SAY GOOD-BYE?
I'M HURT.
IT IS IMPORTANT.
BUT IS IT MOST IMPOR-TANT?
PROMISE ME...
...YOU WILL PROPAGATE.
I KNOW YOU ARE CONSIDERING DYING WITHOUT LEAVING YOUR SEED.
IF YOU HAVE NO OFFSPRING
...
...MY SEED WILL HAVE NOWHERE TO GO.

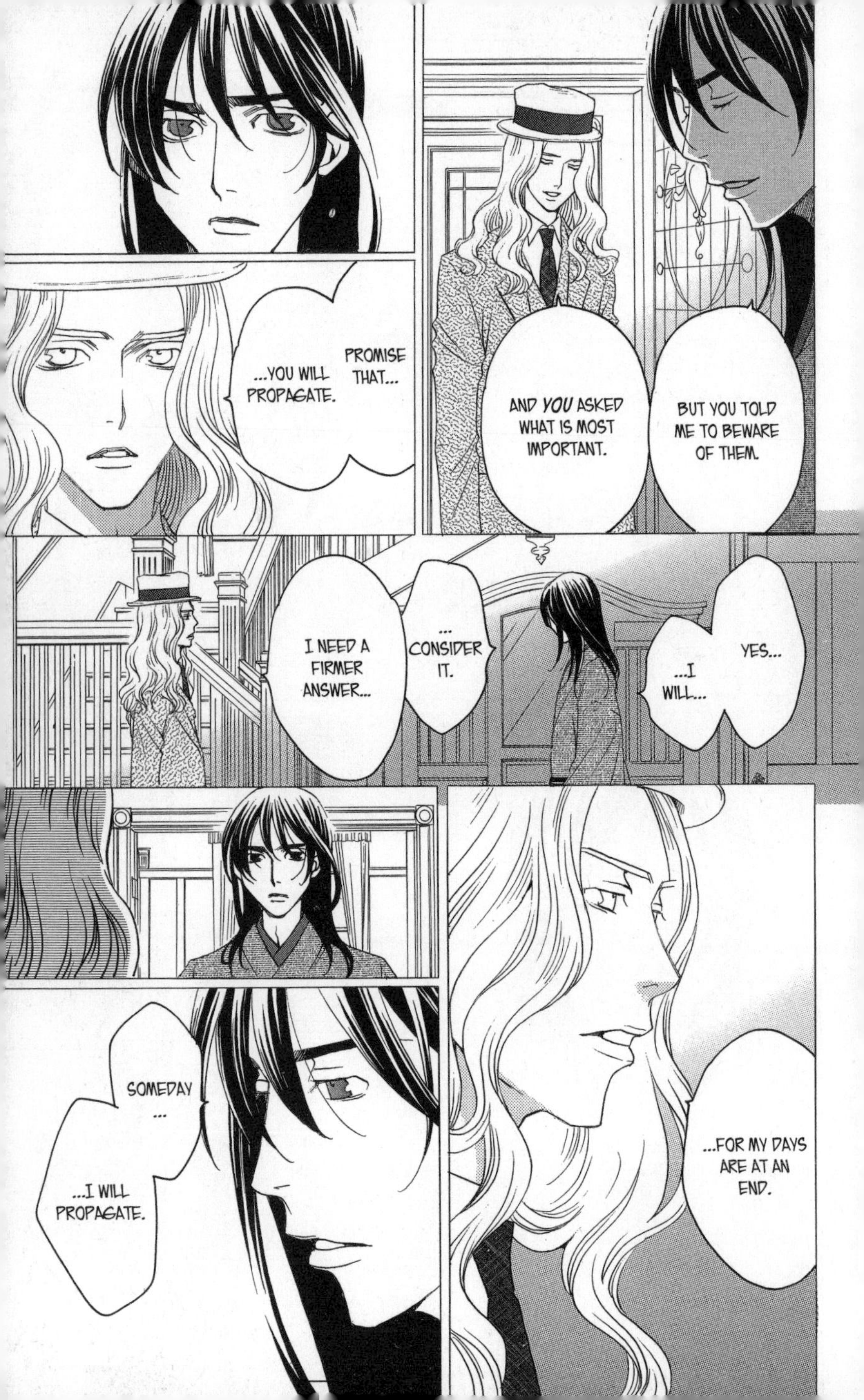
BUT YOU TOLD ME TO BEWARE OF THEM.
AND *YOU* ASKED WHAT IS MOST IMPORTANT.
PROMISE THAT...
...YOU WILL PROPAGATE.
YES...
...I WILL...
...CONSIDER IT.
I NEED A FIRMER ANSWER...
...FOR MY DAYS ARE AT AN END.
SOMEDAY...
...I WILL PROPAGATE.

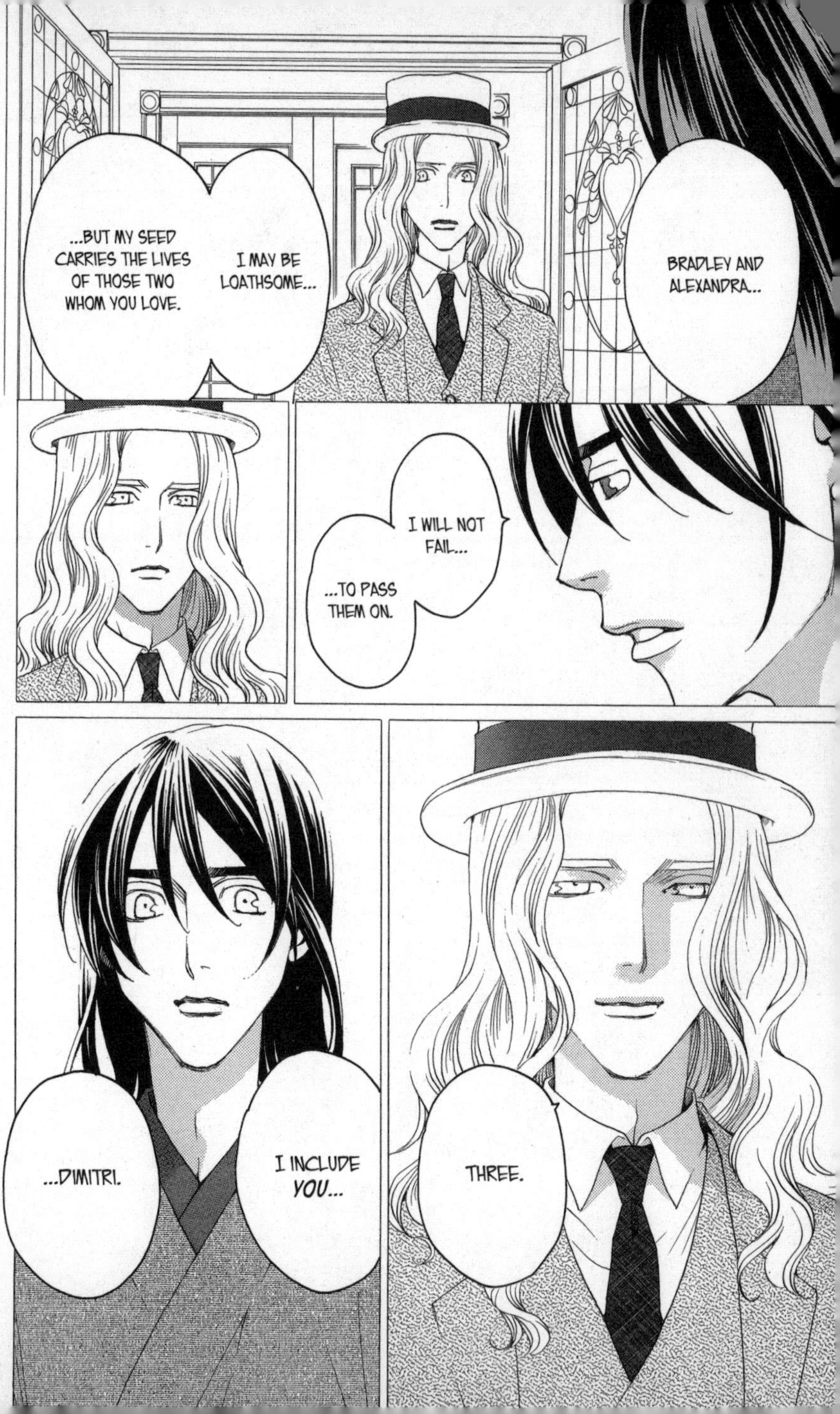
BRADLEY AND ALEXANDRA...
I MAY BE LOATHSOME...
...BUT MY SEED CARRIES THE LIVES OF THOSE TWO WHOM YOU LOVE.
I WILL NOT FAIL...
...TO PASS THEM ON.
THREE.
I INCLUDE YOU...
...DIMITRI.

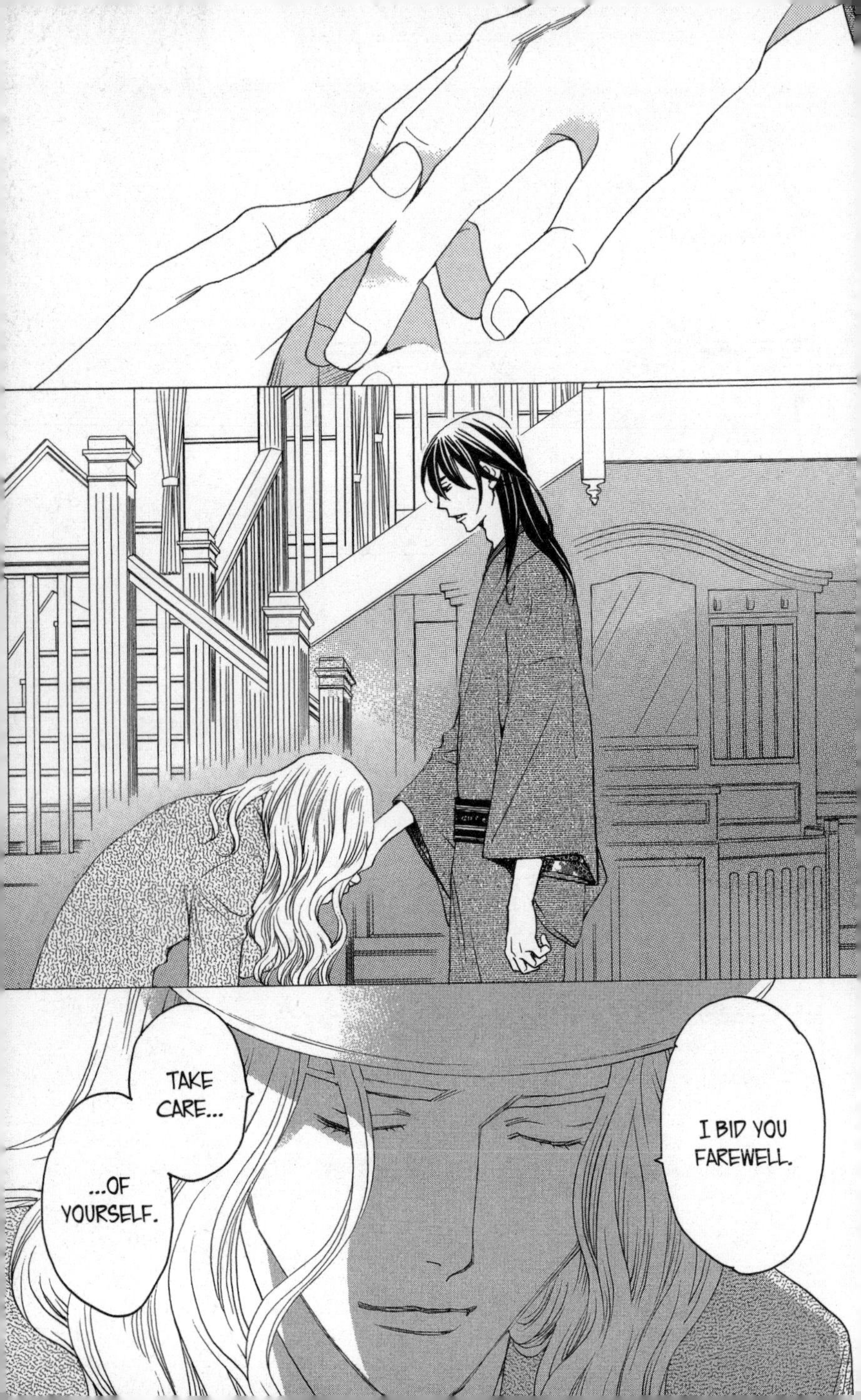
I BID YOU FAREWELL.
TAKE CARE...
...OF YOURSELF.

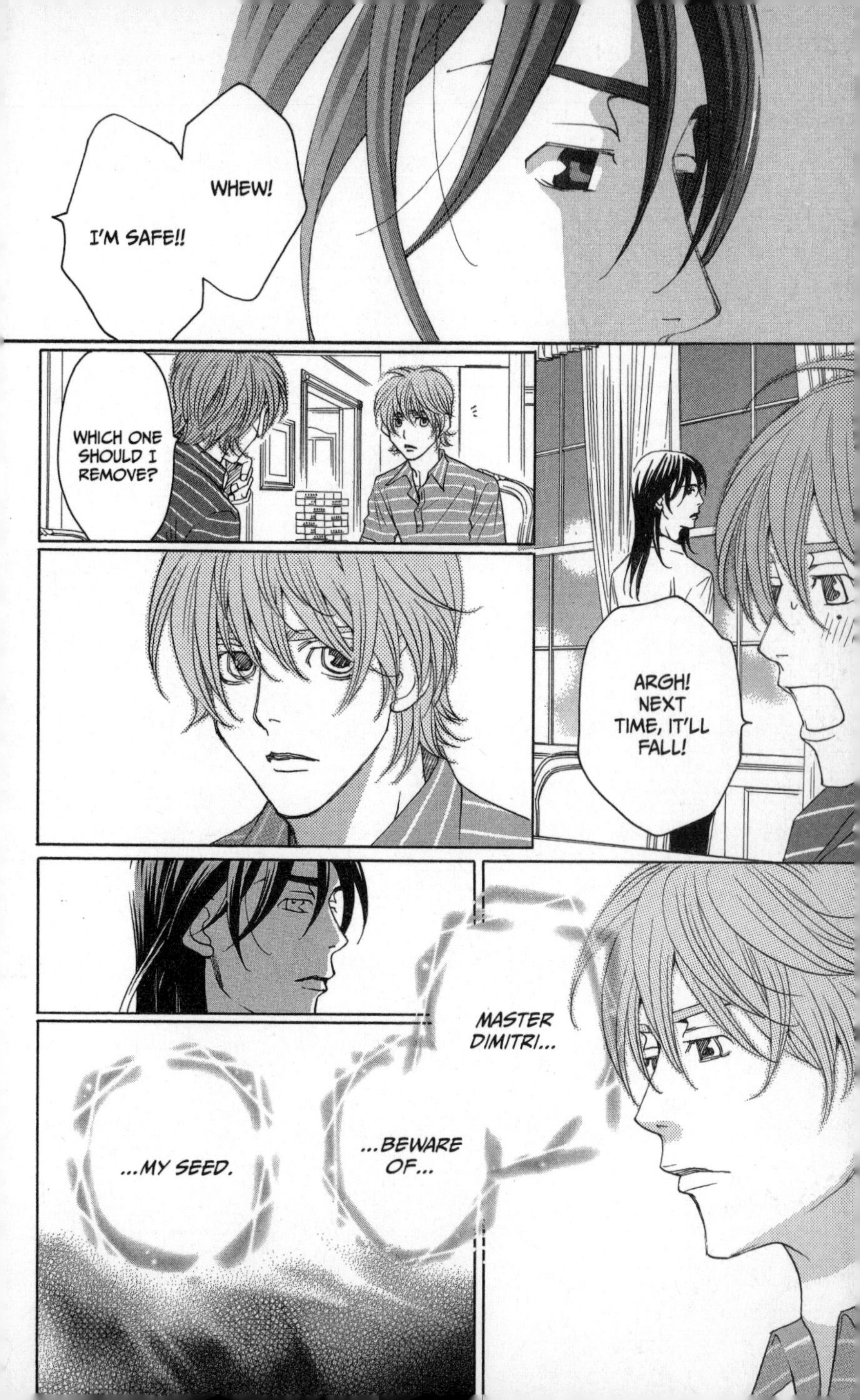
WHEW!
I'M SAFE!!
ARGH! NEXT TIME, IT'LL FALL!
WHICH ONE SHOULD I REMOVE?
MASTER DIMITRI...
...BEWARE OF...
...MY SEED.

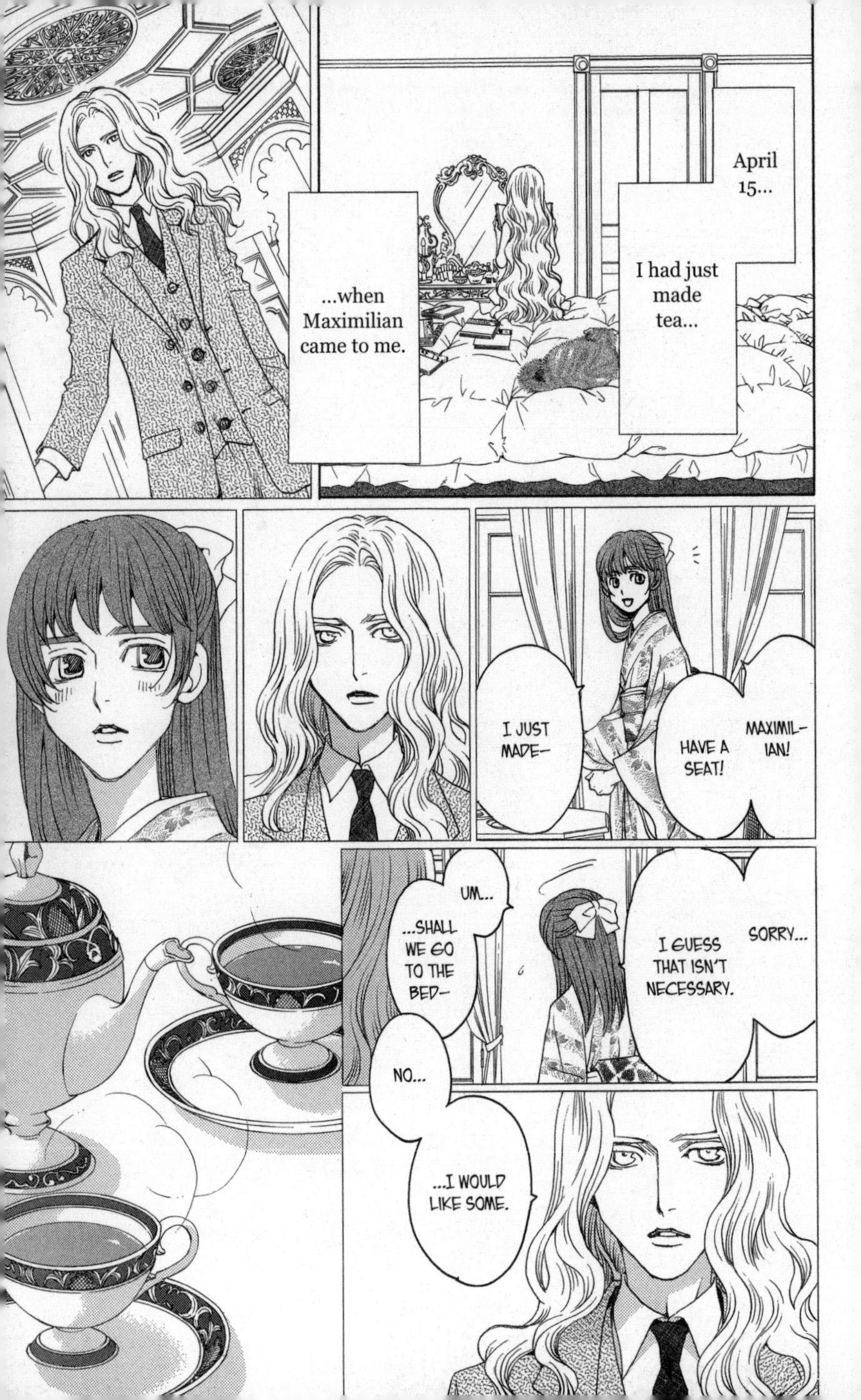
April 15...
I had just made tea...
...when Maximilian came to me.
MAXIMILIAN! HAVE A SEAT!
I JUST MADE—
SORRY... I GUESS THAT ISN'T NECESSARY.
UM... ...SHALL WE GO TO THE BED—
NO...
...I WOULD LIKE SOME.

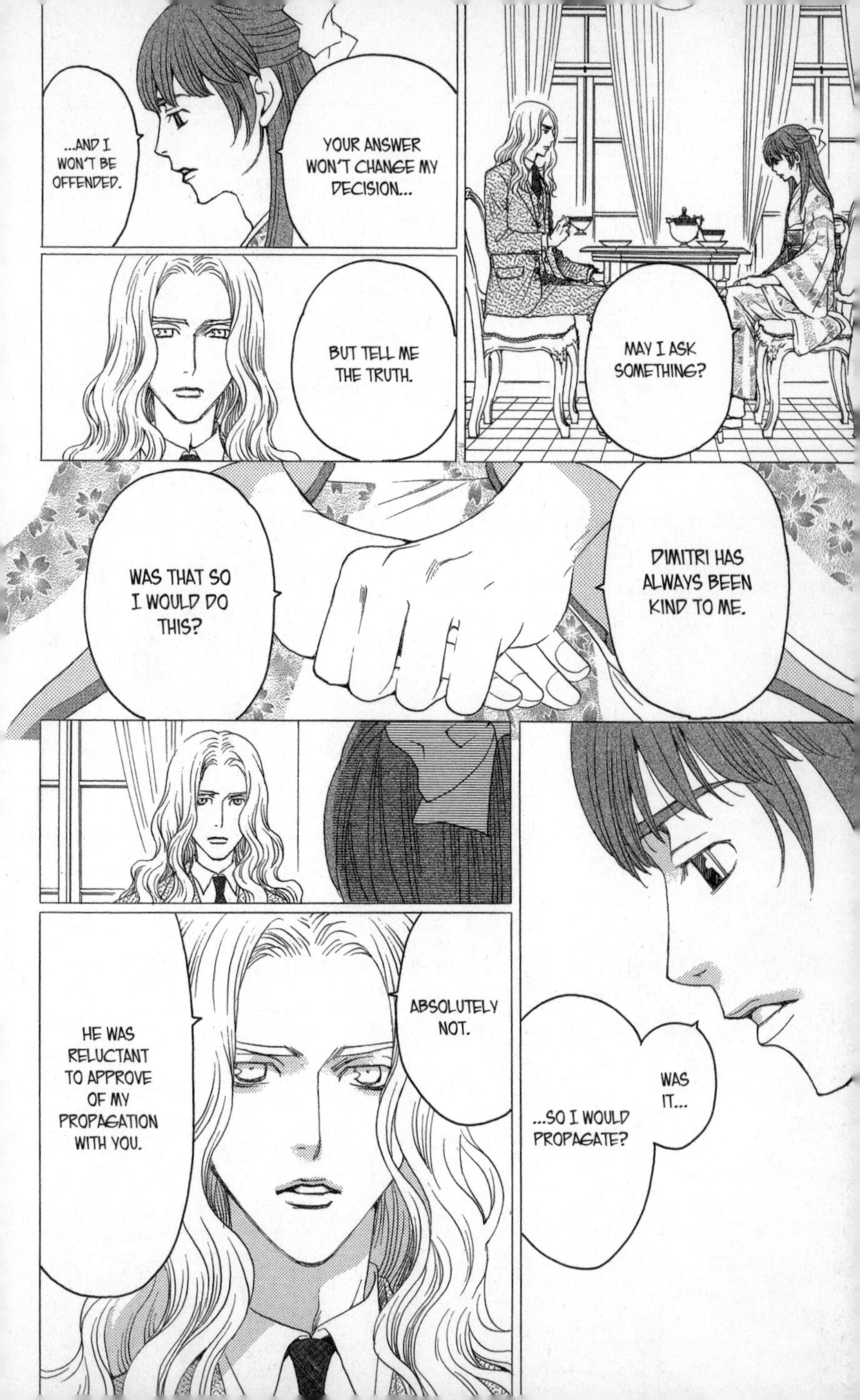
MAY I ASK SOMETHING?
YOUR ANSWER WON'T CHANGE MY DECISION...
...AND I WON'T BE OFFENDED.
BUT TELL ME THE TRUTH.
DIMITRI HAS ALWAYS BEEN KIND TO ME.
WAS THAT SO I WOULD DO THIS?
WAS IT...
...SO I WOULD PROPAGATE?
ABSOLUTELY NOT.
HE WAS RELUCTANT TO APPROVE OF MY PROPAGATION WITH YOU.

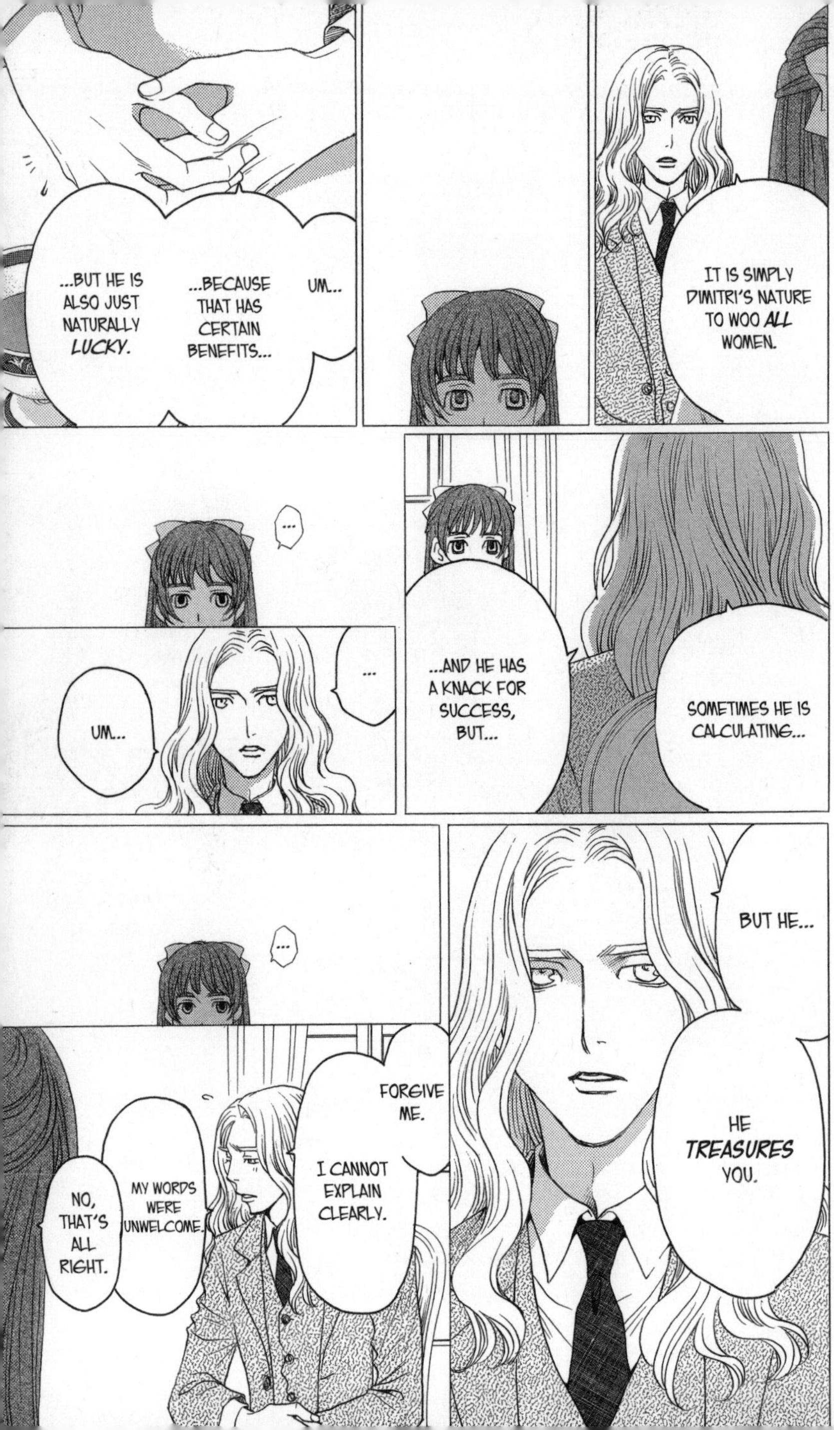
IT IS SIMPLY DIMITRI'S NATURE TO WOO ALL WOMEN.
UM...
...BECAUSE THAT HAS CERTAIN BENEFITS...
...BUT HE IS ALSO JUST NATURALLY LUCKY.
SOMETIMES HE IS CALCULATING...
...AND HE HAS A KNACK FOR SUCCESS, BUT...
...
...
UM...
BUT HE...
HE TREASURES YOU.
...
FORGIVE ME.
I CANNOT EXPLAIN CLEARLY.
MY WORDS WERE UNWELCOME.
NO, THAT'S ALL RIGHT.

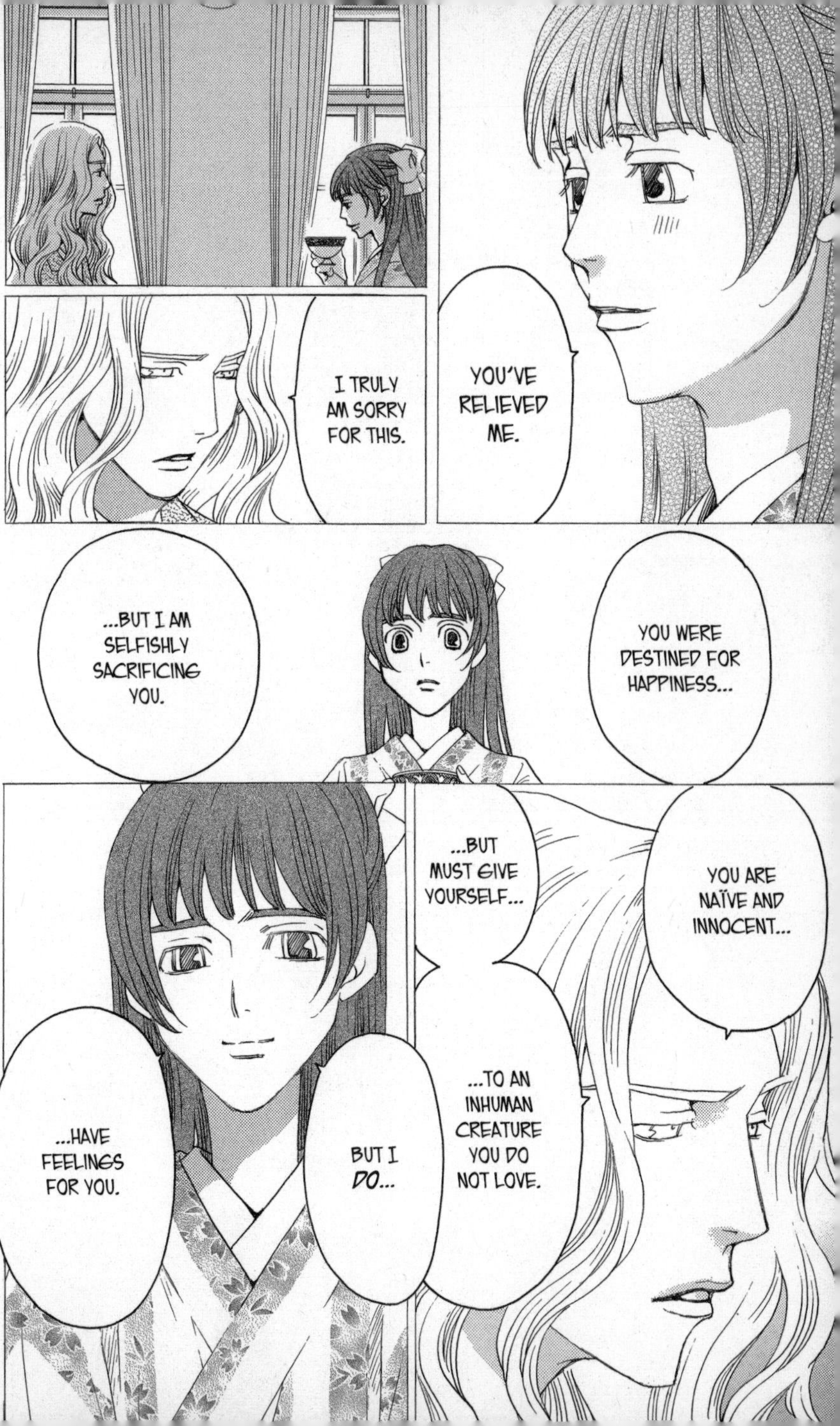
YOU'VE RELIEVED ME.
I TRULY AM SORRY FOR THIS.
YOU WERE DESTINED FOR HAPPINESS...
...BUT I AM SELFISHLY SACRIFICING YOU.
YOU ARE NAÏVE AND INNOCENT...
...BUT MUST GIVE YOURSELF...
...TO AN INHUMAN CREATURE YOU DO NOT LOVE.
BUT I DO...
...HAVE FEELINGS FOR YOU.

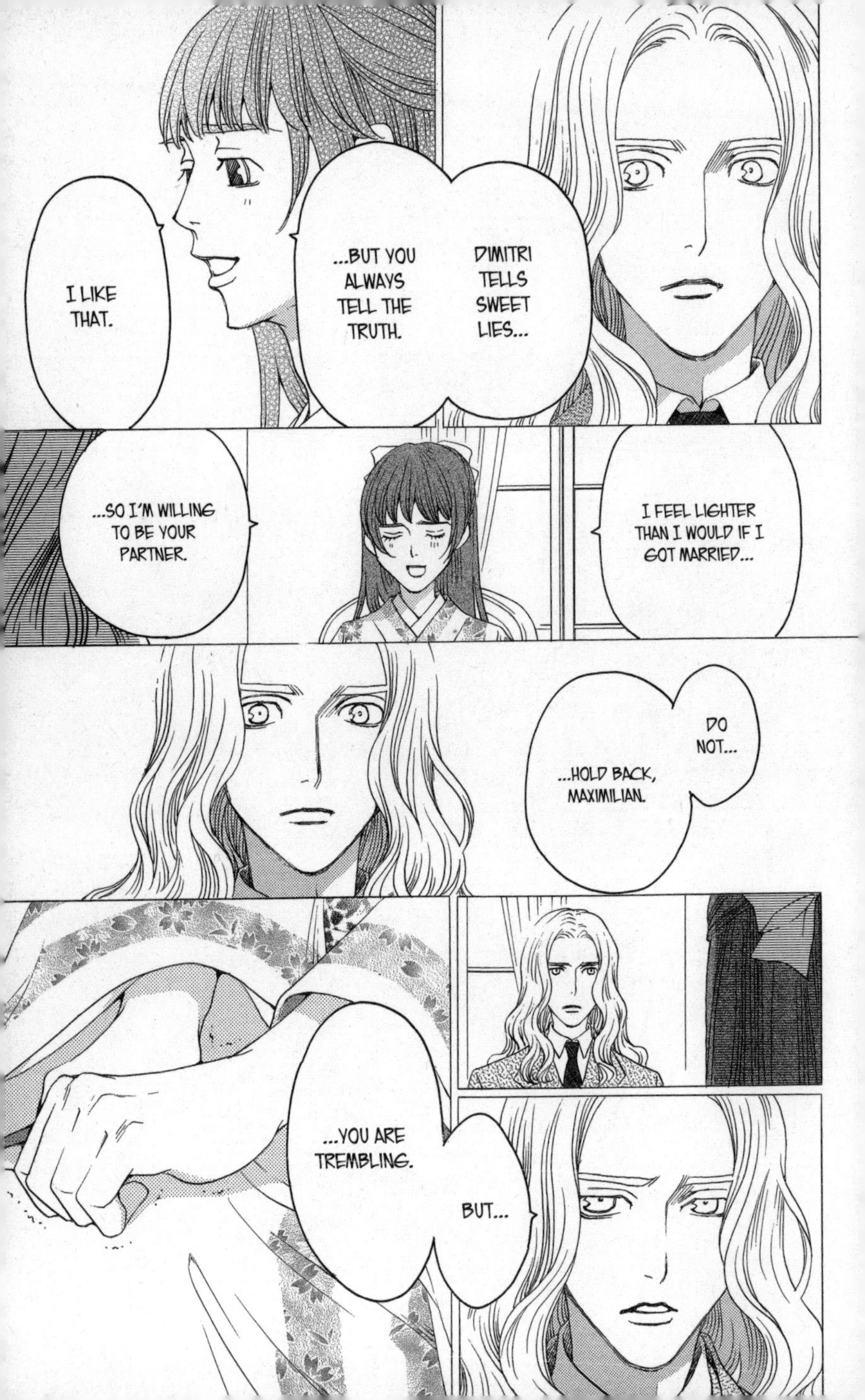
DIMITRI TELLS SWEET LIES... ...BUT YOU ALWAYS TELL THE TRUTH.
I LIKE THAT.
I FEEL LIGHTER THAN I WOULD IF I GOT MARRIED...
...SO I'M WILLING TO BE YOUR PARTNER.
DO NOT... ...HOLD BACK, MAXIMILIAN.
BUT... ...YOU ARE TREMBLING.

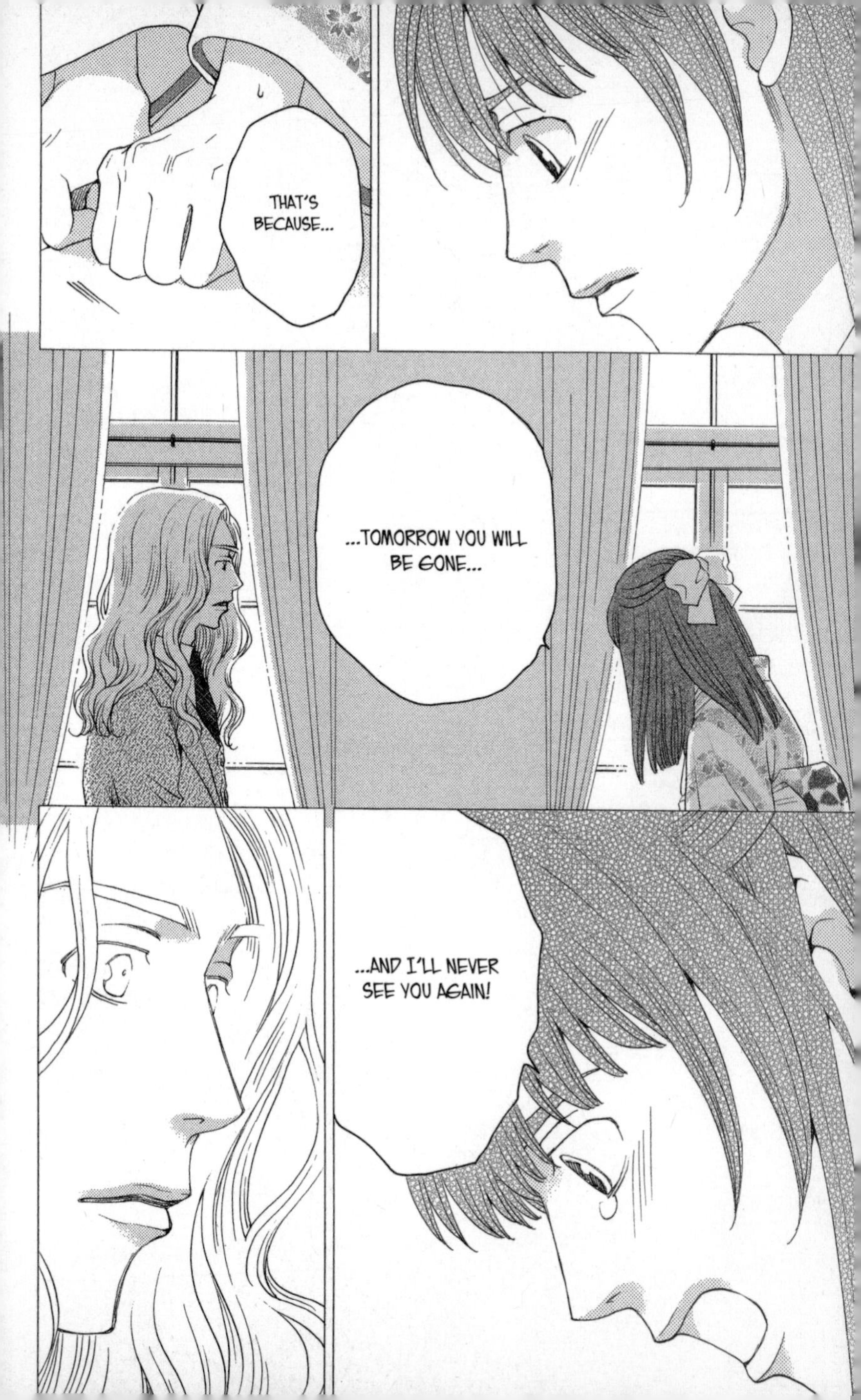
THAT'S BECAUSE...
...TOMORROW YOU WILL BE GONE...
...AND I'LL NEVER SEE YOU AGAIN!

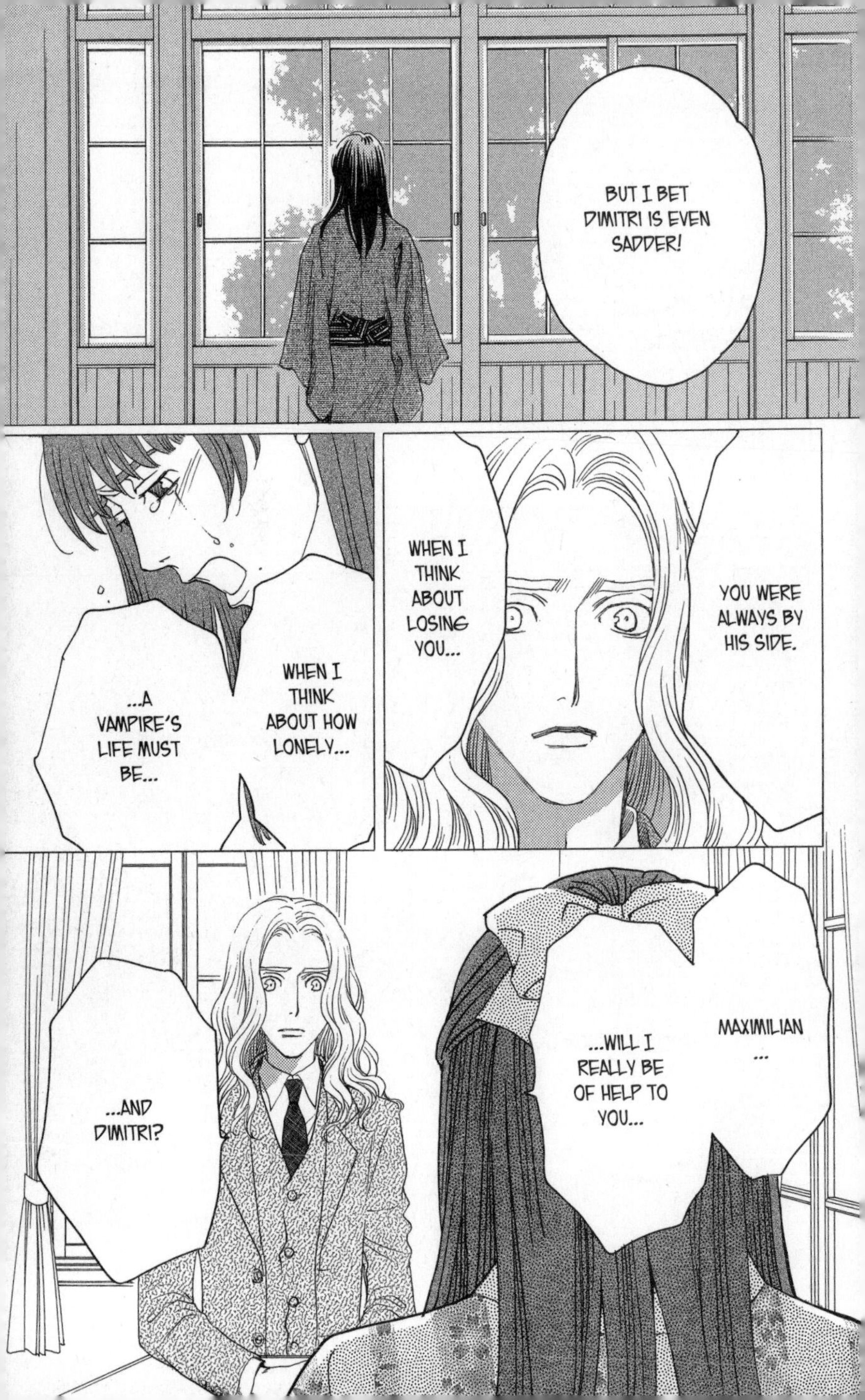
BUT I BET DIMITRI IS EVEN SADDER!
YOU WERE ALWAYS BY HIS SIDE.
WHEN I THINK ABOUT LOSING YOU...
WHEN I THINK ABOUT HOW LONELY...
...A VAMPIRE'S LIFE MUST BE...
MAXIMILIAN...
...WILL I REALLY BE OF HELP TO YOU...
...AND DIMITRI?

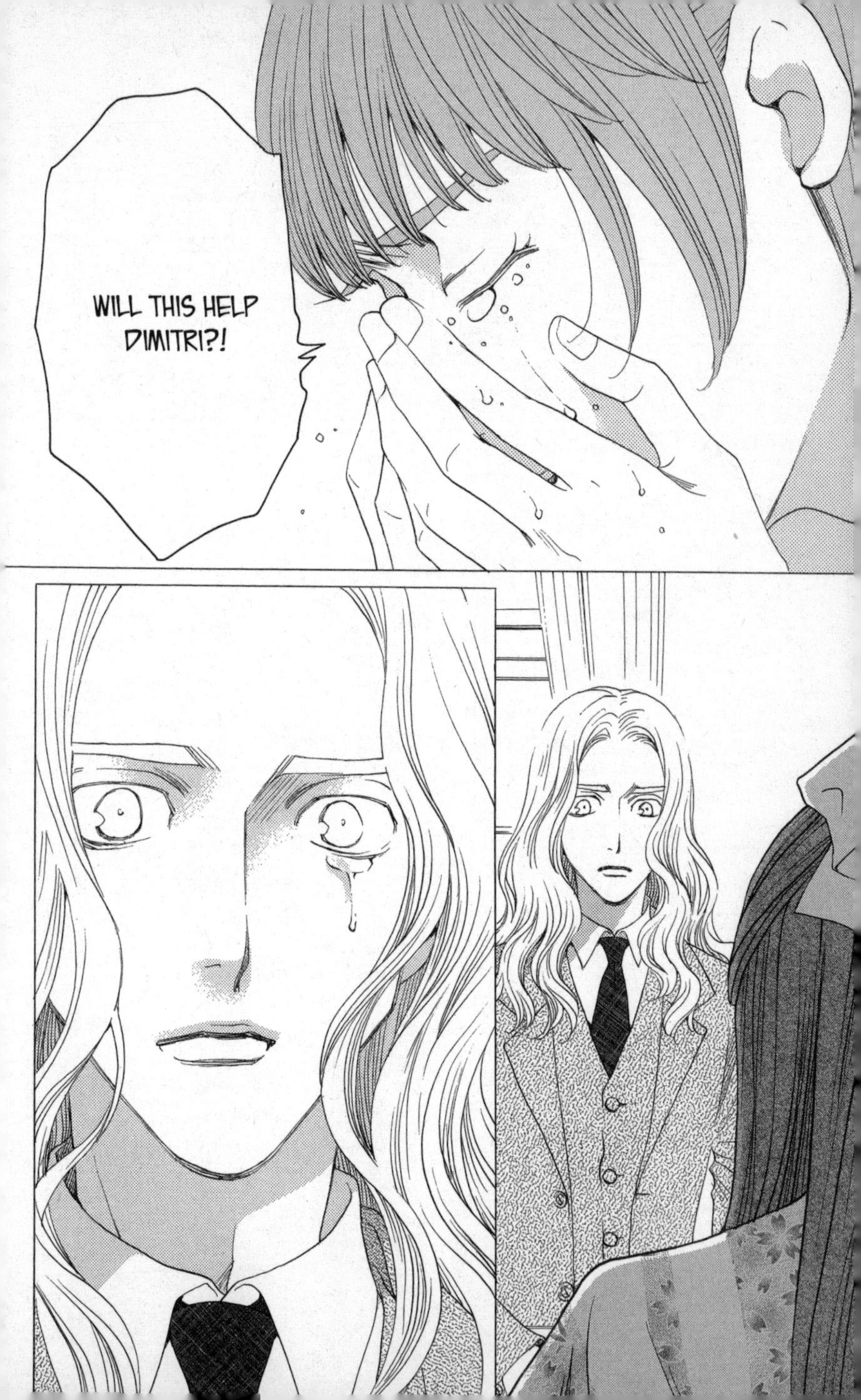
WILL THIS HELP DIMITRI?!

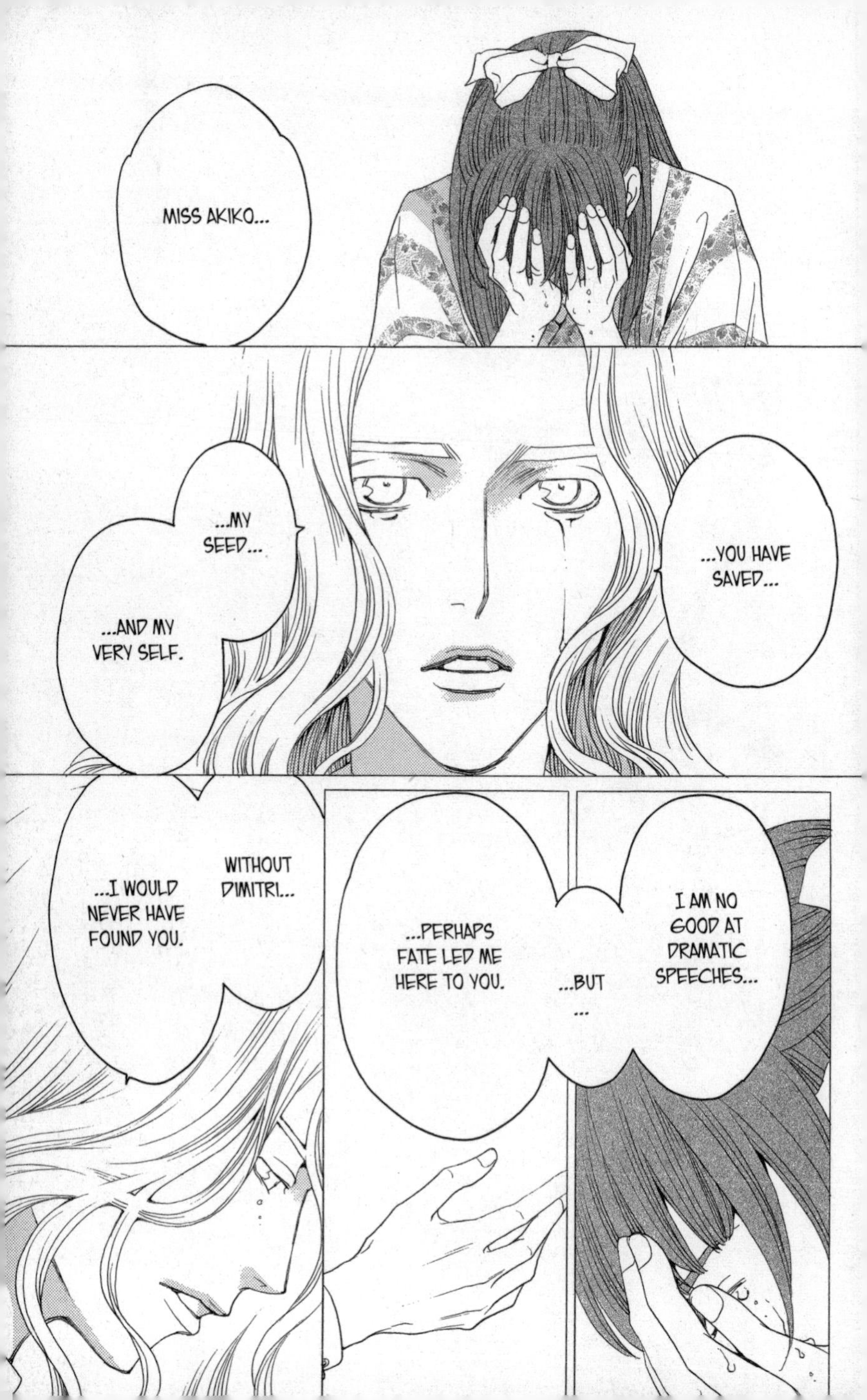
MISS AKIKO...
...YOU HAVE SAVED...
...MY SEED...
...AND MY VERY SELF.
I AM NO GOOD AT DRAMATIC SPEECHES...
...BUT ...
...PERHAPS FATE LED ME HERE TO YOU.
WITHOUT DIMITRI...
...I WOULD NEVER HAVE FOUND YOU.

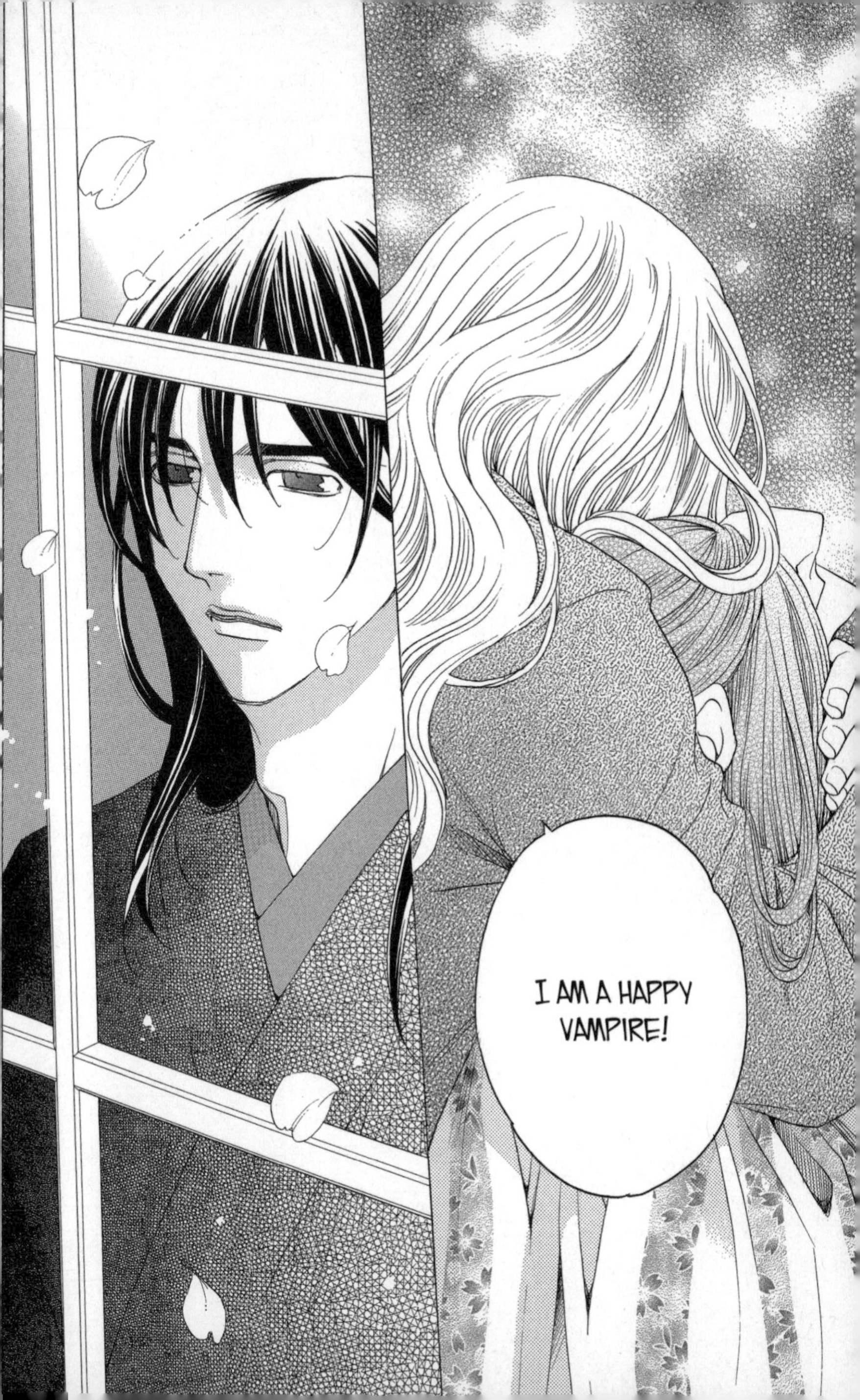
I AM A HAPPY VAMPIRE!

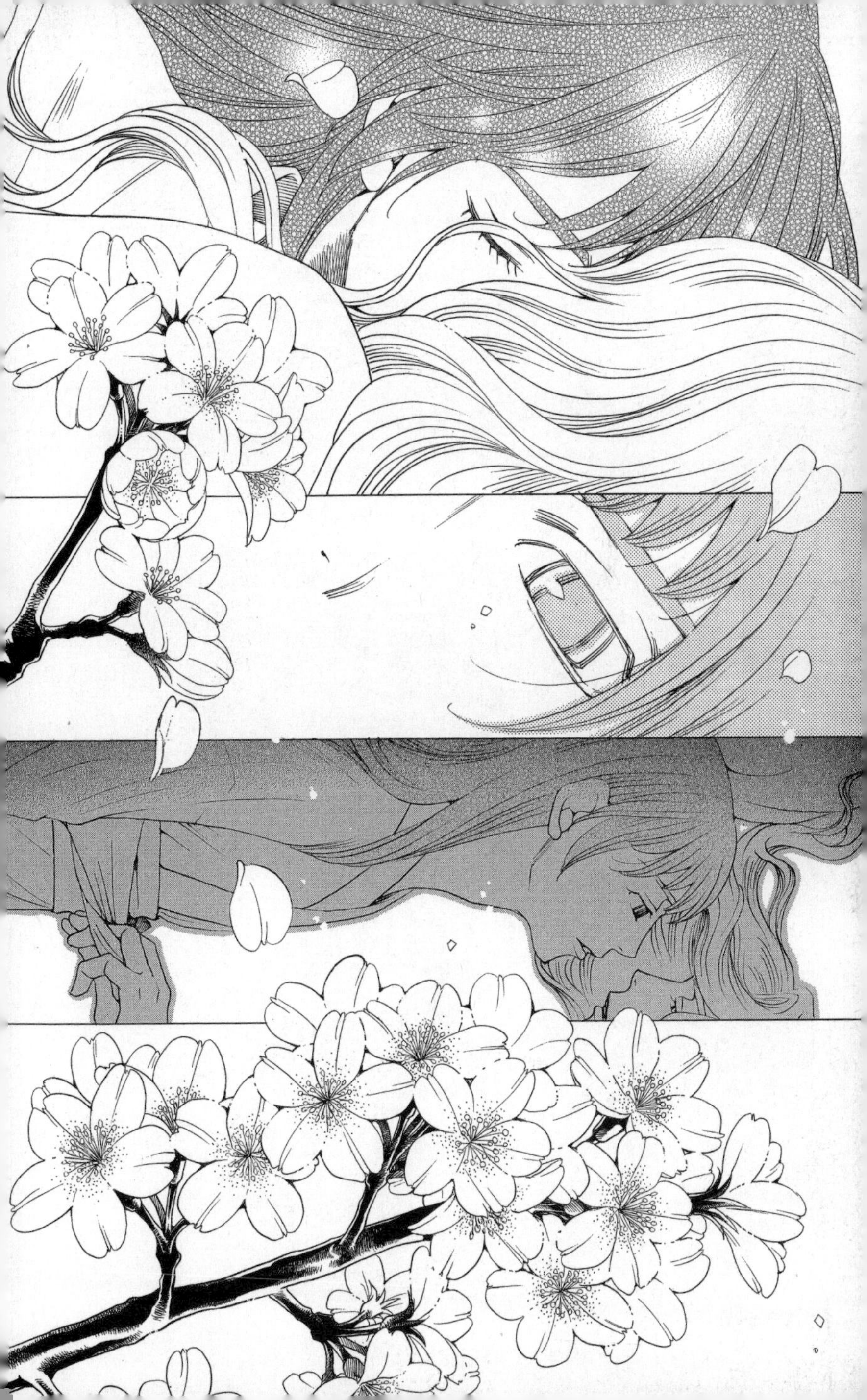

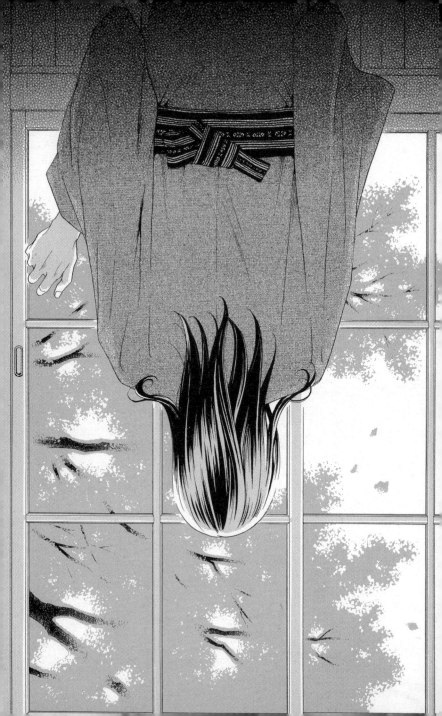

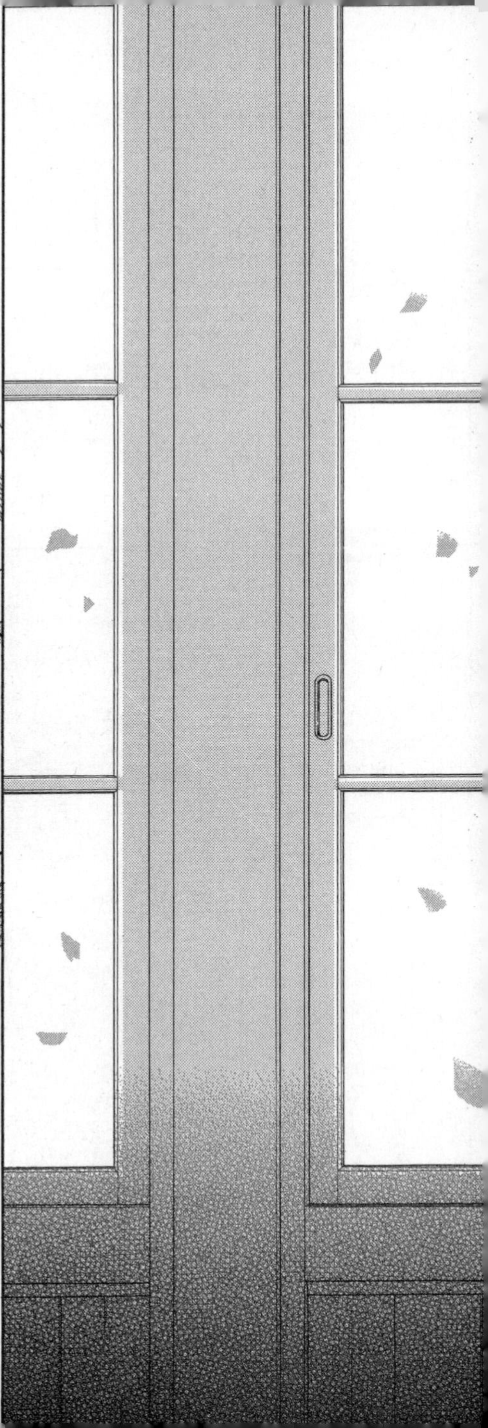

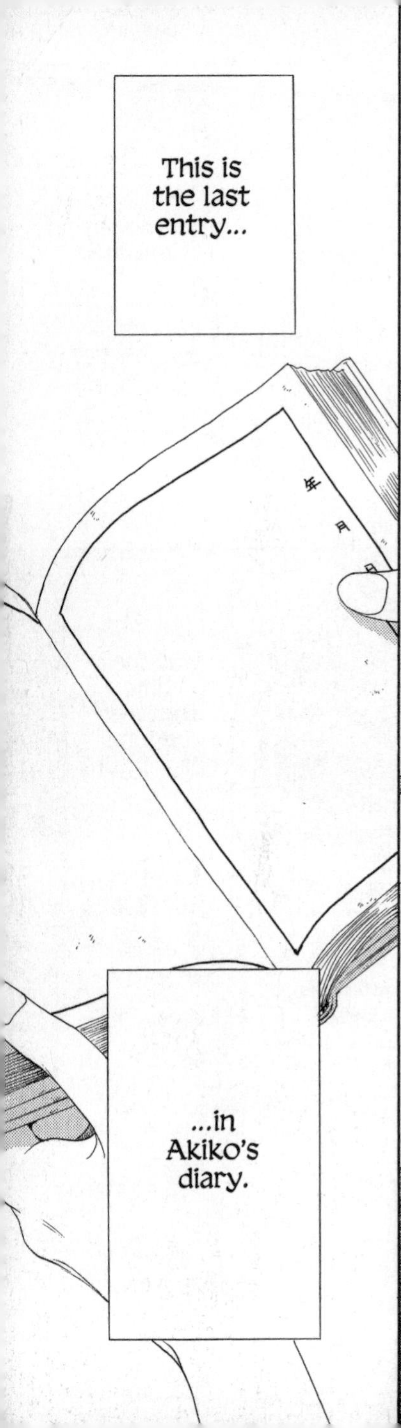
This is the last entry...
...in Akiko's diary.

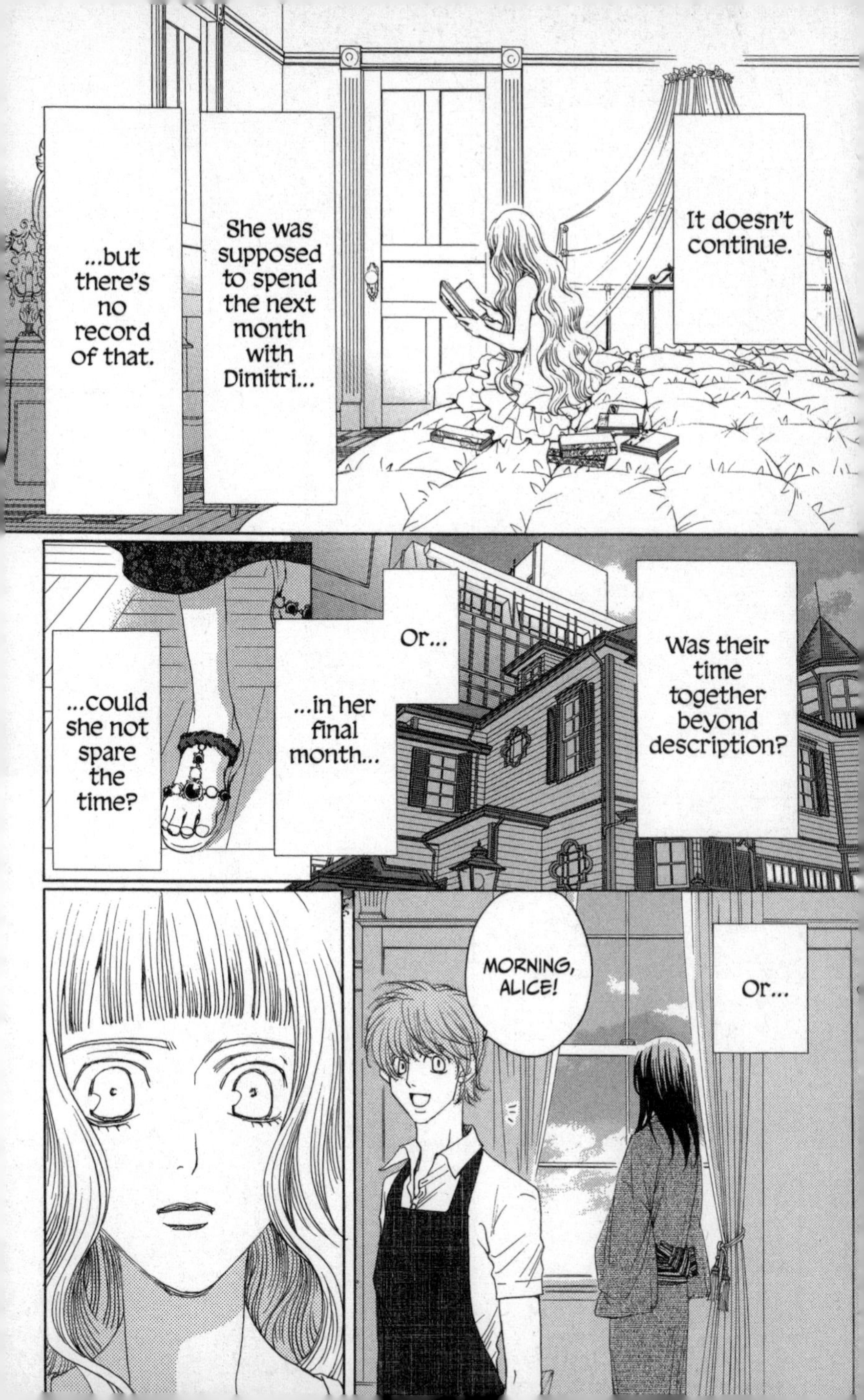
It doesn't continue.
She was supposed to spend the next month with Dimitri...
...but there's no record of that.
Was their time together beyond description?
Or...
...in her final month...
...could she not spare the time?
Or...
MORNING, ALICE!

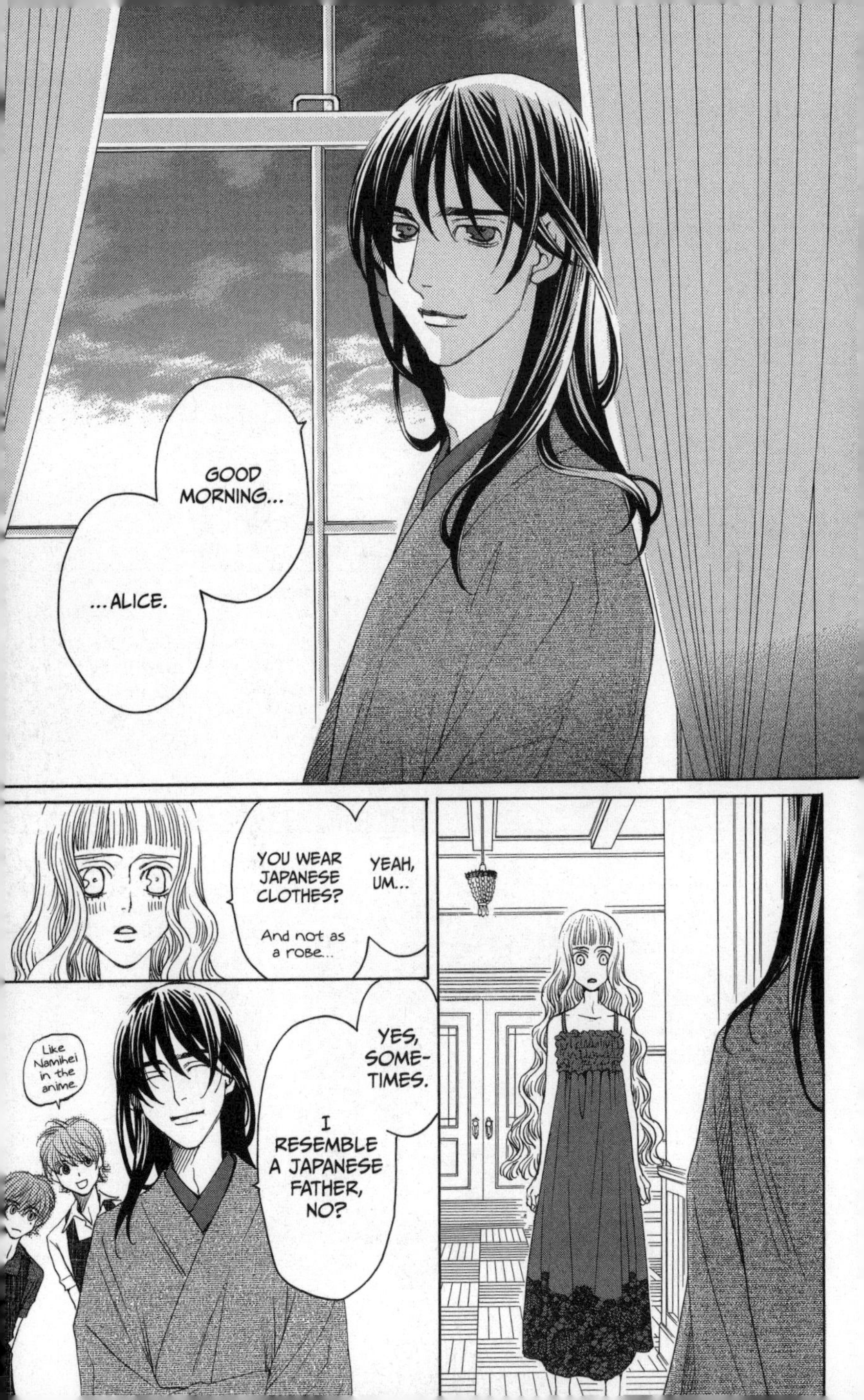
GOOD MORNING...
...ALICE.
YOU WEAR JAPANESE CLOTHES?
And not as a robe...
YEAH, UM...
YES, SOME-TIMES.
I RESEMBLE A JAPANESE FATHER, NO?
Like Namihei in the anime.

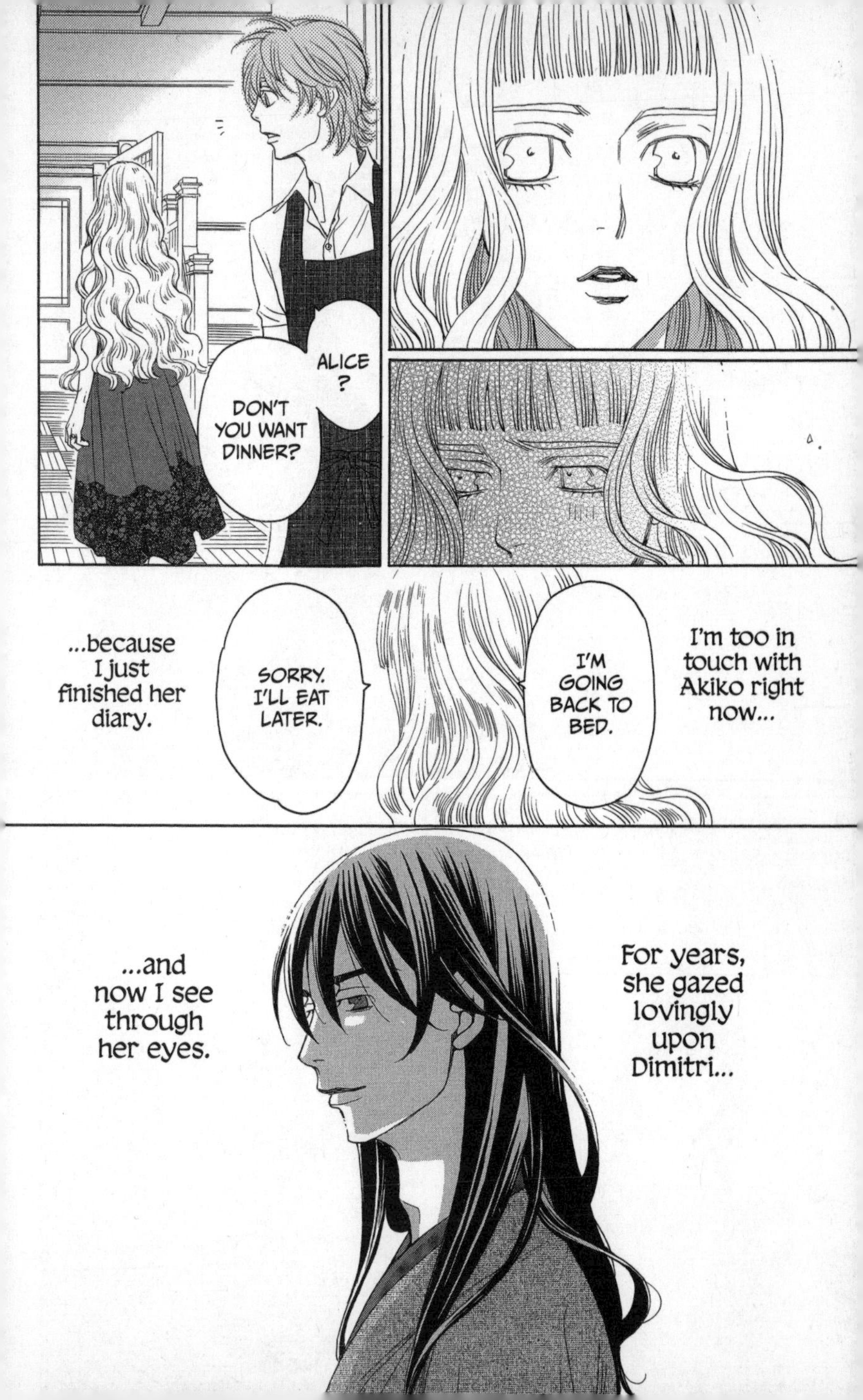
ALICE ?
DON'T YOU WANT DINNER?
I'm too in touch with Akiko right now...
I'M GOING BACK TO BED.
SORRY. I'LL EAT LATER.
...because I just finished her diary.
For years, she gazed lovingly upon Dimitri...
...and now I see through her eyes.

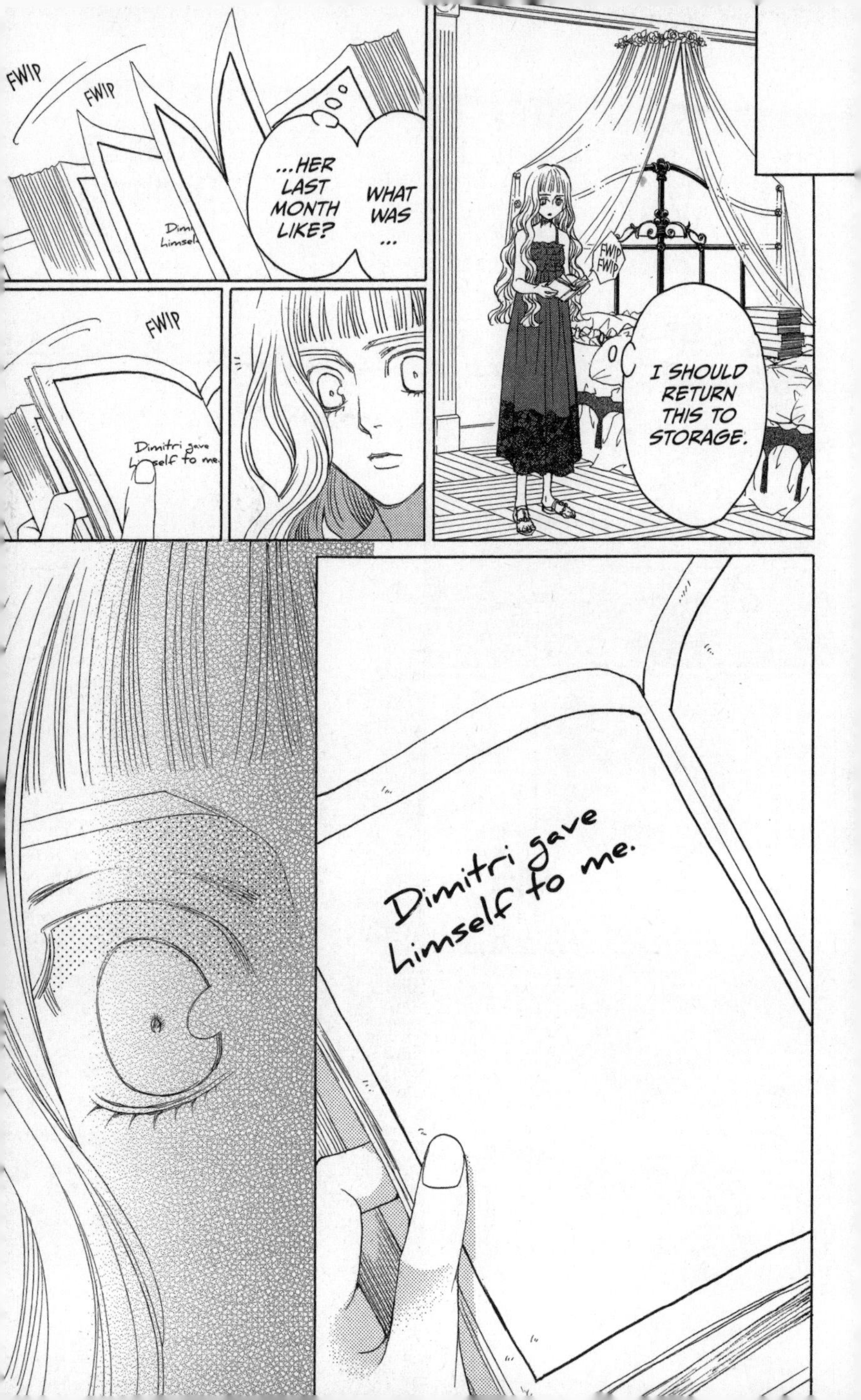
FWIP FWIP
I SHOULD RETURN THIS TO STORAGE.
FWIP
FWIP
WHAT WAS ...
...HER LAST MONTH LIKE?
Dimi
himsel
FWIP
Dimitri gave himself to me.
Dimitri gave himself to me.

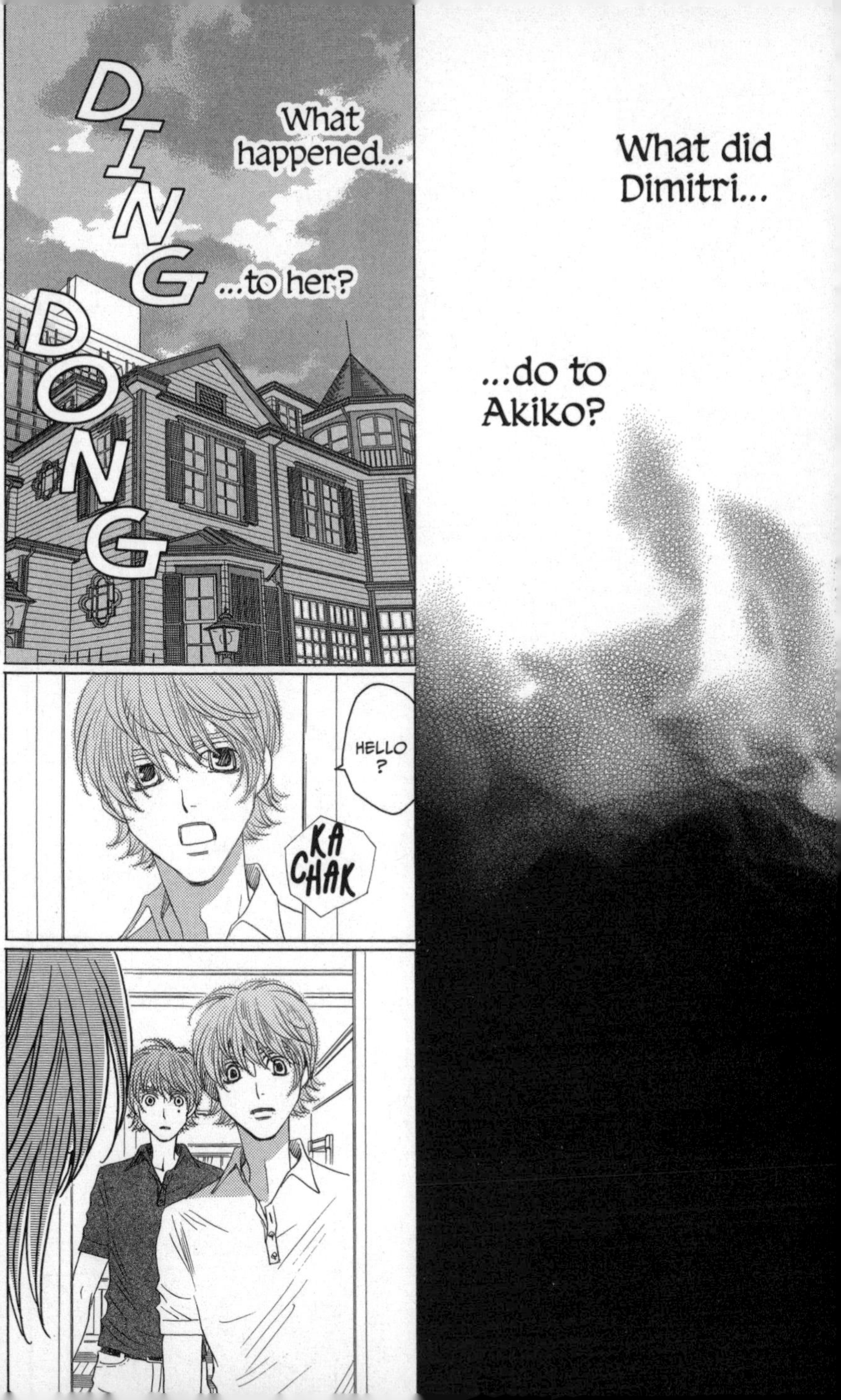
What did Dimitri...
...do to Akiko?
What happened...
DING DONG
...to her?
HELLO?
KA CHAK

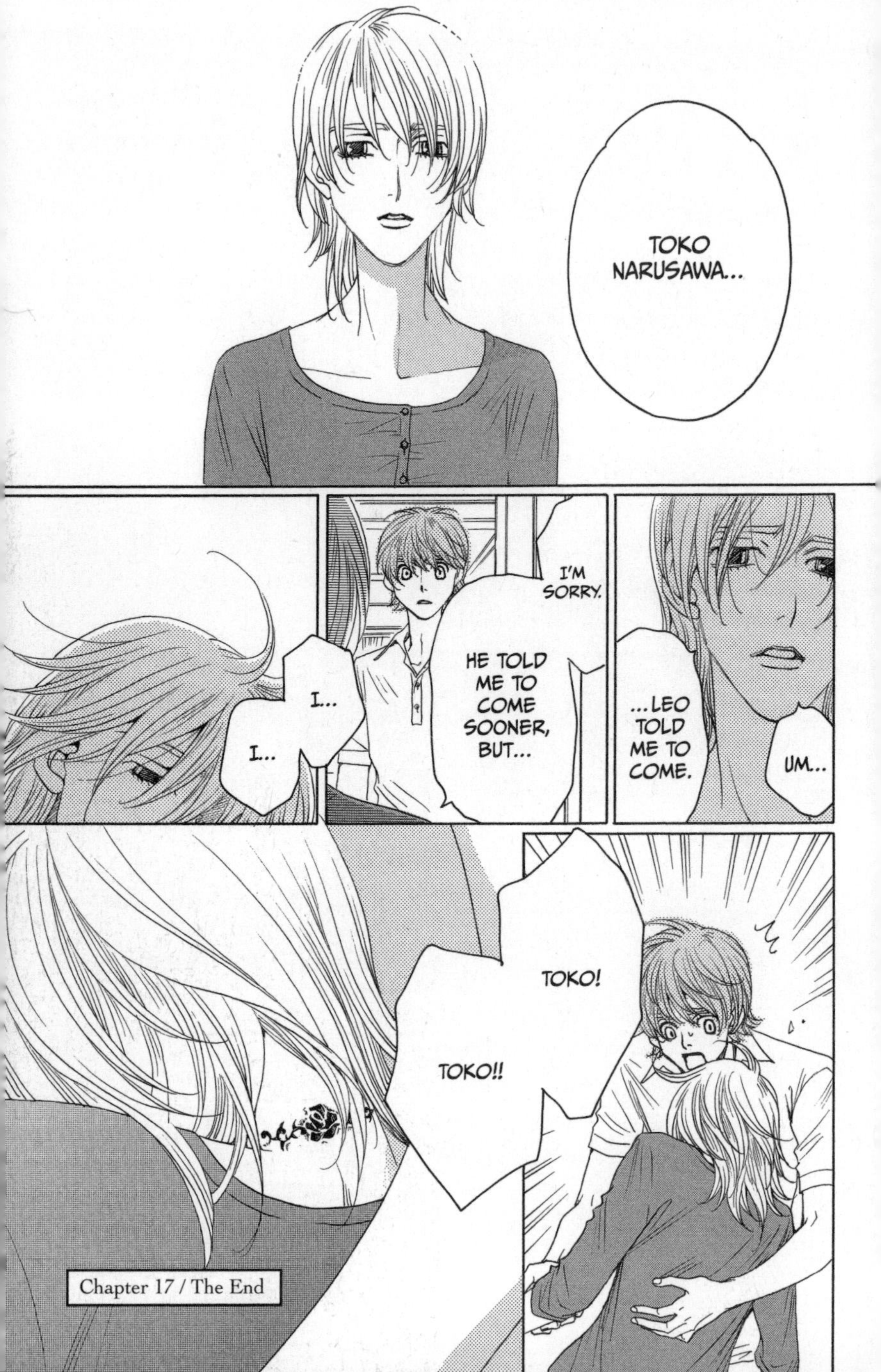
TOKO NARUSAWA...
UM...
...LEO TOLD ME TO COME.
I'M SORRY.
HE TOLD ME TO COME SOONER, BUT...
I...
I...
TOKO!
TOKO!!
Chapter 17 / The End

Black Rose ALICE

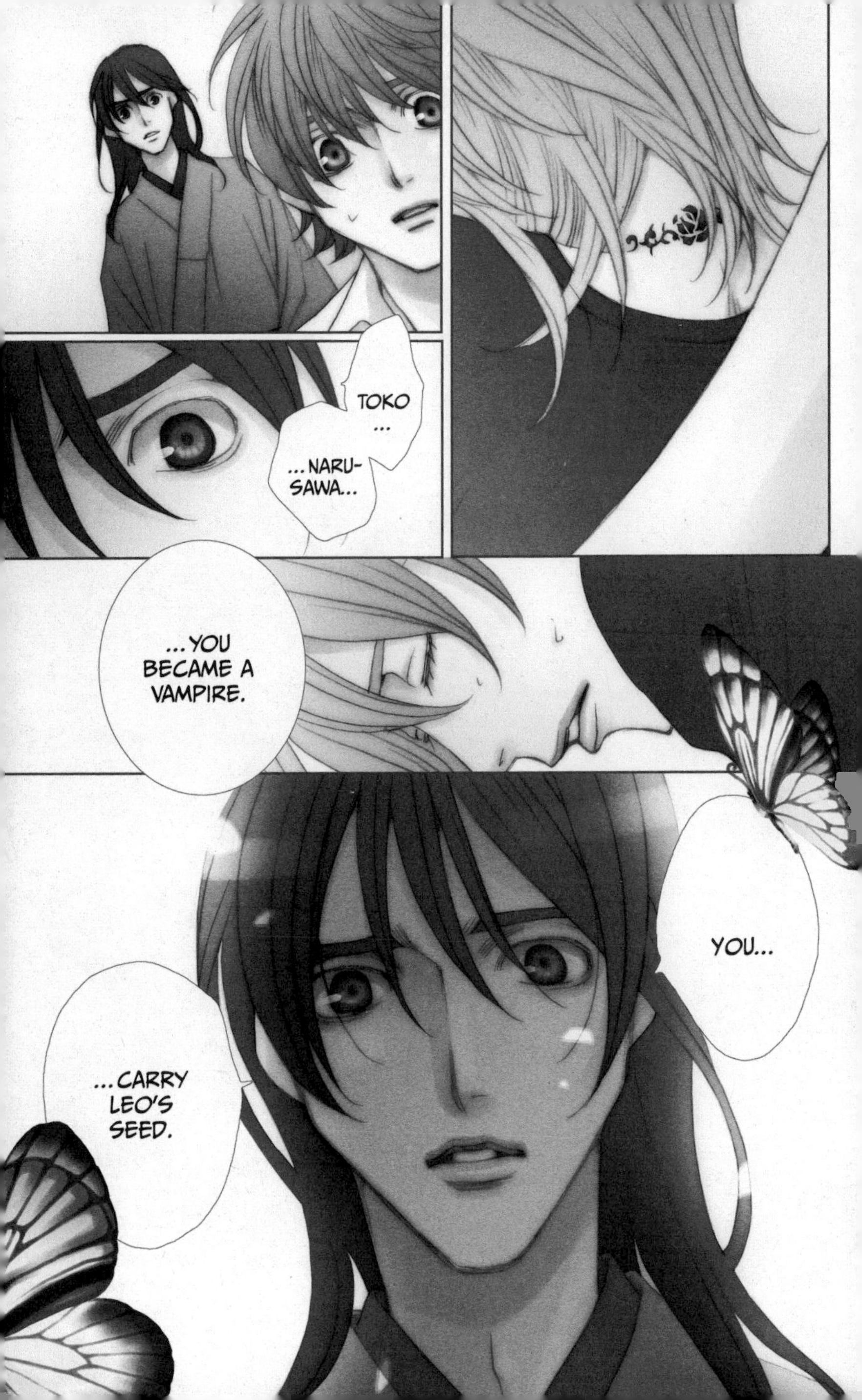
TOKO ...
...NARU-SAWA...
...YOU BECAME A VAMPIRE.
YOU...
...CARRY LEO'S SEED.

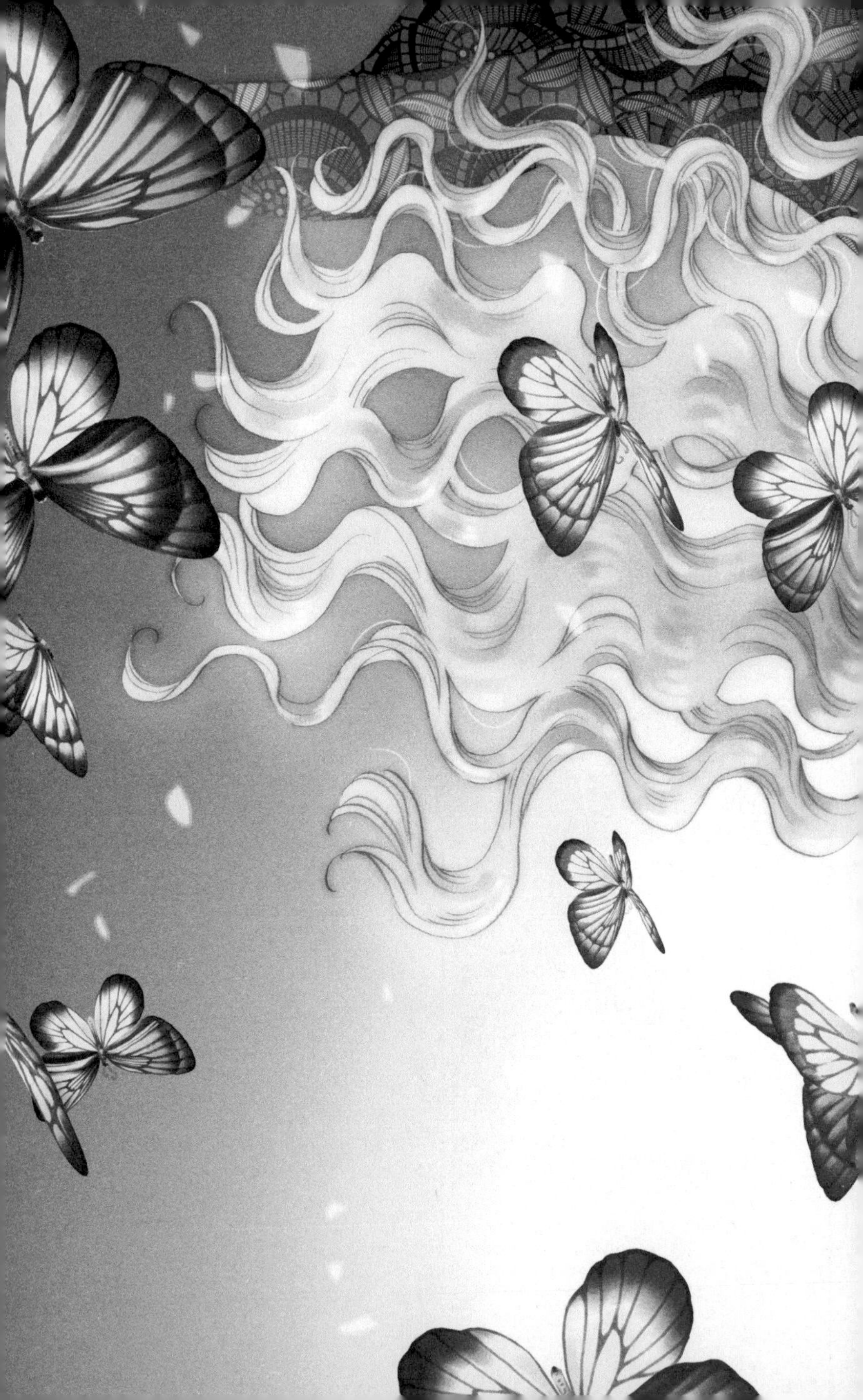

Black Rose Alice
Chapter 18

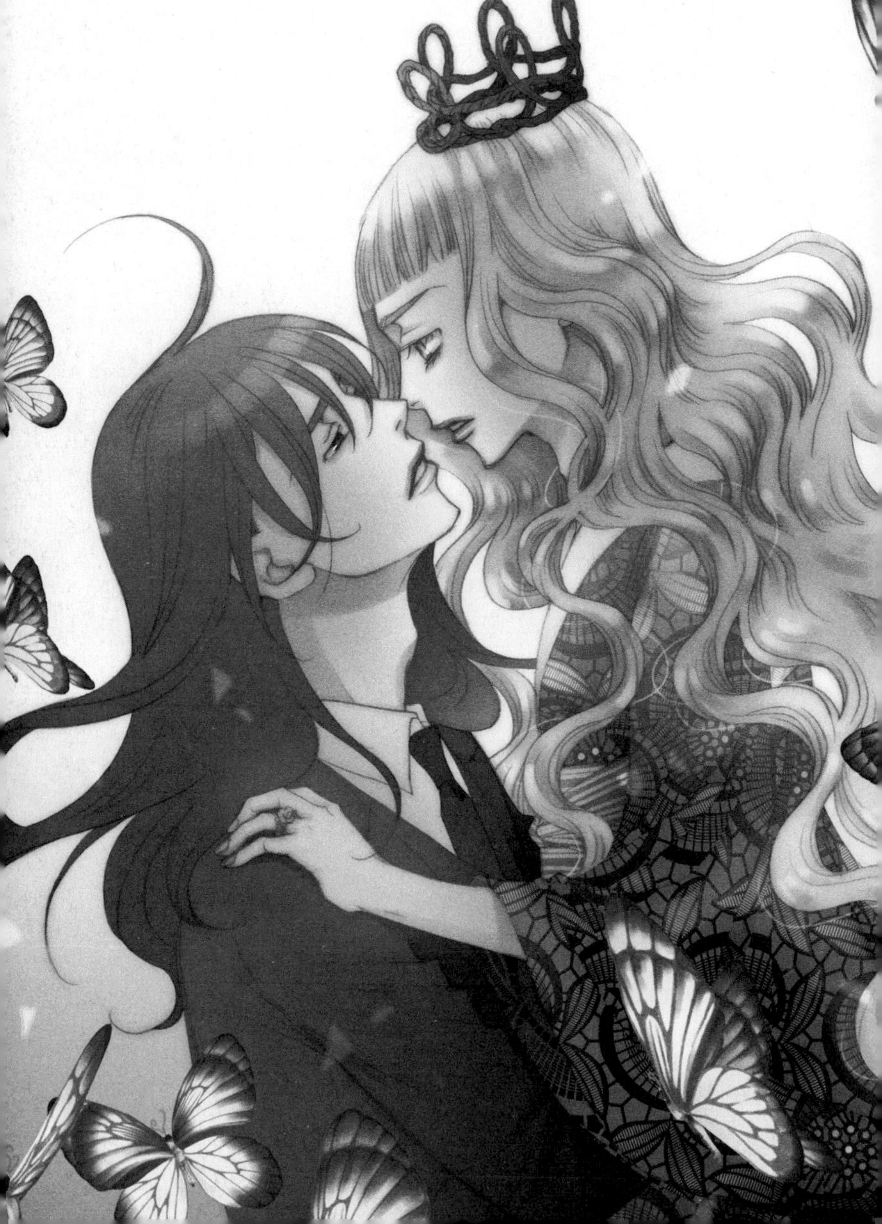

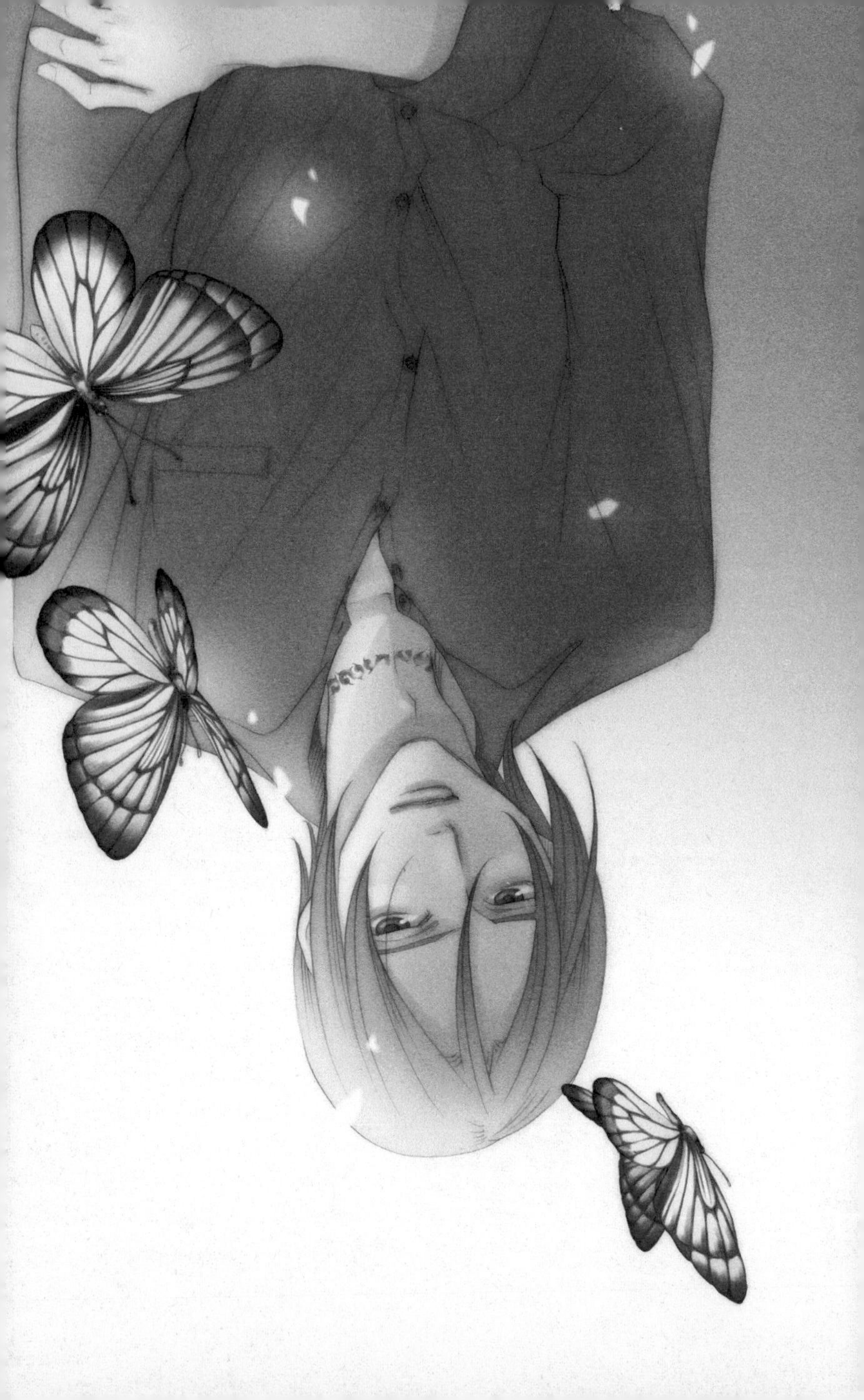

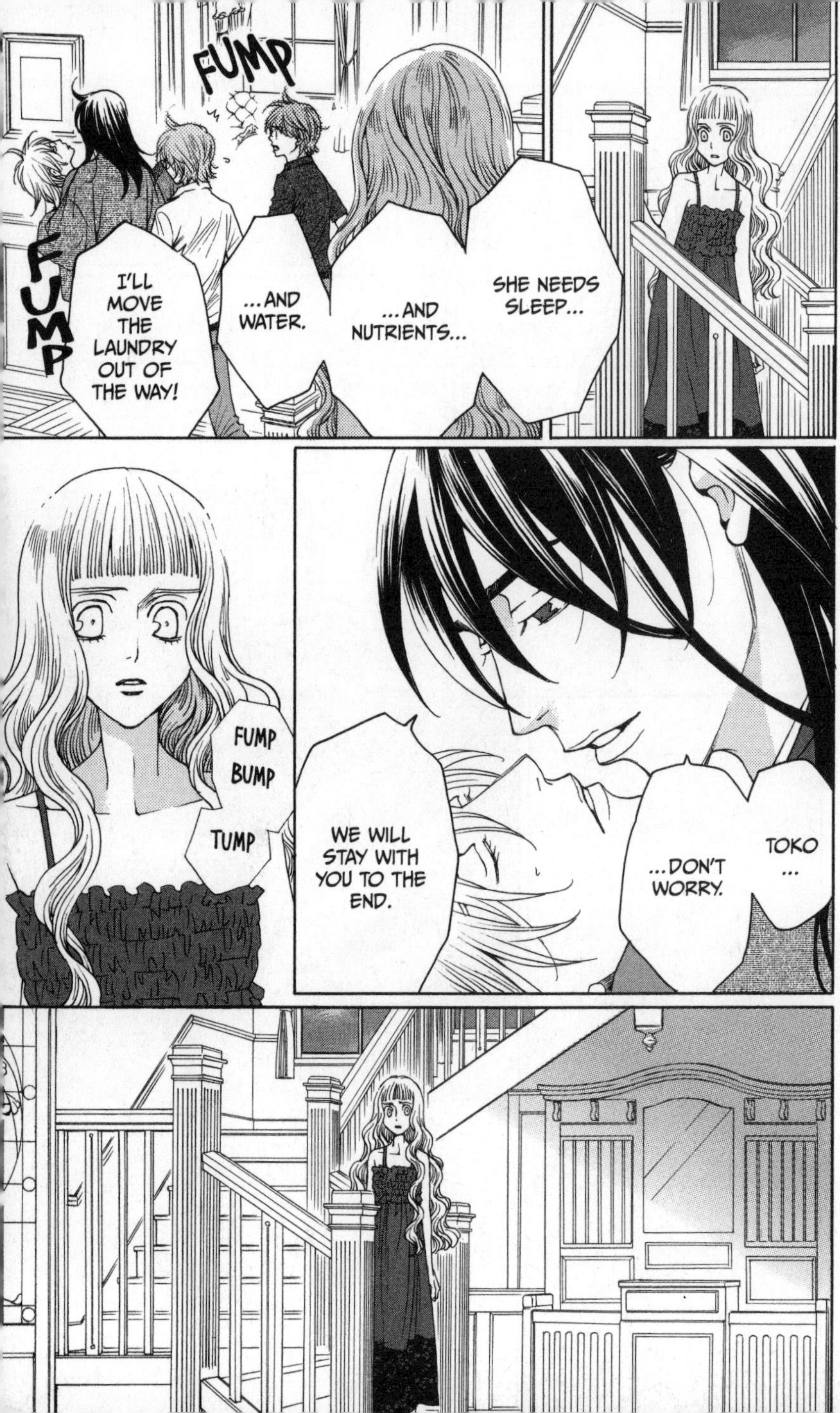
SHE NEEDS SLEEP...
...AND NUTRIENTS...
...AND WATER.
FUMP
I'LL MOVE THE LAUNDRY OUT OF THE WAY!
FUMP
TOKO ...
...DON'T WORRY.
WE WILL STAY WITH YOU TO THE END.
FUMP
BUMP
TUMP

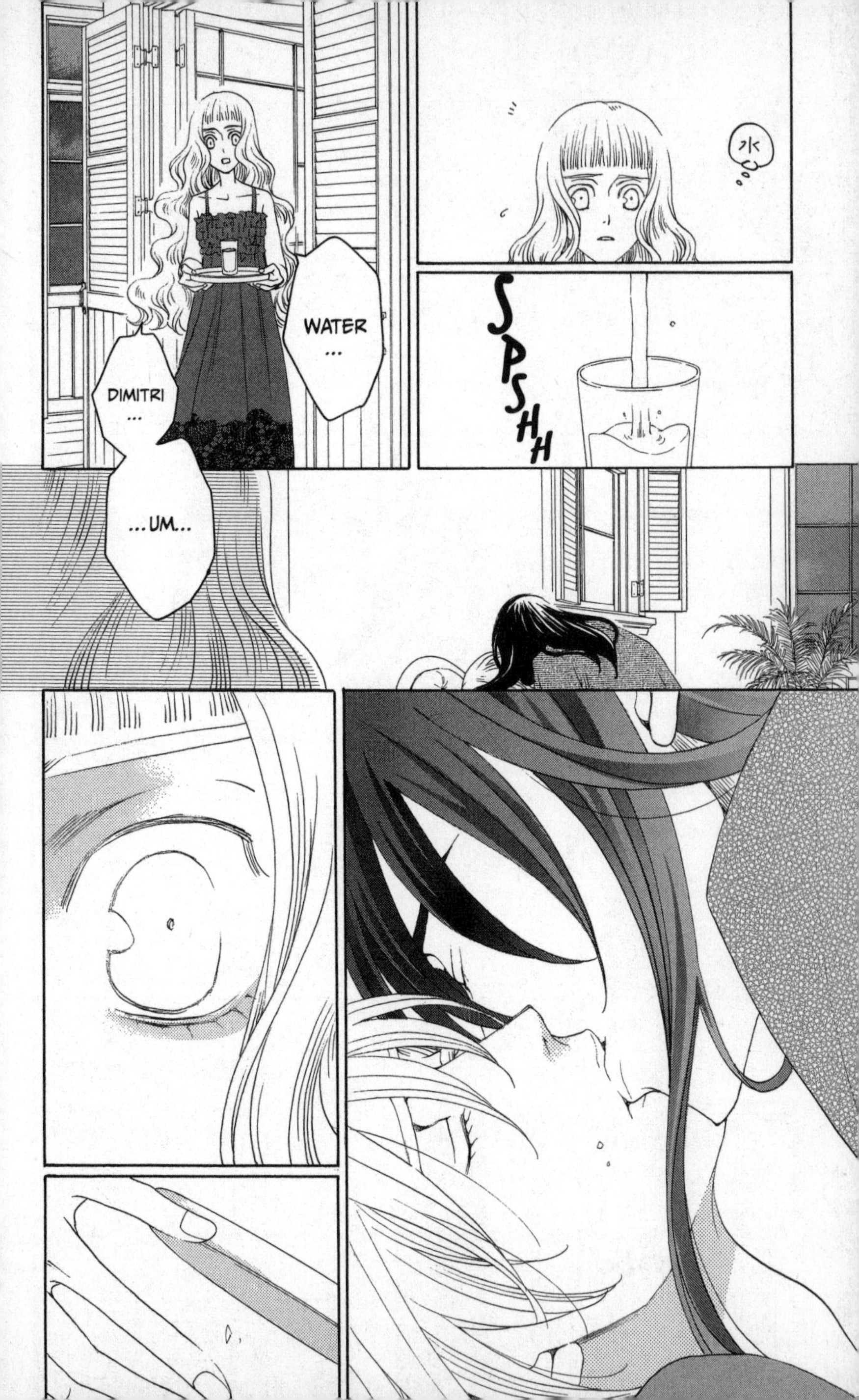
水
SPSHH
WATER ...
DIMITRI ...
...UM...

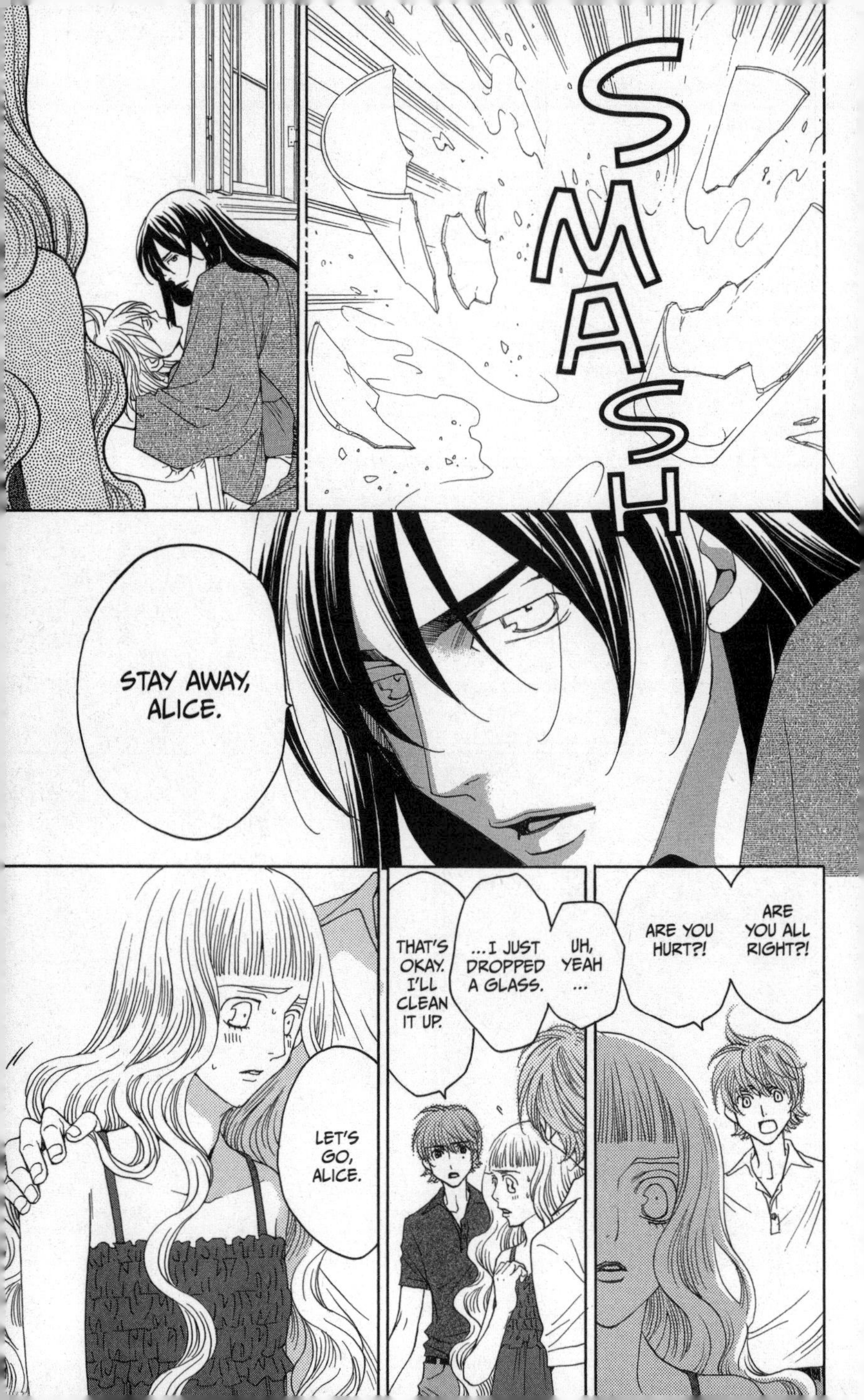
SMASH
STAY AWAY, ALICE.
ARE YOU ALL RIGHT?!
ARE YOU HURT?!
UH, YEAH ...
...I JUST DROPPED A GLASS.
THAT'S OKAY. I'LL CLEAN IT UP.
LET'S GO, ALICE.

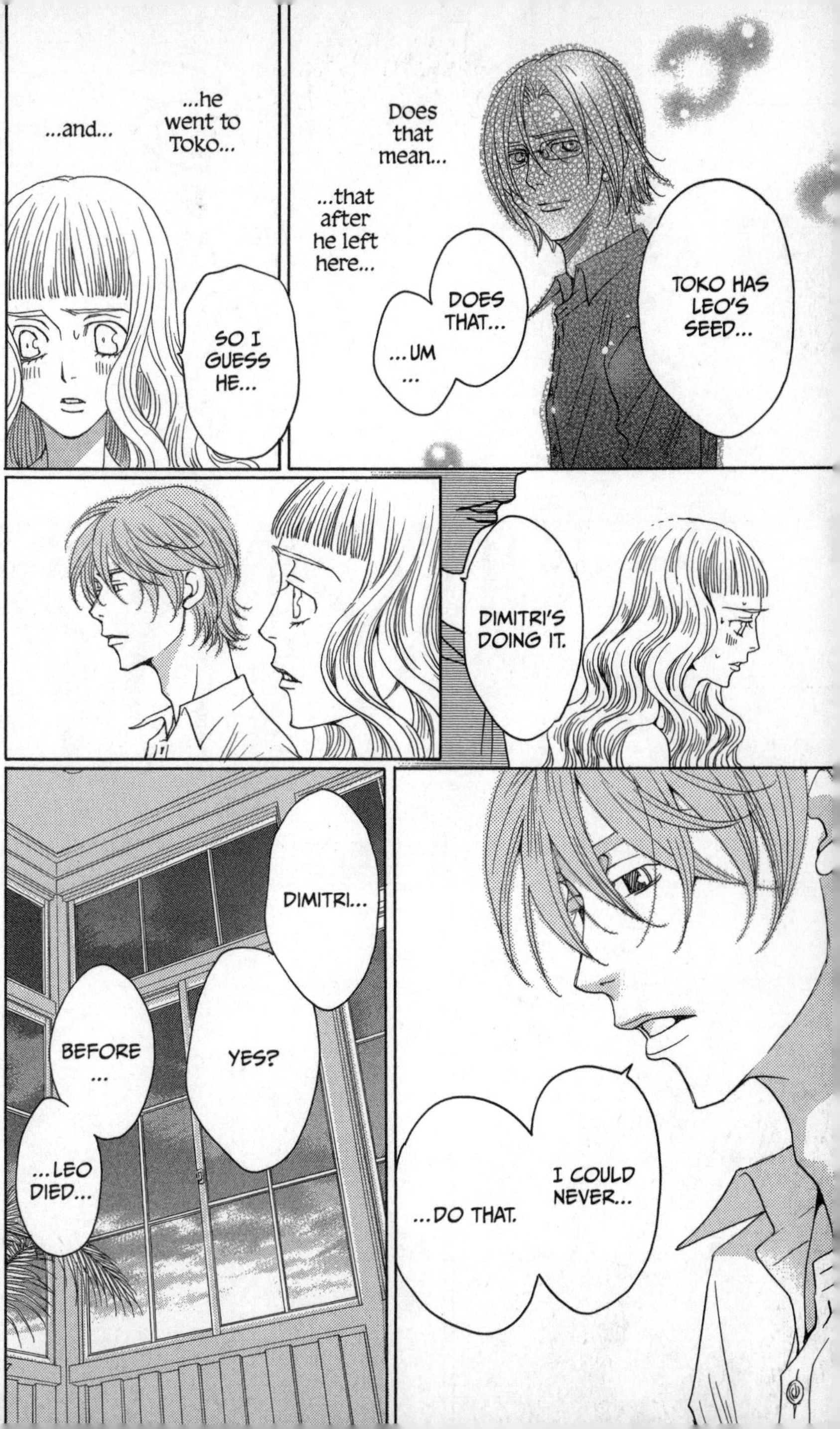
TOKO HAS LEO'S SEED...
DOES THAT...
...UM ...
Does that mean...
...that after he left here...
SO I GUESS HE...
...he went to Toko...
...and...
DIMITRI'S DOING IT.
I COULD NEVER...
...DO THAT.
DIMITRI...
YES?
BEFORE ...
...LEO DIED...

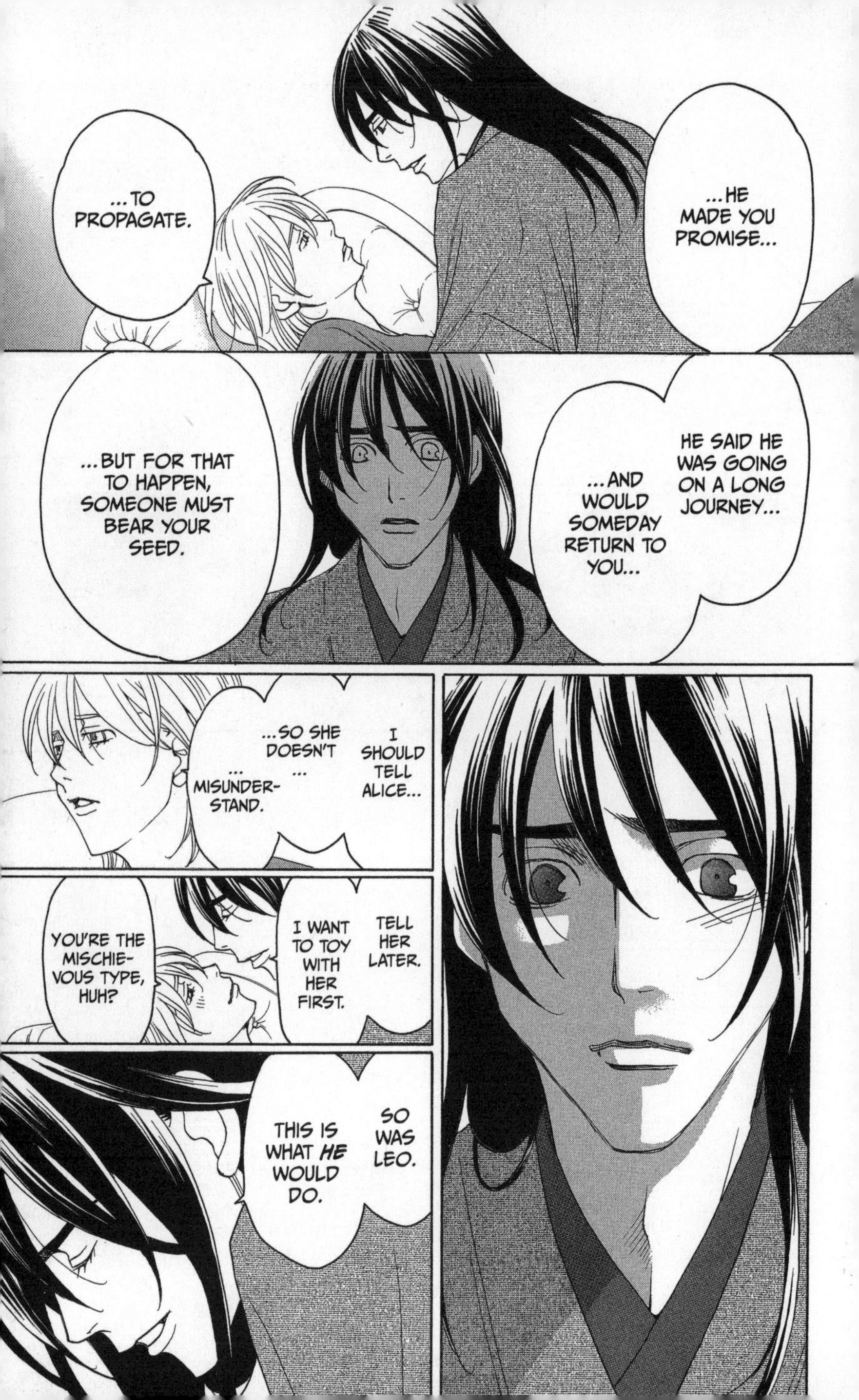
...HE MADE YOU PROMISE...
...TO PROPAGATE.
HE SAID HE WAS GOING ON A LONG JOURNEY...
...AND WOULD SOMEDAY RETURN TO YOU...
...BUT FOR THAT TO HAPPEN, SOMEONE MUST BEAR YOUR SEED.
I SHOULD TELL ALICE...
...SO SHE DOESN'T ... ...MISUNDER-STAND.
TELL HER LATER.
I WANT TO TOY WITH HER FIRST.
YOU'RE THE MISCHIE-VOUS TYPE, HUH?
SO WAS LEO.
THIS IS WHAT HE WOULD DO.

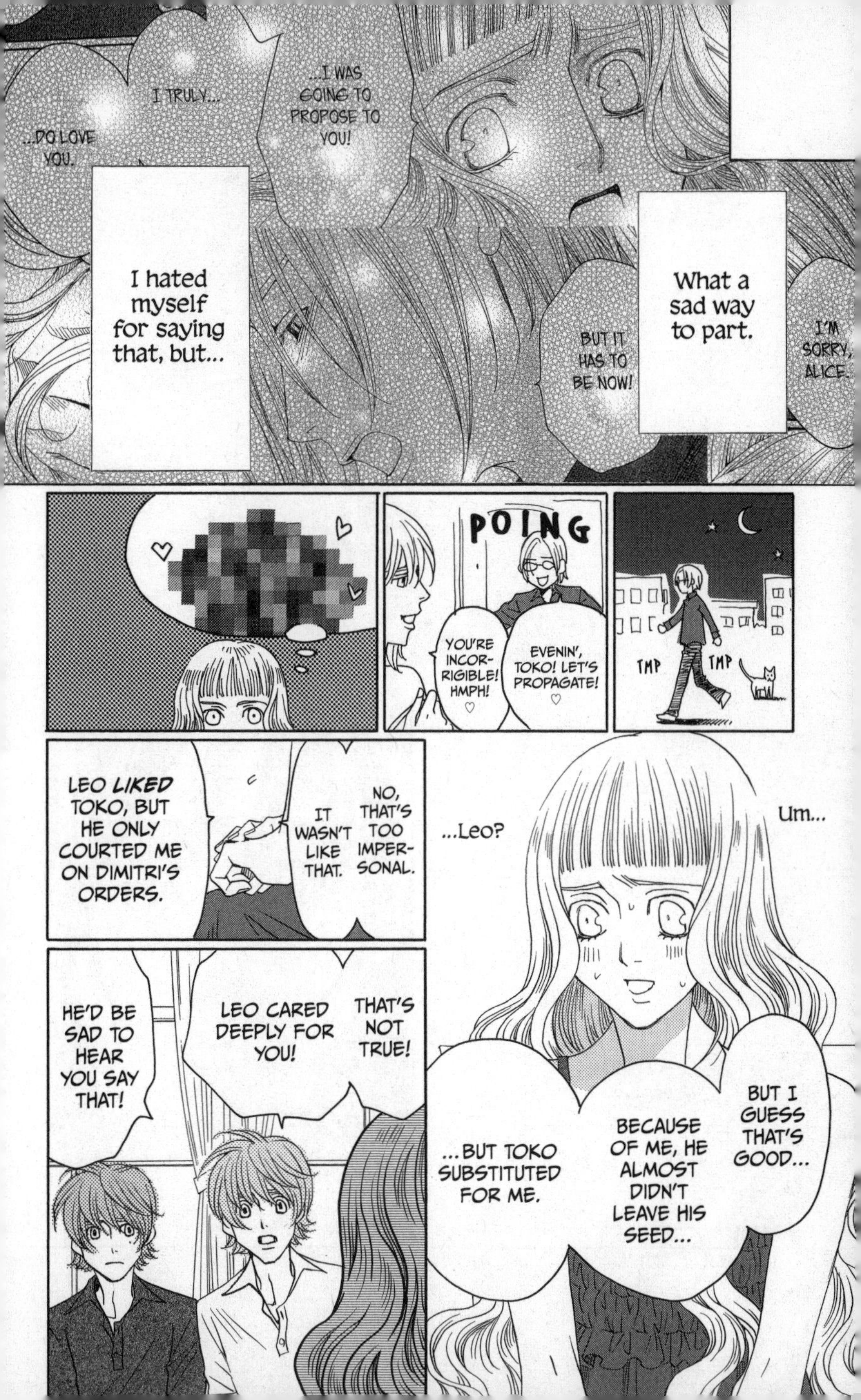
I'M SORRY, ALICE.
What a sad way to part.
BUT IT HAS TO BE NOW!
...I WAS GOING TO PROPOSE TO YOU!
I TRULY...
...DO LOVE YOU.
I hated myself for saying that, but...
TMP TMP
EVENIN', TOKO! LET'S PROPAGATE! ♡
YOU'RE INCORRIGIBLE! HMPH! ♡
POING
Um...
...Leo?
NO, THAT'S TOO IMPERSONAL.
IT WASN'T LIKE THAT.
LEO *LIKED* TOKO, BUT HE ONLY COURTED ME ON DIMITRI'S ORDERS.
BUT I GUESS THAT'S GOOD...
BECAUSE OF ME, HE ALMOST DIDN'T LEAVE HIS SEED...
...BUT TOKO SUBSTITUTED FOR ME.
THAT'S NOT TRUE!
LEO CARED DEEPLY FOR YOU!
HE'D BE SAD TO HEAR YOU SAY THAT!

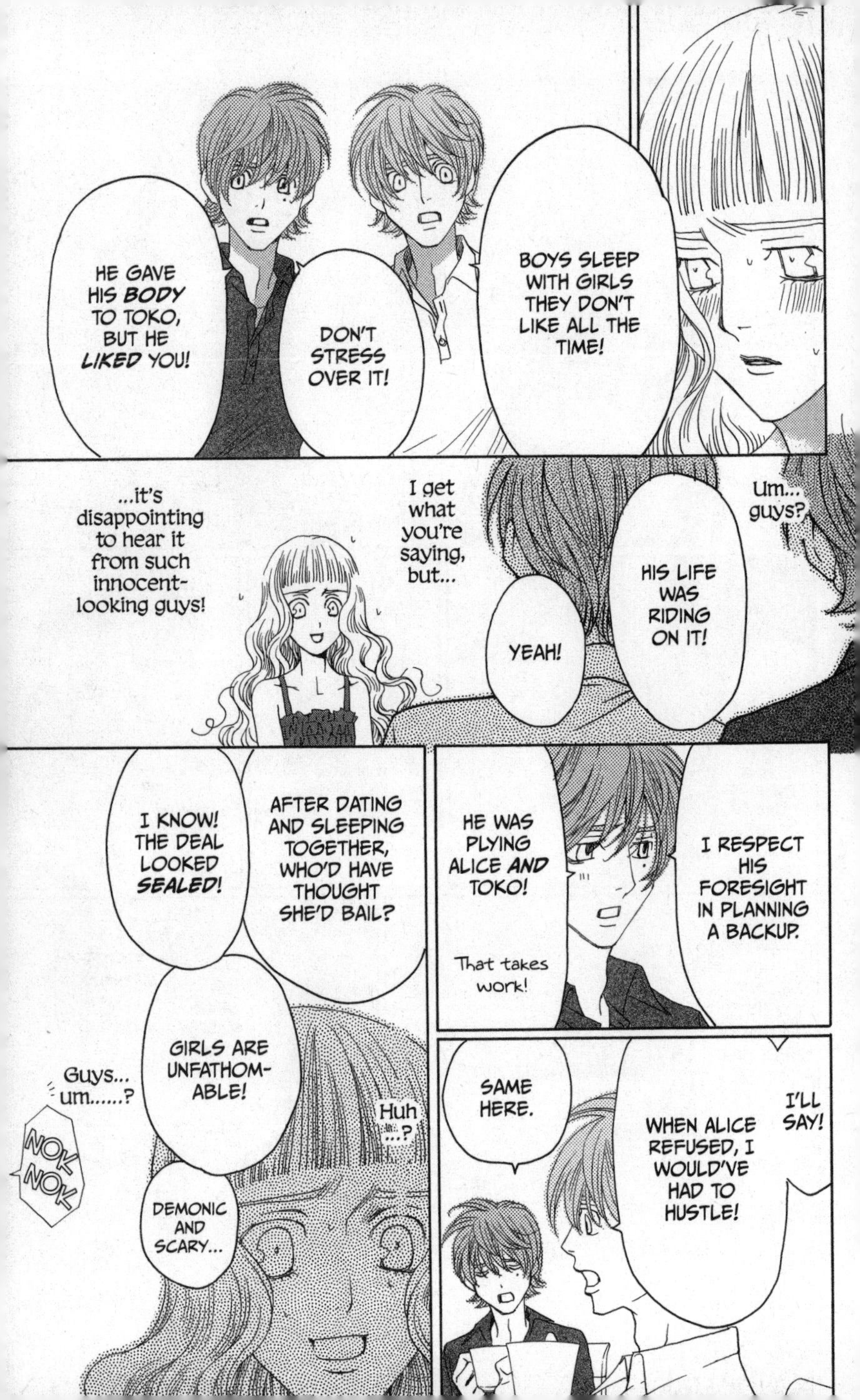
BOYS SLEEP WITH GIRLS THEY DON'T LIKE ALL THE TIME!
DON'T STRESS OVER IT!
HE GAVE HIS **BODY** TO TOKO, BUT HE **LIKED** YOU!
Um... guys?
HIS LIFE WAS RIDING ON IT!
YEAH!
I get what you're saying, but...
...it's disappointing to hear it from such innocent-looking guys!
I RESPECT HIS FORESIGHT IN PLANNING A BACKUP.
HE WAS PLYING ALICE **AND** TOKO!
That takes work!
I'LL SAY!
WHEN ALICE REFUSED, I WOULD'VE HAD TO HUSTLE!
SAME HERE.
AFTER DATING AND SLEEPING TOGETHER, WHO'D HAVE THOUGHT SHE'D BAIL?
I KNOW! THE DEAL LOOKED **SEALED**!
GIRLS ARE UNFATHOMABLE!
Huh ...?
Guys... um......?
NOK NOK
DEMONIC AND SCARY...

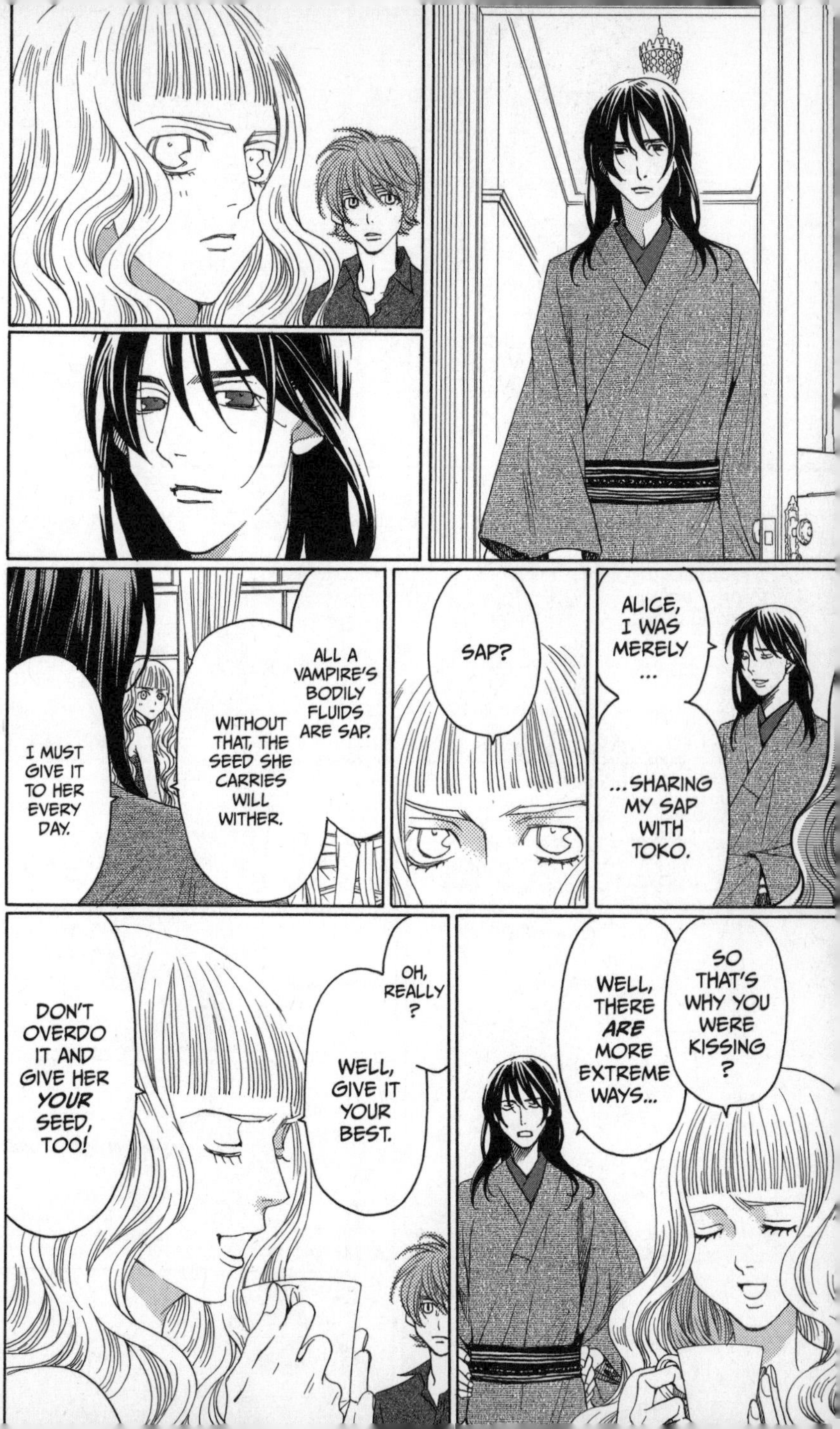
ALICE, I WAS MERELY ...
...SHARING MY SAP WITH TOKO.
SAP?
ALL A VAMPIRE'S BODILY FLUIDS ARE SAP.
WITHOUT THAT, THE SEED SHE CARRIES WILL WITHER.
I MUST GIVE IT TO HER EVERY DAY.
SO THAT'S WHY YOU WERE KISSING?
WELL, THERE *ARE* MORE EXTREME WAYS...
OH, REALLY?
WELL, GIVE IT YOUR BEST.
DON'T OVERDO IT AND GIVE HER *YOUR* SEED, TOO!

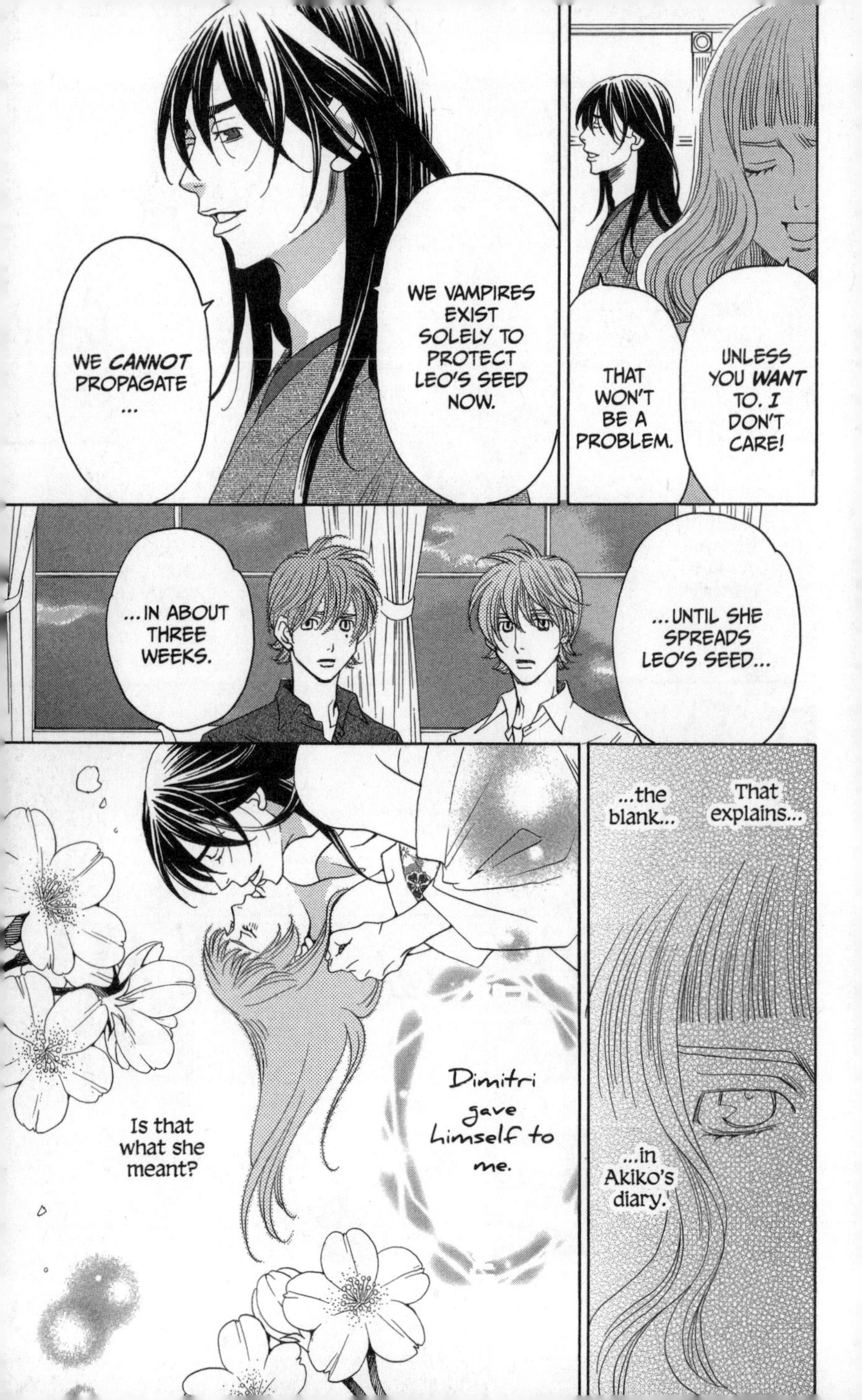
UNLESS YOU WANT TO. I DON'T CARE!
THAT WON'T BE A PROBLEM.
WE VAMPIRES EXIST SOLELY TO PROTECT LEO'S SEED NOW.
WE CANNOT PROPAGATE ...
...UNTIL SHE SPREADS LEO'S SEED...
...IN ABOUT THREE WEEKS.
That explains...
...the blank...
...in Akiko's diary.
Dimitri gave himself to me.
Is that what she meant?

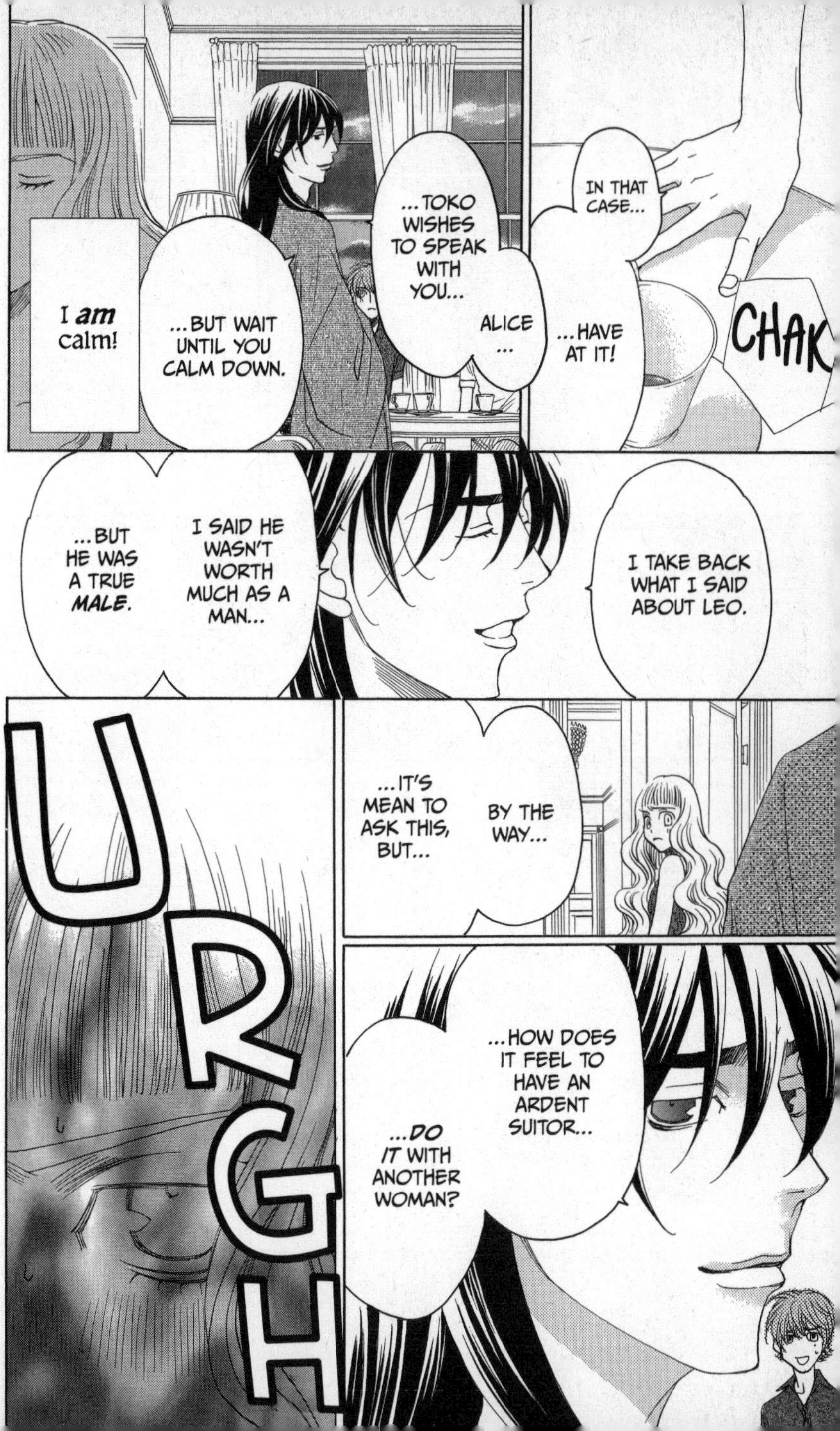
CHAK
IN THAT CASE...
...HAVE AT IT!
ALICE ...
...TOKO WISHES TO SPEAK WITH YOU...
...BUT WAIT UNTIL YOU CALM DOWN.
I *am* calm!
I TAKE BACK WHAT I SAID ABOUT LEO.
I SAID HE WASN'T WORTH MUCH AS A MAN...
...BUT HE WAS A TRUE *MALE*.
BY THE WAY...
...IT'S MEAN TO ASK THIS, BUT...
...HOW DOES IT FEEL TO HAVE AN ARDENT SUITOR...
...*DO IT* WITH ANOTHER WOMAN?
URGH

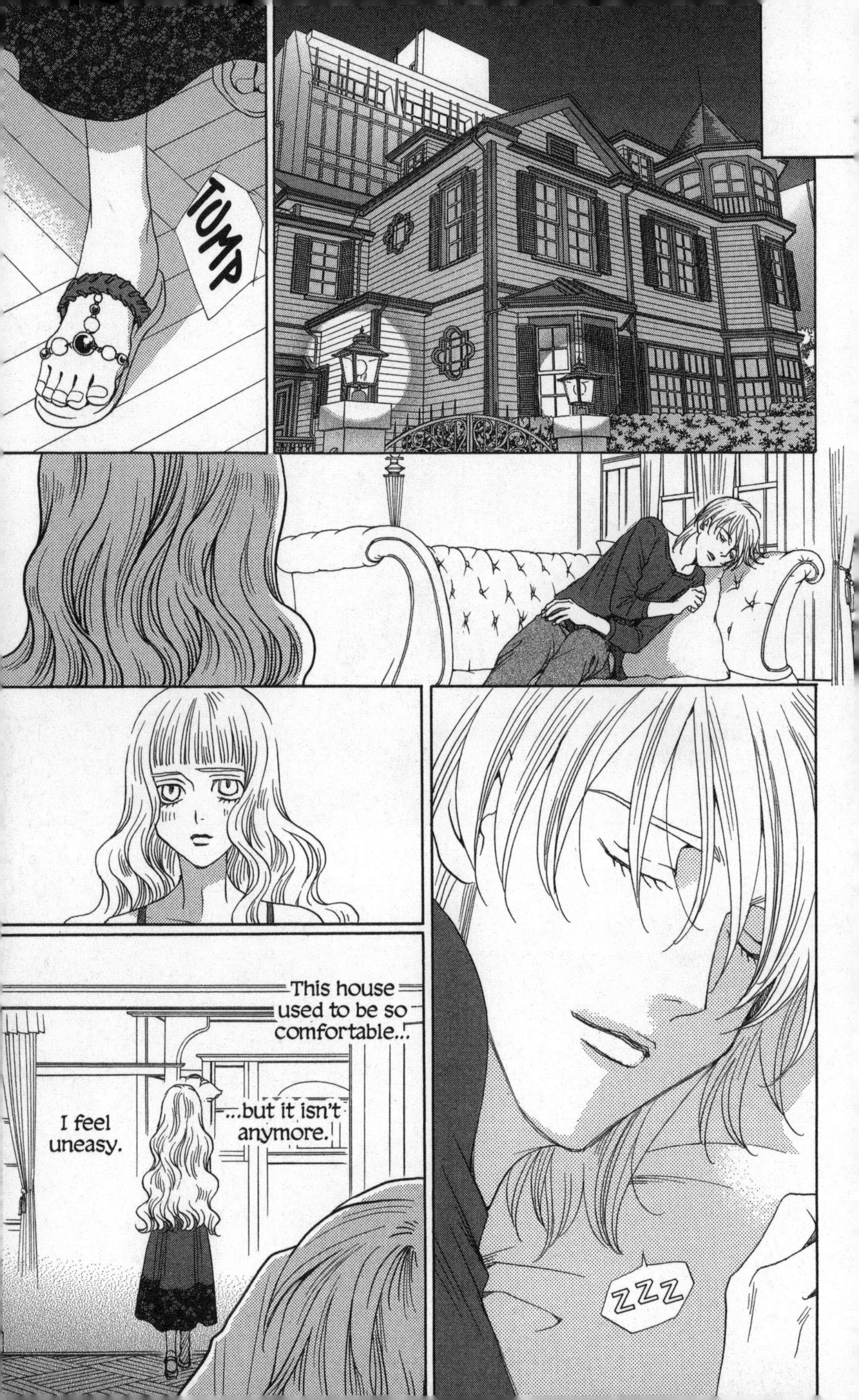
TUMP
ZZZ
This house used to be so comfortable...
...but it isn't anymore.
I feel uneasy.

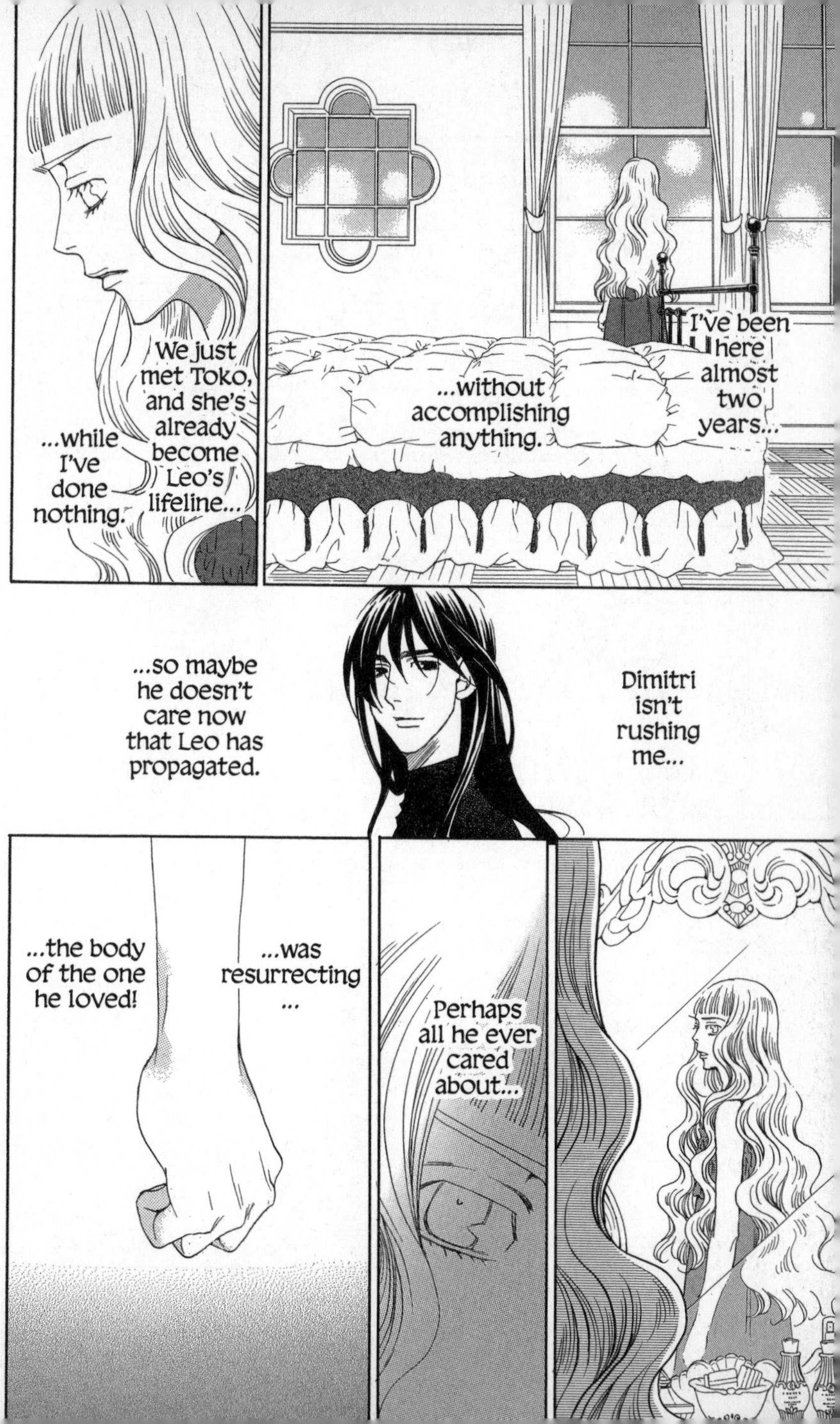
I've been here almost two years...
...without accomplishing anything.
We just met Toko, and she's already become Leo's lifeline...
...while I've done nothing.
Dimitri isn't rushing me...
...so maybe he doesn't care now that Leo has propagated.
Perhaps all he ever cared about...
...was resurrecting...
...the body of the one he loved!

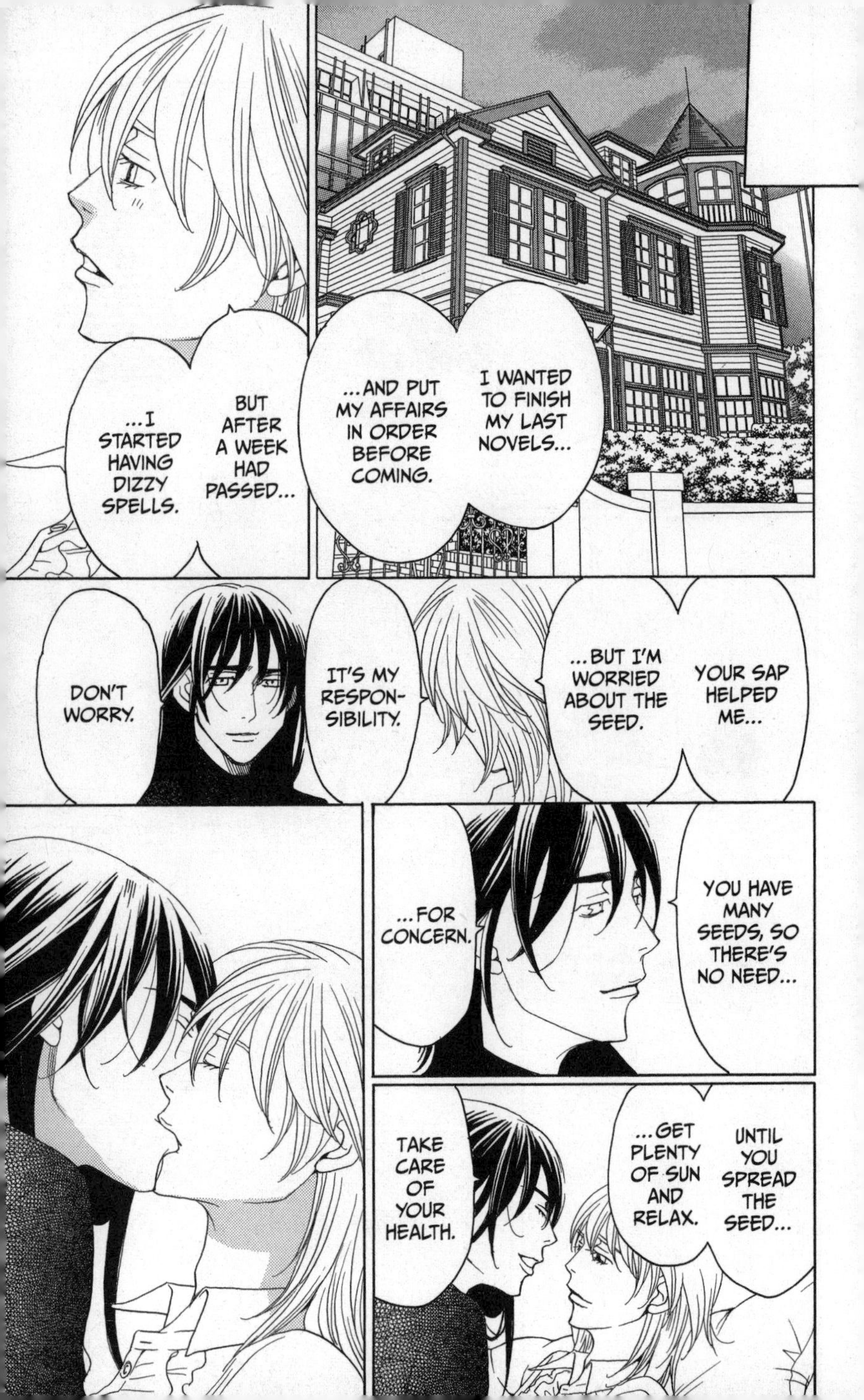
I WANTED TO FINISH MY LAST NOVELS...
...AND PUT MY AFFAIRS IN ORDER BEFORE COMING.
BUT AFTER A WEEK HAD PASSED...
...I STARTED HAVING DIZZY SPELLS.
YOUR SAP HELPED ME...
...BUT I'M WORRIED ABOUT THE SEED.
IT'S MY RESPON-SIBILITY.
DON'T WORRY.
YOU HAVE MANY SEEDS, SO THERE'S NO NEED...
...FOR CONCERN.
UNTIL YOU SPREAD THE SEED...
...GET PLENTY OF SUN AND RELAX.
TAKE CARE OF YOUR HEALTH.

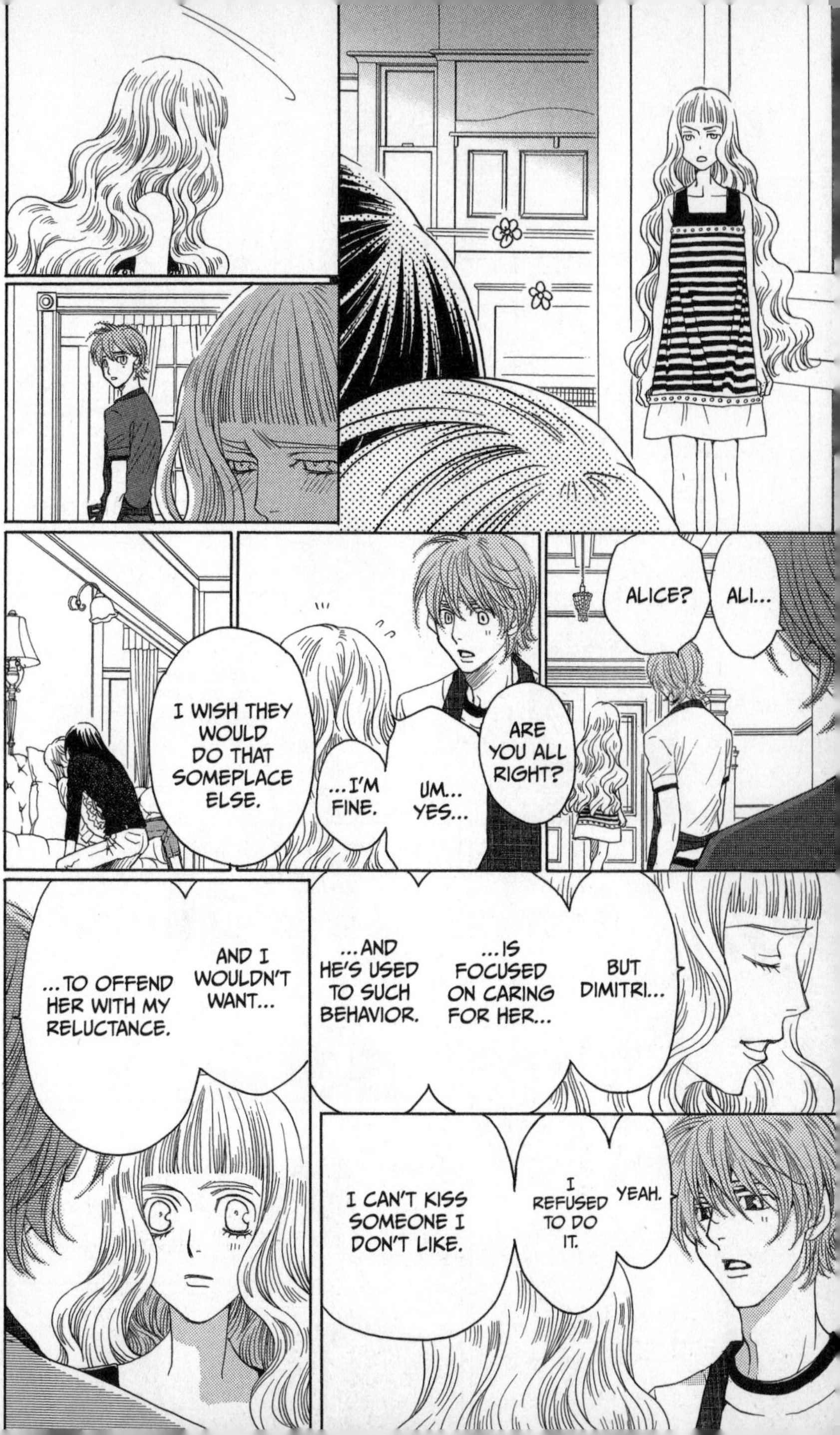
ALI...
ALICE?
ARE YOU ALL RIGHT?
UM... YES...
...I'M FINE.
I WISH THEY WOULD DO THAT SOMEPLACE ELSE.
BUT DIMITRI...
...IS FOCUSED ON CARING FOR HER...
...AND HE'S USED TO SUCH BEHAVIOR.
AND I WOULDN'T WANT...
...TO OFFEND HER WITH MY RELUCTANCE.
YEAH.
I REFUSED TO DO IT.
I CAN'T KISS SOMEONE I DON'T LIKE.

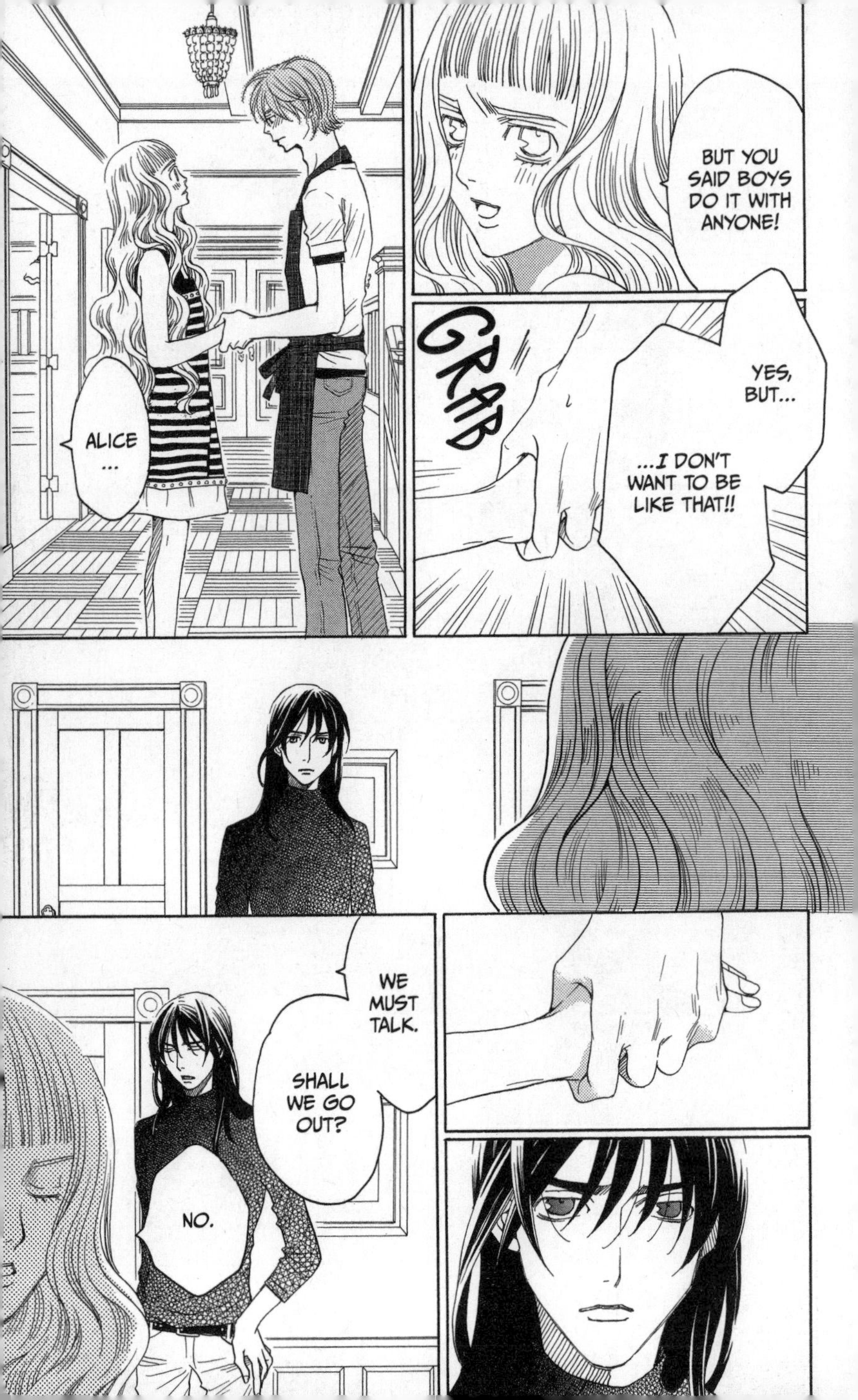
BUT YOU SAID BOYS DO IT WITH ANYONE!
ALICE ...
GRAB
YES, BUT...
...I DON'T WANT TO BE LIKE THAT!!
WE MUST TALK.
SHALL WE GO OUT?
NO.

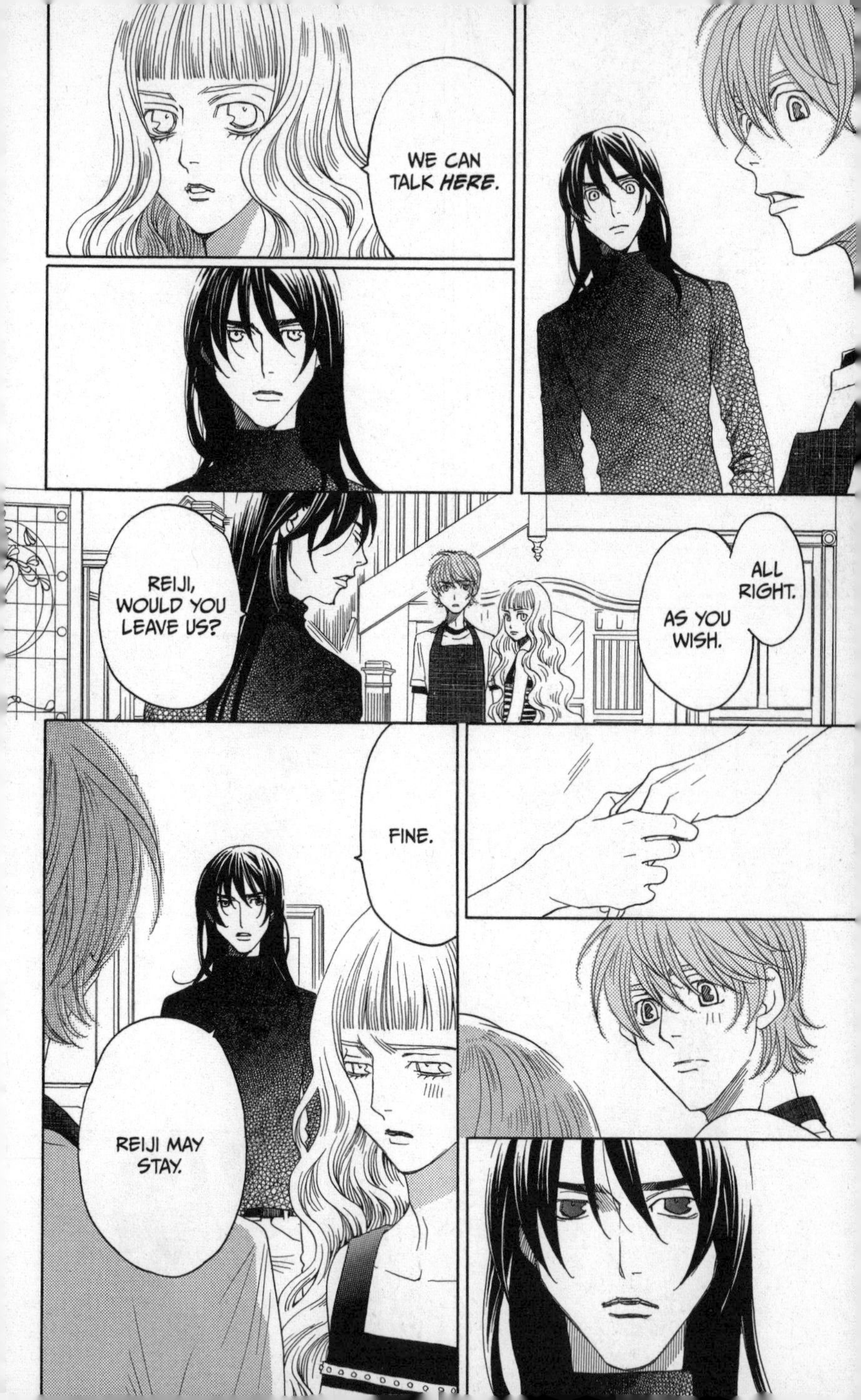
WE CAN TALK HERE.
ALL RIGHT. AS YOU WISH.
REIJI, WOULD YOU LEAVE US?
FINE.
REIJI MAY STAY.

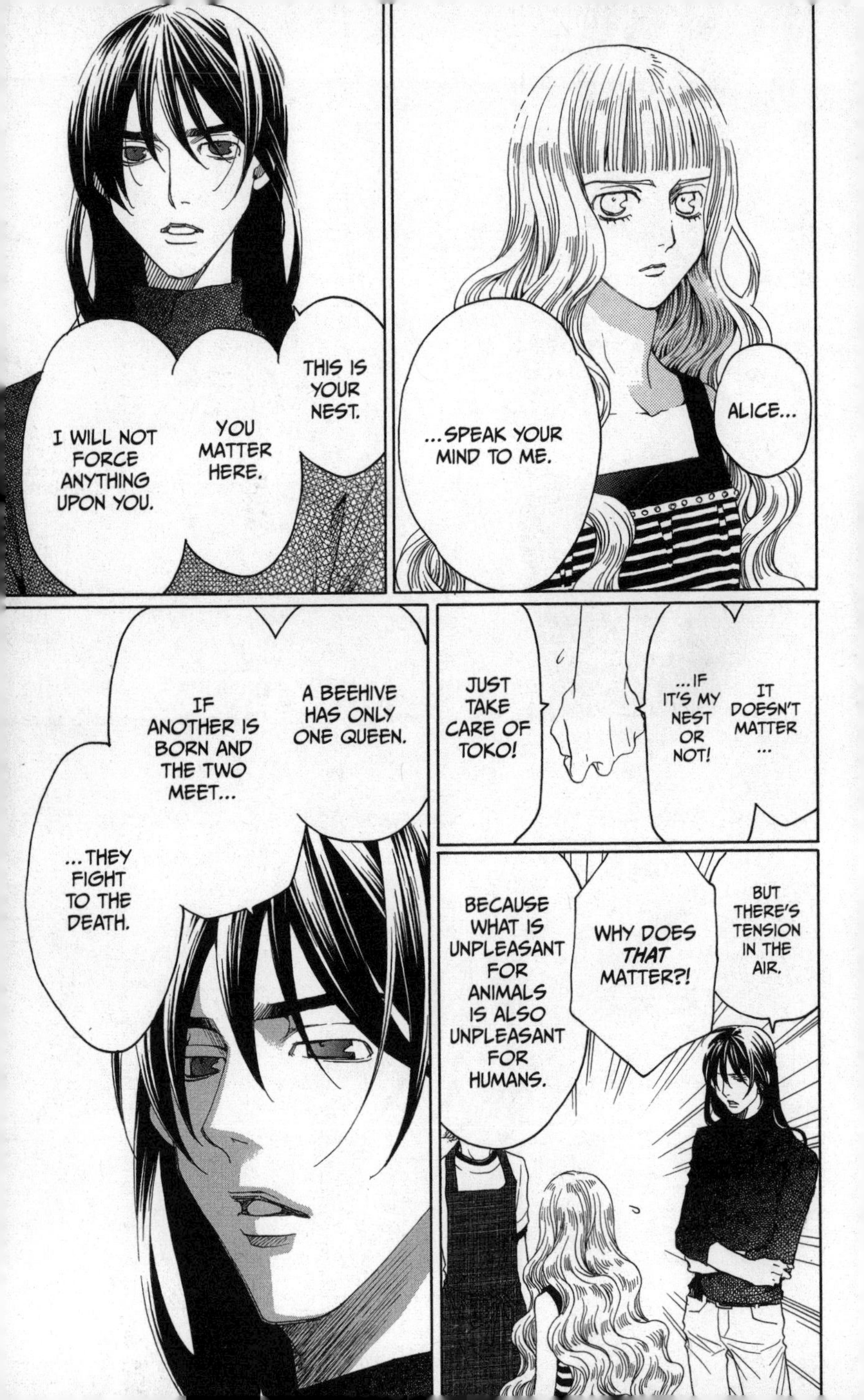
ALICE...
...SPEAK YOUR MIND TO ME.
THIS IS YOUR NEST.
YOU MATTER HERE.
I WILL NOT FORCE ANYTHING UPON YOU.
IT DOESN'T MATTER ...
...IF IT'S MY NEST OR NOT!
JUST TAKE CARE OF TOKO!
BUT THERE'S TENSION IN THE AIR.
WHY DOES *THAT* MATTER?!
BECAUSE WHAT IS UNPLEASANT FOR ANIMALS IS ALSO UNPLEASANT FOR HUMANS.
A BEEHIVE HAS ONLY ONE QUEEN.
IF ANOTHER IS BORN AND THE TWO MEET...
...THEY FIGHT TO THE DEATH.

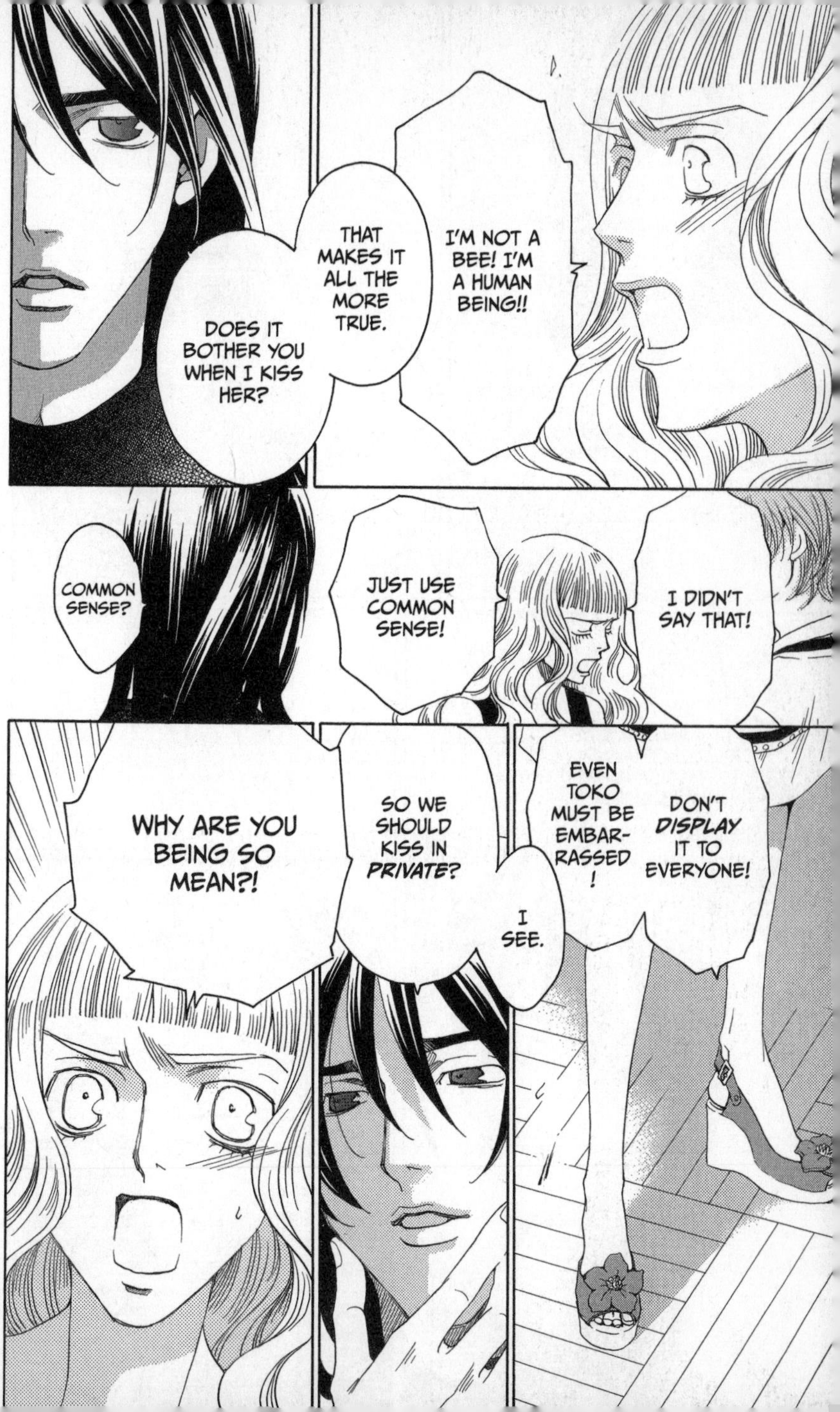
I'M NOT A BEE! I'M A HUMAN BEING!!
THAT MAKES IT ALL THE MORE TRUE.
DOES IT BOTHER YOU WHEN I KISS HER?
I DIDN'T SAY THAT!
JUST USE COMMON SENSE!
COMMON SENSE?
DON'T *DISPLAY* IT TO EVERYONE!
EVEN TOKO MUST BE EMBARRASSED!
SO WE SHOULD KISS IN *PRIVATE*?
I SEE.
WHY ARE YOU BEING SO MEAN?!

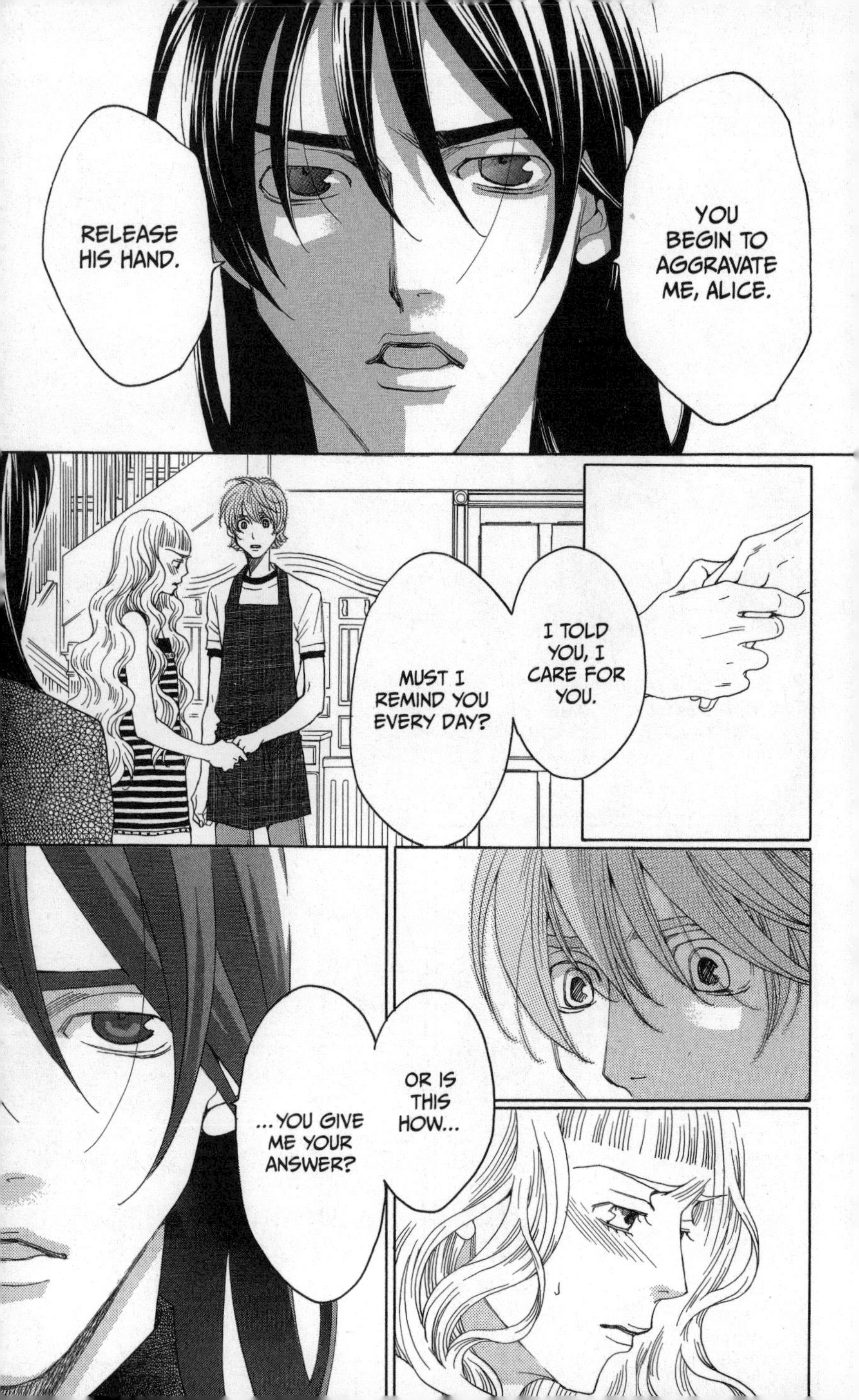
YOU BEGIN TO AGGRAVATE ME, ALICE.
RELEASE HIS HAND.
I TOLD YOU, I CARE FOR YOU.
MUST I REMIND YOU EVERY DAY?
OR IS THIS HOW...
...YOU GIVE ME YOUR ANSWER?

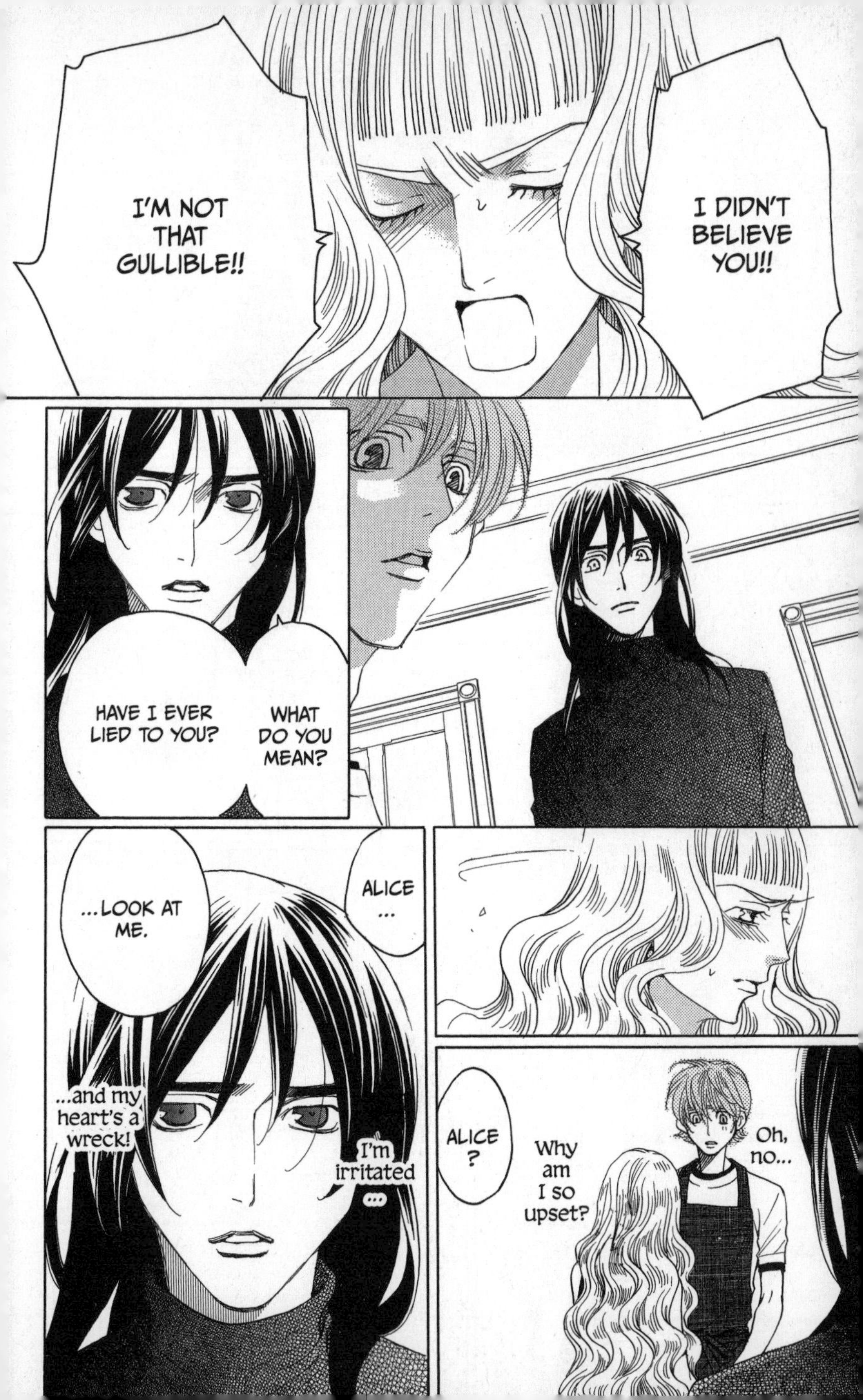
I DIDN'T BELIEVE YOU!!
I'M NOT THAT GULLIBLE!!
WHAT DO YOU MEAN?
HAVE I EVER LIED TO YOU?
Oh, no...
Why am I so upset?
ALICE?
ALICE...
...LOOK AT ME.
I'm irritated...
...and my heart's a wreck!

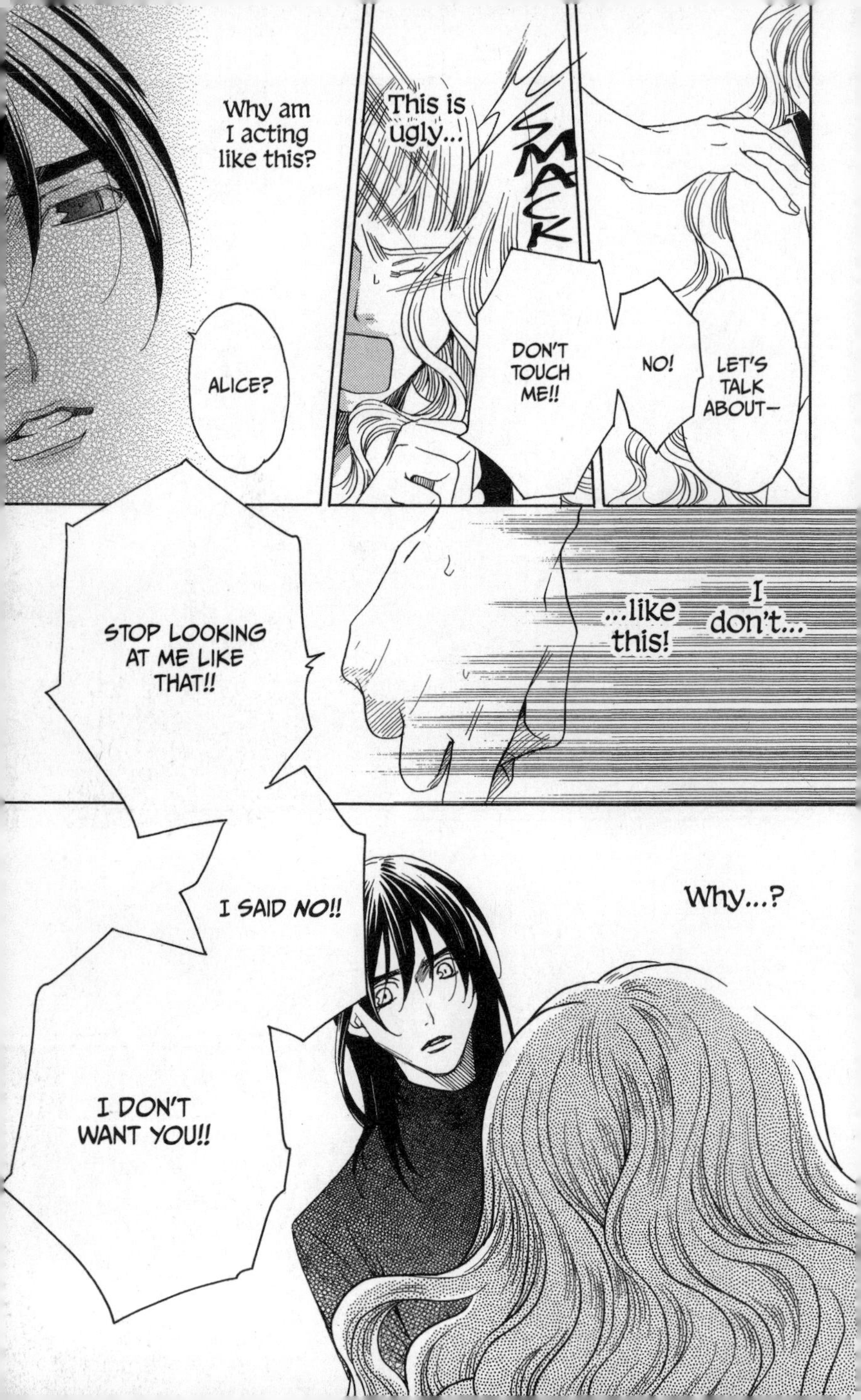
LET'S TALK ABOUT—
NO!
DON'T TOUCH ME!!
SMACK
This is ugly...
Why am I acting like this?
ALICE?
I don't...
...like this!
STOP LOOKING AT ME LIKE THAT!!
Why...?
I SAID NO!!
I DON'T WANT YOU!!

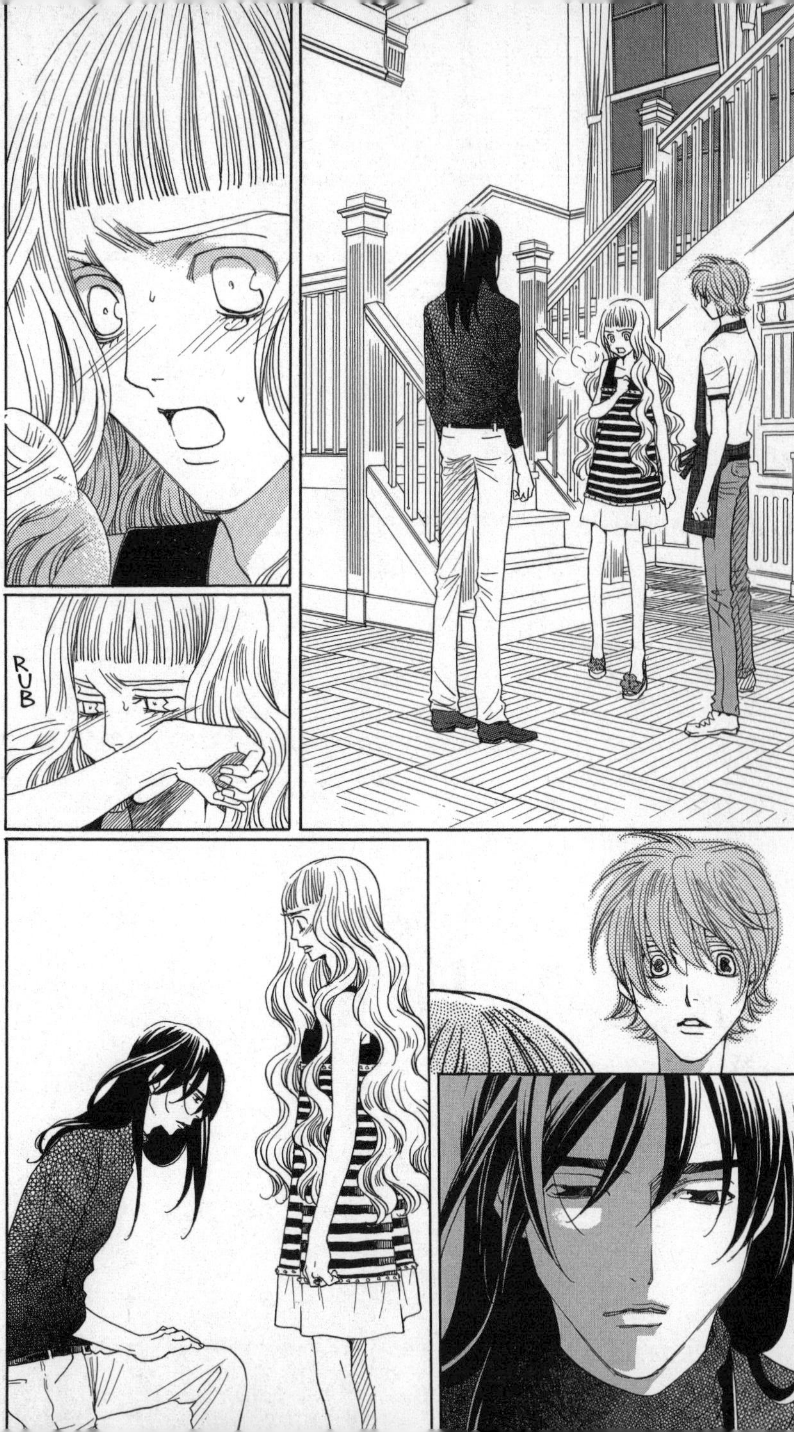
RUB

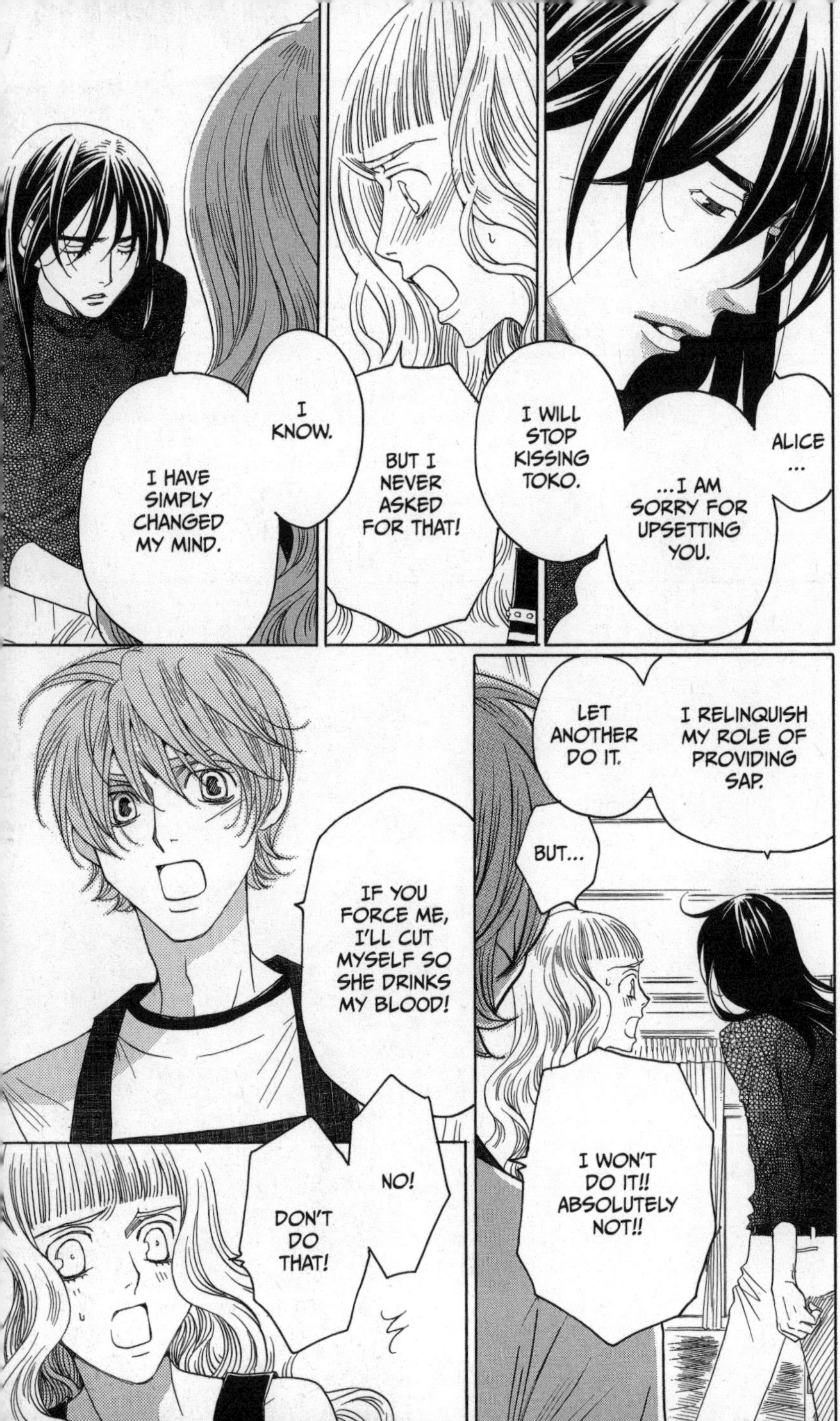
ALICE ...
...I AM SORRY FOR UPSETTING YOU.
I WILL STOP KISSING TOKO.
BUT I NEVER ASKED FOR THAT!
I KNOW.
I HAVE SIMPLY CHANGED MY MIND.
I RELINQUISH MY ROLE OF PROVIDING SAP.
LET ANOTHER DO IT.
BUT...
I WON'T DO IT!! ABSOLUTELY NOT!!
IF YOU FORCE ME, I'LL CUT MYSELF SO SHE DRINKS MY BLOOD!
NO!
DON'T DO THAT!

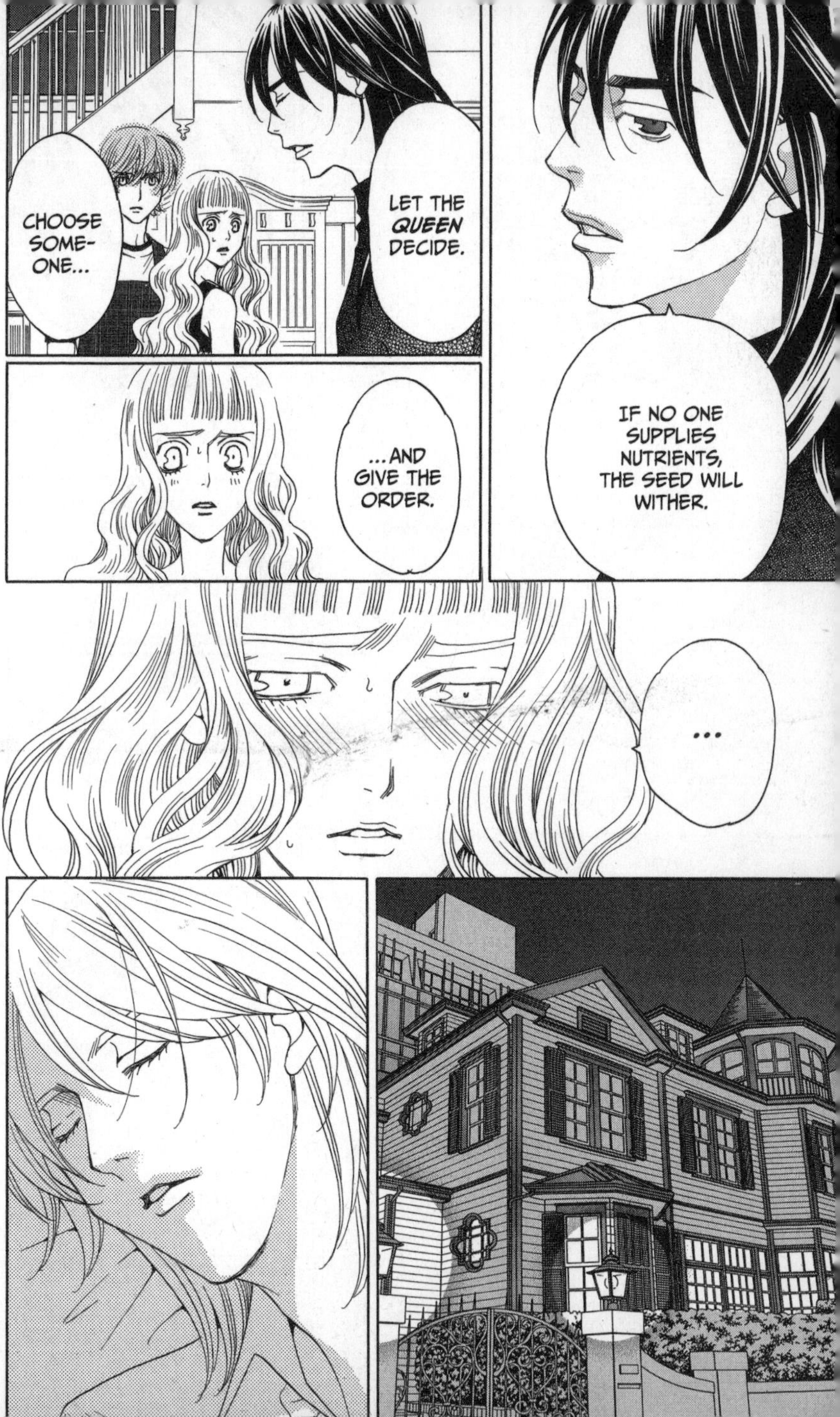
IF NO ONE SUPPLIES NUTRIENTS, THE SEED WILL WITHER.
LET THE *QUEEN* DECIDE.
CHOOSE SOME-ONE...
...AND GIVE THE ORDER.
...

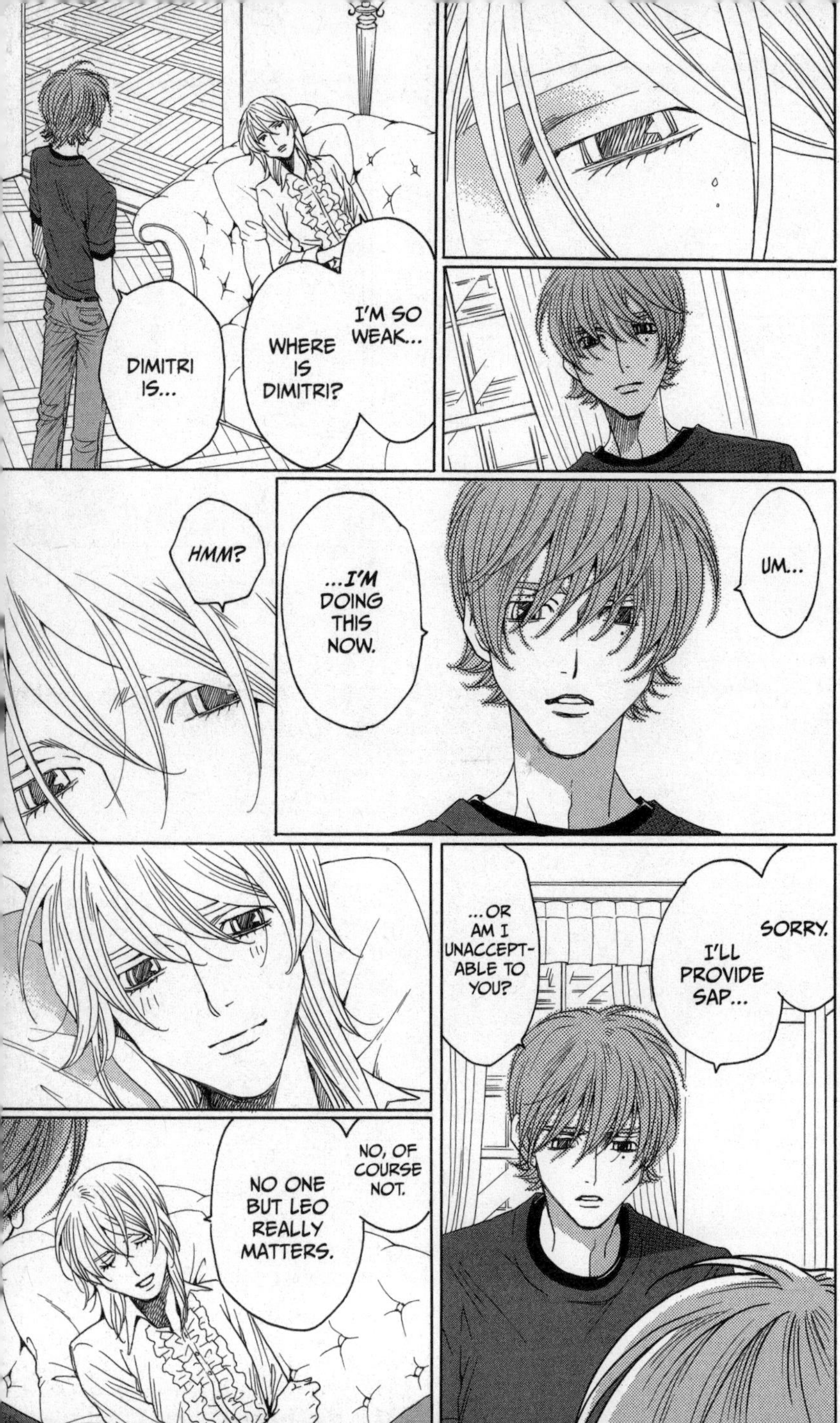
I'M SO WEAK...
WHERE IS DIMITRI?
DIMITRI IS...
UM...
...I'M DOING THIS NOW.
HMM?
SORRY. I'LL PROVIDE SAP...
...OR AM I UNACCEPTABLE TO YOU?
NO, OF COURSE NOT.
NO ONE BUT LEO REALLY MATTERS.

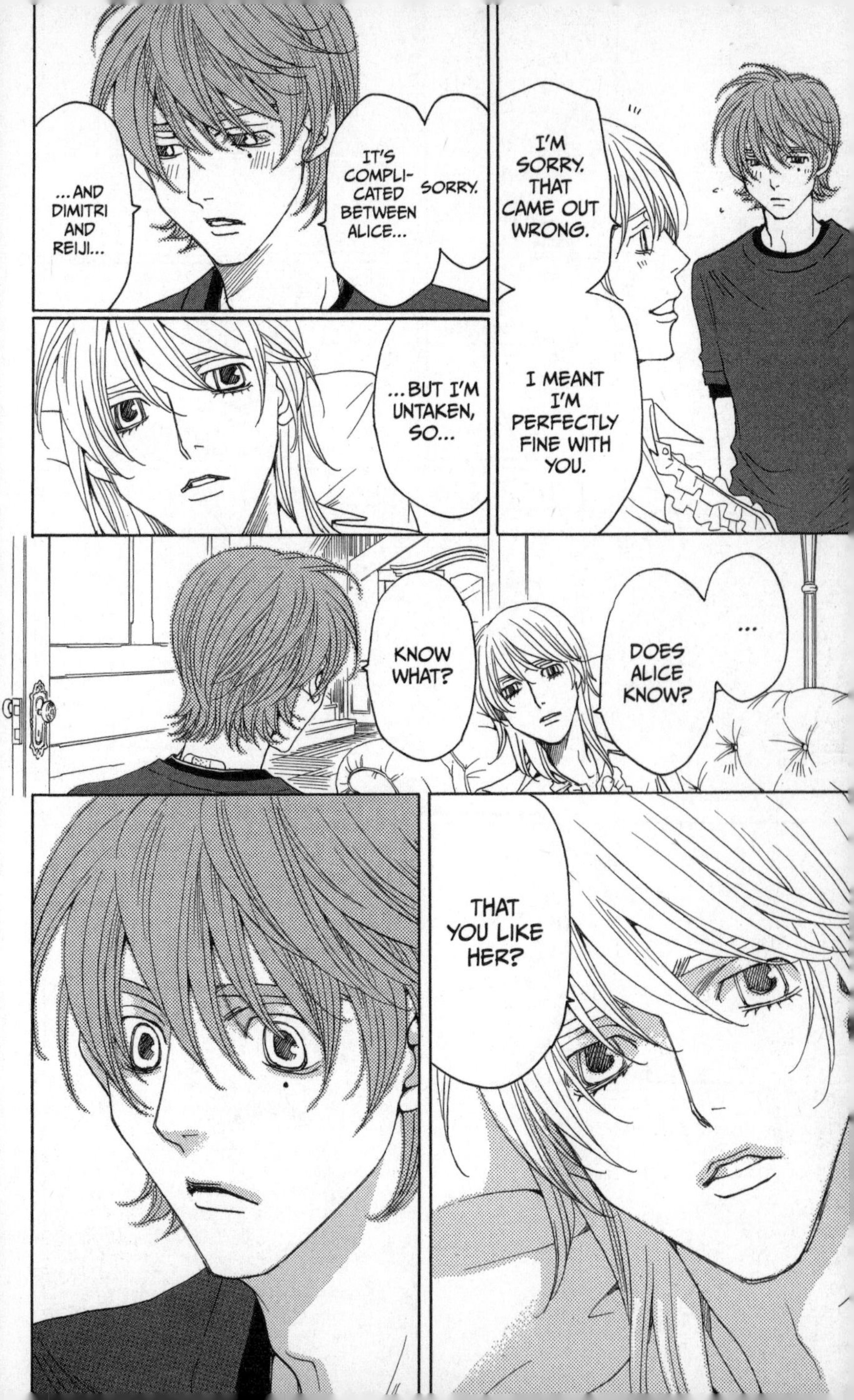
I'M SORRY. THAT CAME OUT WRONG.
I MEANT I'M PERFECTLY FINE WITH YOU.
IT'S COMPLICATED BETWEEN ALICE...
SORRY.
...AND DIMITRI AND REIJI...
...BUT I'M UNTAKEN, SO...
...
DOES ALICE KNOW?
KNOW WHAT?
THAT YOU LIKE HER?

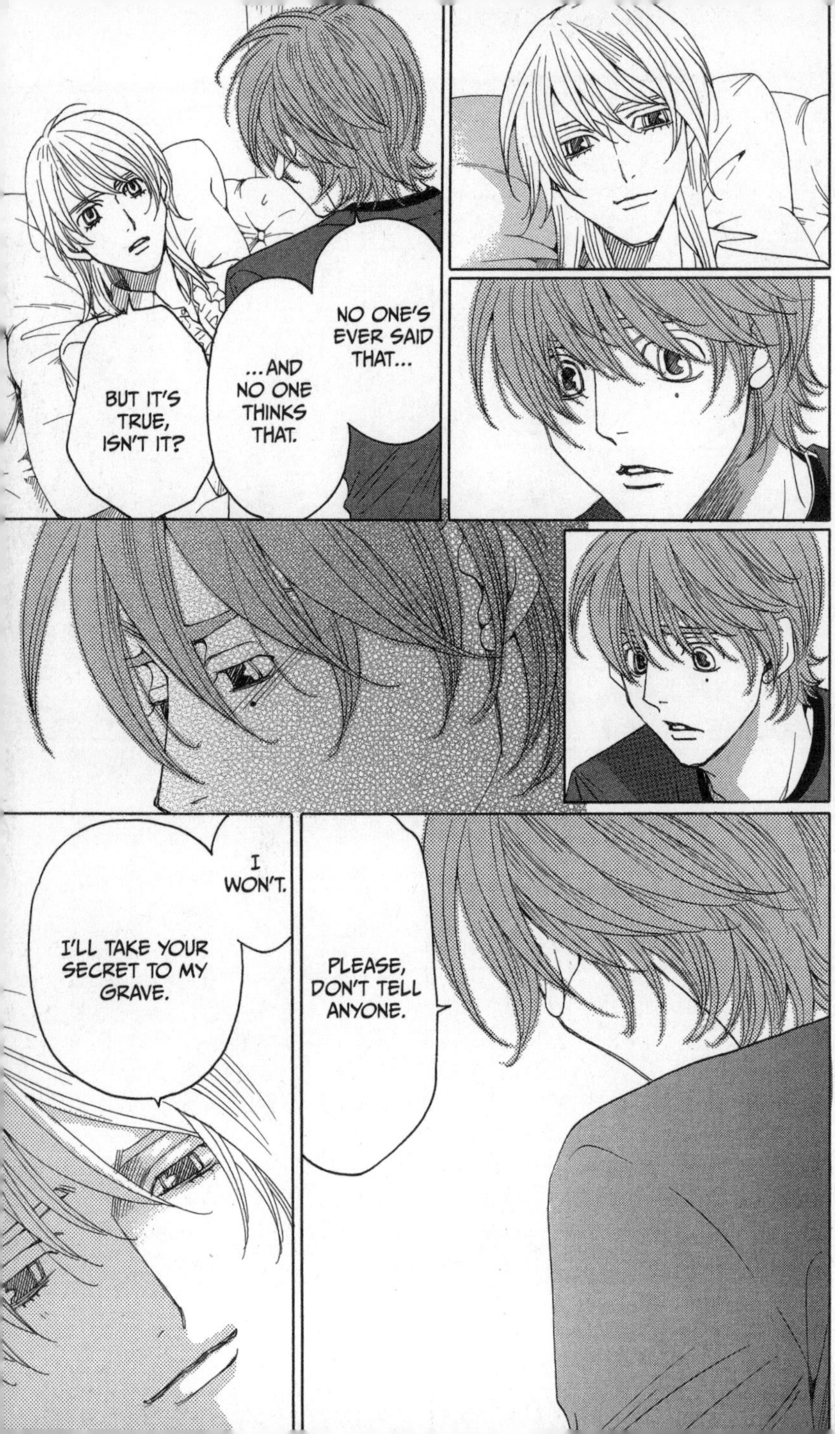
NO ONE'S EVER SAID THAT...
...AND NO ONE THINKS THAT.
BUT IT'S TRUE, ISN'T IT?
PLEASE, DON'T TELL ANYONE.
I WON'T.
I'LL TAKE YOUR SECRET TO MY GRAVE.

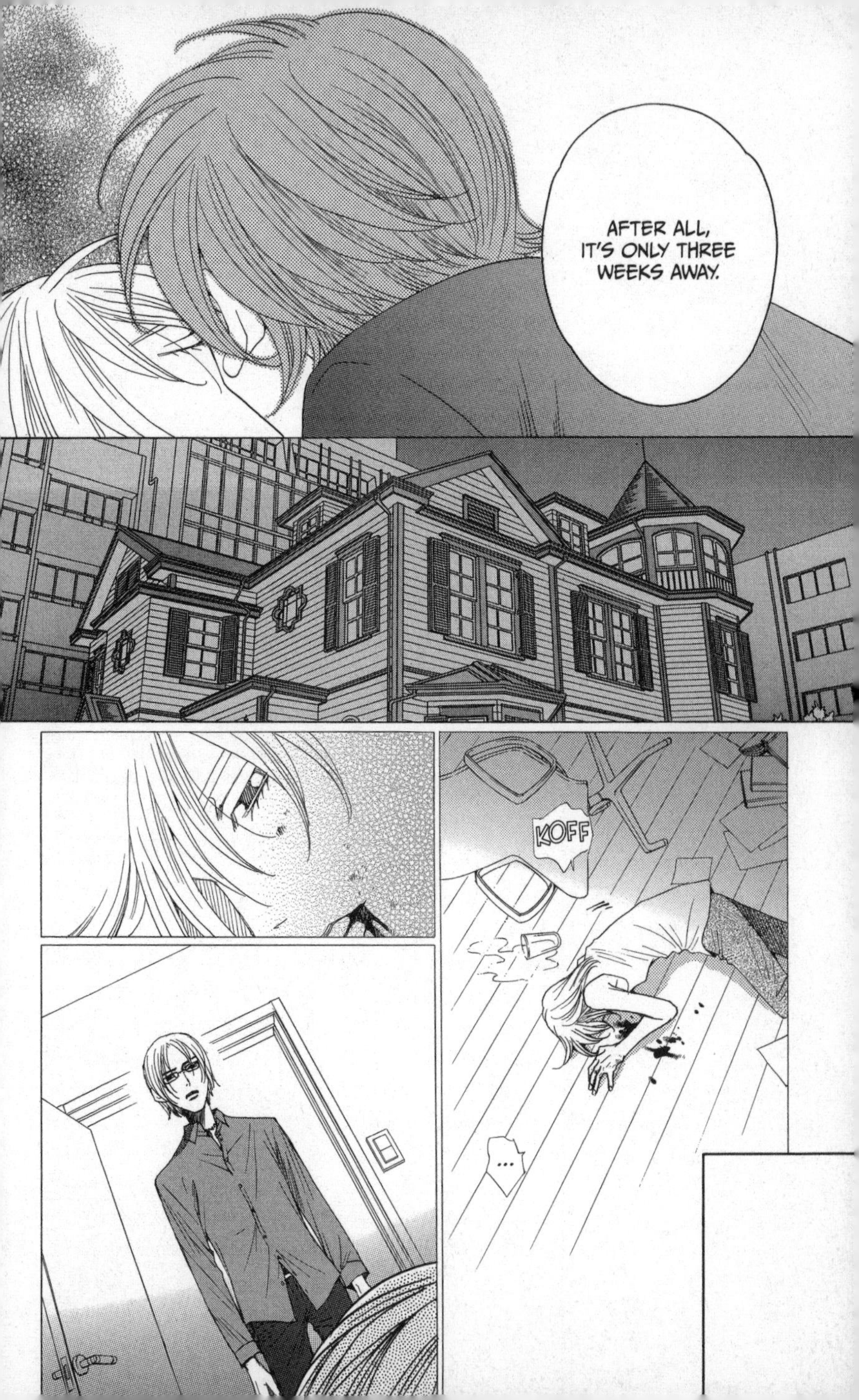
AFTER ALL, IT'S ONLY THREE WEEKS AWAY.
KOFF
...

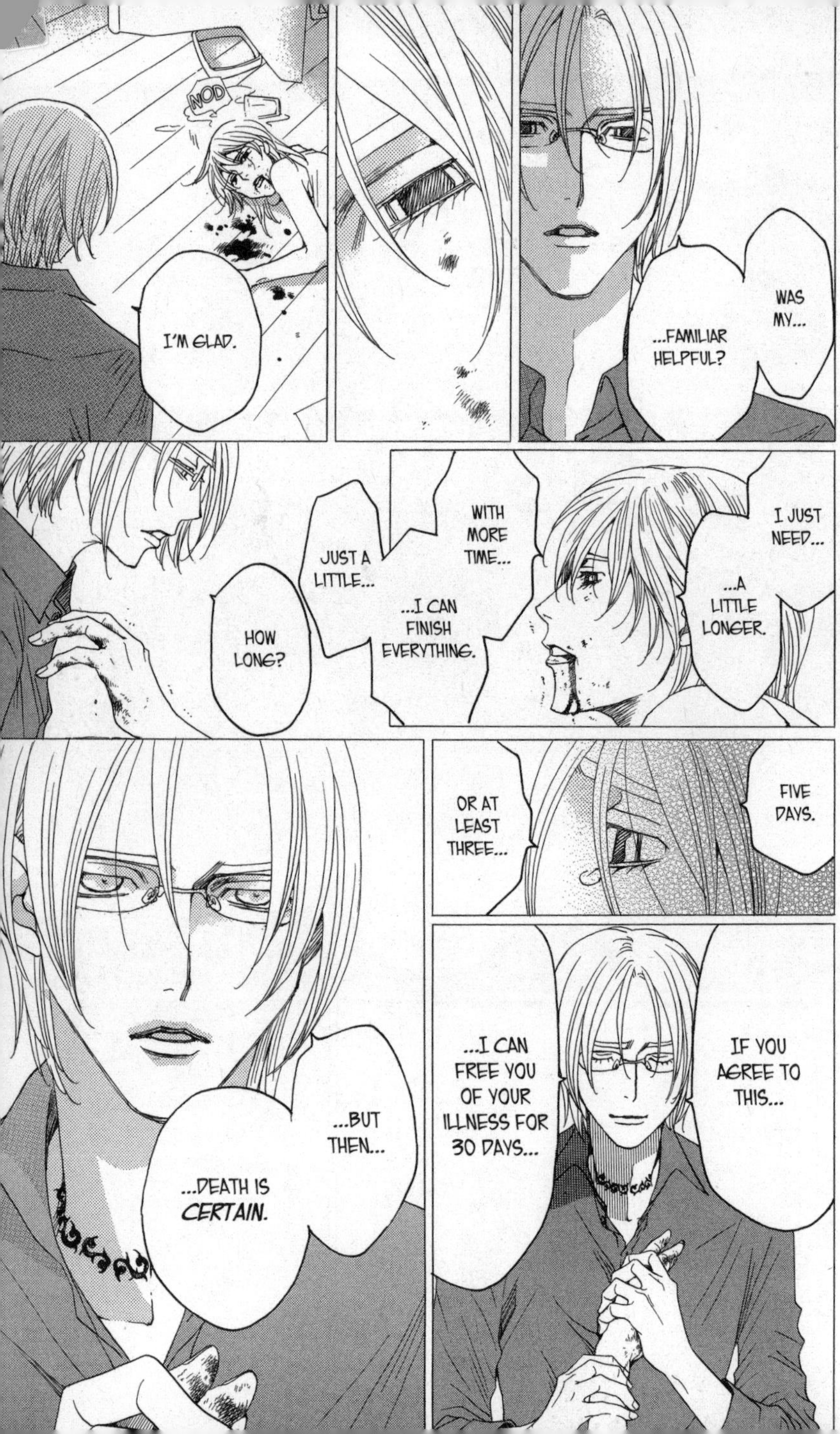
WAS MY...
...FAMILIAR HELPFUL?
NOD
I'M GLAD.
I JUST NEED...
...A LITTLE LONGER.
WITH MORE TIME...
...I CAN FINISH EVERYTHING.
JUST A LITTLE...
HOW LONG?
FIVE DAYS.
OR AT LEAST THREE...
IF YOU AGREE TO THIS...
...I CAN FREE YOU OF YOUR ILLNESS FOR 30 DAYS...
...BUT THEN...
...DEATH IS CERTAIN.

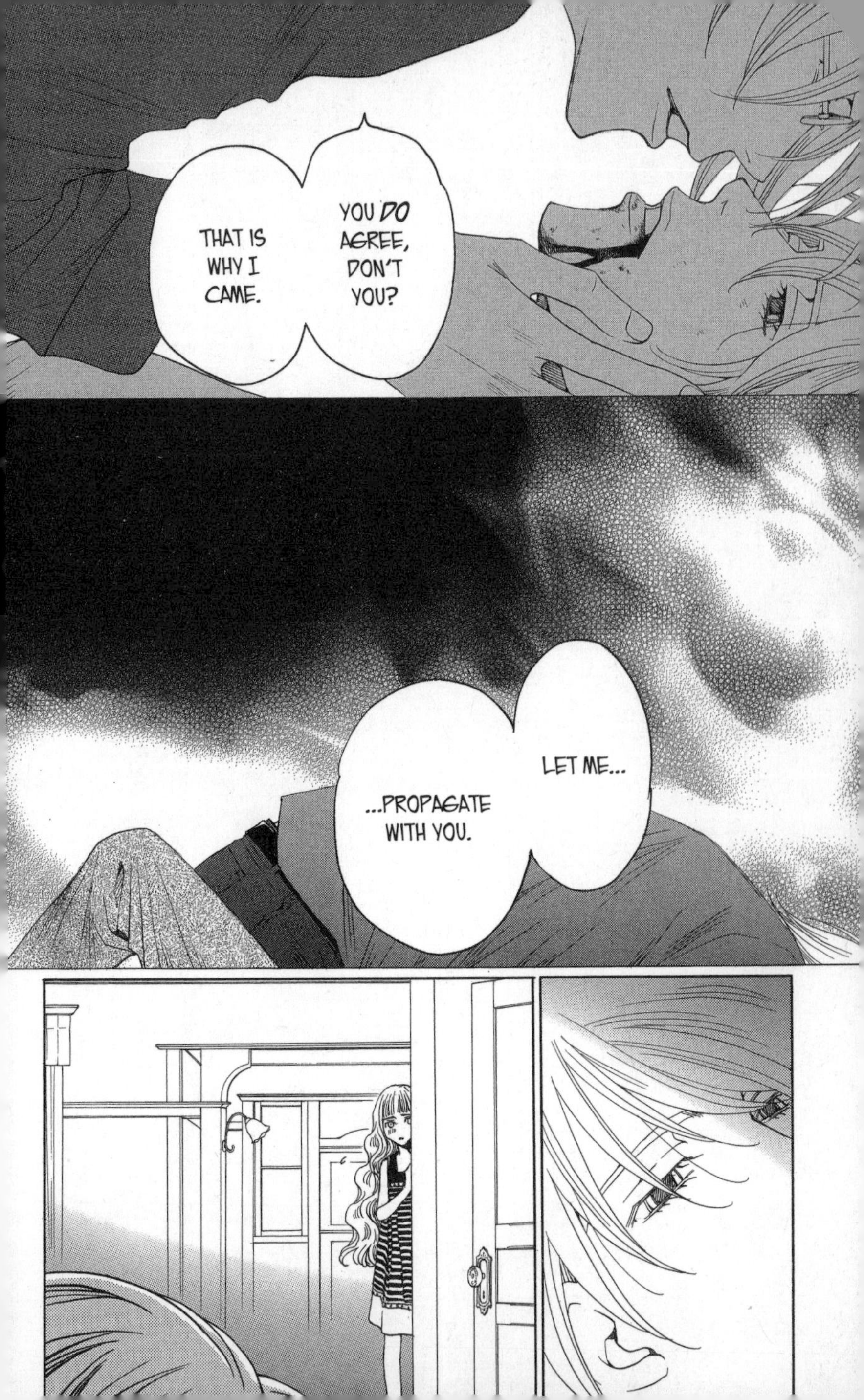
YOU *DO* AGREE, DON'T YOU?
THAT IS WHY I CAME.
LET ME...
...PROPAGATE WITH YOU.

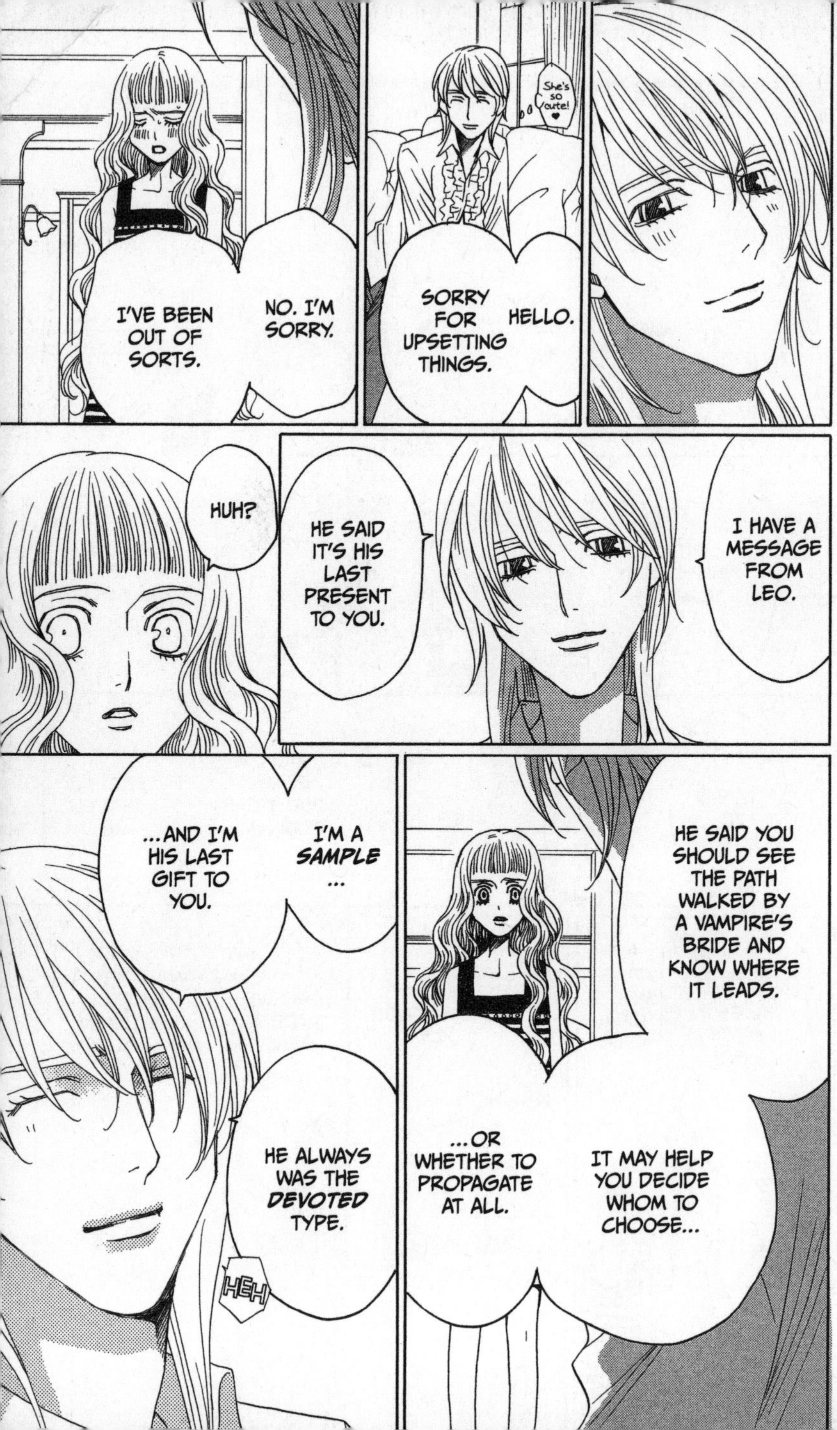
HELLO.
SORRY FOR UPSETTING THINGS.
She's so cute!
NO. I'M SORRY.
I'VE BEEN OUT OF SORTS.
I HAVE A MESSAGE FROM LEO.
HE SAID IT'S HIS LAST PRESENT TO YOU.
HUH?
HE SAID YOU SHOULD SEE THE PATH WALKED BY A VAMPIRE'S BRIDE AND KNOW WHERE IT LEADS.
IT MAY HELP YOU DECIDE WHOM TO CHOOSE...
...OR WHETHER TO PROPAGATE AT ALL.
I'M A *SAMPLE* ...
...AND I'M HIS LAST GIFT TO YOU.
HE ALWAYS WAS THE *DEVOTED* TYPE.
HEH

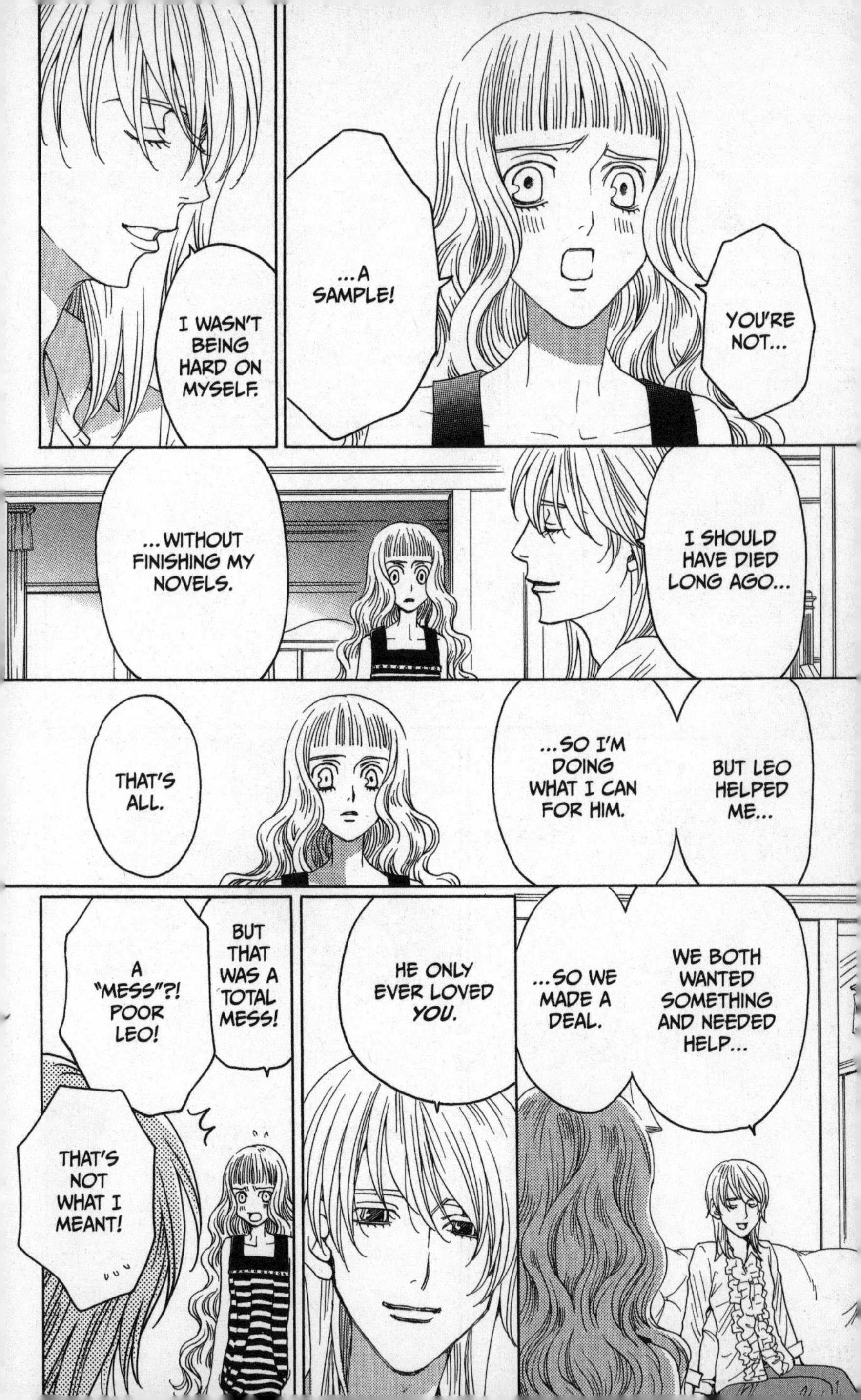
YOU'RE NOT...
...A SAMPLE!
I WASN'T BEING HARD ON MYSELF.
I SHOULD HAVE DIED LONG AGO...
...WITHOUT FINISHING MY NOVELS.
BUT LEO HELPED ME...
...SO I'M DOING WHAT I CAN FOR HIM.
THAT'S ALL.
WE BOTH WANTED SOMETHING AND NEEDED HELP...
...SO WE MADE A DEAL.
HE ONLY EVER LOVED YOU.
BUT THAT WAS A TOTAL MESS!
A "MESS"?! POOR LEO!
THAT'S NOT WHAT I MEANT!

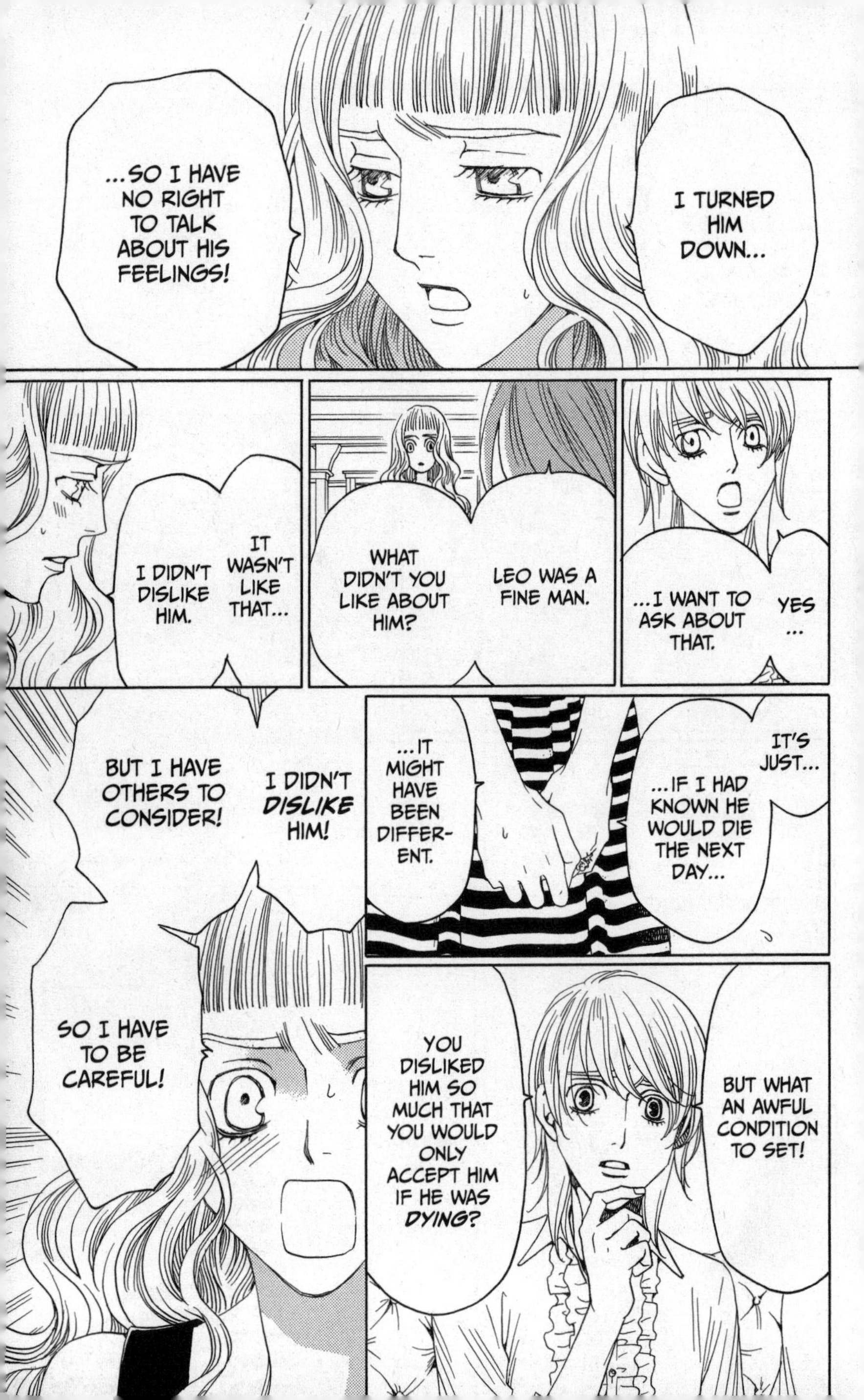
I TURNED HIM DOWN...
...SO I HAVE NO RIGHT TO TALK ABOUT HIS FEELINGS!
YES ...
...I WANT TO ASK ABOUT THAT.
LEO WAS A FINE MAN.
WHAT DIDN'T YOU LIKE ABOUT HIM?
IT WASN'T LIKE THAT...
I DIDN'T DISLIKE HIM.
IT'S JUST...
...IF I HAD KNOWN HE WOULD DIE THE NEXT DAY...
...IT MIGHT HAVE BEEN DIFFER-ENT.
I DIDN'T *DISLIKE* HIM!
BUT I HAVE OTHERS TO CONSIDER!
SO I HAVE TO BE CAREFUL!
BUT WHAT AN AWFUL CONDITION TO SET!
YOU DISLIKED HIM SO MUCH THAT YOU WOULD ONLY ACCEPT HIM IF HE WAS *DYING*?

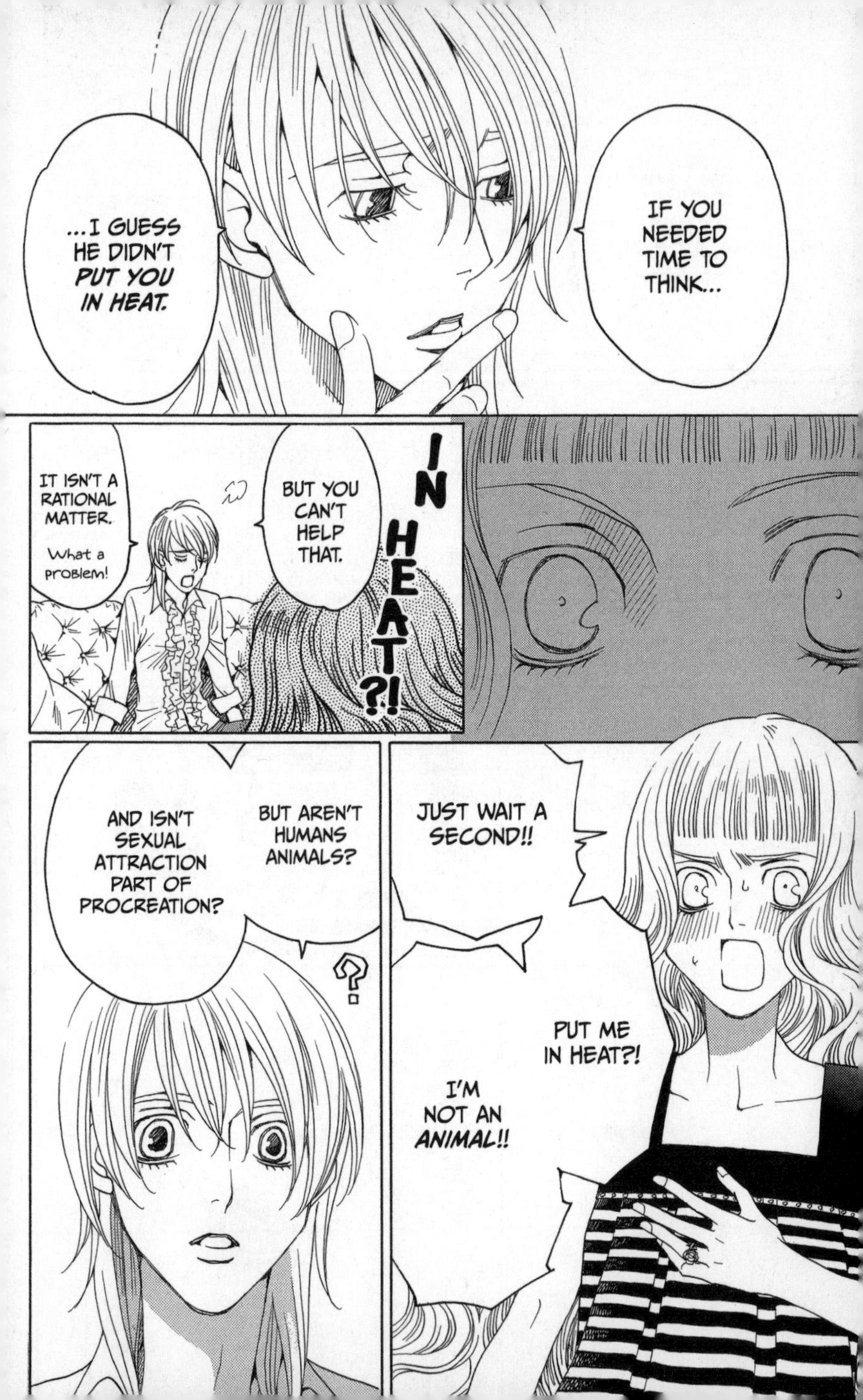
IF YOU NEEDED TIME TO THINK...
...I GUESS HE DIDN'T *PUT YOU IN HEAT.*
IN HEAT?!
BUT YOU CAN'T HELP THAT.
IT ISN'T A RATIONAL MATTER.
What a problem!
JUST WAIT A SECOND!!
PUT ME IN HEAT?!
I'M NOT AN *ANIMAL!!*
BUT AREN'T HUMANS ANIMALS?
AND ISN'T SEXUAL ATTRACTION PART OF PROCREATION?
?

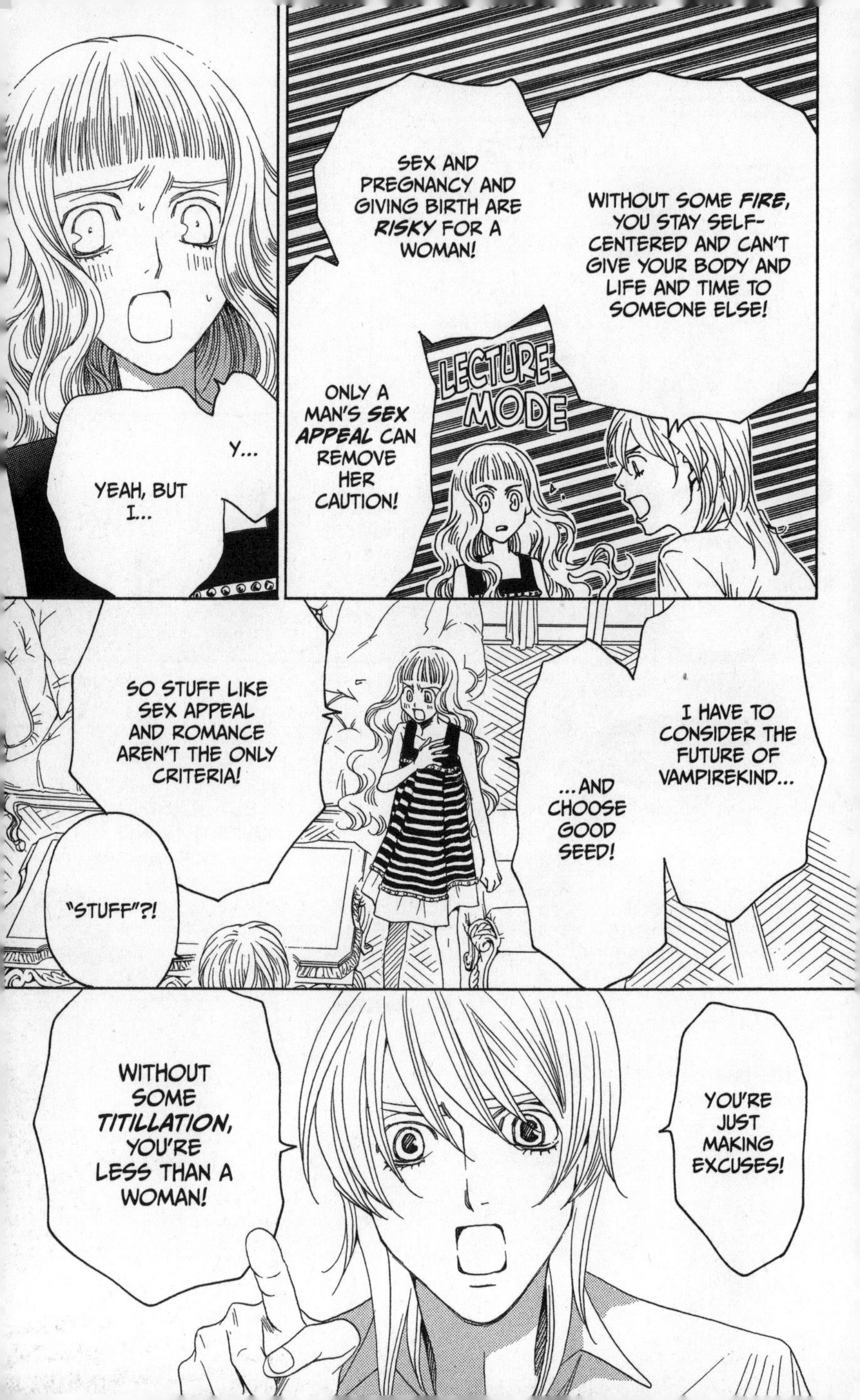
WITHOUT SOME *FIRE*, YOU STAY SELF-CENTERED AND CAN'T GIVE YOUR BODY AND LIFE AND TIME TO SOMEONE ELSE!
SEX AND PREGNANCY AND GIVING BIRTH ARE *RISKY* FOR A WOMAN!
LECTURE MODE
ONLY A MAN'S *SEX APPEAL* CAN REMOVE HER CAUTION!
Y...
YEAH, BUT I...
I HAVE TO CONSIDER THE FUTURE OF VAMPIREKIND...
...AND CHOOSE GOOD SEED!
SO STUFF LIKE SEX APPEAL AND ROMANCE AREN'T THE ONLY CRITERIA!
"STUFF"?!
YOU'RE JUST MAKING EXCUSES!
WITHOUT SOME *TITILLATION*, YOU'RE LESS THAN A WOMAN!

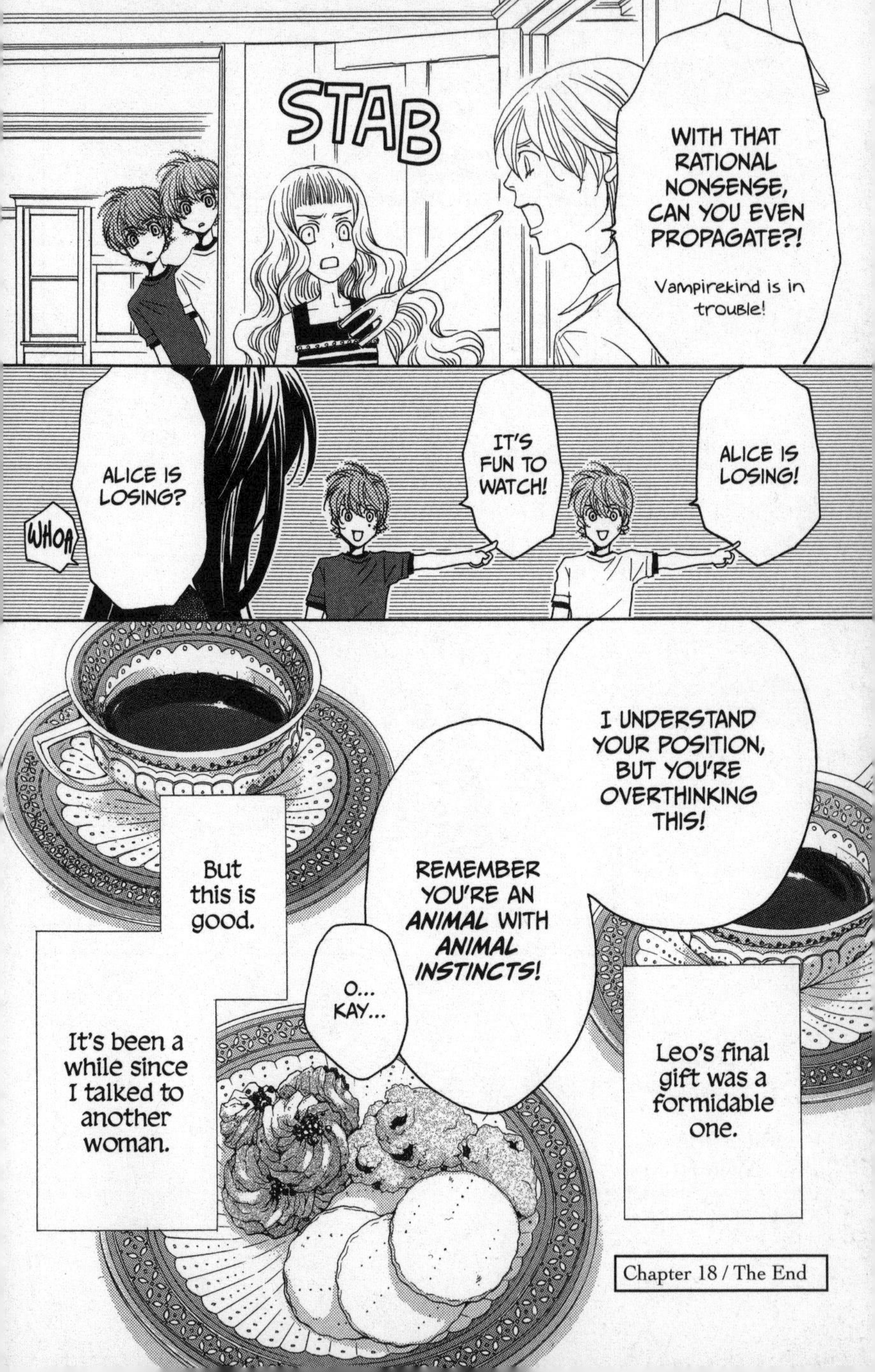
WITH THAT RATIONAL NONSENSE, CAN YOU EVEN PROPAGATE?!
Vampirekind is in trouble!
STAB
ALICE IS LOSING!
IT'S FUN TO WATCH!
ALICE IS LOSING?
WHOA
I UNDERSTAND YOUR POSITION, BUT YOU'RE OVERTHINKING THIS!
REMEMBER YOU'RE AN *ANIMAL* WITH *ANIMAL INSTINCTS!*
O... KAY...
Leo's final gift was a formidable one.
It's been a while since I talked to another woman.
But this is good.
Chapter 18 / The End

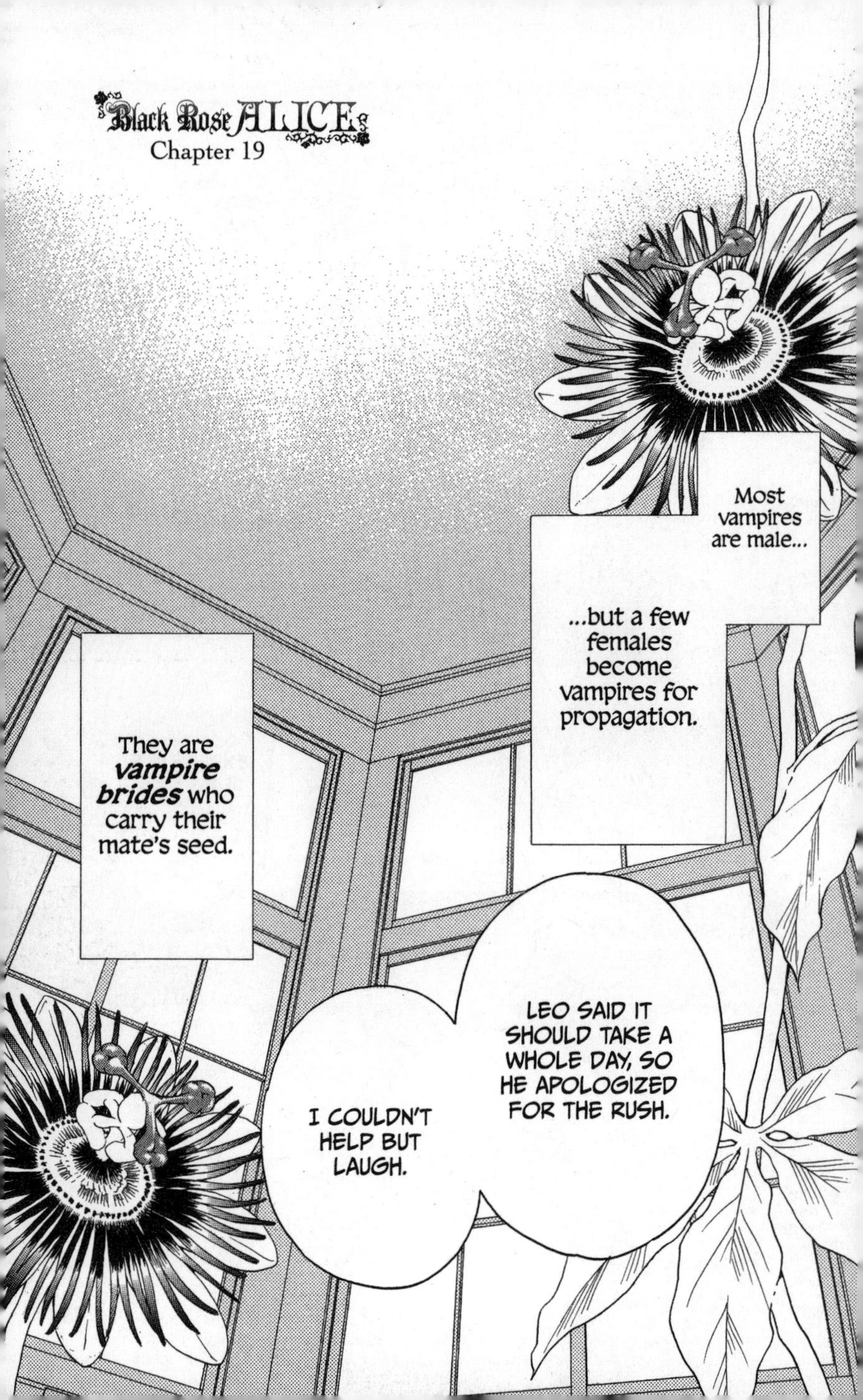
Black Rose ALICE
Chapter 19
Most vampires are male...
...but a few females become vampires for propagation.
They are ***vampire brides*** who carry their mate's seed.
LEO SAID IT SHOULD TAKE A WHOLE DAY, SO HE APOLOGIZED FOR THE RUSH.
I COULDN'T HELP BUT LAUGH.

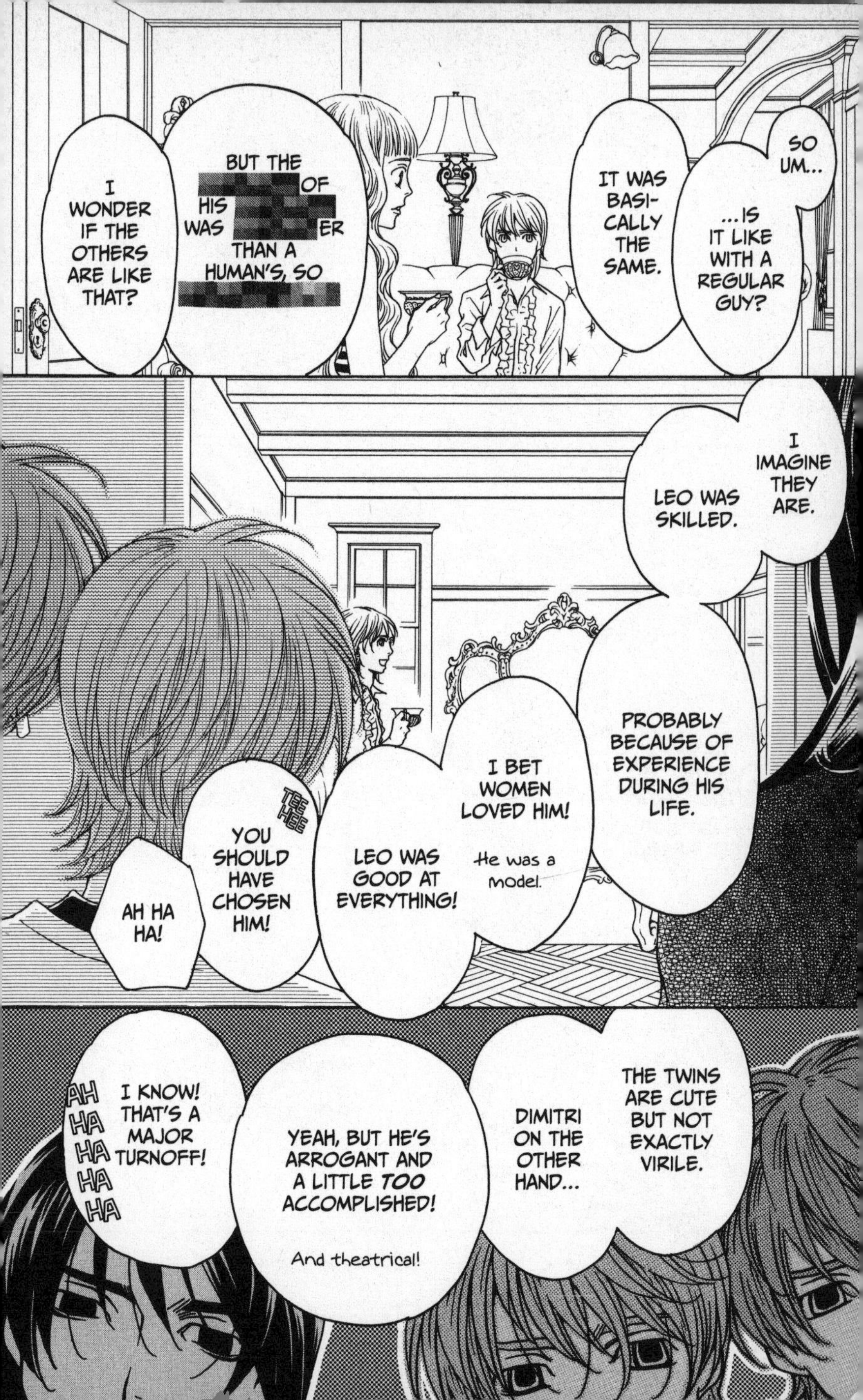
SO UM...
...IS IT LIKE WITH A REGULAR GUY?
IT WAS BASICALLY THE SAME.
BUT THE [redacted] OF HIS [redacted] WAS [redacted]ER THAN A HUMAN'S, SO [redacted]
I WONDER IF THE OTHERS ARE LIKE THAT?
I IMAGINE THEY ARE.
LEO WAS SKILLED.
PROBABLY BECAUSE OF EXPERIENCE DURING HIS LIFE.
I BET WOMEN LOVED HIM!
He was a model.
LEO WAS GOOD AT EVERYTHING!
TEE HEE
YOU SHOULD HAVE CHOSEN HIM!
AH HA HA!
THE TWINS ARE CUTE BUT NOT EXACTLY VIRILE.
DIMITRI ON THE OTHER HAND...
YEAH, BUT HE'S ARROGANT AND A LITTLE *TOO* ACCOMPLISHED!
And theatrical!
I KNOW! THAT'S A MAJOR TURNOFF!
AH HA HA HA HA

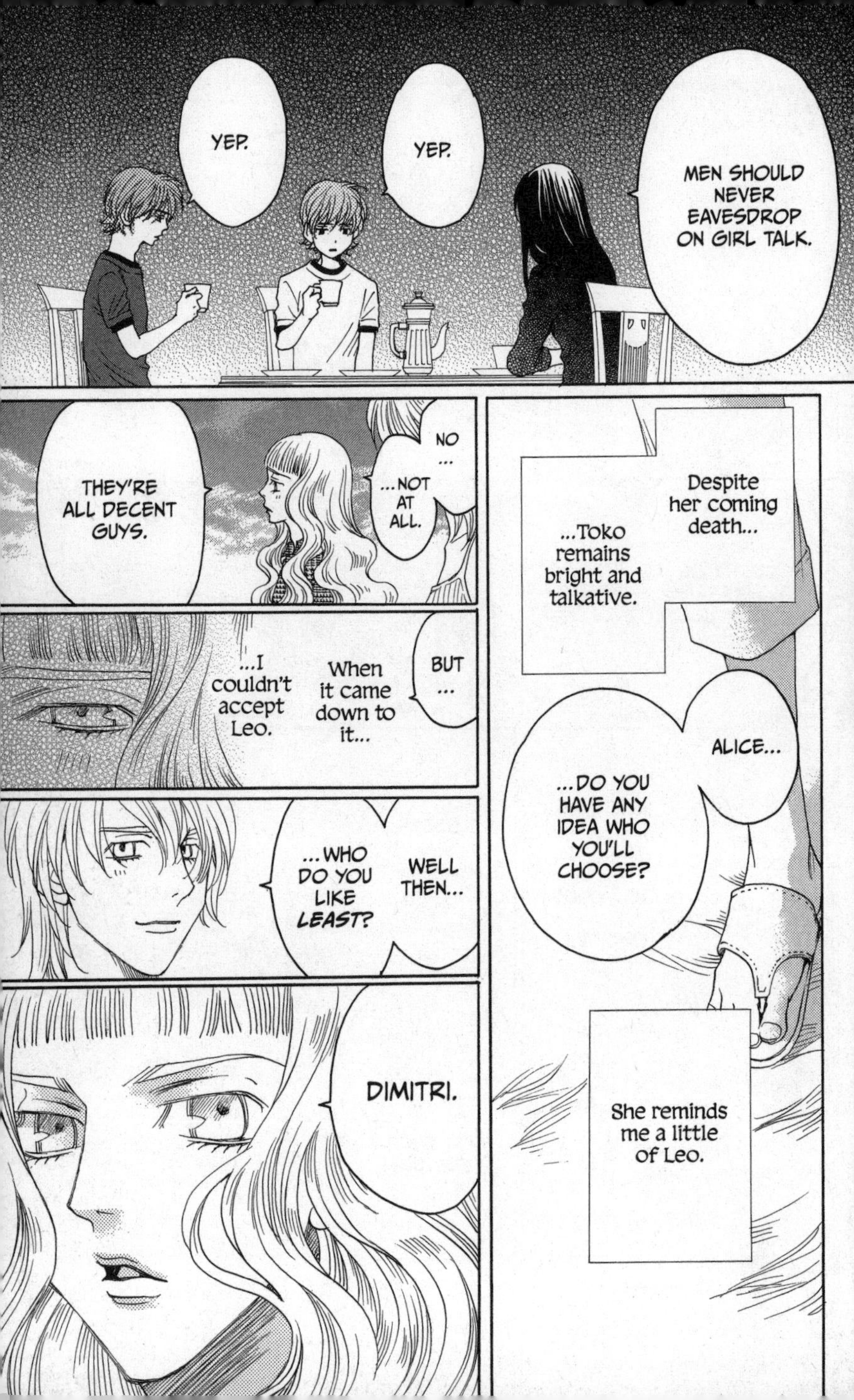
MEN SHOULD NEVER EAVESDROP ON GIRL TALK.
YEP.
YEP.
Despite her coming death...
...Toko remains bright and talkative.
ALICE...
...DO YOU HAVE ANY IDEA WHO YOU'LL CHOOSE?
She reminds me a little of Leo.
NO...
...NOT AT ALL.
THEY'RE ALL DECENT GUYS.
BUT...
When it came down to it...
...I couldn't accept Leo.
WELL THEN...
...WHO DO YOU LIKE *LEAST*?
DIMITRI.

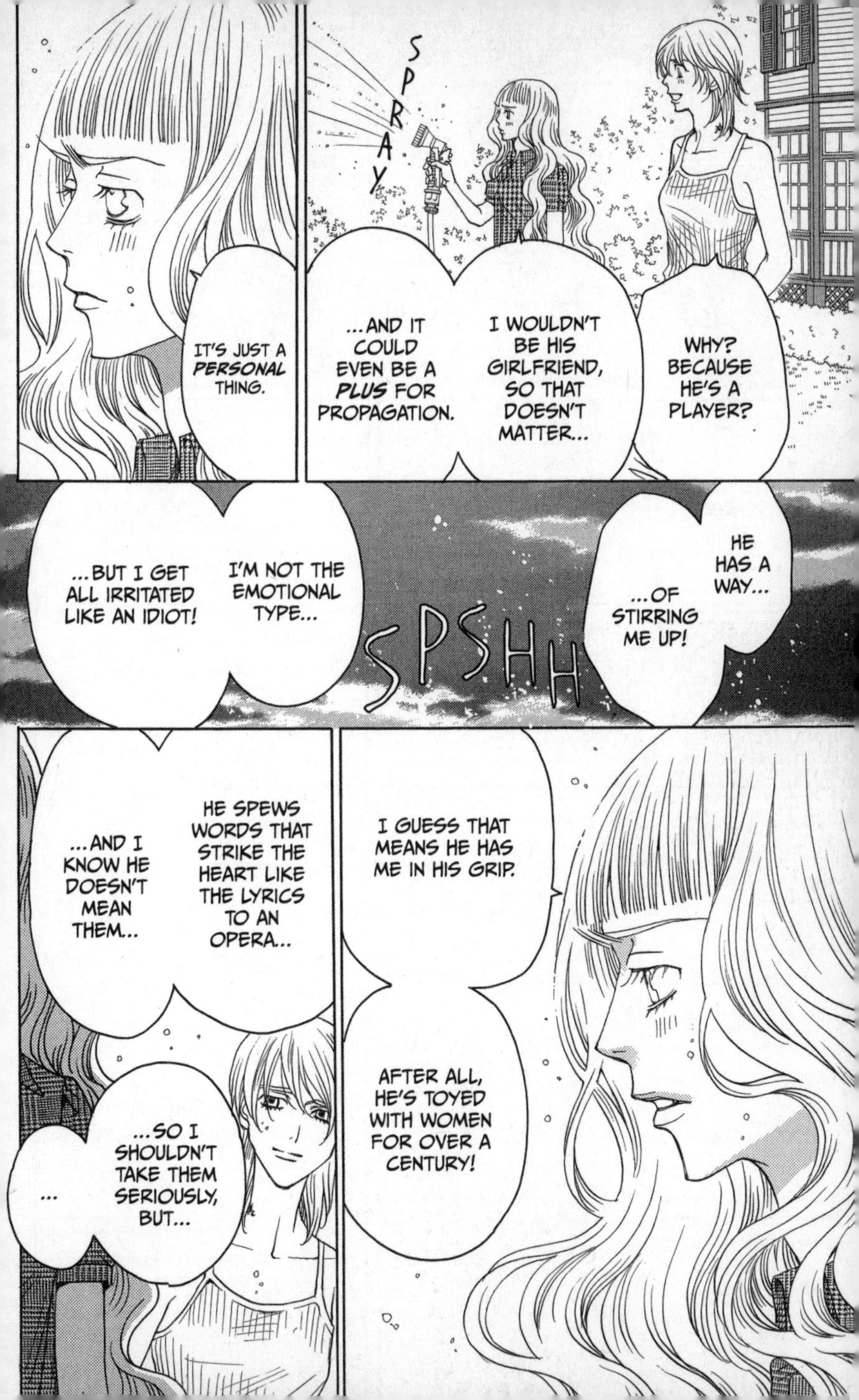
SPRAY
WHY? BECAUSE HE'S A PLAYER?
I WOULDN'T BE HIS GIRLFRIEND, SO THAT DOESN'T MATTER...
...AND IT COULD EVEN BE A *PLUS* FOR PROPAGATION.
IT'S JUST A *PERSONAL* THING.
HE HAS A WAY...
...OF STIRRING ME UP!
SPSHH
I'M NOT THE EMOTIONAL TYPE...
...BUT I GET ALL IRRITATED LIKE AN IDIOT!
I GUESS THAT MEANS HE HAS ME IN HIS GRIP.
AFTER ALL, HE'S TOYED WITH WOMEN FOR OVER A CENTURY!
HE SPEWS WORDS THAT STRIKE THE HEART LIKE THE LYRICS TO AN OPERA...
...AND I KNOW HE DOESN'T MEAN THEM...
...SO I SHOULDN'T TAKE THEM SERIOUSLY, BUT...
...

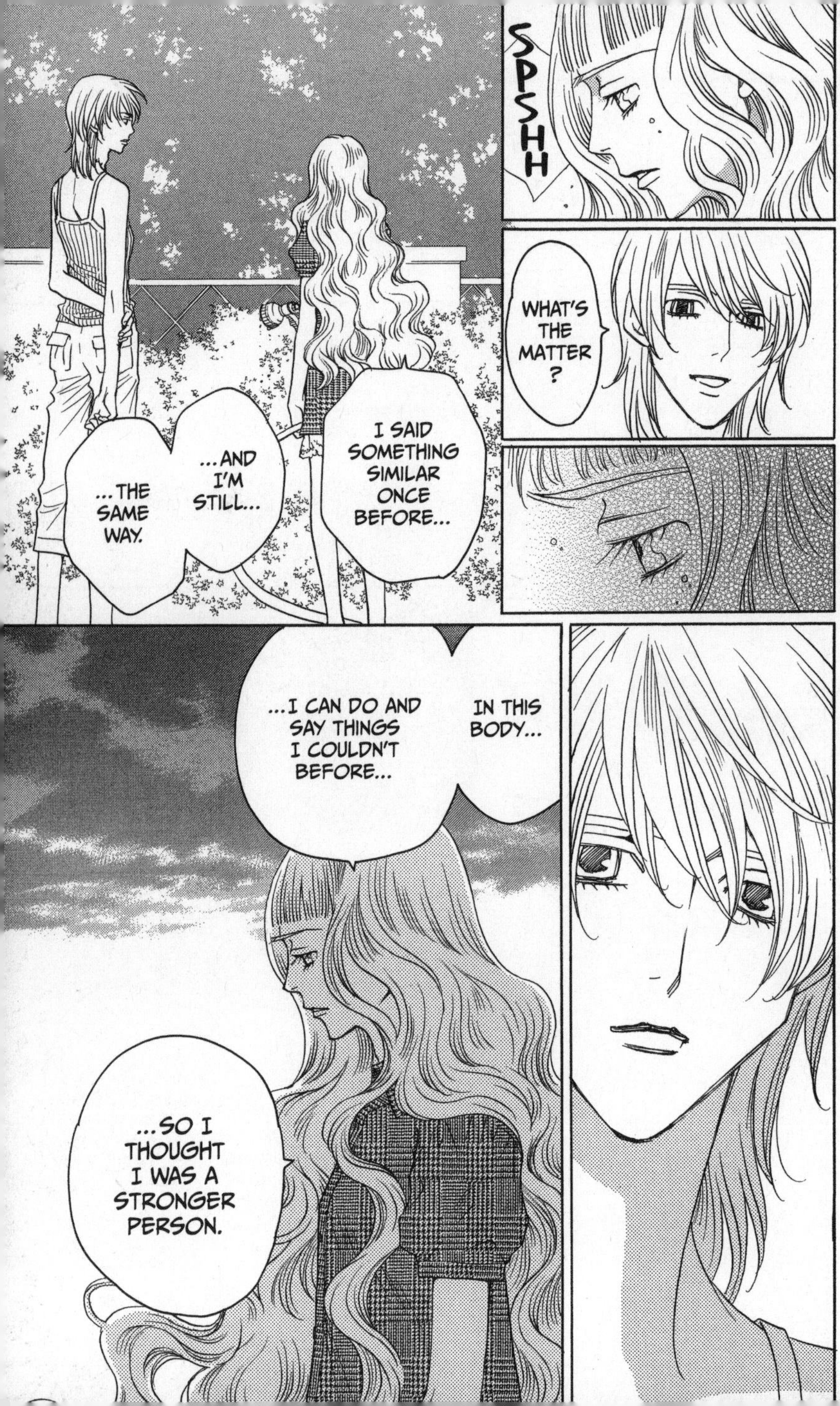
SPSHH
WHAT'S THE MATTER ?
I SAID SOMETHING SIMILAR ONCE BEFORE...
...AND I'M STILL...
...THE SAME WAY.
...I CAN DO AND SAY THINGS I COULDN'T BEFORE...
IN THIS BODY...
...SO I THOUGHT I WAS A STRONGER PERSON.

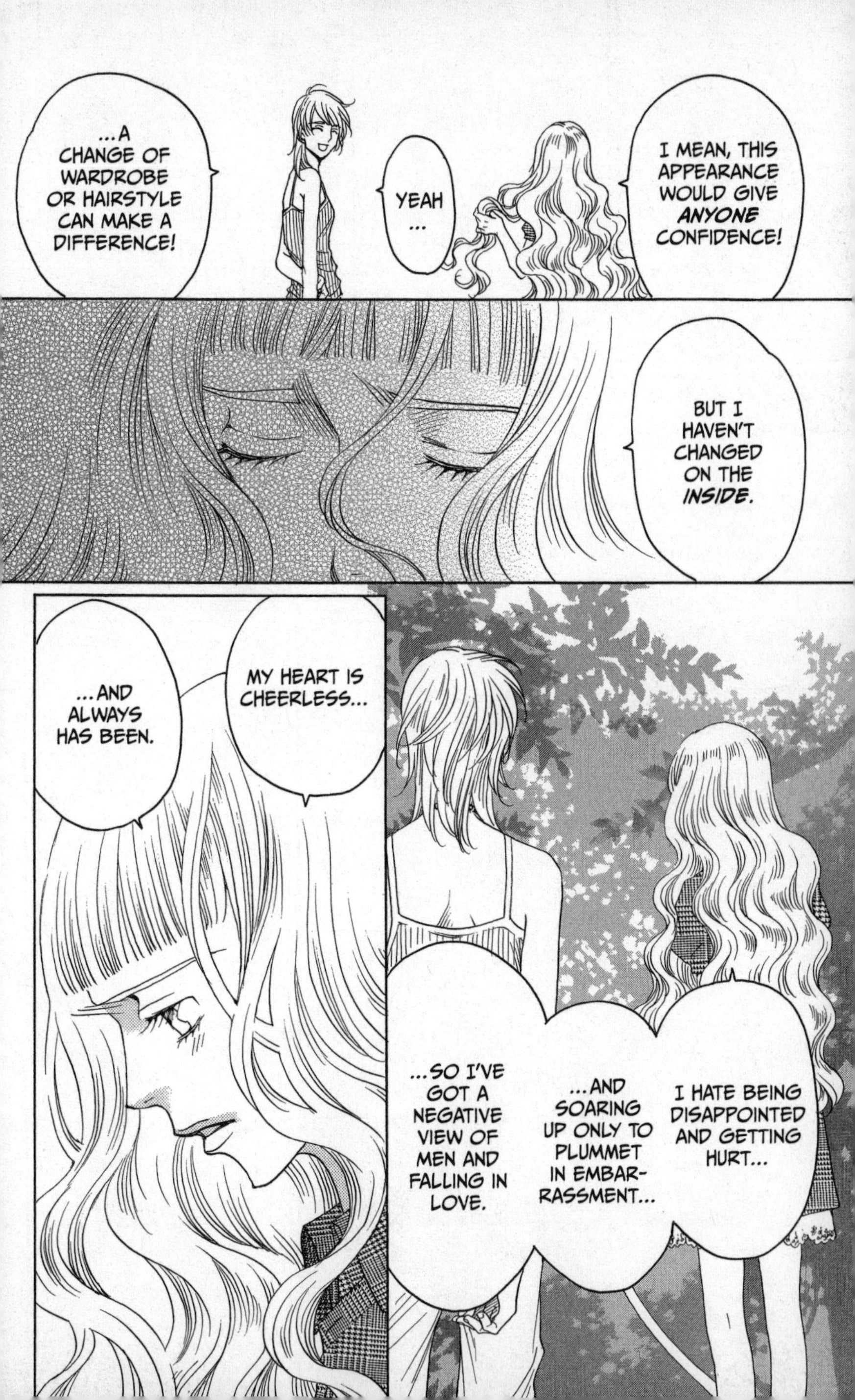
I MEAN, THIS APPEARANCE WOULD GIVE ***ANYONE*** CONFIDENCE!
YEAH ...
...A CHANGE OF WARDROBE OR HAIRSTYLE CAN MAKE A DIFFERENCE!
BUT I HAVEN'T CHANGED ON THE ***INSIDE***.
I HATE BEING DISAPPOINTED AND GETTING HURT...
...AND SOARING UP ONLY TO PLUMMET IN EMBARRASSMENT...
...SO I'VE GOT A NEGATIVE VIEW OF MEN AND FALLING IN LOVE.
MY HEART IS CHEERLESS...
...AND ALWAYS HAS BEEN.

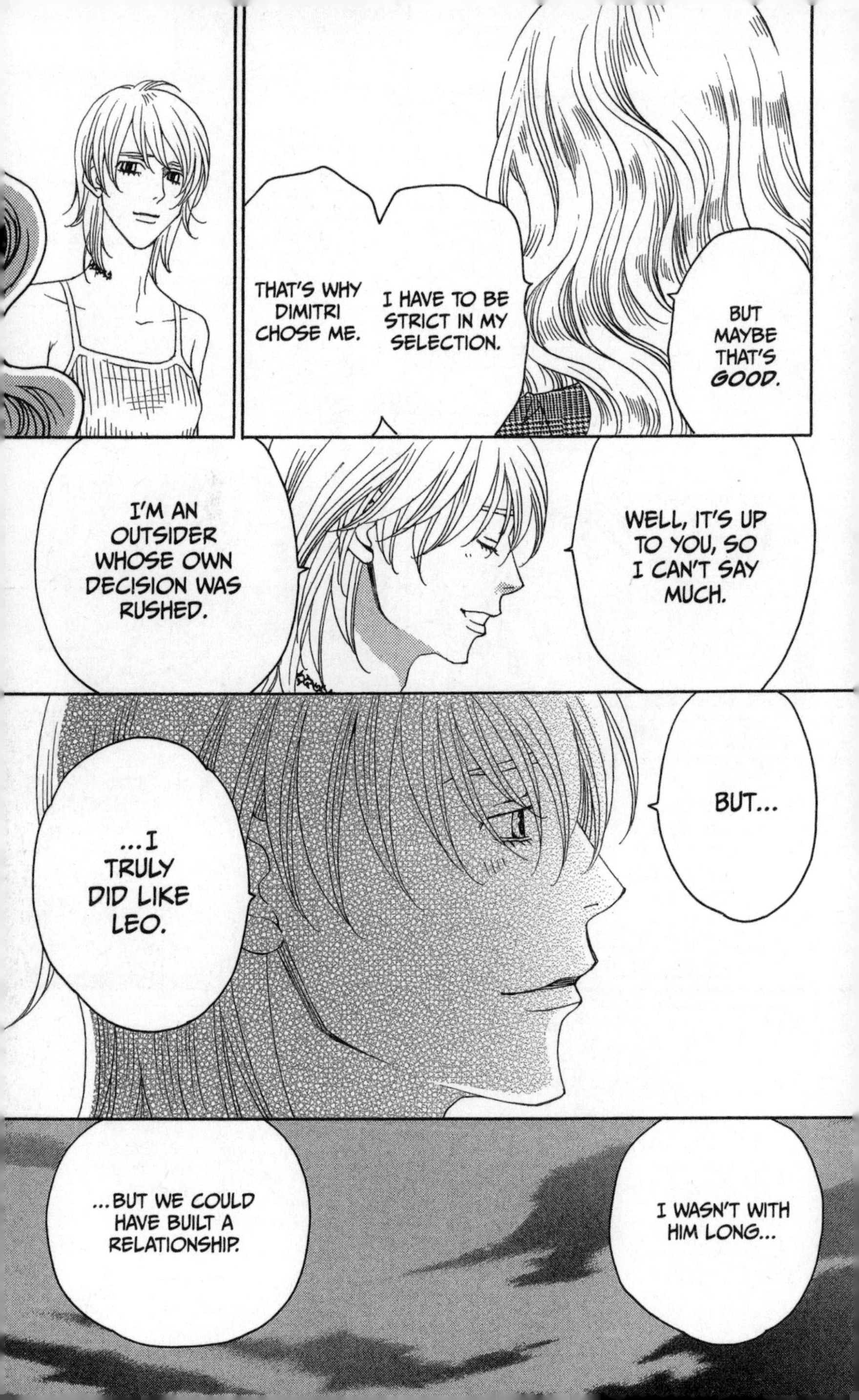
BUT MAYBE THAT'S *GOOD*.
THAT'S WHY DIMITRI CHOSE ME.
I HAVE TO BE STRICT IN MY SELECTION.
WELL, IT'S UP TO YOU, SO I CAN'T SAY MUCH.
I'M AN OUTSIDER WHOSE OWN DECISION WAS RUSHED.
BUT...
...I TRULY DID LIKE LEO.
I WASN'T WITH HIM LONG...
...BUT WE COULD HAVE BUILT A RELATIONSHIP.

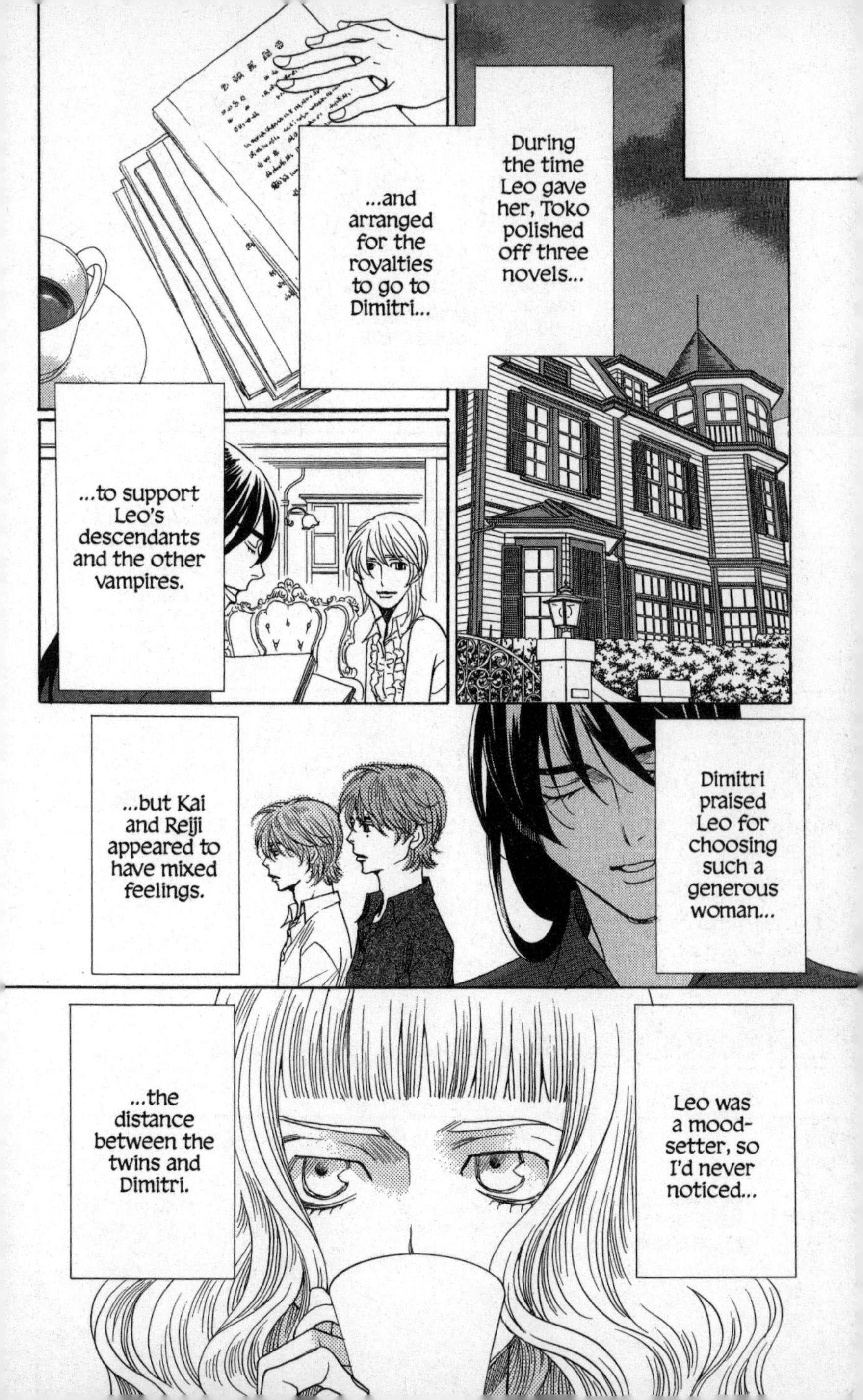
During the time Leo gave her, Toko polished off three novels...
...and arranged for the royalties to go to Dimitri...
...to support Leo's descendants and the other vampires.
Dimitri praised Leo for choosing such a generous woman...
...but Kai and Reiji appeared to have mixed feelings.
Leo was a mood-setter, so I'd never noticed...
...the distance between the twins and Dimitri.

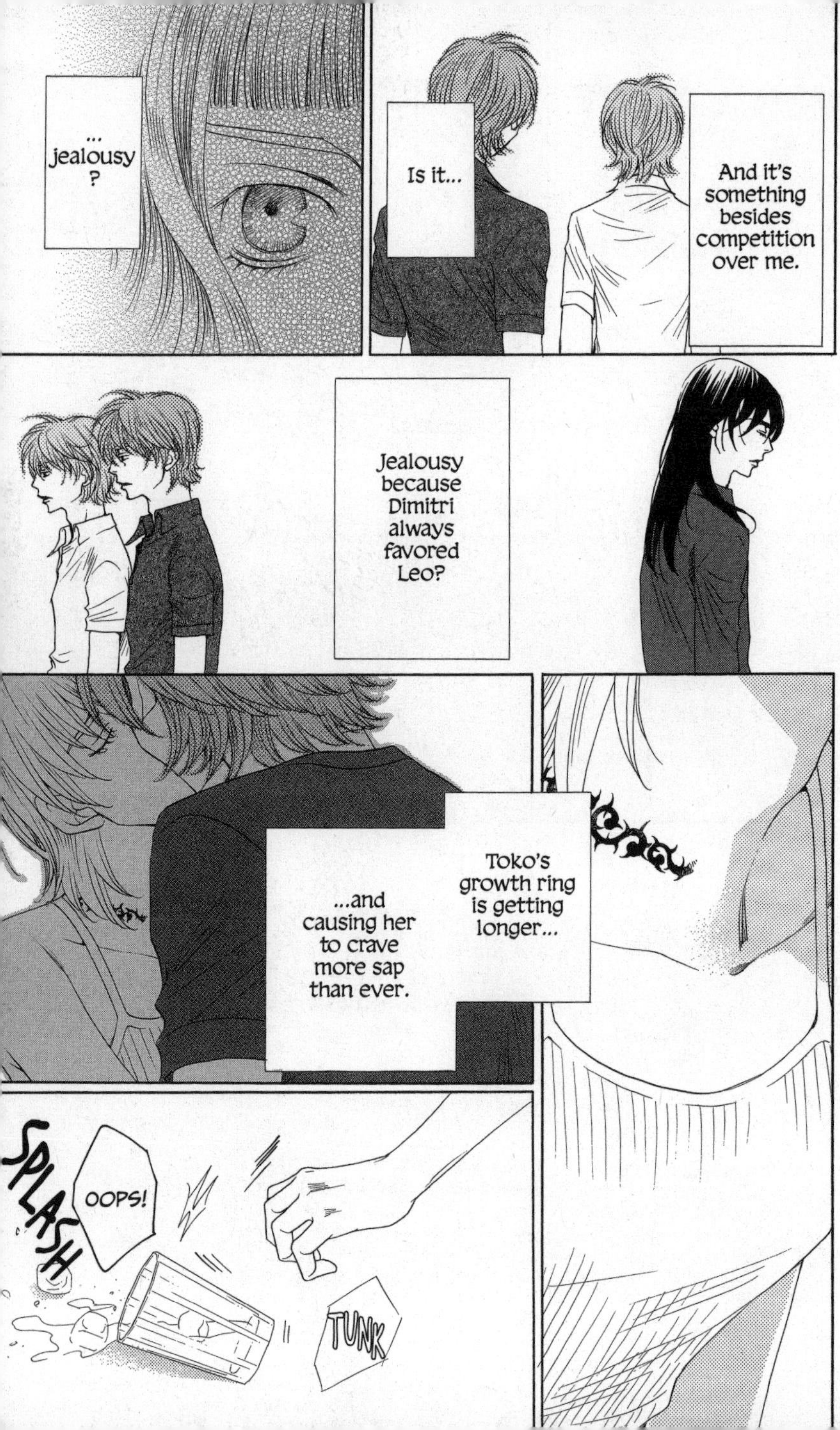
And it's something besides competition over me.
Is it...
...jealousy?
Jealousy because Dimitri always favored Leo?
Toko's growth ring is getting longer...
...and causing her to crave more sap than ever.
TUNK
OOPS!
SPLASH

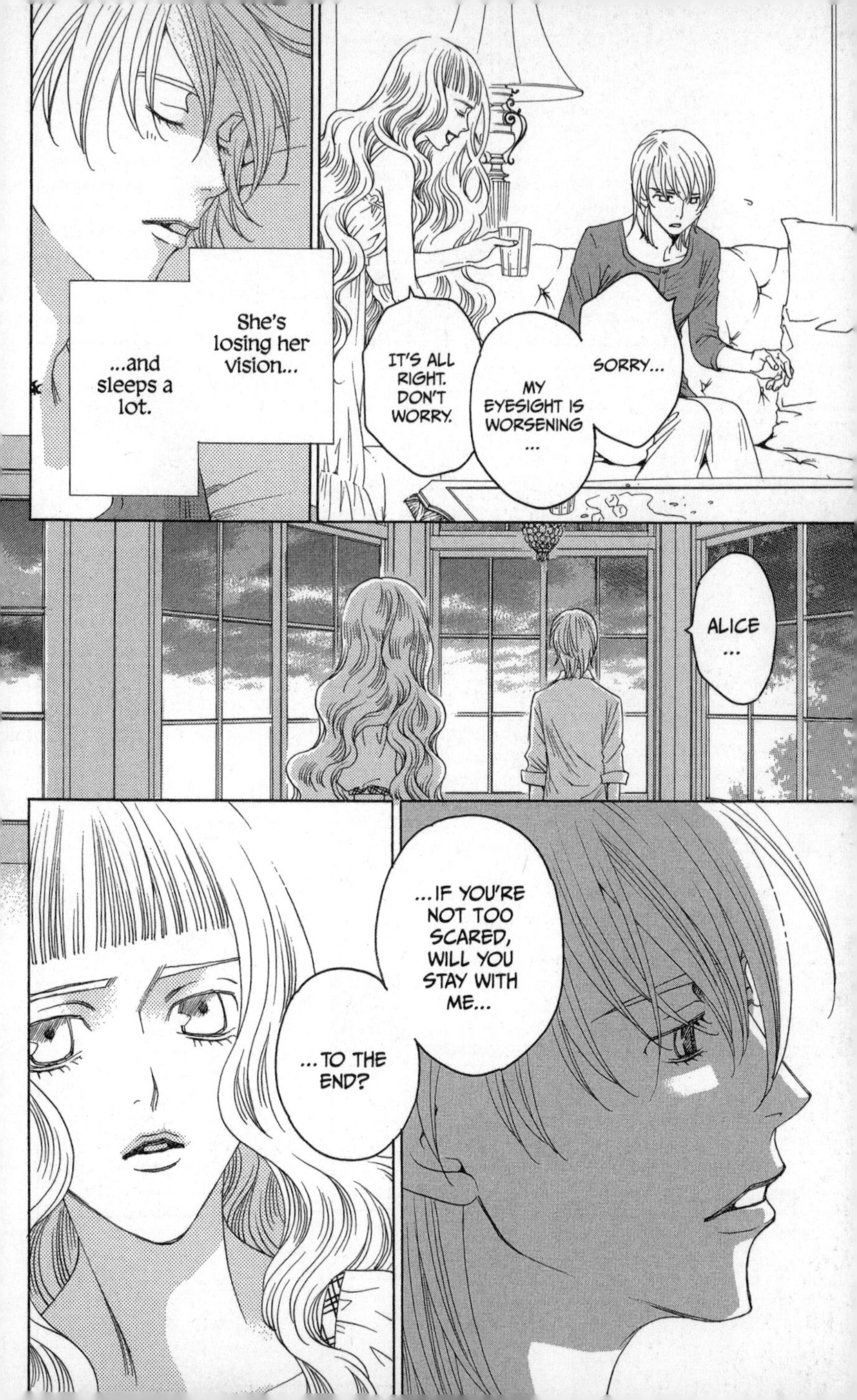
SORRY...
MY EYESIGHT IS WORSENING ...
IT'S ALL RIGHT. DON'T WORRY.
She's losing her vision...
...and sleeps a lot.
ALICE ...
...IF YOU'RE NOT TOO SCARED, WILL YOU STAY WITH ME...
...TO THE END?

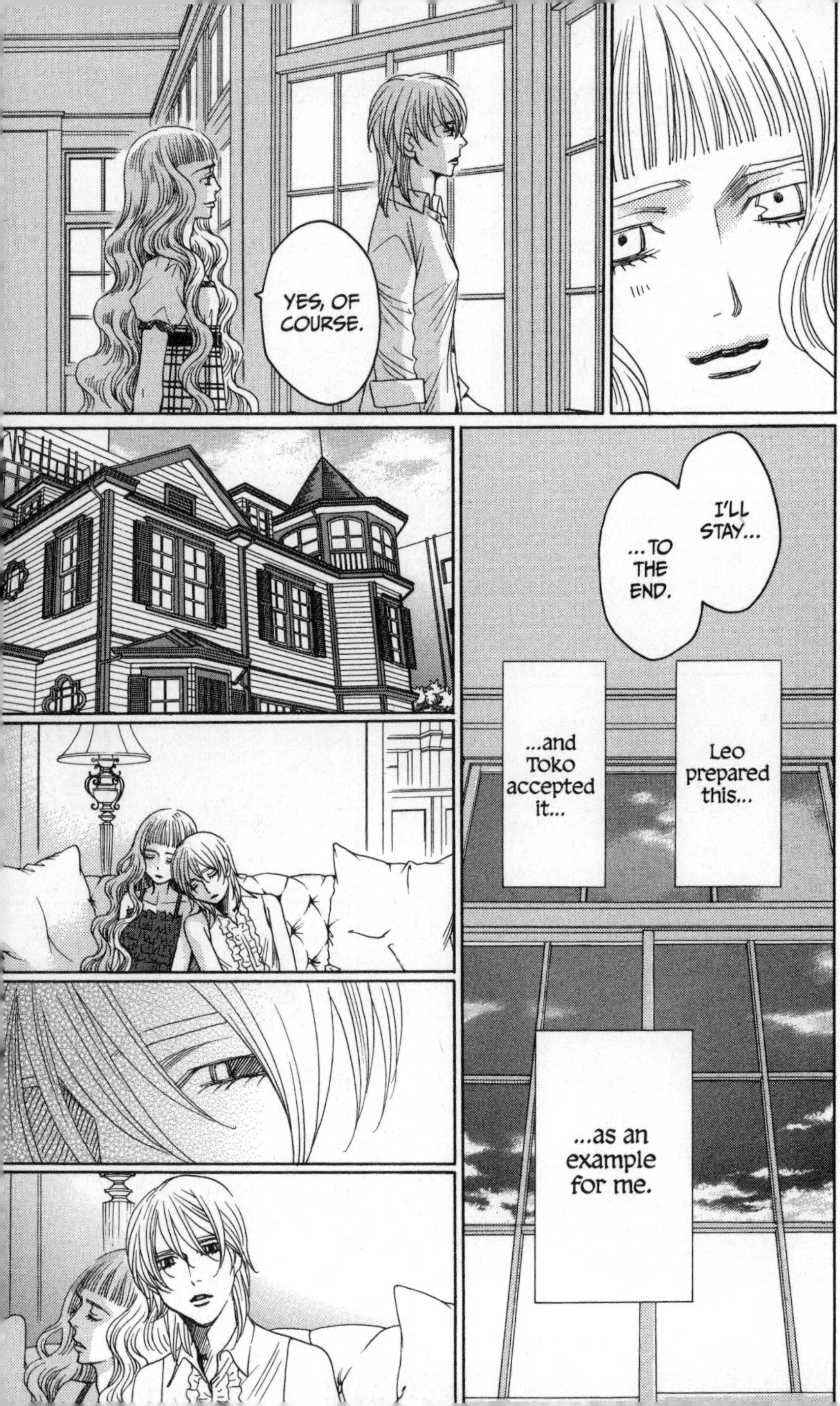
YES, OF COURSE.
I'LL STAY...
...TO THE END.
Leo prepared this...
...and Toko accepted it...
...as an example for me.

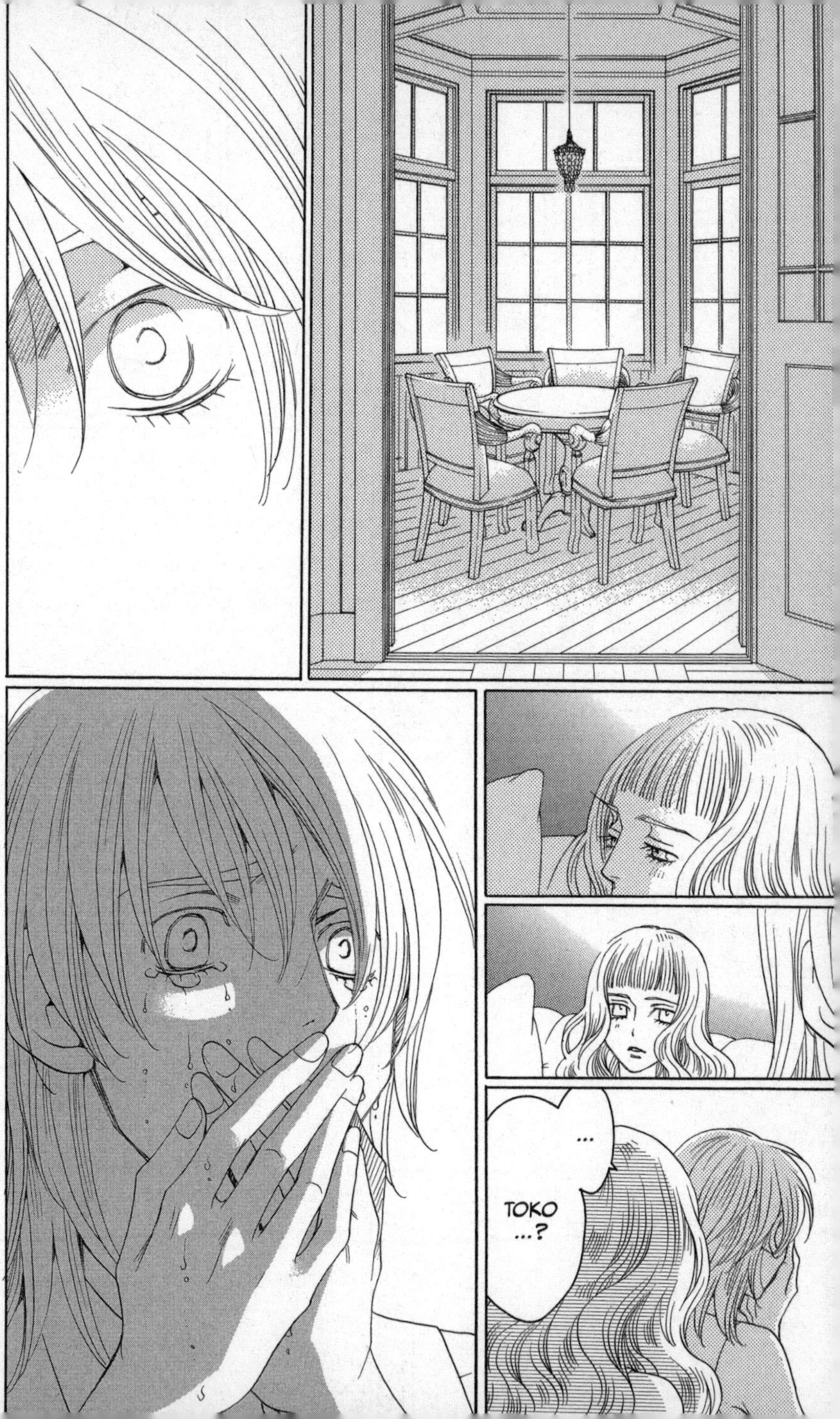
...
TOKO ...?

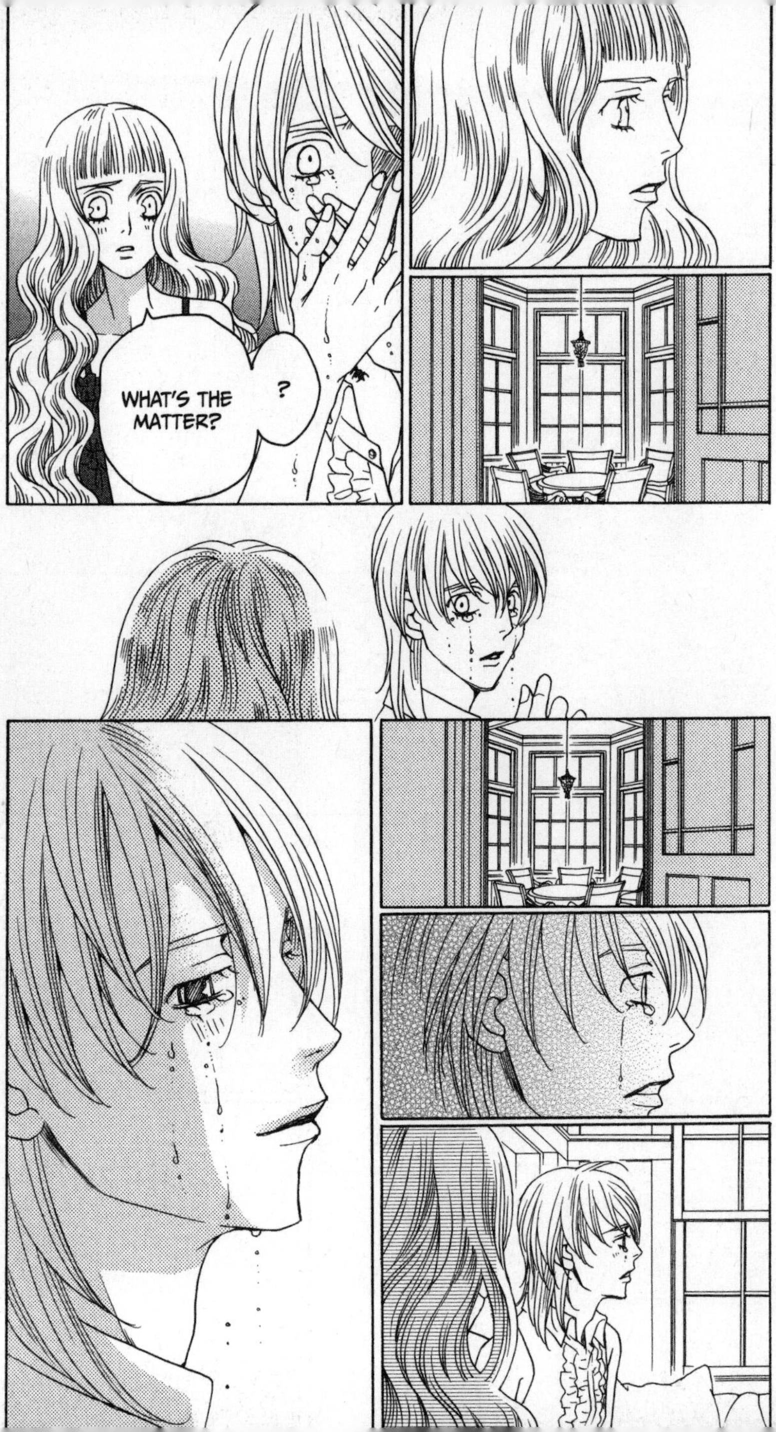
?
WHAT'S THE MATTER?

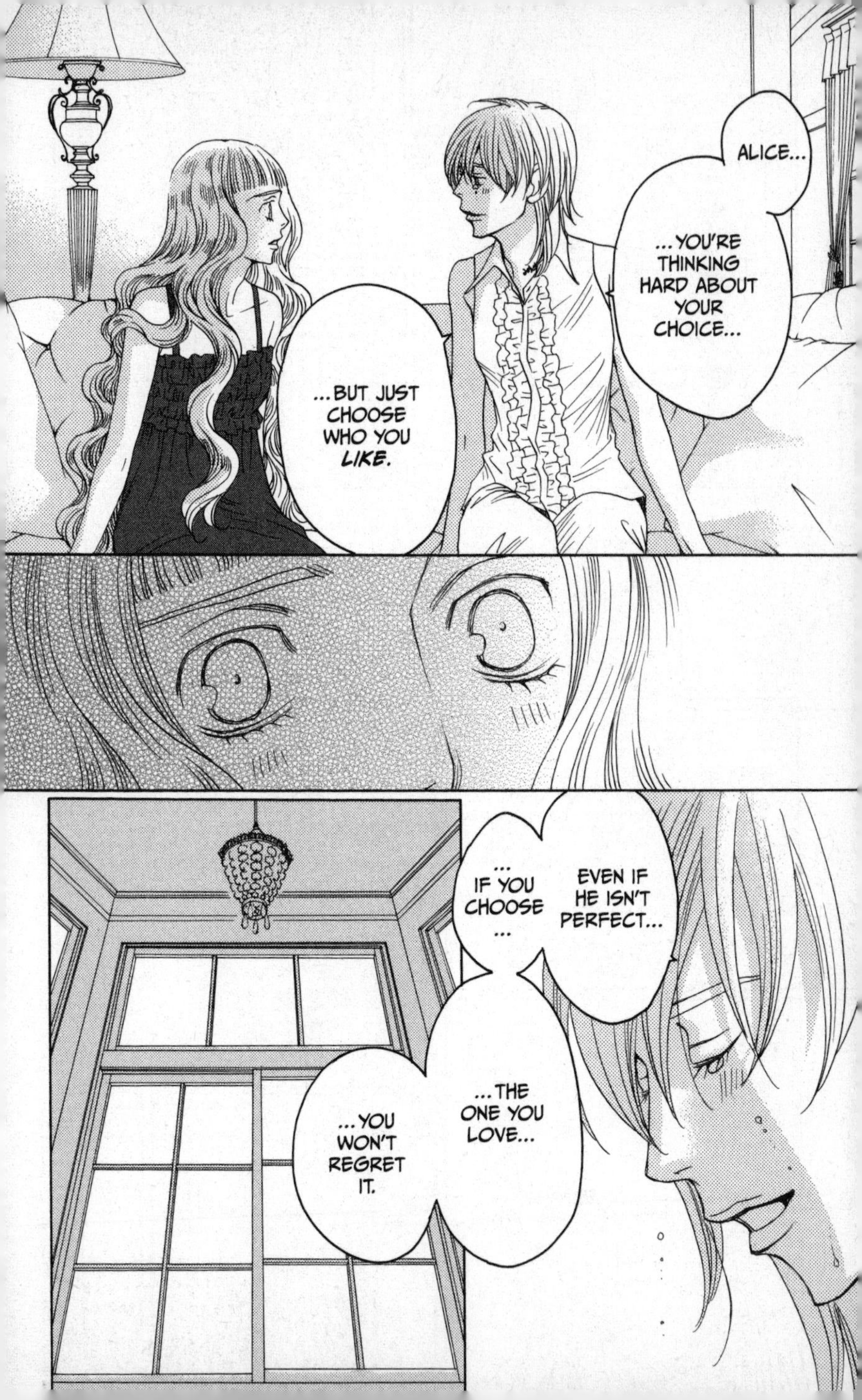
ALICE...
...YOU'RE THINKING HARD ABOUT YOUR CHOICE...
...BUT JUST CHOOSE WHO YOU *LIKE*.
EVEN IF HE ISN'T PERFECT...
... IF YOU CHOOSE ...
...THE ONE YOU LOVE...
...YOU WON'T REGRET IT.

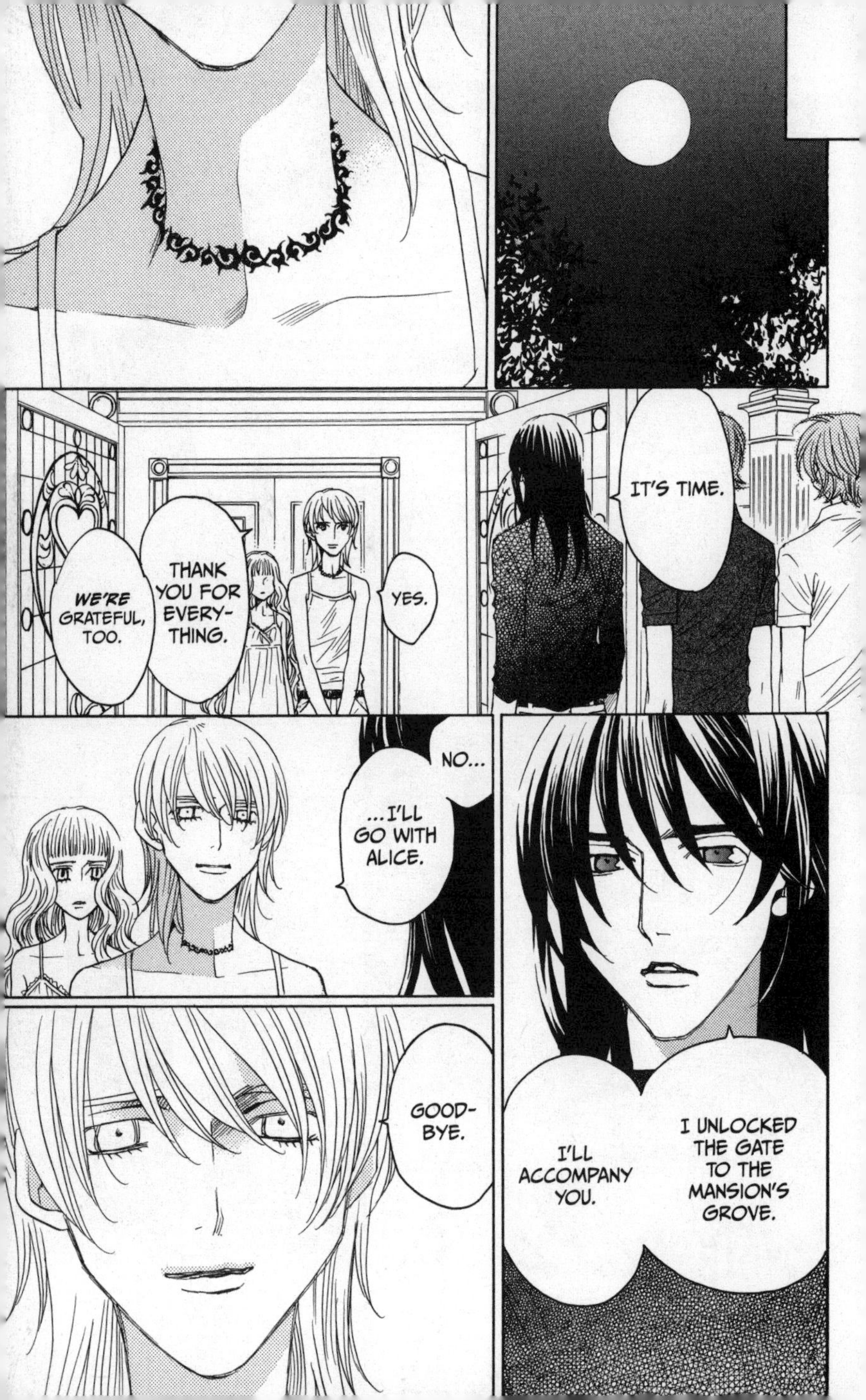
IT'S TIME.
YES.
THANK YOU FOR EVERY-THING.
WE'RE GRATEFUL, TOO.
I UNLOCKED THE GATE TO THE MANSION'S GROVE.
I'LL ACCOMPANY YOU.
NO...
...I'LL GO WITH ALICE.
GOOD-BYE.

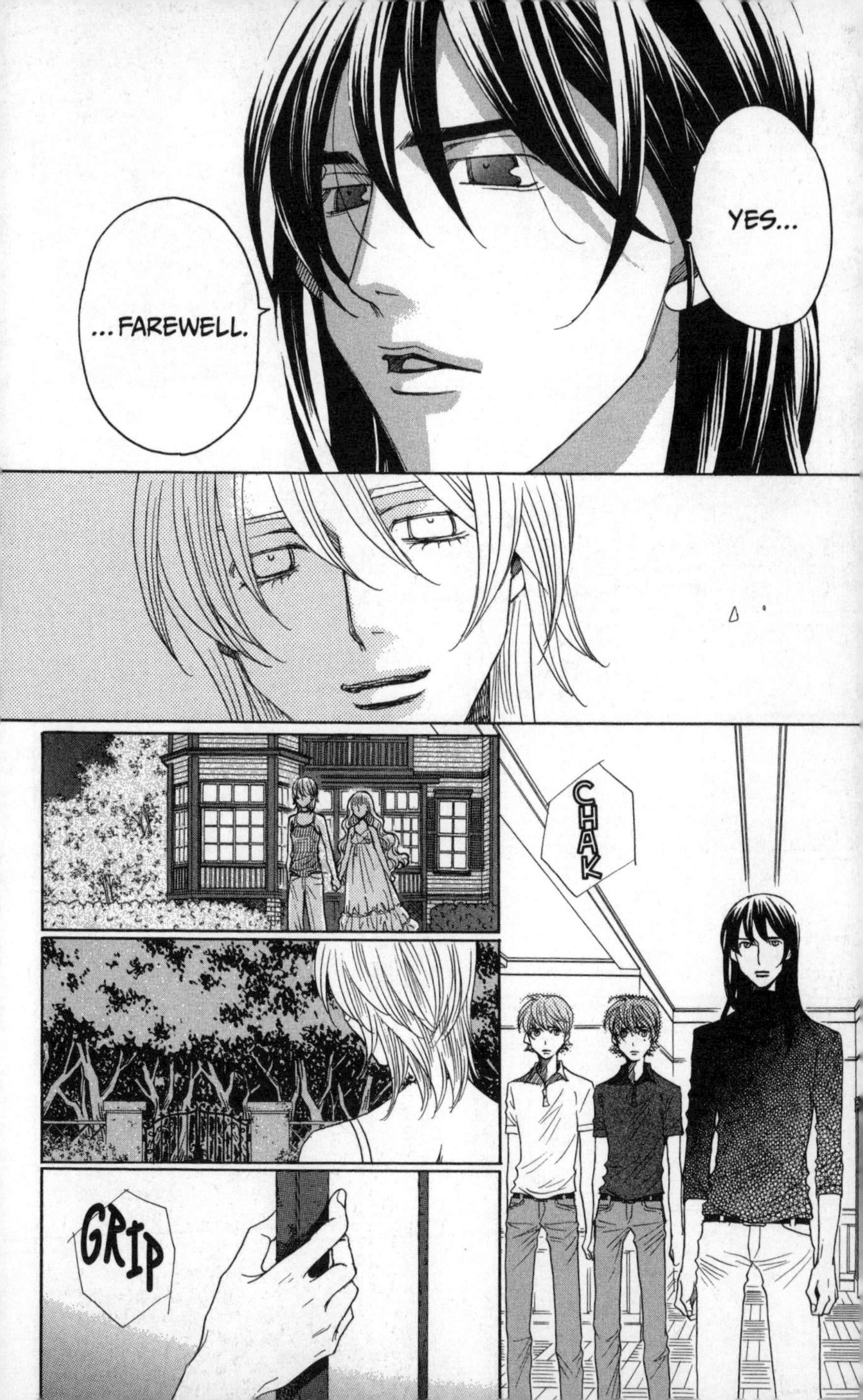
YES...
...FAREWELL.
CHAK
GRIP

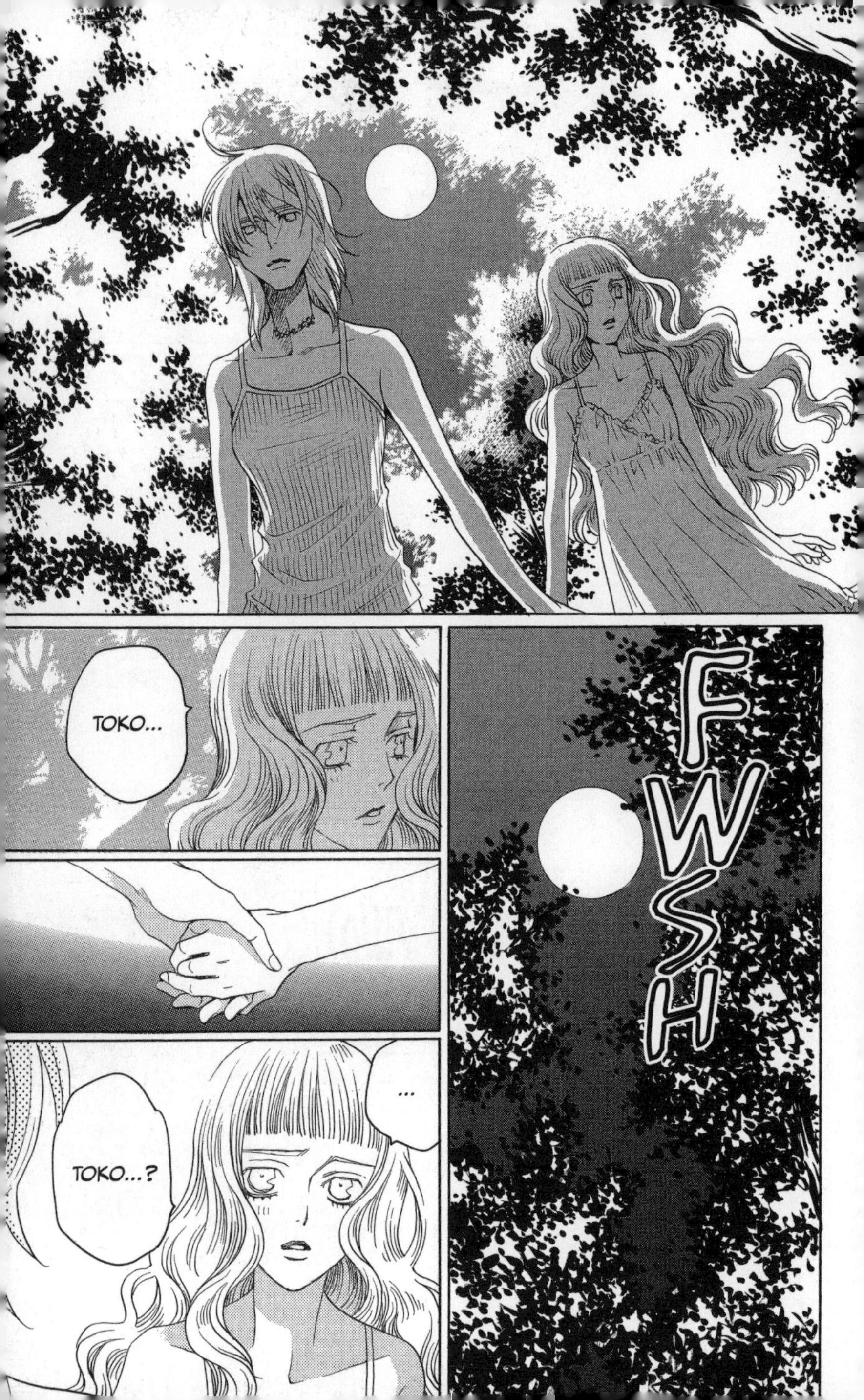
FWSH
TOKO...
...
TOKO...?

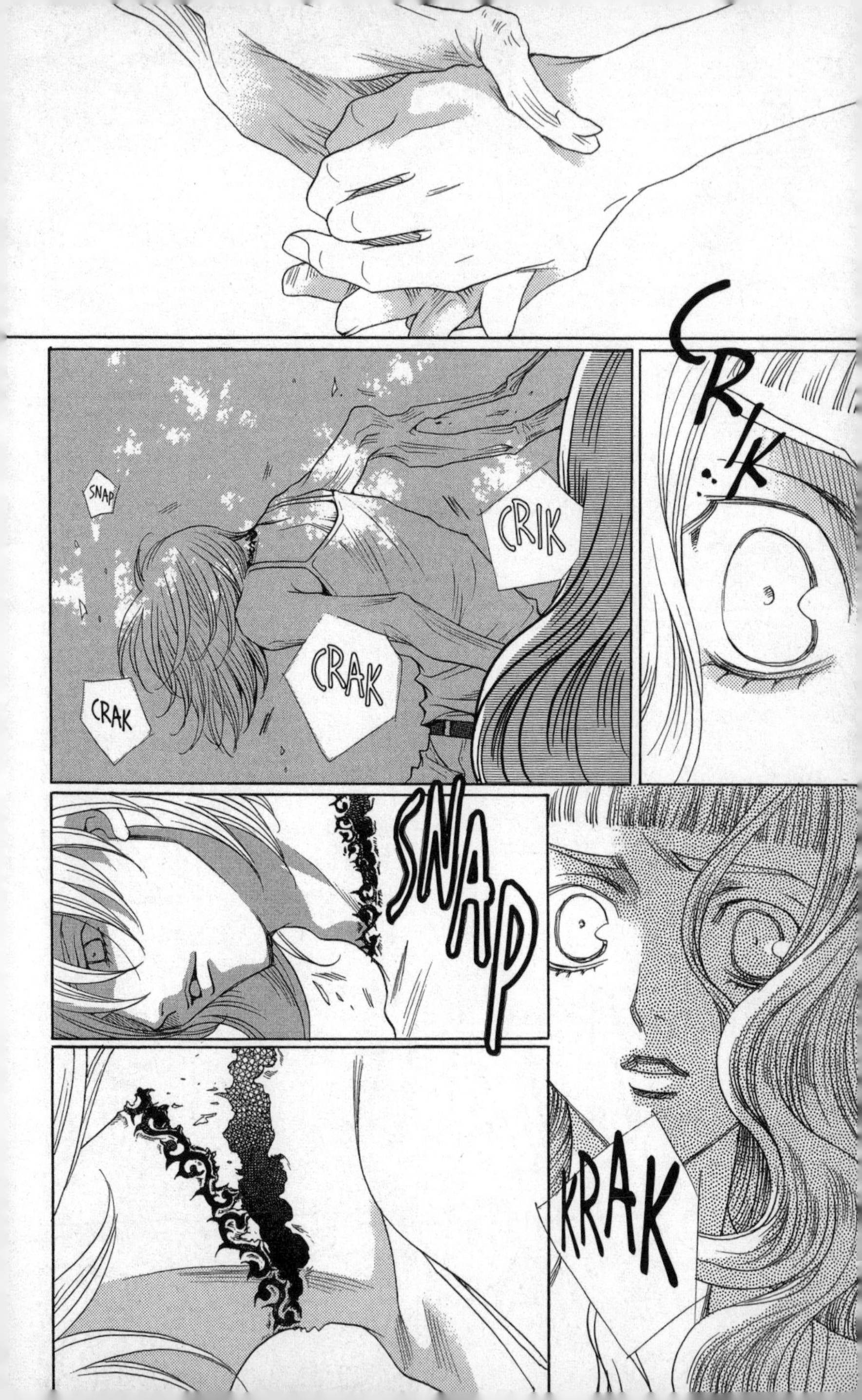
CRIK
SNAP
CRIK
CRAK
CRAK
SNAP
KRAK

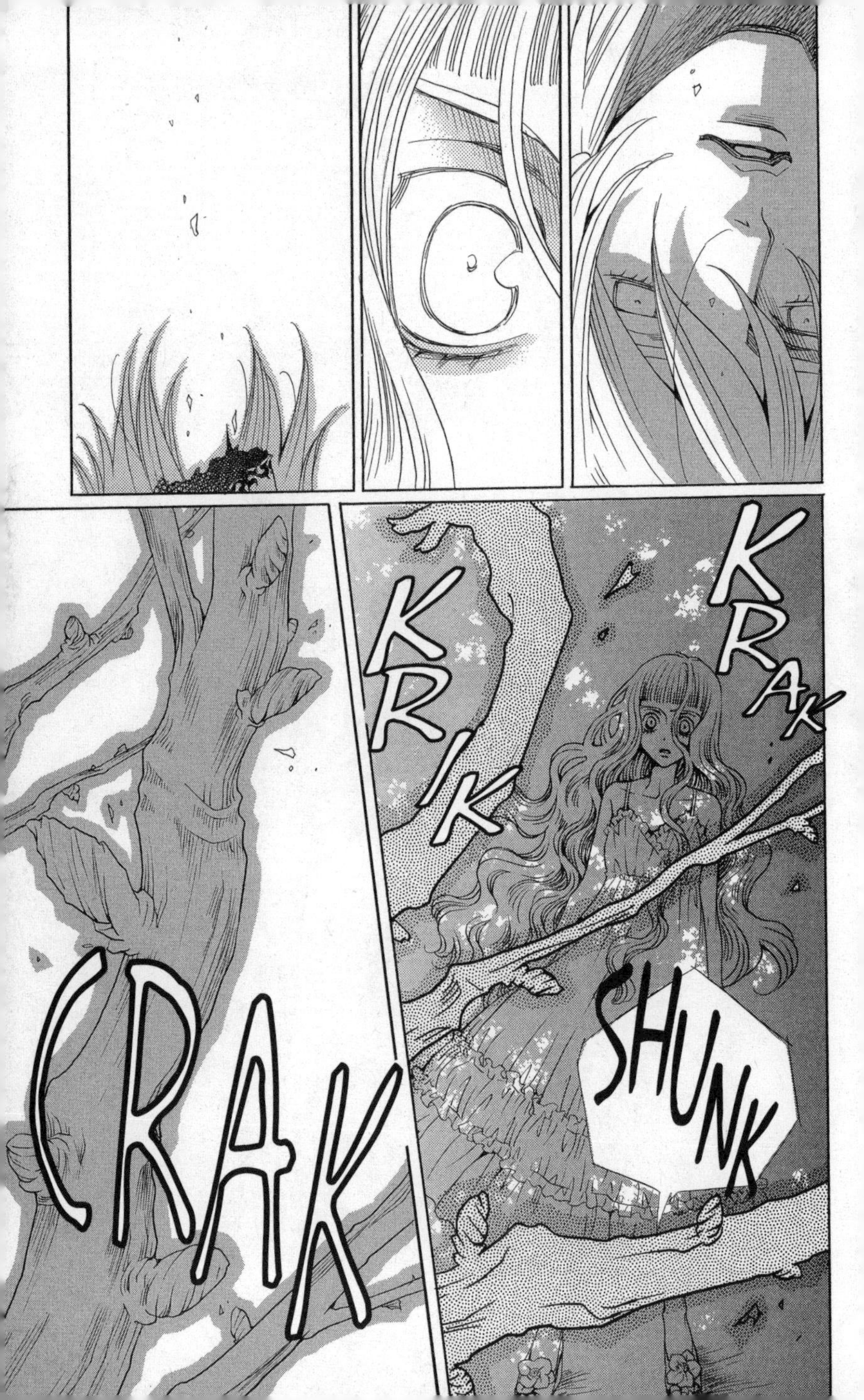
KRAK
KRIK
SHUNK
CRAK

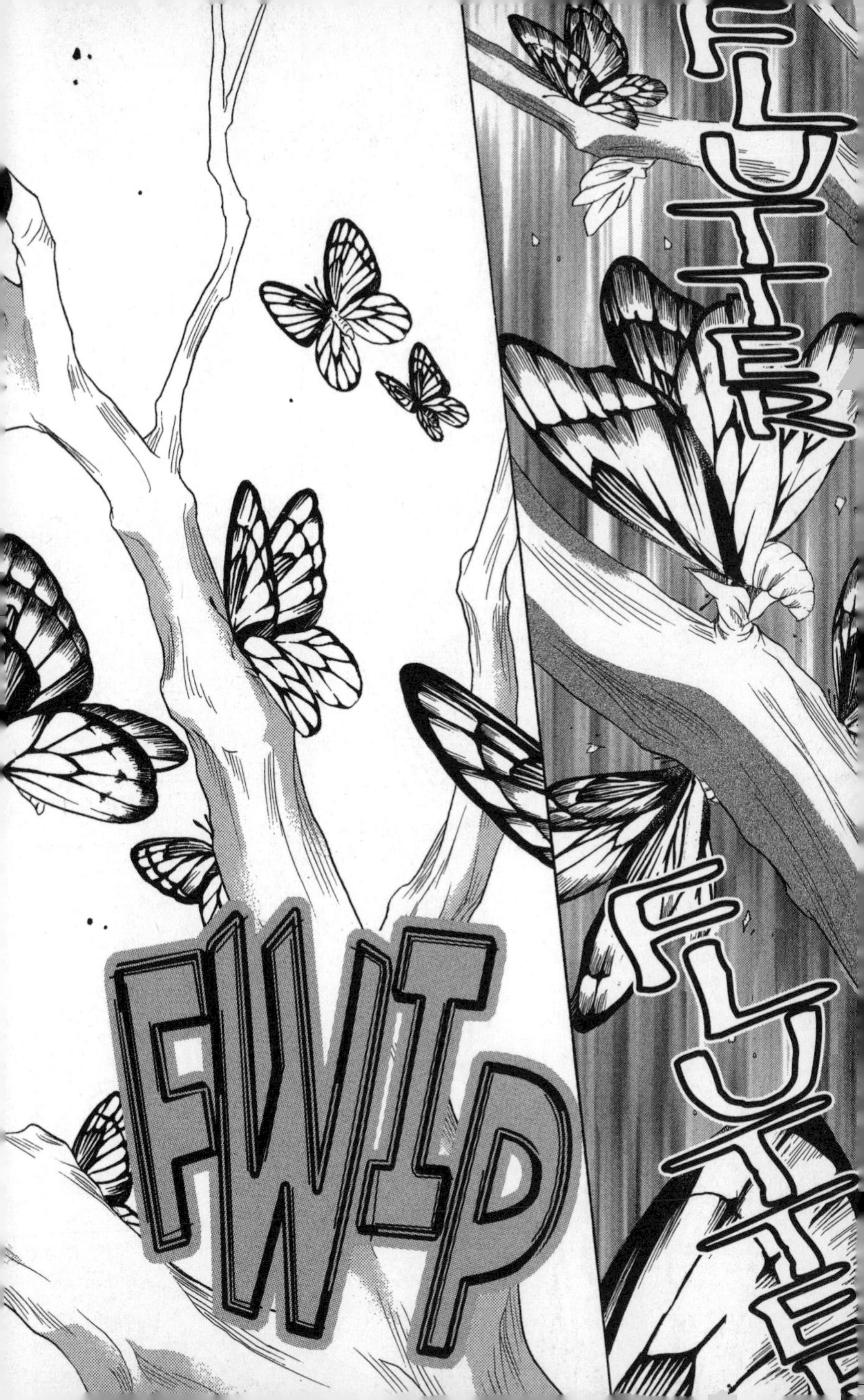
FLUTTER
FLUTTE
FWIP

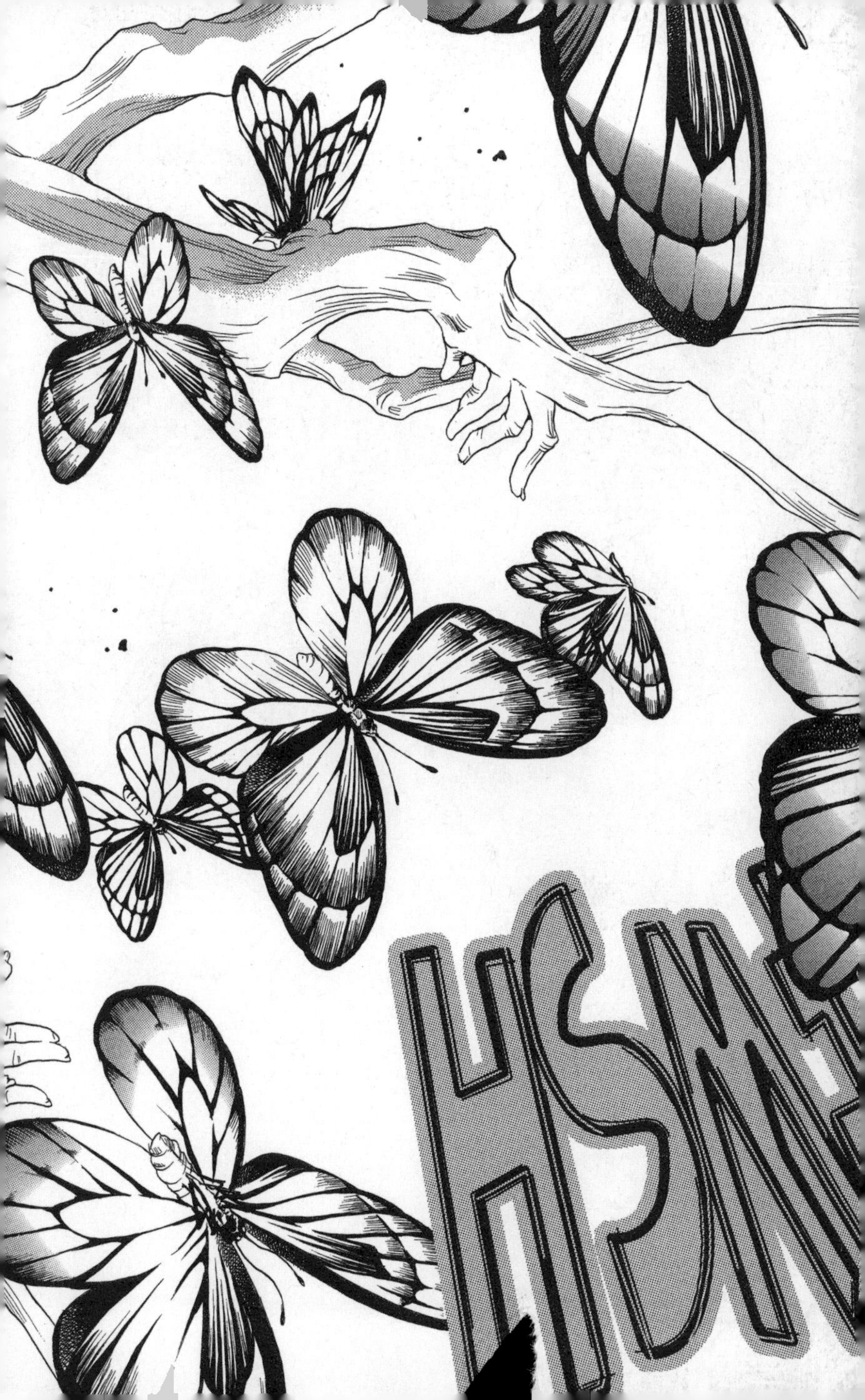

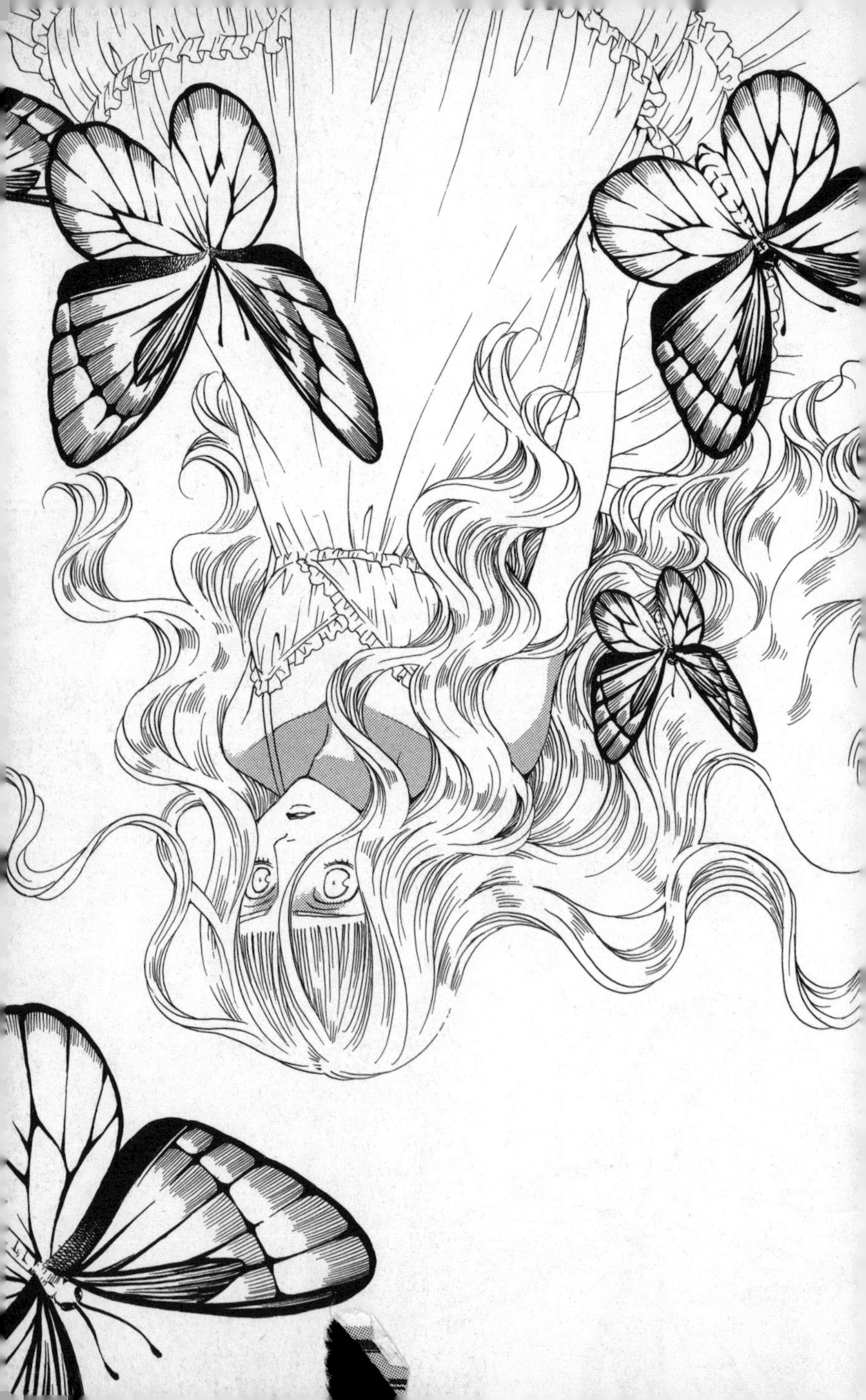

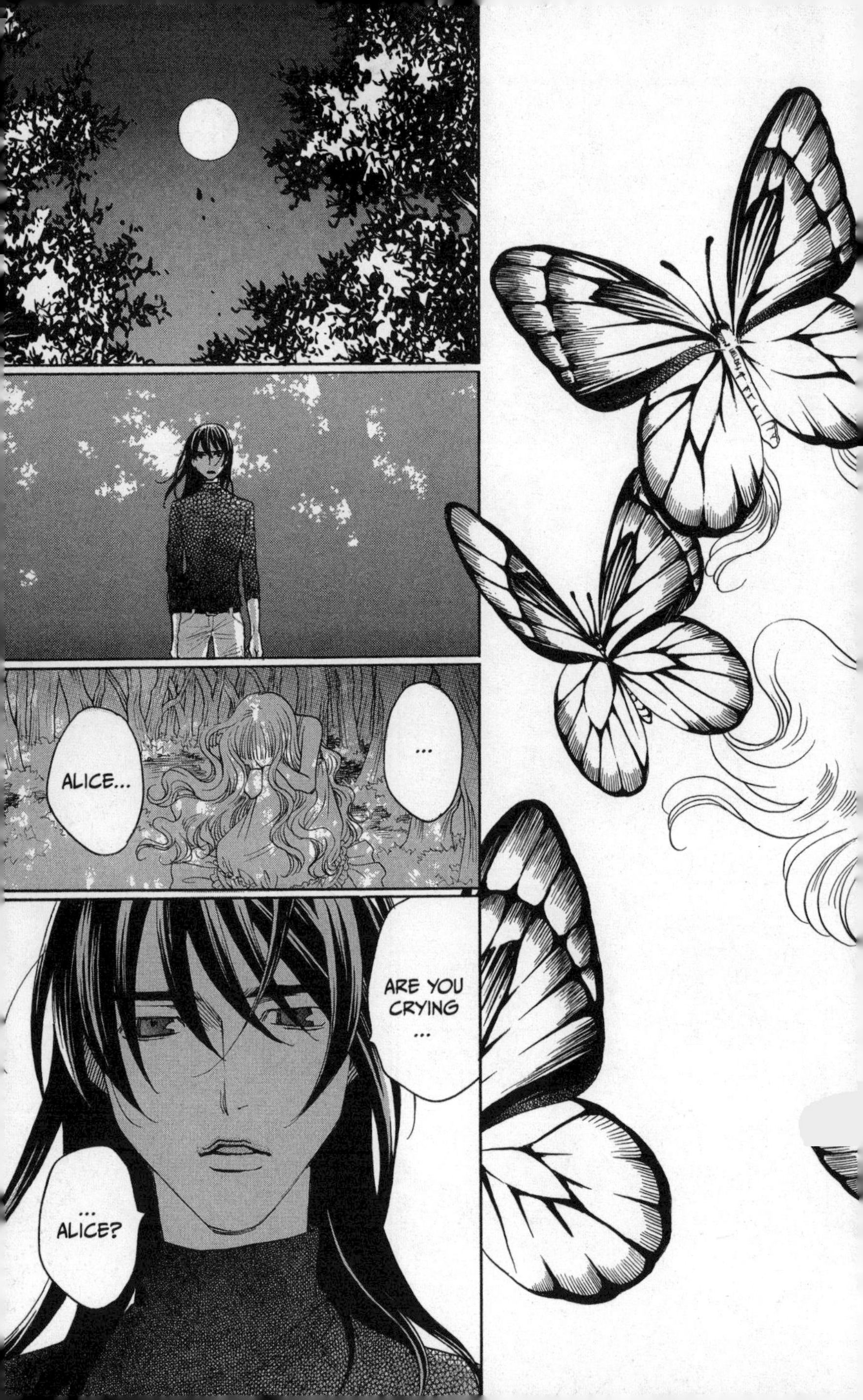
...
ALICE...
ARE YOU CRYING ...
... ALICE?

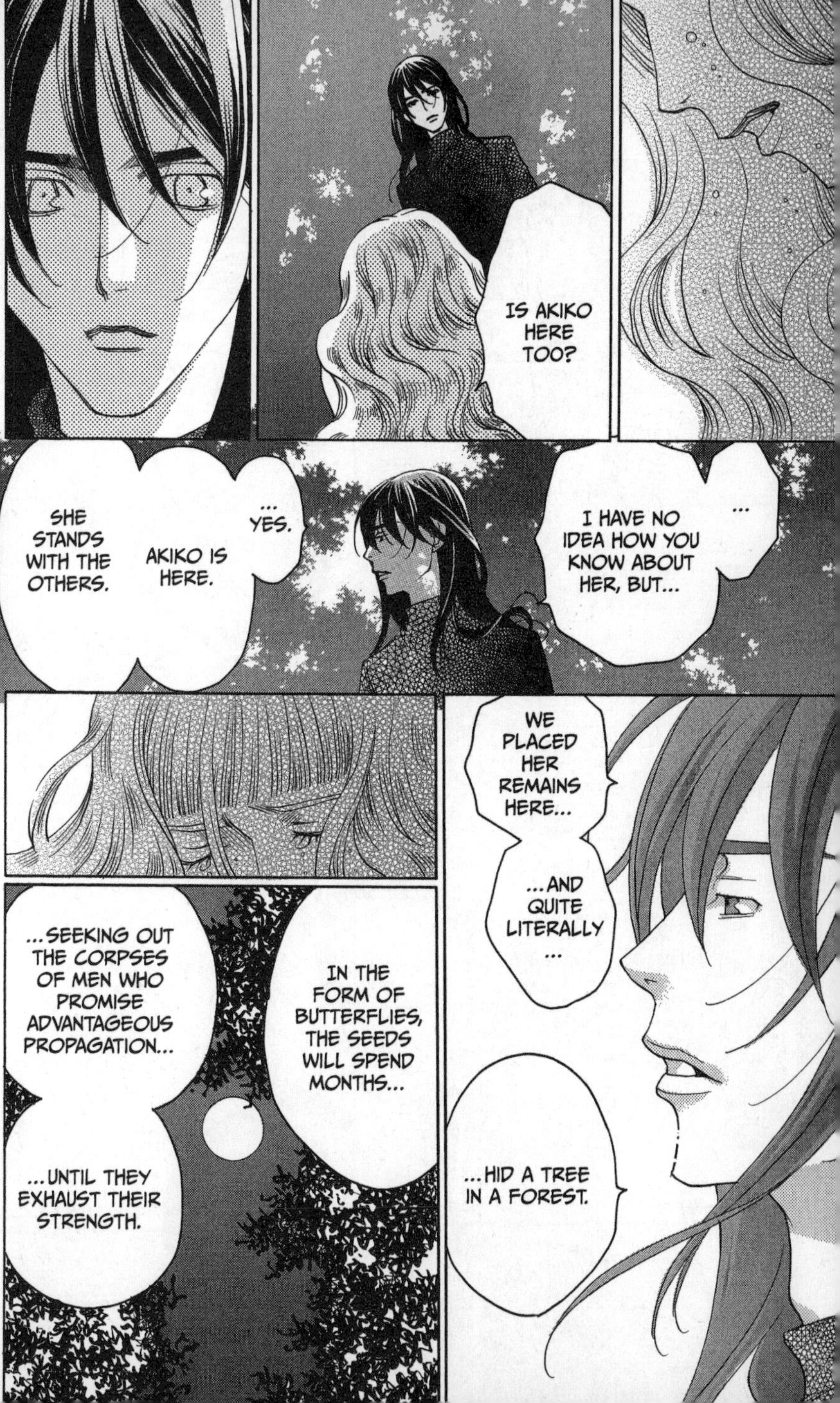
IS AKIKO HERE TOO?
...
I HAVE NO IDEA HOW YOU KNOW ABOUT HER, BUT...
...YES.
AKIKO IS HERE.
SHE STANDS WITH THE OTHERS.
WE PLACED HER REMAINS HERE...
...AND QUITE LITERALLY...
...HID A TREE IN A FOREST.
IN THE FORM OF BUTTERFLIES, THE SEEDS WILL SPEND MONTHS...
...SEEKING OUT THE CORPSES OF MEN WHO PROMISE ADVANTAGEOUS PROPAGATION...
...UNTIL THEY EXHAUST THEIR STRENGTH.

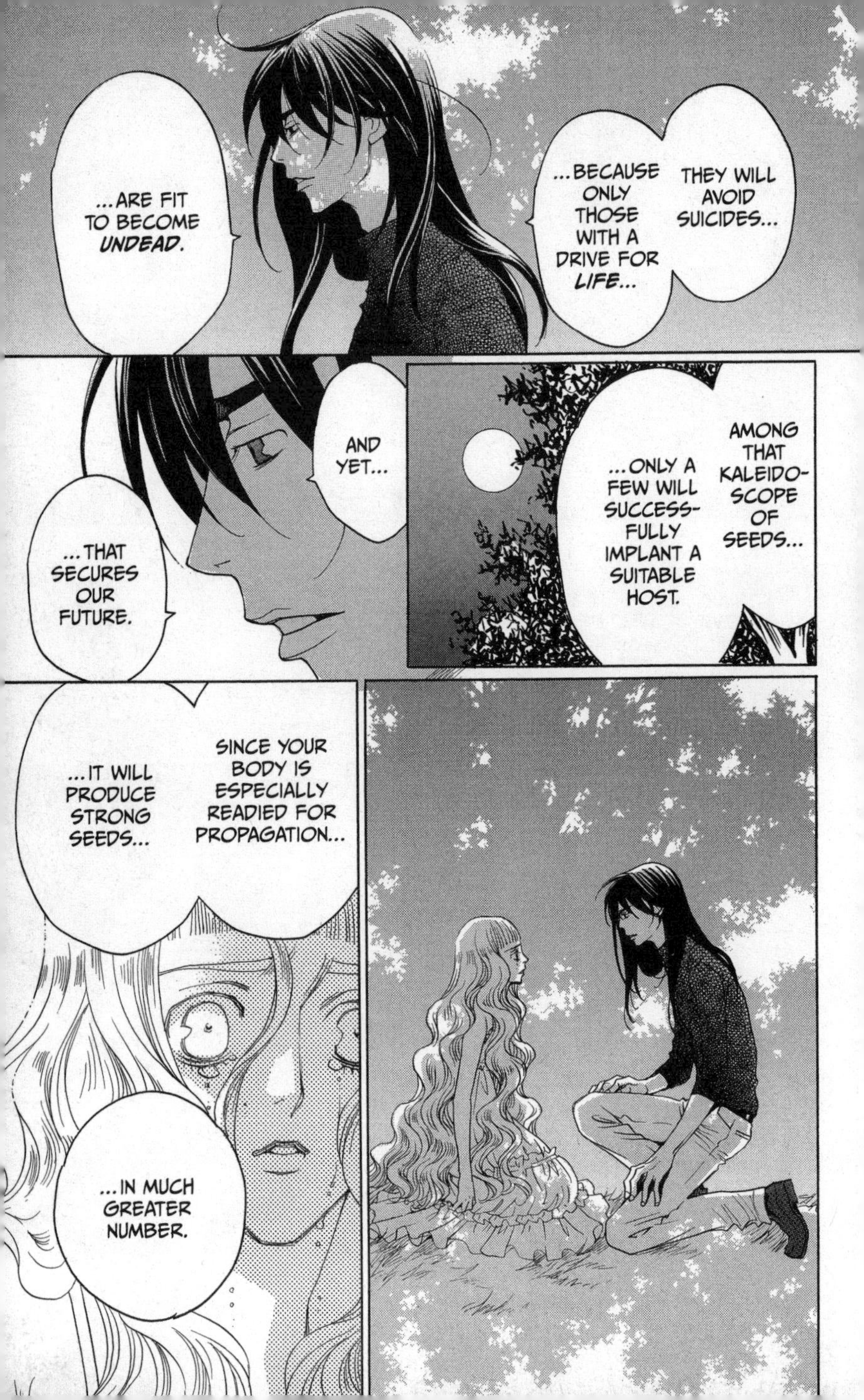
THEY WILL AVOID SUICIDES...
...BECAUSE ONLY THOSE WITH A DRIVE FOR *LIFE*...
...ARE FIT TO BECOME *UNDEAD*.
AMONG THAT KALEIDO-SCOPE OF SEEDS...
...ONLY A FEW WILL SUCCESS-FULLY IMPLANT A SUITABLE HOST.
AND YET...
...THAT SECURES OUR FUTURE.
SINCE YOUR BODY IS ESPECIALLY READIED FOR PROPAGATION...
...IT WILL PRODUCE STRONG SEEDS...
...IN MUCH GREATER NUMBER.

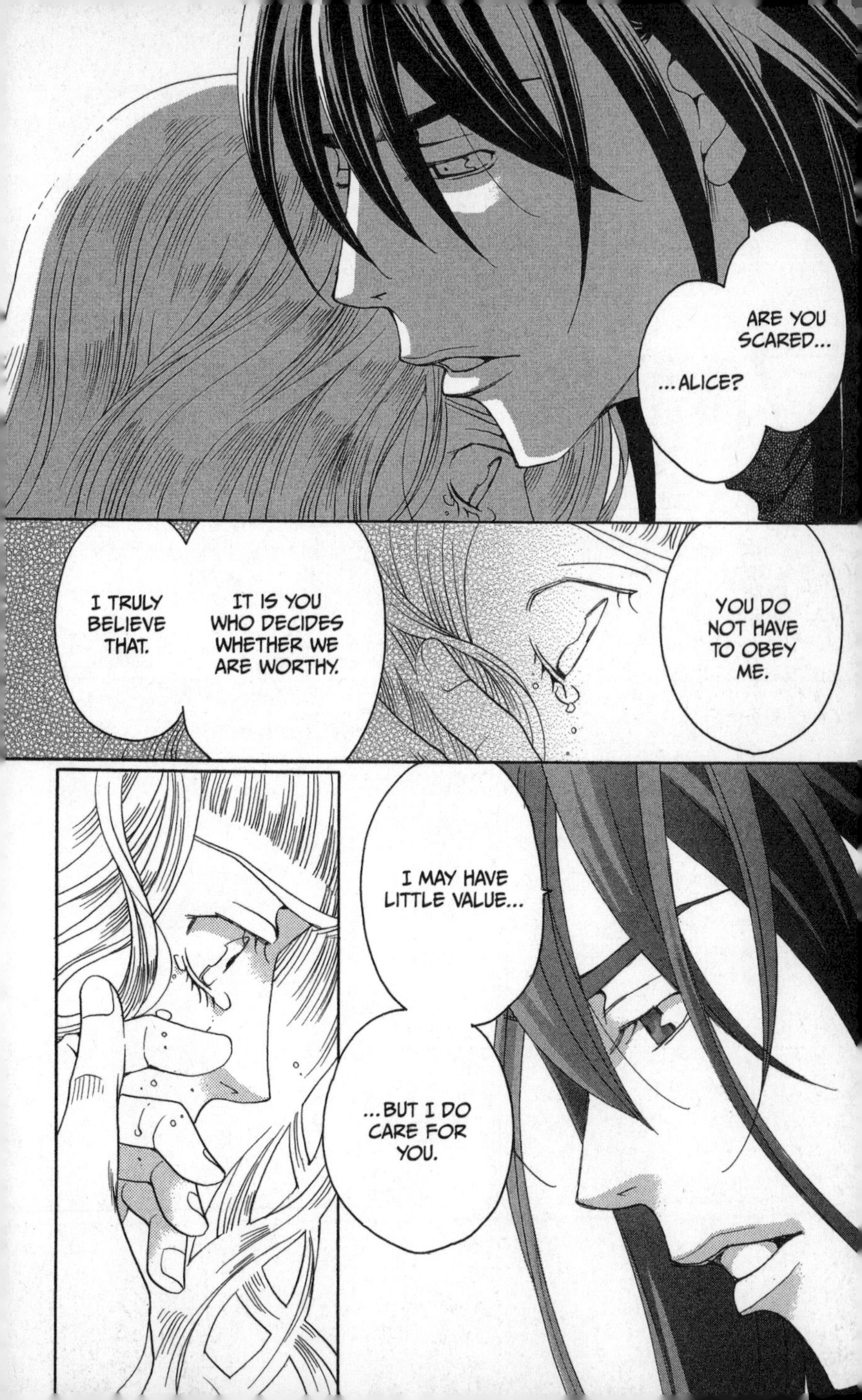
ARE YOU SCARED...
...ALICE?
YOU DO NOT HAVE TO OBEY ME.
IT IS YOU WHO DECIDES WHETHER WE ARE WORTHY.
I TRULY BELIEVE THAT.
I MAY HAVE LITTLE VALUE...
...BUT I DO CARE FOR YOU.

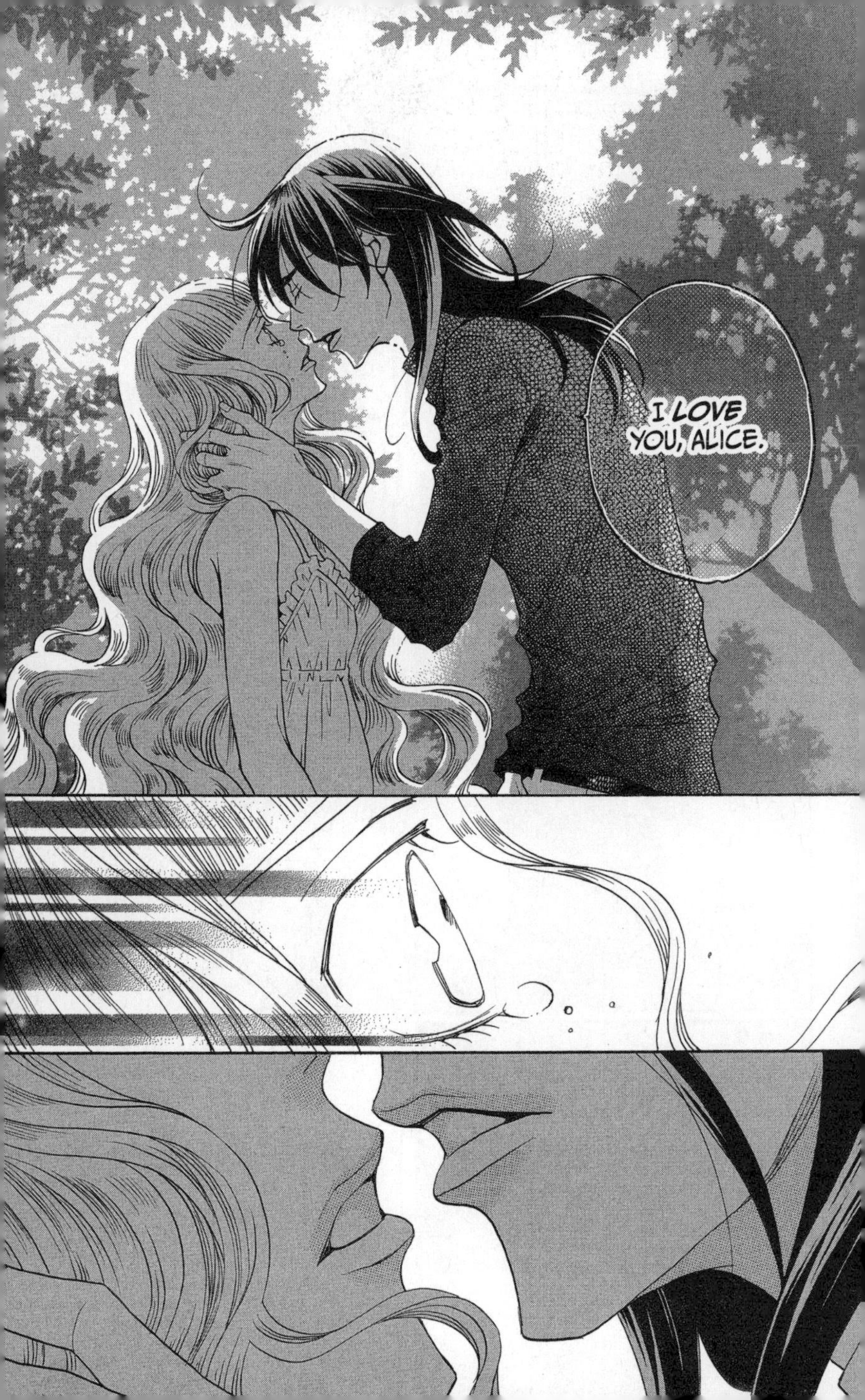
I LOVE YOU, ALICE.

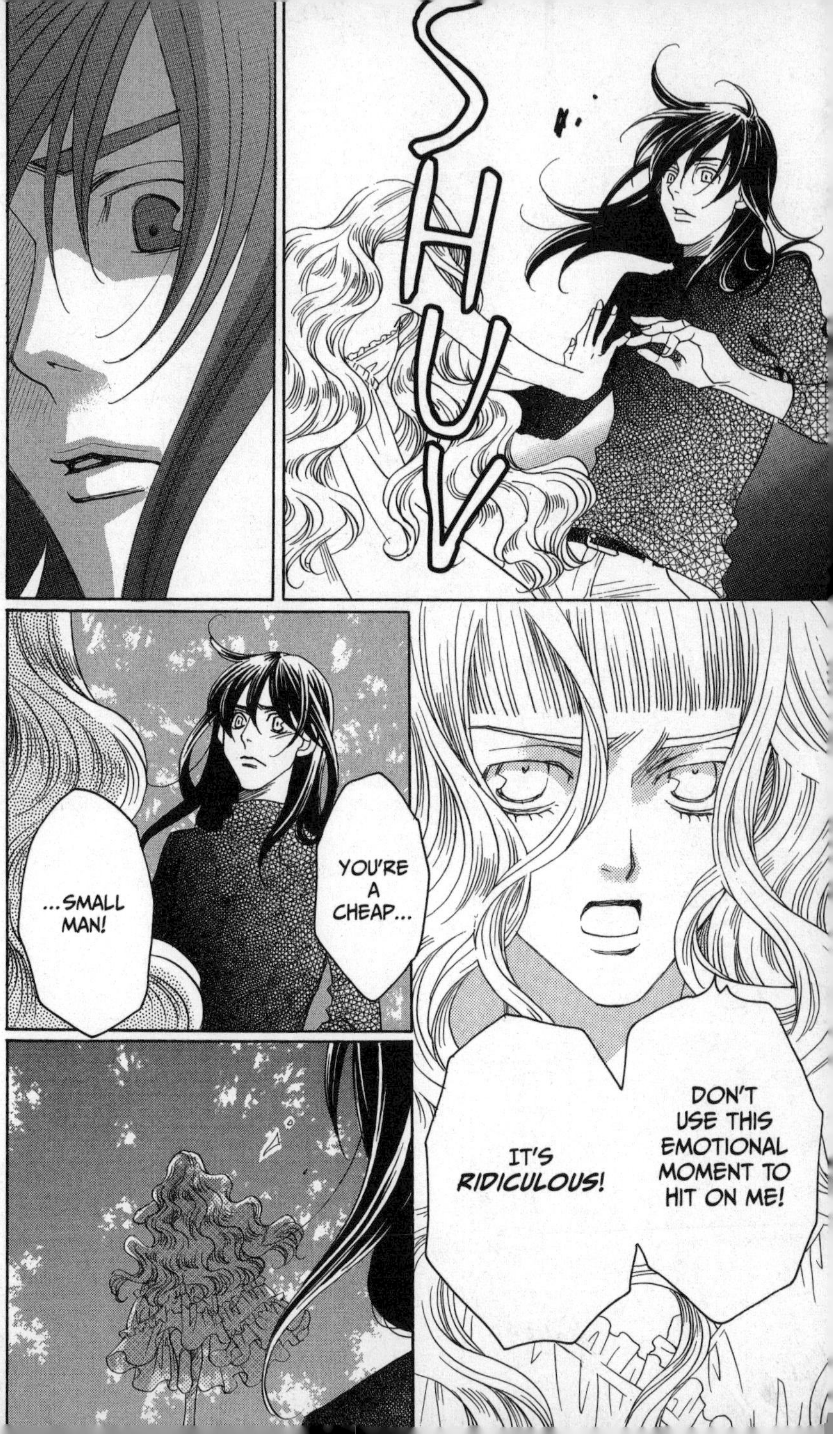
SHUV
DON'T USE THIS EMOTIONAL MOMENT TO HIT ON ME!
IT'S RIDICULOUS!
YOU'RE A CHEAP...
...SMALL MAN!

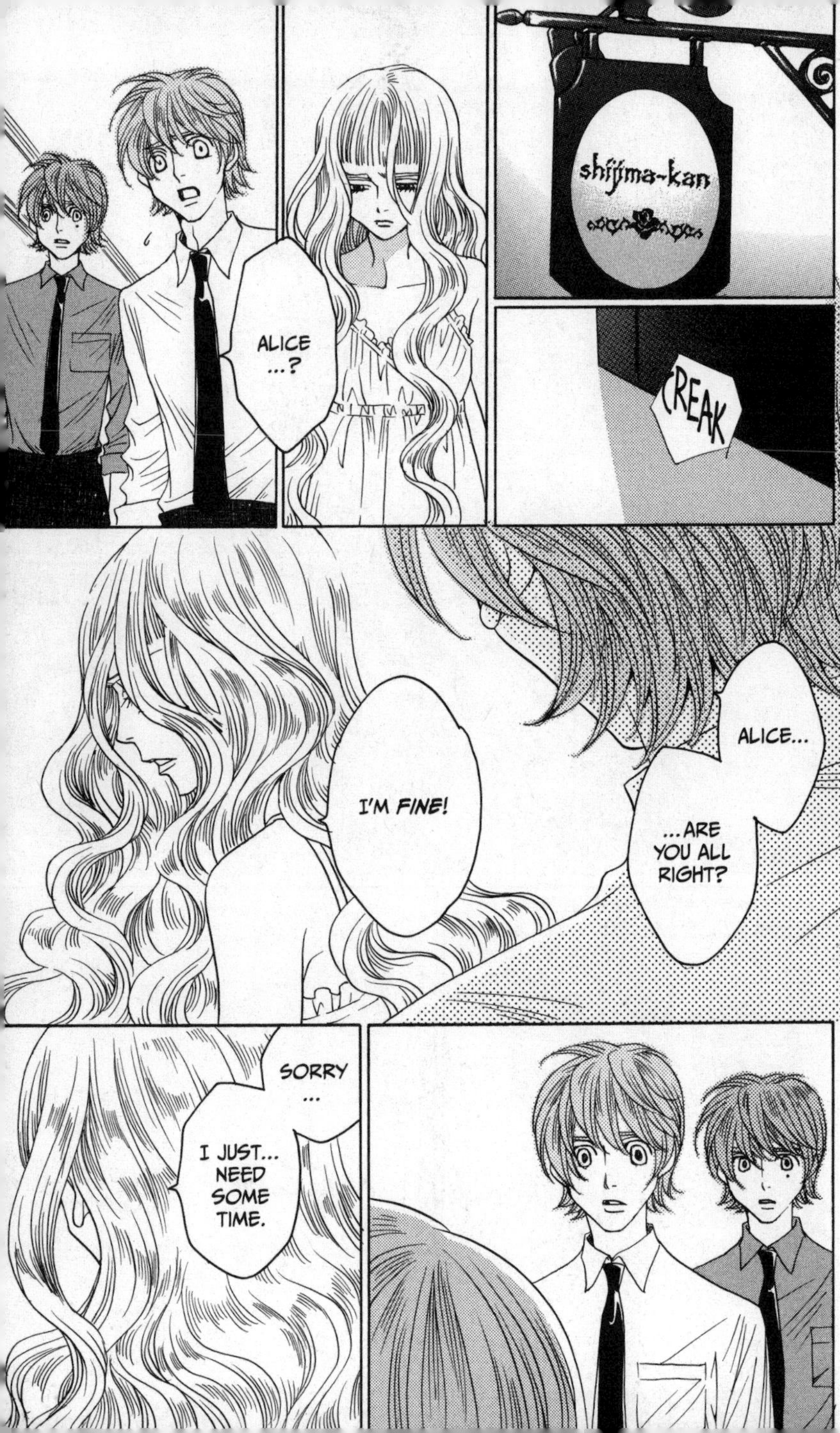
shijima-kan
CREAK
ALICE ...?
ALICE...
...ARE YOU ALL RIGHT?
I'M FINE!
SORRY ...
I JUST... NEED SOME TIME.

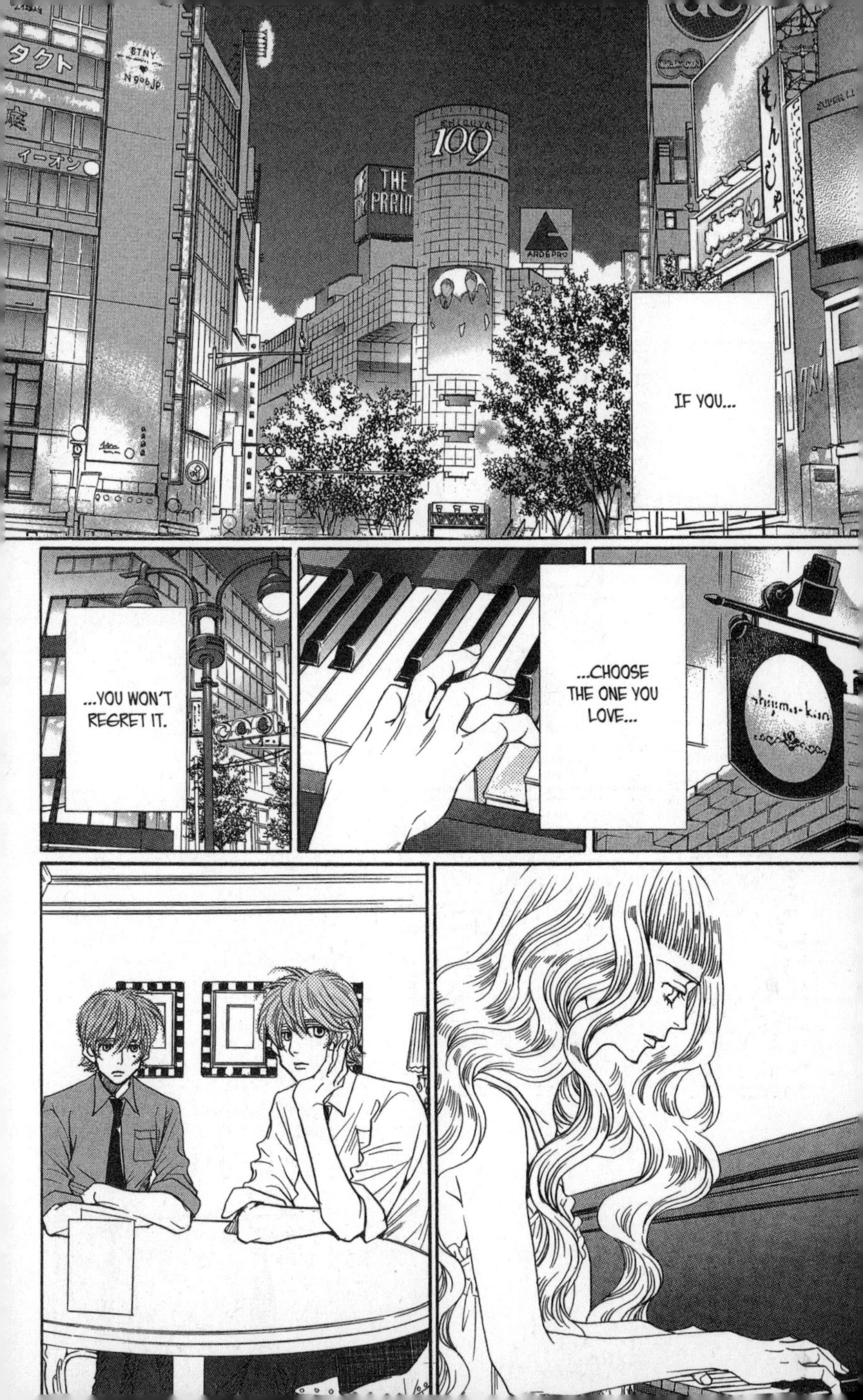
109
ARDEPRO
IF YOU...
...CHOOSE THE ONE YOU LOVE...
...YOU WON'T REGRET IT.

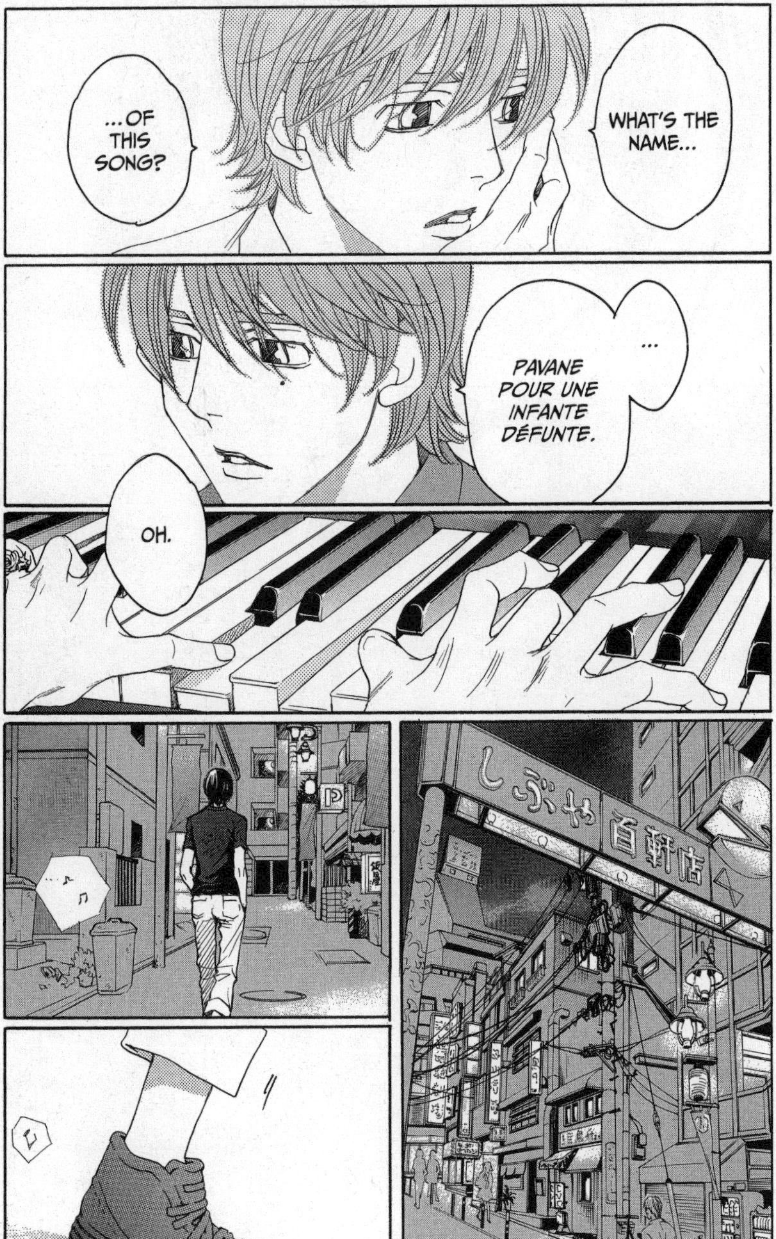
WHAT'S THE NAME...
...OF THIS SONG?
...
PAVANE POUR UNE INFANTE DÉFUNTE.
OH.
しぶや
百軒店

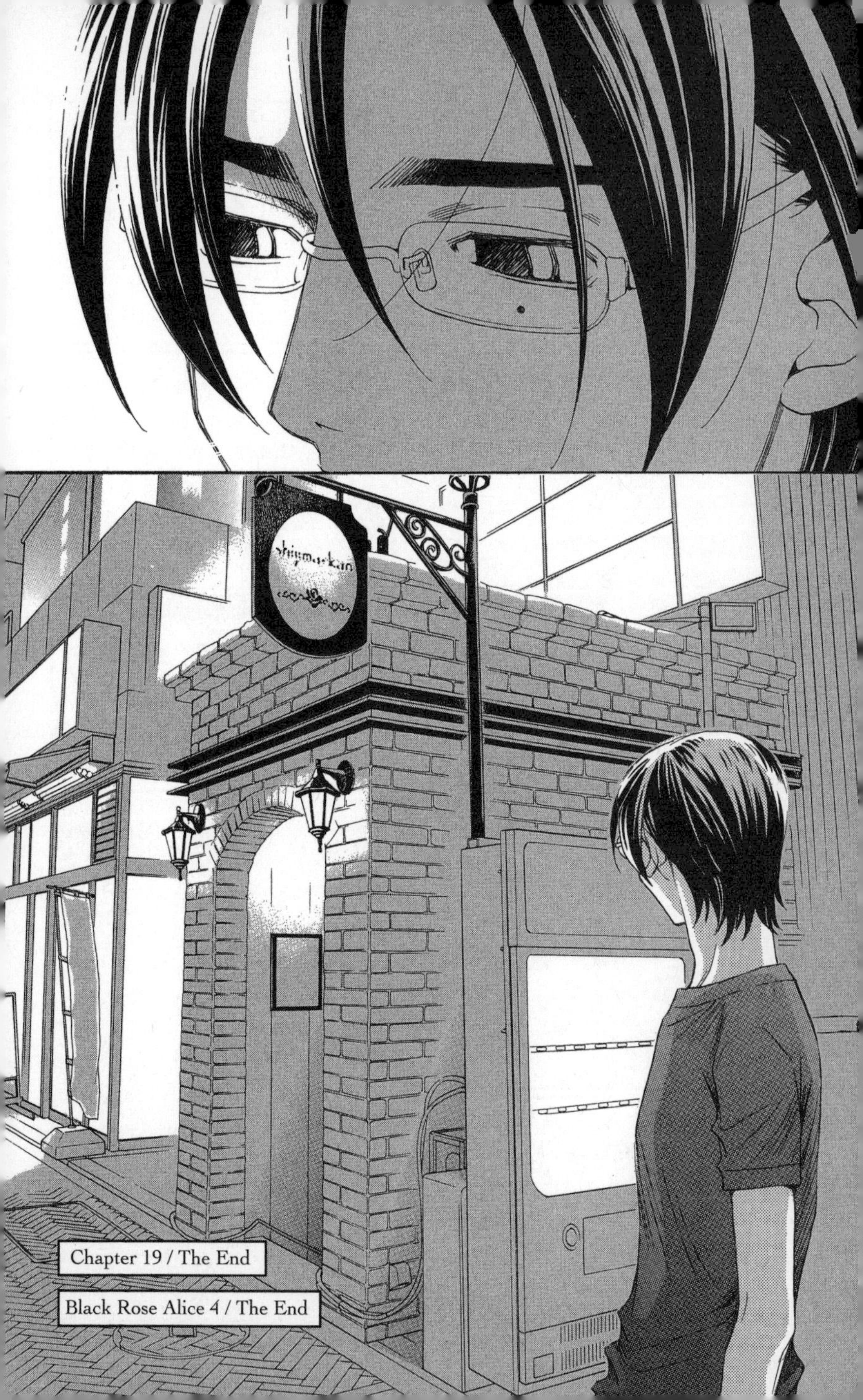
Chapter 19 / The End
Black Rose Alice 4 / The End

For girls too!

For men, results are everything. ♡

CLAP CLAP CLAP

Visit Setona Mizushiro's official homepage:
http://www.page.sannet.ne.jp/setona

I was an only child, so when I was young I always wrote stories or piano songs off on my own. I didn't necessarily want anyone to read or listen to them, I just enjoyed writing, drawing and playing what I wanted to read or hear.

Since I didn't want anyone to see them, I kept them secret from my parents, but as I got older I came to show more consideration for my parents and people around me, so as I created I distinguished between works I would show to others and those I would keep to myself.

I wonder which category the projects I'm working on now fit into? Luckily, they possess elements of both to a certain measure. I've become an adult.

–Setona Mizushiro

Setona Mizushiro's professional debut was *"Fuyu ga Owarou to Shiteita"* (Winter Was Ending), and her series *After School Nightmare* was nominated for an Eisner and recognized by YALSA as a great graphic novel for teens in 2007.

BLACK ROSE ALICE
VOLUME 4
Shojo Beat Edition

STORY AND ART BY
Setona Mizushiro

English Translation & Adaptation/John Werry
Touch-up Art & Lettering/Evan Waldinger
Design/Yukiko Whitley
Editor/Pancha Diaz

BLACK ROSE ALICE Volume 4
© 2010 SETONA MIZUSHIRO
All rights reserved.
First published in Japan in 2010 by Akita Publishing Co., Ltd., Tokyo
English translation rights arranged with Akita Publishing Co., Ltd.

Printed in the U.S.A.

Published by VIZ Media, LLC
P.O. Box 77010
San Francisco, CA 94107

10 9 8 7 6 5 4 3 2 1
First printing, May 2015

www.viz.com   www.shojobeat.com

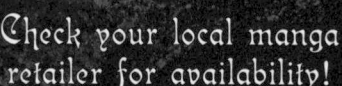

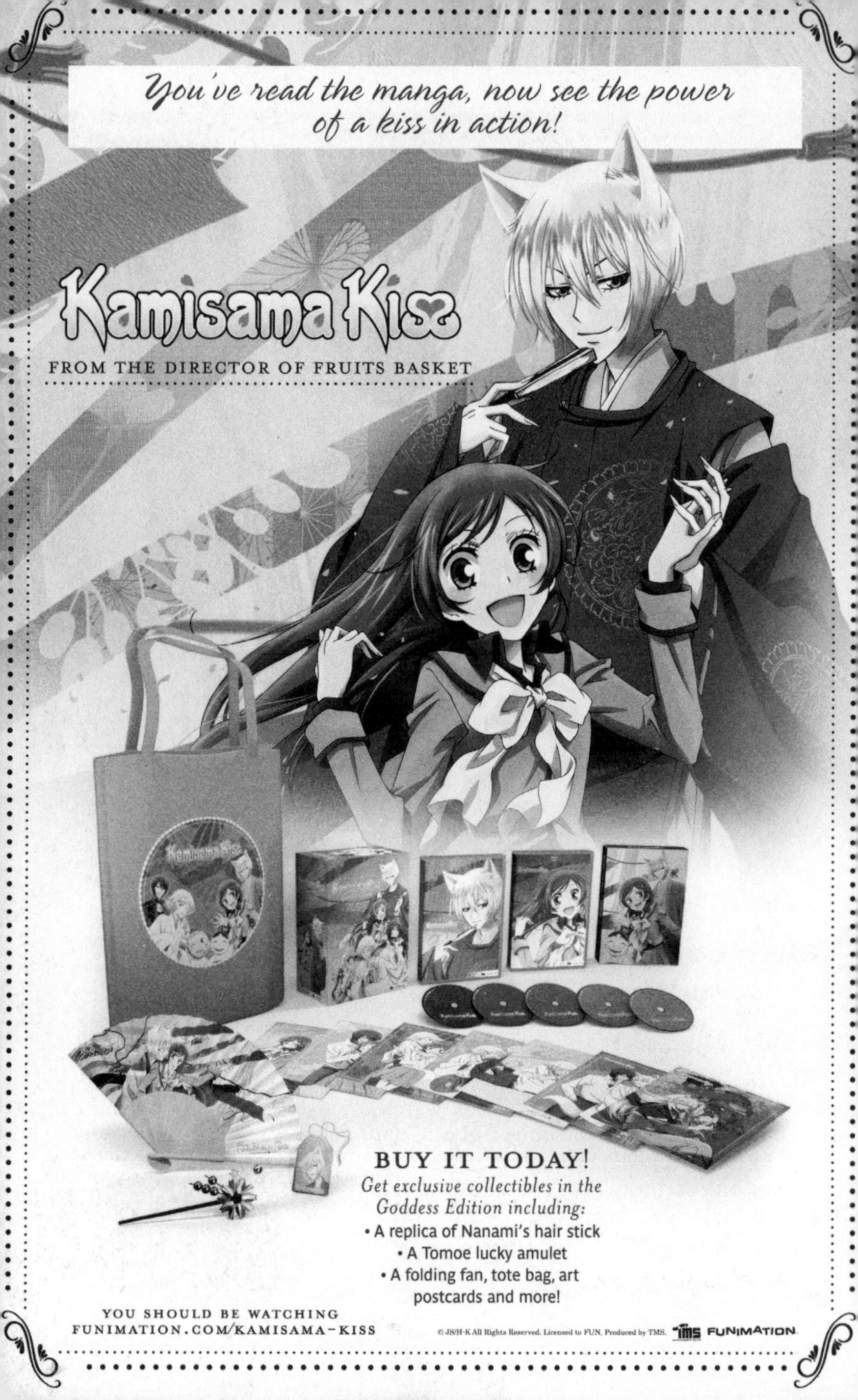
You've read the manga, now see the power of a kiss in action!
Kamisama Kiss
FROM THE DIRECTOR OF FRUITS BASKET
BUY IT TODAY!
Get exclusive collectibles in the Goddess Edition including:
• A replica of Nanami's hair stick
• A Tomoe lucky amulet
• A folding fan, tote bag, art postcards and more!
YOU SHOULD BE WATCHING
FUNIMATION.COM/KAMISAMA-KISS
© JS/H-K All Rights Reserved. Licensed to FUN, Produced by TMS.
TMS FUNIMATION

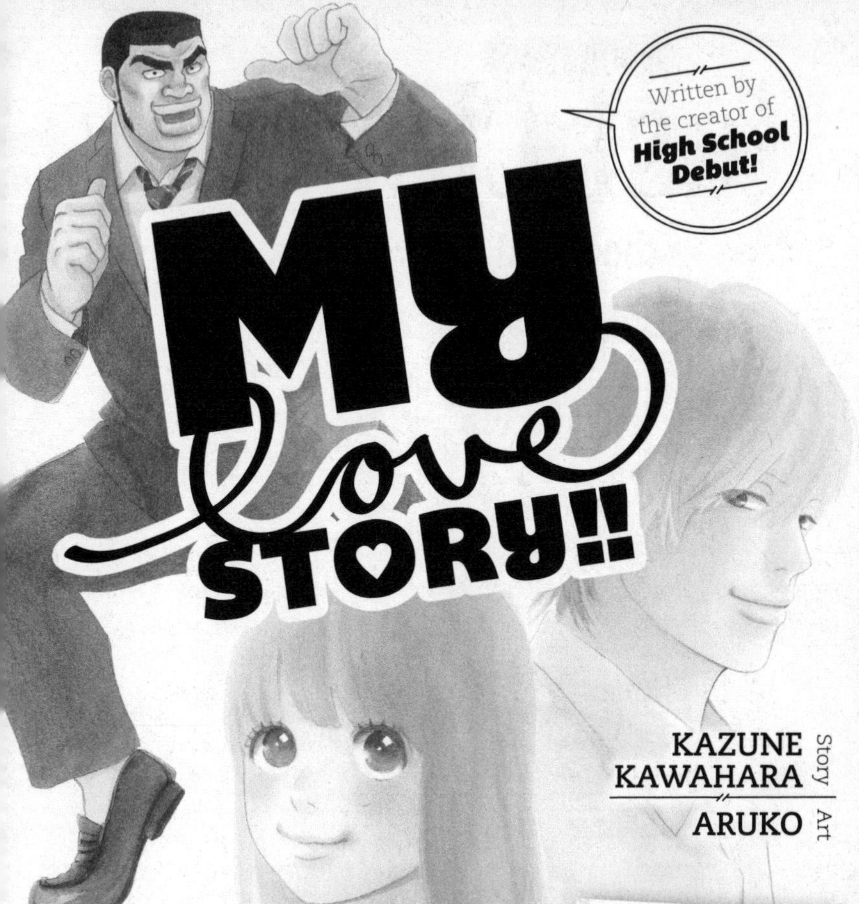

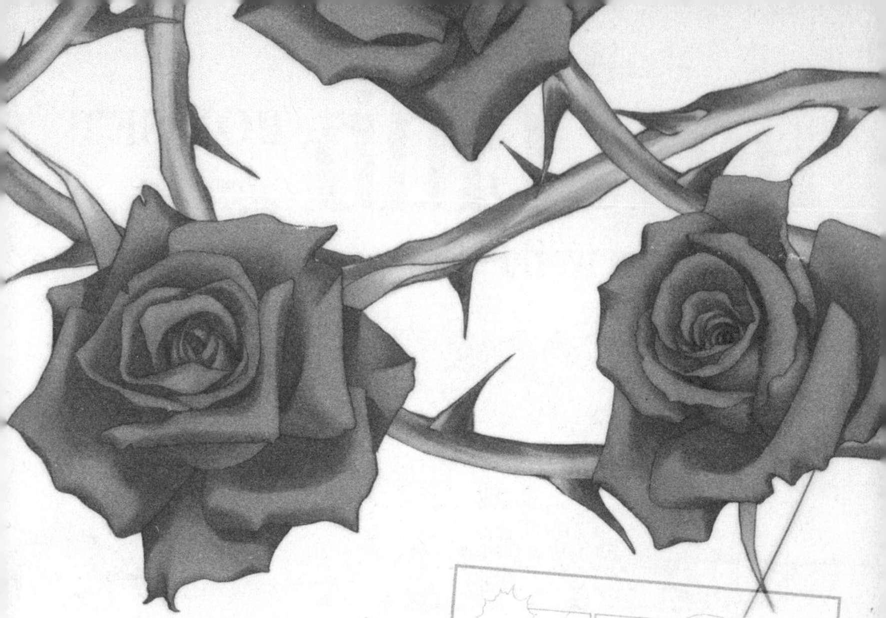

This is the last page.

In keeping with the original Japanese comic format, this book reads from right to left—so action, sound effects, and word balloons are completely reversed. This preserves the orientation of the original artwork—plus, it's fun! Check out the diagram shown here to get the hang of things, and then turn to the other side of the book to get started!

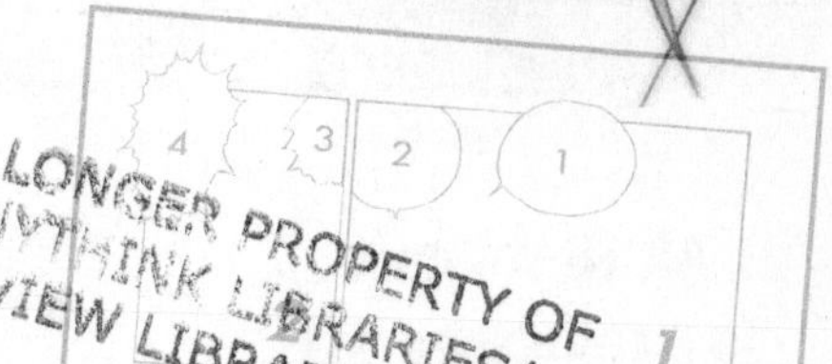
1
2
3
4
1
2
3
4
5
6
7
8
9
5